PAUL SCHNEIDER

Witness of Buchenwald

PAUL SCHNEIDER

Witness of Buchenwald

A Biography by
Rudolf Wentorf

Translated by Daniel Bloesch

REGENT COLLEGE PUBLISHING
Vancouver, British Columbia

Paul Schneider: Witness of Buchenwald

Copyright © 2008 Daniel Bloesch

Published 2008 by Regent College Publishing
5800 University Boulevard, Vancouver, BC V6T 2E4 Canada
Web: www.regentpublishing.com
E-mail: info@regentpublishing.com

Regent College Publishing is an imprint of the Regent Bookstore <www.regentbookstore.com>. Views expressed in works published by Regent College Publishing are those of the author and do not necessarily represent the official position of Regent College <www.regent-college.edu>.

Book design by Robert Hand

Library and Archives Canada Cataloguing in Publication

Wentorf, Rudolf
Paul Schneider: witness of Buchenwald / by Rudolf Wentorf; Daniel Bloesch, translator.
Translation of Paul Schneider: Der Zeuge von Buchenwald.

ISBN 978-1-57383-417-9

1. Schneider, Paul, 1897–1939. 2. Reformed Church—Germany—Clergy—Biography. 3. Evangelische Kirche der Altpreussischen Union. Kirchenprovinz Rheinland—Clergy—Biography. 4. Anti-Nazi movement—Germany—Biography. 5. Christian martyrs—Germany—Biography. 6. Buchenwald (Germany: Concentration camp). I. Bloesch, Daniel W. II. Title.

BX9469.S35W413 2008   284'.2092   C2008-901142-2

Scripture quotations marked (NIV) are taken from the HOLY BIBLE, NEW INTERNATIONAL VERSION®. NIV®. Copyright © 1973, 1978, 1984 by International Bible Society. Used by permission of Zondervan. All rights reserved.

Back cover: Eberhard Bethge quotation is from *Dietrich Bonhoeffer: A Biography*, rev. and ed. Victoria Barnett, trans. Eric Mosbacher et al. (Minneapolis: Fortress Press, 2000), 568.

Every effort has been made to obtain appropriate permissions for this publication.

TABLE OF CONTENTS

FOREWORD

During the 1980s I had the blessing of living and studying in Germany for four years. At that time there were many (now elderly) persons with whom I came into relationship who had themselves experienced life during the Third Reich. Knowing that I was an American, moreover a pastor and graduate student in theology (with special interest in Dietrich Bonhoeffer and Martin Niemöller), it was striking how often and regularly the conversation would turn toward their memories of and reflections on life in the time of Hitler. It became my acute sense that forty years after the ending of the Second World War there remained much that was still churning and unresolved in the consciences of these dear German people. Their meeting with an American pastor occasioned deep and highly personal processing of what had been experienced during the years of National Socialism.

Inexorably, it seemed, the encounter would eventuate in discussion about how it could have been possible for someone like Hitler to succeed in carrying forth policies that in retrospect are unimaginable. While the judgment of history has made clear the horror and abomination of the Nazi regime, what has seemed less than clear is how the German people themselves could have allowed such a ruler to prevail. How could so many decent people have become bystanders as the repression continued to worsen? More pointedly, my conversation partners were still asking themselves so many years later: How could it have been possible for me and my family to remain silent and not have done more to resist? At times the conversations nearly took on the character of private confession. I found myself in the awkward predicament of listening to stories that stirred deep memories of anguish, while remaining uncertain about how to respond. Was listening enough? Dare I offer spiritual care, even absolution? And, if so, by what authority?

The case of Pastor Paul Schneider, amply documented in this book, demonstrates exactly how the nightmare of National Socialism prevailed. By examining this particular instance of harassment, persecution, and murder, we get a glimpse of the dynamics that led the majority of people to avoid the most critical issues through the well traveled road of compliance. It took not only clear insight into the meaning of events as they rapidly unfolded but also courage to risk saying "No" to the lure of popular patriotism. What is more, this case demonstrates in vivid detail the miracle of resistance on the part of the few.

The political humiliation and economic hardship borne by the German people in the wake of the Versailles Treaty during the Weimar Republic was enormous. The provisions of the Versailles Treaty at the end of World War I required the surrender of significant territory and colonies, severe limits on the German military, the requirement for unilateral admission of guilt for the war, and punitive reparation payments. Together these conditions laid the foundation for an impossible set of challenges to be negotiated by the fledgling experiment in German democracy based on the Weimar Constitution. Throughout the 1920s, both the left wing and right wing political parties took aim at the failures of the Weimar government. Although initially the greatest threats to the new political order came from the side of communism, by the beginning of the 1930s the clearest danger became the growing popularity of the right wing National Socialist party under the organization of its charismatic leader, Adolf Hitler.

Fueled by the economic chaos created by runaway inflation and the rampant unemployment of the Great Depression, the National Socialist party made steady gains in a series of elections, leading to Hitler's accession to power on January 30, 1933. Hitler's politics were able to exploit the widespread resentment over the consequences of the Versailles Treaty. Moreover, he was able to name the identifiable scapegoats in the community of the Jewish people, whom he blamed for Germany's malaise. Hitler's appeal may seem unimaginable knowing the wreck his leadership created for the victims of his policies through genocide and war. Yet desperation in times of economic and political crisis regularly provokes populations to grasp for desperate measures. Hitler promised to revive German pride and the nation's infrastructure at a time when people were ready to grasp for any—even an illusory—solution that had both an enemy to blame and a populist-sounding agenda. This proved to be a deadly confluence of contributing factors.

If it had been successfully implemented early on, successful resistance to the Nazi regime might have unfolded through collective organization on the part of Christians. For Christians this was the missed opportunity of the Confessing Church, to which Paul Schneider belonged. Already in November 1933 German church leaders, who were in opposition to the initial policies of the Hitler government, aligned with Pastor Martin Niemöller to form the Pastors Emergency League. This was the first organization established to counteract the co-option of the Protestant Church by the National Socialist government. Those who orchestrated the subsuming of church governance into the Nazi machinery became known, by contrast, as the "German Christians."

By January 4, 1934 the German Christian Reich Bishop Ludwig Müller issued an order forbidding public criticism of the church administration and its policies. In opposition to such measures, the Confessing Church was organized around the articles of faith articulated in the Barmen Declaration, adopted May 29–31, 1934. The strategy of the Hitler regime at the end of 1934 and into 1935 was to appease the resistors by altering the most egregious policies and removing the most objectionable leaders, all toward the end of breaking down the opposition. Because most of those in the Confessing Church chose not to persist in their resistance when they thought the worst was over (at least for themselves), the policy of temporary appeasement was successful towards the long term goal of total domination. The failure of the church opposition to maintain cohesion in its ranks led to the erosion of its strength and left many to suffer the fatal consequences, including Pastor Schneider. Where collective resistance failed to persist, individual Christians were left to their own defenses.

This biography of Pastor Paul Schneider extensively documents the pressures and dilemmas faced by a common pastor in standing up to the local, regional, and national apparatus of National Socialism. It reveals both the subtleties and the relentlessness encountered by those who chose to resist. It gives a glimpse into the workings of the Nazi apparatus in extending its reach of total control. And finally it shows the ultimate consequence suffered by those daring to raise their voices against the machine. What makes Rudolf Wentorf's work so valuable to readers in the English speaking world is the combination of thorough biographical information about Pastor Schneider with exacting detail about the process enacted against him on the part of his enemies. Once Schneider had been identified as a resistor, the political apparatus did not relent in its persecution, even seeing him as a threat to its hegemony after his death.

The story of resistance began when the session of Schneider's congregation posed what seem to be innocent questions about the scheduling of Nazi youth activities in such a way as to conflict with youth participation at worship. While this appeared to be a legitimate enough objection based on church tradition, this act placed Schneider on the radar screen of the Nazi apparatus. When Schneider took the further step of posting on the signboard of the church notices which challenged Nazi authority over youth activities, the confrontation escalated to a new level. Soon a few members of the congregation joined the fray, providing reports to Nazi officials about critical remarks made in the pastor's announcements and sermons. It is striking already in 1933 how daring the Nazi hierarchy had become in seeking to intimidate the established church. Within a few months of taking power, Nazi officials felt secure enough in their authority to begin to issue threats about the need to remove or transfer Pastor Schneider. Consistory (i.e., judicatory) officials in the meantime sought to remain neutral and avoided coming to Schneider's defense, counseling him toward restraint in matters deemed controversial.

Pastor Schneider's efforts to exercise the ancient practice of church discipline in relation to participation in the Lord's Supper pushed the conflict to a new level. The dissent of a single elder from the congregation, added to the other points of tension, eventually precipitated in Schneider's transfer to another pastorate. In the process Schneider became a marked man. His advocacy for the Confessing Church, including the reading and posting of announcements from it, created new provocation from the beginning of his service in his new parish. When Schneider objected to the interruption of a Christian funeral by a Nazi sympathizer who publically introduced Nazi ideology into the burial service, Pastor Schneider became embroiled in a long and heated debate about the proper authority of the church in relationship to state control. At every step of the way, Schneider grounded his convictions on the truth of the Gospel of Jesus Christ. But the Nazi regime knew no other gods than those which blessed its own ideology.

Pastor Schneider continued to resist Nazi interference with church business by refusing to allow church participation in the display of the national flag or in the ringing of the church bells on nationalistic occasions. Notice was made of his refusal to offer a Nazi salute at the beginning or end of confirmation instruction hours at the local elementary school. He understood the grave threat posed to Christianity by the Hitler cult. New charges were made against the pastor by members of his parish loyal to the Nazi regime and new cases of church discipline were invoked. Every attempted explanation was turned on its head against him. When at Christmas time in 1936 pagan religious rites were commended for use in the local Protestant school, a new stage was reached in the confrontation between church and state. Vigorous protest was raised by Schneider and his congregations against the introduction of Germanic mythology into the celebration of Christmas. The reader notes well the steady escalation in the number and kind of issues which the state pressed upon the local church and pastor.

On the last Sunday before Lent in 1937, Pastor Paul Schneider delivered his final regular sermon to his congregations. Schneider was taken into "preventive detention" by the Gestapo and eventually banned from returning to the Rhineland and his parish. Hearing the call of God to continue his pastoral ministry, Schneider defied the deportation order and returned to preach in his congregations on October 3. He was arrested again on that day and sent to Buchenwald concentration camp on November 27, 1937. Even at Buchenwald, Schneider continued his protest against Nazi tyranny, refusing to salute the flag and preaching in a loud voice to the inmates even from a cell in solitary confinement. Because of his defiance—we might call it faithfulness—Schneider was tortured and executed in July 1939. Those who knew him in the concentration camp testified to his boldness to the end. Even after Schneider's death, the persecution did not cease, with Nazi obfuscations made about the cause of death, harassment at the time of his funeral, and unjust complications about the support of his widow and children.

This book documents in stunning detail the process of persecution against Schneider, a common parish pastor, and his uncommon response, based on his commitment to the Christian faith. The role played by the Consistory of the church in the whole affair is one of the most haunting aspects of the whole account. At its best, the church hierarchy remained neutral in the state's harassment of Schneider. As the process proceeded toward its tragic conclusion, however, there is overwhelming evidence of the Consistory's willing cooperation in the measures taken by the state against him. The documentation depicts in clarity how a local pastor was left to his own devices in seeking to stand firm in the defense of the Christian message. This book shows exactly how it was not only possible, but even advisable for people to remain silent in the face of the threat of the sort of harassment and persecution exacted against Schneider, lest they become the next victims.

Several times Wentorf makes reference to "positive Christianity"—a Christianity purged of Jewish influence and combined with nationalistic zeal and pagan Germanic elements—as the Nazi religion. It was this perversion of authentic Christianity that Schneider opposed at every turn. The Confessing Church provided theological grounding for such a protest. But as the Confessing Church collapsed in the mid-1930s, pastors like Schneider were left to fend for themselves in standing up to the Nazi machine. Many were crushed in the process. In the case of Pastor Schneider, we see how relentless was the pursuit of total control and how fragile the network of resistance.

Positive Christianity bears a family resemblance to more recent versions of civil religion. Virtually every state must and does appeal to religious sources to legitimize its policies, making claims to divine authority. While rarely is the fusion of national hubris with divine sanction as potent as in the case of Nazi Germany, in every nation the church needs to examine its role in serving as an agent for legitimizing state policies. In many instances, it may be hard for the faithful to distinguish between the core articles of Christian faith and the tenets of civil religion. The overidentification of church and state has plagued the history of the church in various instances throughout the centuries. We are reminded again of the responsibility of Christians to serve God above all things and to know the difference between the worship of God and the worship of the state. This case teaches us how the church needs to devise both theological and ethical criteria by which to offer or withhold its blessing of state policies.

The researching and writing of this book by Rudolf Wentorf is a gift to all those who seek to comprehend and learn from the lessons of Nazi Germany for the life and witness of the Christian church. The attention to detail through the elaborate documentation, organized according to Schneider's biography, provides a research tool and extensive case study of great merit. This volume serves as the standard work for interpreters of Paul Schneider and his legacy. In its own way, this book takes an important place alongside the masterful theological biography of Dietrich Bonhoeffer by Eberhard Bethge. The flawless translation of the book by Daniel Bloesch makes the work accessible to English speaking readers at a time when fascination with the church's response to Nazism continues to flourish. Regent College Publishing has undertaken a project of lasting value through the publication of this excellent translation.

Craig L. Nessan
Dubuque, Iowa
June 25, 2008

In memoriam:

Pastor Paul Schneider
(1897–1939)

who died in the Buchenwald concentration camp near Weimar
as a martyr of the Protestant Church

and to his sons

Pastor Dietrich Schneider
(1927–1960)

and

Dr. Gerhard Schneider
(1933–1960)

A serious automobile accident for which they were not responsible
put an end to their lives in this world. Thus they followed their father
into eternity at an early age.

I

INITIAL REMARKS

The Lettner Publishing Company in Berlin published the documentation "Trotz der Höllen Toben" on the 70th birthday of Pastor Paul Schneider on August 29, 1967. As early as the fall of 1953 the wife of Paul Schneider presented her impressive little book *Der Prediger von Buchenwald*[1] published by the same company. Both publications did not serve to glorify a human being, but wanted to bear witness to the good news that God is announcing the new age of his invincible Kingdom in the midst of this passing age.

The ways of God in dealing with individual human beings and with his world of nations may often cause a lack of understanding, even hostility. This world, as long as it persists in maintaining its distance from God, cannot react in any other way because the one who throws the world into confusion is still playing his diabolical game in it; the following pages bear witness to it.

The illusory powers within the world that are up to their mischief in the world are inspired by the Adversary. It is their intention to set the standard for the world. But history is continually teaching us how limited the power of these impotent forces really is. It was Paul Schneider who testified to the world through his ordeal in the solitary confinement cell of the Buchenwald concentration camp near Weimar that God is the Lord, who in spite of everything sets the standard and enables human beings to be his visible witnesses before the whole world.

In that oppressively hot summer of 1939 I was with my bride in the Lüneburg Heath, a region we are very fond of. Messages from the Confessing Church

---

[1] M. Schneider, *Der Prediger von Buchenwald* (Berlin, 1953; 11th ed., Berlin, 1964); a new edition was published by Neuhausen, Stuttgart, 1985 (we will use the following abbreviation: *Prediger*).

were delivered by hand from one person to the next. In the worship services the brothers and sisters for whom the Gestapo had stretched out its hands were remembered in intercessory prayer. In the days when the world was rushing toward war, we received the shocking news that Pastor Paul Schneider, who had always been remembered in the prayers of the church while in detention, had gone home to the Lord in the Buchenwald concentration camp near Weimar on July 18. We were more than dismayed; dark foreboding filled our hearts. These events pursued me and left behind a number of questions as I looked at the outer and inner structure of our church. But my thinking has matured as a result of these events and given me the certainty that God is sending two clear signals in the midst of the appalling darkness, far from all diplomatic and legal experimentation and far from those who hide behind laws and decrees: a signal that hearts have hardened and another signal that makes itself known in suffering discipleship.

No one can shirk the responsibility of defining his or her position on these witnesses of faith.

This book would like to motivate Protestantism to rethink and redefine its relationship to its martyrs, for it was these martyrs who bore witness to what endures in life and in death and to where our actual security in life and in death can be found. Our martyrs show us the spiritual dimension, the source of our church's life. They called the church and are still calling it today to order its life by the gospel and are among those who are a constant thorn in the conscience of the church.[2]

---

[2] The official weekly journal of the "Protestant Church in Germany" in its edition of January 15, 1948 mentions for the first time the following names of ministers and theologians who lost their lives in concentration camps or in prisons: E. Behrend, D. Bonhoeffer, H. Hesse, E. Kasenzer, J. Perels, P. Richter, P. Schneider, L. Steil, W. Sylten, F. Weissler. Later these names were mentioned: M. Gauger, F. Müller, E. Sack, H. Buttersack, H. Koch, G. Maus, H. Jacoby, K. F. Stellbrink. Until January 15, 1948 the Protestant Church in Germany had not kept track of those men and women who had to lose their lives for the sake of the faith. In the course of the last few years the church has begun to reflect anew on the criteria that should be used to determine who may or may not be considered a martyr of the church. Who would now not want to add Hermann Stohr to the list of martyrs? It is reasonable to assume that Paul Schneider would have made the same decision as Hermann Stohr did if he had been called on to go to war for the Nazi state. He could never have taken an oath to Hitler. More and more he saw in National Socialism a diabolical, unjust state. So a *Heil Hitler!* ("Long live Hitler!") never crossed his lips. (However, compare the greeting he

On July 1, 1523 the young Augustinian monks Heinrich Voes and Johann Esch were publicly burned at the stake because they openly declared their allegiance to the Reformation of the church kindled by Luther. Afterwards Luther wrote in a letter:

> To all dear brothers and sisters in Christ who are in Holland, Brabant and Flanders together with all believers in Christ, grace and peace from God our Father and our Lord Christ.
>
> Praise and thanks be to the Father of all mercy who lets us see again his wonderful light at this time which until now was hidden because of our sin, making us subject to the horrible power of darkness, erring so miserably and serving the Anti-Christ. But now the time has come again . . . for you have been given the privilege not only of hearing the gospel and recognizing Christ before the whole world, but to also be the first who suffer shame and disgrace, fear and distress, prison and danger for the sake of Christ; and your lives have reaped such a full harvest of fruit and strength because you have poured out your own blood and affirmed the gospel in this way, especially since the two noble gems of Christ in your fellowship, Hinricus and Johannes, disregarded the risk to their lives in Brussels so that Christ may be praised with His Word . . . . Because we see the present misery and distress and have such strong, comforting promises, so let us renew our hearts, be of good courage and joyfully allow the Lord to slaughter us. He said it; he will not lie. "Even the hairs on your head are numbered." And although our adversaries shout at these saints and call them Hussites, Wycliffians and Lutherans and will boast of murder, that should not surprise us, but strengthen us all the more; for Christ's cross must have blasphemers.[3]

In this context I would like to point out in advance the devotional recorded at the end of this portrayal of Paul Schneider's life. This devotional provoked the anger of the Gestapo. Hans Asmussen explained there: "Paul Schneider is one of those souls under the altar (Rv. 6:11) who rest there until the number

---

used in one letter: *Sieg Heil!* ["Victory Salute"], or: "With a German salute!") He also always refused to salute the flag, because the Swastika was a "criminal symbol" for him.

[3] M. Luther, *Ausgewahlte Werke*, vol. 3, *Sendbrief an die Christen in Niederland* (München, 1950), p. 61.

of their fellow servants and brothers who were to be killed as they had been was completed."[4] Christian martyrs for the faith differ from other victims of tyrannical regimes by the fact that with their dedication they bear witness to the victory of the crucified and risen Lord who has overcome the world.

In an academic sense Paul Schneider was not a theological teacher of our church, he did not earn any university degree, and yet the word of Holy Scripture especially applies to him: "Remember your leaders, who spoke the Word of God to you. Consider the outcome of their way of life and imitate their faith. Jesus Christ is the same yesterday and today and forever."[5]

The church of the Word is challenged to ask today whether the village pastor of Dickenschied and Womrath who became the pastor of Buchenwald still has something to say to it. Today we cannot keep hiding the fact that Protestantism has a hard time dealing with those women and men who have clearly told the state what is the state's and the church what the church's task is in this age. The theologians are challenged to ask what value the uncompromising declaration of the gospel has as the ultimate, unchanging truth that decisively shapes their spiritual actions, apart from any diplomatic considerations. Academic theology is challenged to ask where it sees the actual purpose of its work and what language it uses to describe the actions of the martyrs.

Our martyrs for the faith want to help us make sure that our view of the future, our view of life and eternity, is not obscured in the midst of this age that is passing away. They teach us that in fact no human being can avoid the Christ who is present always and everywhere.

This work would like to make a modest contribution to an understanding of Christian martyrdom by shedding light on an act of resistance in the "Third Reich" motivated by the Christian faith. I would also like to show that church diplomacy becomes estranged from the church itself when it is pursued only to preserve its own church structures and when it does not serve people by proclaiming the salvation offered in the gospel. The documents are willing and eager to give us information on this without any ifs and buts. Evaluating the documents is a task best left to the reader. Gerhard Besier has detailed

---

[4] *Prediger*, 237.

[5] Hb. 13:7 (NIV)

the present state of research on this subject in his essay "The Beginnings of a Political Resistance in the Confessing Church."[6]

I want to especially thank Mrs. Schneider in Dickenschied for her valuable help in conceiving this work. She not only explained the facts of the events, but also again and again entrusted her conversation partners with the task of probing the spiritual dimensions of the events in Dickenschied and Womrath at that time. Paul Schneider's companions in suffering to whom I owe a special debt of gratitude are listed by name.

I would also like to thank the Leipzig church historian Professor Kurt Meier for the valuable suggestions he made in the course of our correspondence. The name of Professor Klaus Scholder must also not be omitted. Although he was called home too early, he showed a steadfast interest in this work throughout his life and expressed it by offering suggestions in personal and telephone conversations. Professor Gerhard Besier whom I have already mentioned is one of the historians to whom the undersigned owes a debt of gratitude. I also want to thank Professor Carsten Nicolaisen in Munich. It is more than just a duty for me to mention the fact that my teacher Professor Kurt-Dietrich Schmidt who was called home many years ago must also be included in this circle.

Likewise, I also want to warmly thank archivist Pastor Dietrich Meyer who is in charge of the archives of the Protestant Church in the Rhineland. He gave a special measure of support to this work.

I would also like to express my gratitude to the employees of the Federal Archives in Koblenz, the officials of the Hessian State Archives in Wiesbaden as well as the administrations of the universities in Giessen, Marburg and Tübingen. The head office of the high school in Giessen and the pastorate in Hochelheim are a part of my circle of supporters. They all helped me in my search for evidence with great dedication.

I am also grateful to the board of directors of the "National Memorial" in Buchenwald near Weimar for the honorable care they have given to this place of memories. A visit there has given me many important insights.

I gratefully remember my encounters in Dickenschied with Professor Claude Foster of West Chester University (USA). I ask God's blessing on his Schneider studies and a continuation of our good collaboration.

---

[6] G. Besier, *Ansatze zum politischen Widerstand in der Bekennenden Kirche—zur gegenwartigen Forschungslage,* in *Der Widerstand gegen den Nationalsozialismus,* ed. v. J. Schmadeke and P. Steinbach (Munich and Zurich, 1986), p. 265ff.

I warmly thank Pastor Gerd Westermeyer in Dickenschied for always being willing to help.

My colleague in the church district of the Lauenburg Duchy, Pastor Bruno-Hermann Vahl, has accompanied this work with great interest and active help. I would especially like to thank him for this with brotherly affection.

The Protestant Church in the Rhineland, the church district of Simmern-Trabbach and the Savings and Loan Association in Simmern supported the book with a grant to defray the printing costs. I would sincerely like to thank all of them for this help that is not taken for granted.

I would also like to thank the Neukirchen Publishing Company, especially Dr. Christian Bartsch, for his many efforts on behalf of this project as he accompanied it through the publication process.

Rudolf Wentorf
Seedorf am Schaalsee
On the 50th anniversary of
Paul Schneider's death
July 18, 1989

2

THOUGHTS THAT ARE ALWAYS
PRESENT

The question of how it was possible for National Socialism to captivate such wide sections of the German people who were recruited from both the white-collar and blue-collar workforce will always be accompanied by an embarrassing, even anguished undertone. What compounds the problem is that the intelligentsia in Germany failed, and not only there. It also failed in Europe and even in America, apart from small groups of intellectuals.[1]

---

[1] I will mention several individuals from the chorus of prophetic voices: a) The Kiel professor O. Baumgarten wrote a book seven years before Hitler seized power which was sent to every Protestant clergyman in Germany *(The Cross and Swastika)*. "The perpetual search to find guilt and darkness in the Jews corrupts the noble, bright character of proud Christians. And the poisoning of the German national soul by the demonstrable unkindness of this polemic is to be lamented more than the deleterious consequences of the Anti-Semitic agitation for our national, cultural life. The Swastika and the cross are mutually exclusive. There is no swastika excluding the Jews for those who live under the cross of Christ, who died for all without distinction and thus lives for all without distinction. 'There is neither Jew nor Greek, slave nor free, male nor female, for you are all one in Christ Jesus'" (Gal. 3:28 NIV; p. 36); b) *Sonntagsblatt des arbeitenden Volkes,* published by the Federation of Religious Socialists, "Christentum und Faschismus sind unvereinbar," Nr. 48, Nov. 30, 1930, volume 12; c) H. Sasse, *Kirchliche Zeitlage,* in *Kirchliches Jahrbuch für die deutschen evangelischen Landeskirchen* (1932), p. 30ff (reprinted in Ders., *In statu confessionis,* ed. F. W. Hopf (Berlin, 1975), p. 251ff.); d) compare with K. Meier, *Der Evangelische Kirchenkampf,* 3 vols. (Halle and Göttingen, 1976–1984); e) K. Scholder, *Die Kirchen und das dritte Reich,* 2 vols. (Frankfurt/M. and Munich, 1977–1985); f) D. Bonhoeffer was among those who very early warned of the danger of National Socialism. Compare on this topic: E. Bethge, *Dietrich Bonhoeffer. Theologe-Christ-Zeitgenosse* (Munich, 1986); g) compare on the question of resistance, G. Besier, *Ansätze zum politischen Widerstand in der Bekennenden Kirche,* note 7. Compare also K. Meier, *Die historische Bedeutung des Kirchenkampfes für den Widerstand*

The initiators of the "National Socialist German Workers' Party" clearly revealed in their publications long before 1933 how they envisioned the state to be structured after a takeover by the Nazis when they would be giving the orders in Germany. Alfred Rosenberg, later the chief ideologue of the NSDAP, expressed himself in these terms as early as 1922 in "The Nature, Principles and Goals of the NSDAP": "The only idea that is able to unite all the classes and denominations of the German nation is the new, yet ancient world view that is based on the spirit of the German community that had been buried for so long. This world view is called National Socialism."[2]

---

im Dritten Reich. Zeitgenössische und aktuelle Aspekte der Urteilsbildung in Ders., *Evangelische Kirche in Gesellschaft, Staat und Politik 1918–1945* (Berlin, 1987), p. 132ff.; h) in this context we should also point out the Altona Confession. K. Scholder comments on this: "The Altona Confession was always overshadowed by the famous Barmen Confession. But what Barmen owes to Altona has often been ignored. It was by no means only an 'unclear preliminary statement,' but the first step the church took to clarify the battle lines. The young Berlin professor D. Bonhoeffer was right when he came to speak of the Altona Confession with almost unreserved joy at the conclusion of his seminar in the winter semester of 1932/33. Indeed, in what direction would the Protestant Church have gone if this had not also been said and heard in this way at the threshold of the Third Reich?"(*Die Kirchen und das dritte Reich,* vol. 1 [Frankfurt/M, 1977], p. 237f.). This confession was promulgated on January 11, 1933 after extensive preliminary work on the basis of incidents that occurred on July 17, 1932 in Altona. Twenty-one Altona pastors had signed it before then. Compare also K. Meier, *Der Evangelische Kirchenkampf,* vol. 1, ibid., p. 361; i) W. Hunzinger, in *Neue Blätter für den Sozialismus* (ed. E. Heitmann, F. Klatt, A. Rathmann, P. Tillich [1931]), p. 176f.: "The vital question addressed to the Protestant Church is whether it will say No to a deification of man just as passionately as it says No to Communism and nationalism." Hunzinger continues: "Their existence as a Protestant church at the very least will depend on whether in both cases it speaks the word that it is called to speak, the Word of the God who alone deserves honor and praise—in uncompromising determination—even if it would have to become an isolated church as a result." K. Scholder correctly notes that these sentences sound "like an anticipation of the Barmen Declaration of 1934" (*Die Kirchen und das dritte Reich,* vol. 1, ibid., p. 175f.); j) compare also H. Strathmann, *Nationalsozialistische Weltanschauung* (Nurnberg, 1931); k) W. Schwarz, "What Significance does the Tension between National Socialism and Protestant Christianity have for Apologetics and the Proclamation of the Word? Based on a lecture that was given at the Silesian Conference for Homeland Mission and Apologetics in Krummhübel on May 7, 1931" in *Wort und Tat,* Issue 3, *Apologetische Zentrale* (Berlin-Spandau, 1931).

    [2] Compare A. Rosenberg, *Wesen, Gründsätze und Ziele der NSDAP* (Munich, 1922), p. 58. In the foreward he notes, "National Socialism considers this character training as a key problem of our time. Even 'programs' can only achieve their purpose when they flow

In 1927 Adolf Hitler expressed the unmistakable idea that the foundation of National Socialist thought and action would be the folkish world view because it corresponds to "the innermost desire of nature, since it restores that free interplay of forces that must lead to a continual increase in mutual discipline until finally by taking possession of this earth the best race is given the go-ahead to take action in all fields, some of which will be above it, others of which will be outside of it. We all suspect that in the distant future problems will face man that can only be dealt with by a superior race as a master race, and it will be called on to assume this task based on the resources and possibilities of a whole globe."[3]

Hitler saw in his worldview the offensive weapon he needed to advance his idea of controlling the state and human beings. He openly expressed what significance it had for his thought and action. "The worldview is intolerant and can not be content with the role of one party among others, but imperiously demands its own exclusive and complete recognition as well as the complete rearrangement of public life according to its views. Therefore, it cannot tolerate the simultaneous existence of any group that advocates the earlier state of affairs."[4]

The Old Testament and Jesus himself bind Christianity and Judaism together. Hitler was an Anti-Semite possessed by a diabolical passion and as such he invariably rejected the Old Testament as well. The ultimate conclusion of his struggle against Judaism was that he also had to struggle against Christianity as well. In *Mein Kampf* we read, "Thus I believe today that I am acting according to the plan of the all-powerful Creator: By resisting the Jews, I am fighting for the work of the Lord . . . ."

In a speech given on April 12, 1922 Hitler told what significance Jesus had for him:

> I tell you, my Christian experience points me to my Lord and Savior as
> a fighter. It points me to the man who, once lonely and only surrounded

---

from this spiritual rebirth. Insights gained from human reason can only be given their true basis through this rebirth. With this objective in mind, the 'Nature, Principles and Goals' was sent out as the first publication of the NSDAP in 1922 . . . ." This work is an important document of contemporary history and supports the thesis I have proposed.

[3] A. Hitler, *Mein Kampf,* 95–96th ed. (München, 1934), p. 422.

[4] Ibid., p. 506.

by a few followers, understood these Jews and called on his followers to fight against them. As the true God he was not the greatest One as a silent sufferer, rather he was the greatest One as a fighter! In unbounded love I read as a Christian and human being the verse that proclaims to us how the Lord finally brought himself to take the whip and drive the money changers, the brood of vipers out of the temple! Deeply moved, I recognize today, after two-thousand years, his tremendous struggle for this world against the Jewish poison most powerfully by the fact that he had to bleed to death on the cross for it.

The phrases "according to the plan of the all-powerful Creator . . . Christian experience . . . my Lord and Savior . . . the true God . . ." are purely rhetorical statements that had no meaning or value for him. The so-called National Socialist worldview did not go beyond a pure dualism of good (Aryan) and evil (Jews). The concept of the concentration camp is already found in an article by Hitler that the "*Völkische Beobachter*" published on March 13, 1921. We read there, "Let us prevent the Jews from undermining our people, if necessary, by seizing its pathogens and putting them in concentration camps."

These examples should suffice to show what ideas were alive in Hitler. Using these ideas, he set his sights on taking over the state. At the same time they illustrate the claim Hitler made when National Socialism appeared on the scene, taking Austria and Germany as their starting point. His first and foremost concern was to give new meaning to the existing values of his time.

The "heralds" of the National Socialist worldview, a political religion that was devoted to the state, appeared in public with an enormous amount of confidence as a result of their mastery at playing the demagogue. As demagogical jugglers they were masterful at making fun of or criminalizing all existing morals, behaviors and customs that were not agreeable to them. In the political realm they deliberately confused patriotic, nationalistic and socially minded thinking and action with National Socialist thinking and action. They needed the national and social slant to give its new, Germanic worldview a foothold in the German nation. Strictly speaking, the label National Socialism is misleading because from the very beginning it was not defined either by national, social or socialist ideals.[5] It would be more honest and in the end more

---

[5] The National Socialist ideologues understood by "world view" a kind of religious system of thought by which they sought to elevate their blood and soil theory to metaphysical heights.

understandable to speak of "Hitlerism." Yet following the general usage we will stick with the term "National Socialism."

On its "march through the institutions" National Socialism at first did not pay much attention to the churches. There were orders from the top leadership of the NSDAP to the subordinate party offices not to bother with church affairs. Such directives were a part of the National Socialist strategy.

On February 24, 1924 Hitler announced the party platform of the NSDAP with its 25 points that was drafted by Anton Drexler with the assistance of Gottfried Feder. The much quoted 24th point, which played a role in the church struggle time and again, states:

> We demand freedom for all religious confessions in the state as long as they do not endanger its existence or violate the Germanic race's sense of morality and moral values. The party as such advocates the position of a positive Christianity without tying itself to any particular denomination. It fights against the Jewish-Marxist spirit in us and outside of us and is convinced that a lasting recovery of our nation can only take place from the inside and on this basis: service before self.[6]

The question that makes us uneasy again and again is this: Why didn't the Christian churches with their hosts of theologians sit up and take notice in time? For what does "the sense of morality and moral values of the Germanic race" mean, or the "Jewish-Marxist spirit" under the cover of the phrase, "The party as such advocates the position of a positive Christianity"?

In this context the Protestant church must allow the question of whether it had not once again remembered the times when it could live comfortably with the alliance between "throne and altar" during the "national uprising" ordered by the Nazis in 1933. Had it not seen the Weimar Republic as a destabilizing phenomenon of the times after the emigration of the Kaiser? Had it not backed the policy of preserving traditional structures instead of reforming them (just as it backed a policy of restoration after 1945)? Was it not irresponsible in listening to those pseudo-nationalistic voices in the interests of preserving its own power at the beginning of Nazi rule? Had it not for this reason become incapable of taking action? Of course, there had been voices in the church that

---

[6] G. Feder, *Das Programm der NSDAP und seine weltanschauliche Grundgedanken* (München, 1930).

had warned them early about National Socialism (see note 1). Although they were diverse in their theological thinking, they were all united in their rejection of National Socialism—and this was not only true since 1933, as we have said. After everything was clear, the church was warned later by the memorandum of the "Confessing Church" in 1936 and also at the first convention of the Confessing Synod of the Protestant Church of the Old Prussian Union which convened from December 16–18, 1936 in Breslau, at which Günter Jacob gave a talk on the subject "Church or Sect?"[7] But the churches officially recognized by the state were not represented there.

It is an especially regrettable phenomenon that the official church governments that ruled until the end of the war simply disappeared after 1945 without confessing that they had gone astray, just as the state government did as well.

On the basis of available documents we will follow the journey of a Rhenish pastor's life. Although he grew up in a nationalistic and patriotic home, he quickly discerned what was concealed under the mask of National Socialism's "nationalistic" posture. He measured National Socialism by what he had to say to the people of his time as a servant of the divine Word.

---

[7] Printed in G. Jacob, *Die Versuchung der Kirche. Theologische Vorträge der Jahre 1934–1944* (Göttingen, 1946).

3

PARENTS AND CHILDHOOD

The range of hills known as the Soon Forest gave the old parish village of Pferdsfeld its picturesque background.[1] Paul Robert Schneider was born there on August 29, 1897 at one o'clock in the afternoon as the son of the pastor and his wife who lived there. His uncle Pastor Walther Schneider baptized him in the manse on September 29 of the same year (*Michaelis*, the Wednesday after the 15th Sunday of Trinity, as it is recorded in the baptismal registry). His baptismal verse was: "Sons are a heritage from the Lord, children a reward from him" (Ps. 127:3 NIV). The reason why the baptism was administered in the manse and not in the church was probably his mother's poor state of health.

His father, Gustav Adolf Schneider, born on January 13, 1858 in Elberfeld, lost his mother at the age of fifteen months and was placed in the care of his maternal grandparents. In their house his aunt Maria, a teacher in Elberfeld, took a special interest in the boy. She was considered to be a faithful and committed member of the Reformed congregation located there.

Pastor Krummacher confirmed Adolf Schneider although he often attended the worship services of Pastor Kohlbrügge with his aunt in the "Dutch Reformed Free Church" to which he felt drawn. The reason why he was nevertheless confirmed in his ancestral church could probably be found in the discipline that is characteristic of serious Reformed congregations.[2]

---

[1] The village Pferdsfeld no longer exists today. The residents were relocated because of the noise from military jets.

[2] Compare on this subject the "Heidelberg Catechism," the confessional document of the Reformed congregations with its questions and answers phrased in a way that facilitates the learning process. After several abortive attempts Kohlbrugge received permission through a royal edict to establish a "Free Reformed Church" in Elberfeld.

The concept of "discipline," i.e., "church discipline" as well, had a special importance in the later pastoral life of Adolf Schneider. He possessed a solid theological and liberal arts education. He completed his theological studies at the universities of Bonn, Leipzig and Tübingen. Prominent names such as Johann Tobias Beck are found in the long list of his theological teachers.

His clumsy and introverted nature often caused him great trouble. Nevertheless, his children never denied him the respect they owed him in spite of their strict upbringing.

The mother of Paul Schneider, Elisabeth, nee Schnorr, was born on August 8, 1863 in Düsseldorf. Very early in her life she lost her parents, who owned a hotel in the Rhine metropolis. Together with her sister she was placed in an orphanage in Mülheim an der Ruhr, in which she later worked as a teacher herself. Her marriage to Adolf Schneider took place in 1888; after two stillborn deliveries she was allowed the privilege of giving birth to three healthy boys: Adolf in 1891, Paul in 1897 and Hans in 1901. A friend of the Schneider family reports, "His mother was the sunshine of the house. I never met her when she was sad or complaining although a serious case of jaundice was a source of great torment for her until her early death in 1914. She was a generous woman, a brave personality, pious in a heartfelt way and inventive in providing a happy childhood for her children in spite of all her inhibitions. The three boys were allowed to tame ravens, catch squirrels, keep frogs, in short, to enjoy all the animals that were within their reach . . . ."[3] While they were still in Pferdsfeld, her husband had acquired a small carriage for her which was first pulled by a donkey and then by a pony so that his wife could share his joy in the beauty of nature and its creatures. Although she was soon confined to her armchair, his sick mother was still able to fulfill her duties as a housewife and gave her family the security that always remained a loving memory for her children. For her son Paul she was the epitome of true inwardness. In later years he wrote, "She remained the joyful soul of our house as long as she could sit among us."* At this point we must also remember their faithful maid Sophie who served both pastoral families (Adolf and Paul) with sacrificial loyalty from their days in Pferdsfeld until after the death of Paul Schneider.

---

[3] Information personally given to the author.

4

SCHOOL YEARS

When Paul Schneider was of school age he started elementary school in Pferdsfeld; on the side he also received private instruction from his father. As a result he was able to transfer into the third class of the high school in Kreuznach as an eleven year-old. During the week "he lived . . . for a year in a strictly managed boarding school," as he later wrote. Saturday was a day he and his fellow students awaited with great longing, for immediately after the last class they boarded the train that was to bring them to their families and the freedom they offered.

In 1910 Pastor Adolf Schneider requested a transfer from Pferdsfeld to Hochelheim in the church district of Wetzlar[1] by Easter. The family hoped that the climate in Hochelheim would be more beneficial to their mother than the harsh climate of the Hunsrück. From Hochelheim Paul could travel daily to the high school in Giessen. Paul very soon explored the country around the parish, the fields, meadows and forests. He enjoyed taking the spade and the rake to work in the parish garden, and he showed great skill in farm work as well. A love for nature and its creatures was always noticeable in him.

On the fifth Sunday of Lent—it was March 24, 1912—Paul Schneider was examined by his father in the church at Hochelheim and confirmed on the following Palm Sunday. The father gave his son these profound words of Jesus to take with him on his journey through life: "For this reason I was born, and for this I came into the world, to testify to the truth. Everyone on the side of truth listens to me."[2] In retrospect we must recognize that this verse was a

---

[1] The church districts of Braunfels and Wetzlar, also called synods, belonged to the "Protestant Church of the Rhine Province" even though they were located on Hessian territory.

[2] John 18:37 (NIV)

prophetic statement that became a reality in the life of Paul Schneider. But who could have even remotely guessed then that this confirmand was the one who would be chosen to testify to the truth of the gospel in the "bunker" of Buchenwald?

His school years passed without any problems as his grades kept on file in Giessen confirm. Paul Schneider was not yet eighteen years old when he volunteered for military service, which was also according to the plan of his patriotic, nationalistic father who was loyal to the Kaiser. Beforehand he passed his school-leaving examination that he had taken on June 29, 1915 in Giessen as he was about to enter military service. In the school files "medicine" is mentioned as his desired career.

He later described how he felt when the First World War broke out and how the first months after that shaped up for him:

> The war that had just broken out found me as a seventeen year-old student in my eighth year of secondary school and brought the first unrest into my inner life as my nationalistic instincts were stirred. This nationalistic excitement was channeled in a somewhat different direction by the loss of my dearly beloved mother; in the second year of the war I entered the army as a volunteer dragoon after a brief period of first-aid training.

5

MILITARY SERVICE

On August 2, 1915 Paul Schneider joined the dragoon regiment Nr. 5 in Hofgeismar as a volunteer. On November 10, 1915 he was dispatched to Russia, joining the field regiment, and was wounded there on March 22, 1916. His transfer from the main first-aid unit to the third reserve military hospital in Frankfurt an der Oder took place on the same day. On April 18, 1916 he was already back with his unit in Hofgeismar. It is significant for the next stage of his journey that on April 29, 1916 as a soldier in Giessen Paul Schneider applied to the "Grand-Ducal State University," seeking to be enrolled as a student of philosophy and theology. By taking this step he confirmed that he had given up his plan to study medicine at that point in his life.

His registration number was handed out on May 13, 1916. From then on Paul Schneider was no longer listed in the military files as a graduate from secondary school, but as a university student. We read in his resume:

> In the winter of 1915/16 I was slightly wounded in Russia, and received the iron cross 2nd class. After making a full recovery, I returned to my unit in Hofgeismar for half a year. In the fall of 1916 I set out as a private first class for the western front, joining the heavy artillery, where I became familiar with several different theaters of war by the end of the war. After receiving the usual promotion to the rank of sergeant for a one-year volunteer, I wore the uniform of a lieutenant of the reserves for the final eight months. My discharge to the home front and the outward collapse of the fatherland found me determined to devote myself to the study of theology.*

On December 19, 1918 Lieutenant Paul Schneider was given his discharge papers in the office of the Soldiers' Council of the infantry-artillery regiment Nr. 20 in Prussian Bahrenfeld near Hamburg. He noted: "I was happy when I had the discharge papers in my pocket . . . ." For a day he had a look around the city of Hamburg and then returned to his father's manse in Hochelheim, repulsed by the hustle and bustle of life in the big city.

6

UNIVERSITY

From Hochelheim Paul Schneider takes up the study of Protestant theology. Later he writes:

> I am not able to cite a particular circumstance that motivated me to choose the study of theology unless it was an inner inclination. The joyous confidence my mother had in God as she bore her serious case of jaundice to the end, and her selfless, caring love certainly developed the first seeds of religion in me. After I had passed my school-leaving examination, I was still determined to study medicine. Differences of opinion with my army buddies, especially during the time I was a lieutenant, and the conviction that no other force could help strengthen our nation torn by inner conflict or a divided humanity more than religion, led me—still more instinctively than consciously—to make the decision to become a servant of religious proclamation.*

He further notes:

> So I began my study of theology in Giessen. As I immersed myself in this study, what I had vaguely felt until then became clearer and more conscious convictions. I spent the first two semesters in Giessen and through Professor Bousset I gained a strong impression of the seriousness and truthfulness of critical theology, just as I also became familiar with its weaknesses and biases.*

Pastor Emil Weber, a personal friend and fellow brother of Paul Schneider for many years, reports:

From our time together in secondary school we had a heart-felt friendship that was almost in danger of breaking up during the semesters we studied in Giessen as a result of the radical liberalism to which Paul had totally dedicated himself. Not a day passed without heated theological discussions on the way to and especially from the university to the railroad station and on the train. Because he was so intense, Paul could forget to get off the train, and I often had to admonish him to do so. He continued the discussion from the running board and jumped off the train as it began to move. Paul's zeal for the truth went to the extreme. He would have even sacrificed our friendship to it if he thought it were necessary. But today I believe that our battles were the preparation he needed for his later transformation which came to light in just as clear and strong a fashion.[1]

When he was already a pastor and was preparing to take over his father's pastorate in 1926, Paul Schneider made this statement about the religious instruction of his school days:

In school a liberal religious instruction had disabused me of the priestly-mysterious aspect of religion that had always seemed to me like superstition in religion or in the stories of the New Testament. So at times the study of theology appeared to me in friendly colors.**

The son of a fellow student of Paul Schneider who now lives in the United States confirmed the fact that tensions arose between Paul's parents and his teacher on the basis of this liberal religious instruction.

It has been an unshakable fact of Paul Schneider's life at all times that when he had logically thought through intellectual and spiritual problems that were on the agenda at the time and was able to determine his position, he then consistently advocated this position. At the end of the first half of his first semester in Giessen he notes in his diary: "I have a hard time getting used to new things considering my ponderous and slow manner. So the first part of the semester was at first emotionally distressing for me. The new way of dealing with intellectual issues, the way one was expected to totally fend for oneself " is what caused him grief.**

---

[1] *Prediger,* p. 19.

He takes himself to task in a critical spirit and discovers that something must change in him. So he takes up the struggle against himself, enters the "Wingolf"[2] and notes:

> In addition, I joined the Wingolf. Is this fraternity worth the sacrifice of time? Is the benefit I gain commensurate to the time I invest? These questions and my tendency to seek solitude, to shy away from social activities, make me almost shrink back from it. But my inner sense of duty that tells me to overcome my innate propensity to dream and seek comfort, still keeps me faithful to the colors of black-white-gold.**

This entry ends with the momentous sentence, "If you are undecided between two things, then choose the one that is less comfortable for you." At first Paul Schneider does not really feel comfortable in his new surroundings; he writes, "A hopeless feeling of being a stranger in my new circumstances makes me travel home often."**

He knows about his tendency to be a loner and to be awkward. His fellow students want to help and "order" him to take dancing lessons to compensate for his social shortcomings. Although he devotes himself to fraternity life in the first semesters, he notes, "I am not an active supporter of the fraternity."** His father also comes over to Giessen from Hochelheim for certain events. In this way he participates in the life of Paul's fraternity as "the old gentleman."

In spite of all his reservations Paul Schneider still occasionally seems to take pleasure in what his fellow students have "ordered" him to do. He reports:

> Dancing possesses social, educational value; one comes across as being smarter, more skillful, and freer. One learns the gift of conversation more easily, which is necessary to make life easy and bearable in every situation. One becomes more physically agile. Perhaps dancing also brings many a young man out of an abnormal position in relation to the opposite sex into a normal, pure, healthy one.**

The diary also gives information on how he himself views "the opposite sex." On the occasion of a party organized by the fraternity he notes:

---

[2] The "Wingolf" understands itself as a student fraternity on a Christian basis.

Reni is sitting and standing with the other ladies in the stands. Afterwards I went home with my father. How awkwardly I carry on a conversation with Reni, and yet I long to be close to her. It is a mixture of some fear, joy and longing that draws me to her. She is very smooth and smart and tactful, always saying just the right thing . . . and extremely tastefully . . . dressed; how different I must become to be worthy of her. And how natural her demeanor is, whether she is talking to Sophie or to my father or with strangers. The next morning I pick her up and she looks so fresh again in a different dress (white crepe with a blue ribbon), even more beautiful than the day before, in the white lace dress . . . Reni is delightful.**

Paul Schneider always knew how to live life to the full; sanctimonious behavior was weird to him. His relationship to "the opposite sex" was like that of any normal young man.

On October 2, 1919 Paul enrolls in the Philipps University in Marburg. But in the summer semester of 1920 we find him in Tübingen. His later wife writes of this time:

The housing shortage is great; he asks the Weilheim manse to take him in. For the first time he experiences a large family circle and is welcomed into the family. His modest, peaceful, then again boyish, high-spirited nature reminds the family of the minister's son who was killed in the war. Two young people daily walk to the city, he goes to the university, she goes to the women's vocational school. During their lunch break they meet in a canoe on the Neckar River and are living a dream, totally absorbed in an unspoken happiness. Two years pass until they totally find each other and from that time on they walk hand in hand through a four-year engagement period: both a comforting staff and sweet burden to each other.[3]

Paul Schneider was able to wait so that at a later time he could bring his Margarete home with great joy.

We read in his resume about the summer semester: "It has been of less significance to me theologically and was devoted more to exploring the country and people of southern Germany. An ethics seminar taught by Professor Heim

---

[3] *Prediger*, p. 21.

made a lasting impression on me."* Paul Schneider also took his seminar called "An Introduction to the Theology of Schleiermacher and Ritschl" and Professor Schlatter's "New Testament Seminar" as well as a lecture titled "An Explanation of Jesus' Sayings in Luke." Schlatter did not speak to Paul Schneider in Tübingen; the reason would probably be found in the Swiss dialect cultivated by Schlatter. Later, in the seminary in Soest, he worked through Adolf Schlatter's biblical interpretations with great benefit as a "candidate of theology."

Yet before he goes to Tübingen from Marburg, he and his fellow students in Marburg are called to participate in a special mission. Paul Schneider notes:

> Once again I put on the gray coat in early 1920 when the government called the Marburg students to put down a rebellion in Thuringia. These four weeks in Thuringia made me recognize the far-reaching significance of the social question for our nation.*

From Tübingen he returns to Marburg where he completes his final semesters. He writes:

> My appreciation for religion was enhanced by the diverse offerings there in my final semesters. Professor Budde made the Old Testament precious and valuable to me by bringing out the organic link between Old and New Testament piety. The longer I heard Professor Julicher lecture, the more I learned to look up to him. He combined the comforting strains of a heart-felt, positive piety with his enormous knowledge and the often sharp criticism that flowed from it, but never let his students get stuck in the criticism. Professor Otto also captivated me and many of my friends by the numinous depth that he gives to every dogmatic question about the sharp contrast between positive and liberal, and by his masterful ability to make psychological analyses. The seminars of Professor Stephan led me to think and work systematically.*

Paul Schneider was always prepared to learn about contemporary social issues. He never forgot the social injustice he saw and experienced in Thuringia and it left a mark on him.

The whole situation in Germany at that time was more than worrisome; the horrifying effects of the lost war could be felt everywhere. The student Paul Schneider struggled to discern the way he was called to go. He felt the statement made by Professor Kruger during a welcome home ceremony for students who had returned home from the war pointed the way ahead for him: "We are not called to be masters, but servants and leaders of the nation."**

Already during his first semesters in Giessen Paul Schneider began to take issue with the socialism of those days, drawing a distinction between socialism and Bolshevism. He writes: "Bolshevism is a frightening specter before our eyes." He laments the lethargy of the student body that is not facing the challenges of the time and is not seeking any answers to the burning issues of the day. He himself diligently attends lectures and actively participates in the discussions about the subjects they dealt with. After one such lecture he remarks:

> Bolshevism is a contradiction in terms since a condition that can only be determined by the love of the individual for the general public and his good will is to be introduced by violence. This desire to introduce it violently can ultimately not support the idea that the representatives of this violent introduction, of the whip and the strikes, meet these prerequisites for the establishment of the social state. But still no change in attitude occurs solely by introducing external socialization, and so the socialization would have to turn into a permanent dictatorship of the proletariat, which would achieve nothing because the prerequisite for socially just conditions, a socially-minded attitude based on morality, is given even less in the proletariat than in the middle-class. If the nation becomes moral, then its people do better, then we come closer to a socially just state that emerges totally of its own accord.**

Paul Schneider thinks from the New Testament's point of view—something that is always noticeable in his thought. The statements of the New Testament are at first always addressed to the individual in order to enforce the love commandment as well as the whole Decalogue. The sum of individuals who know they are under an obligation to the love commandment, as well as to the commandments as a whole, build the foundation for the socially just state.

Paul Schneider searches for the reasons that have caused the unrest in the German working class. He writes on this subject:

> Man needs physical and intellectual work, and the more he is culturally developed, the more urgent intellectual activity becomes. Likewise, this was a need for the proletariat whose satisfaction was not guaranteed by the social conditions prevalent before the war and . . . this is one of the motives for revolution.**

In another entry we can read: "For only by pursuing intellectual work does man rise above the animals."** He sees man as a whole—body, and soul and spirit—and lets his thought and action be determined by this. These are certainly ideas of a young theology student, but they already reveal what view of man lived in him. Thus he demands that "all human beings share in the intellectual wealth of humanity."**

At that time Paul Schneider joins the "National Student Federation" and thus remains in the tradition of his parents' home without continuing it uncritically. He strives for social behavior in the people of his time that is inspired by the biblical message in which the concept of violence no longer has any place.

Schneider's father came from the Reformed tradition and imparted this to his son within the Protestant United Church. Paul Schneider was of a self-critical and critical nature. So it was inevitable that in the course of his continuing spiritual growth he developed a more reserved relationship to fraternity life: "O bad times! Still no bright spot on the horizon! Still no ray of hope! What helps somewhat is the work, and celebrating festivals there! Founder's Day Celebration! Is it right to join in the celebration?"**

The economic, ethical and political consequences of the lost war hit Protestantism hard. The question of God's justice was passionately discussed. I hope two statements will provide background information on this subject.

1. The officiating court preacher Ernst von Dryander interpreted Romans 8:31 ("If God is for us, who can be against us?") in the worship service before the famous session of the Reichstag on August 4, 1914 in the Berlin Cathedral. He said among other things:

> Looking up to the state that educated us, to the fatherland in which the roots of our strength lie, we know we are entering a battle for our culture against the lack of culture, for civilized German behavior against barbarism, for the free German personality bound to God against the instincts of the disorderly masses . . . . And God will be with our righteous weapons! For German faith and German piety are closely linked to civilized German behavior . . . .[4]

---

[4] B. Doehring, ed., *Eine feste Burg—Predigten und Reden aus eherner Zeit,* vol. 1 (Berlin, 1914), p. 14f.; compare also K. Scholder, *Die Kirchen und das dritte Reich,* vol. 1, p. 7.

2. Johannes Schneider, editor of the "Church Yearbook 1919," expresses his helplessness after the signing of the Versailles Peace Treaty and writes:

> Where has God's justice gone? The question is tormenting thousands, even those who long ago recognized and lamented the inner decline of our nation, its worship of mammon, its pursuit of pleasure, and could observe the marks of God's righteousness in the signs of the times. Are the others better? Is not the worship of mammon an American import? Is not cold-hearted egotism England's gift, and is not moral decline, together with the insatiable hatred expressed in their nasty treatment of us, a typically French characteristic? Do we not see a triumph of lies and a success of meanness that was rare even in the darkest times of history? Is Schiller's saying really true: The history of the world is the judgment of the world? If yes, then righteousness does not judge . . . .[5]

The mood in the population had hit rock bottom in those days; even the church could not offer any direction. In this situation Paul Schneider made his decision in Marburg and left the fraternity.

> In this instance I cut the bond between me and them on my own initiative, since I attacked the fraternity's code of conduct and the forms this institution takes (the foundations of fraternity life), believing they are in need of reform. The main thing was the drinking code. I could have easily stayed in the fraternity in spite of this, but I am quite happy to have time and strength for other things.**

But Paul Schneider still belonged to the Wingolf in Giessen. Membership in a fraternity was limited only to the particular location of the university and independent of one's place of residence and one's later place of study.[6]

In July 1924 he writes to his future father-in-law who suffers from the burden of the lost war just as his own father does:

---

[5] *Kirchliches Jahrbuch* 46 (1919), p. 312. Also on this subject: K. Scholder, *Die Kirchen und das dritte Reich,* vol. 1, p. 8.

[6] Membership in a fraternity remains tied to the location of the university as long as the member or the fraternity want it. A change in one's place of study or graduation does not change anything.

The incomprehensible life we live is greater than we, and in spite of all our strength it is no use to fight against it, it does not rest until it has cast us down and broken us. Life says: not as you will, but as I will. And in time man is given a completely different direction. He must go through collapse and death and emptiness, through despair and bitter pain. But the rebuilding, this is what makes man blessed and happy, and he has to only gradually get used to this joy. He must also be strong to handle this joy so that he will not lose it in exuberance.[7]

On August 29, 1921 Paul Schneider reports to the consistory of the Rhine Province in Koblenz for his first theological examination. In the midst of his preparations for the examination he notes:

Hochelheim, Feb. 28, 1922

The art of living must be learned anew every day. Here there is never a sense of being finished, of being "out of the woods." Our life must be like continual military service; we must "always be on duty." Without this readiness the trials we face will become our master, we will lose our sense of direction and before we know it, we will have succumbed to depression. If you believe you are standing, watch out that you haven't already fallen! I am cramming for the examination and notice how even this little, finite goal of passing the examination gives me strength and perseverance.

I would have never thought that I could sit for days behind the books. And I think I've stayed physically fresh while studying. I will again have to change my ideas about the relationship between the spirit and the body. It is the spirit that builds the body. Perhaps I stressed the necessity of personal hygiene in such a one-sided manner that it revealed a lack of faith. I practiced asceticism and yet I did not get control of my situation or myself. You looked for the health of "body and soul" only on the periphery, on the surface and not first in prayer, with God, as the most profound and original source.

Work builds and preserves man. If this is true of physical labor, should it not be even truer of spiritual labor? If it were possible for me to fill my day totally with spiritual labor, would I still need muscle power to keep my health? If the spirit and the will can do everything, truly, it

---

[7] *Prediger*, p. 22.

must also be able to build an appealing dwelling, without health fads .
. . . Can not God give me strength, as much as he wants, as much as I
need, and throw all "reasonable moderation" overboard? So it is left to
me to live my life totally from God, the reasonable and wonderful, all-
powerful and kind-hearted One. I want him to tell me what I should
do, how I have to live, and forego all my own standards. Lord God,
show me my goal, the goal of my life and my work! What counts then
is using my strength to achieve this goal and making it subservient to
him, knowing that so much of what is now so dark must become light.
My God and Father, please give me this liberating outlook!**

Under April 2, 1922 we find out:

I am facing the test (the date for it is April 6). I hope more and more
that I am able to place the result and the further course of my life in
God's hand. For a while I was filled with great restlessness, energy and
drive only to see it suddenly give way to an emptiness and tiredness
that made me think I had nothing left in my spiritual possession. But
it is also more the coming and going of my awareness of God and his
assistance that often throws me for a loop without having a desire to
intervene in my own inner struggle of faith.**

The intensity of this inner struggle is what drives him into a kind of
"melancholy and anxiety." Slowly Paul Schneider grows into a special, indeed,
personal relationship with his God so that his wife can later report:

On a day before Christmas a ray of the eternal light penetrates into
his soul, a great rejoicing begins, and for a long time he lives on this
"spiritual excitement and the spiritual emotions it engendered"; the
knowledge that God can cause light to shine remains in him.[8]

Remembering these inner events he himself writes later:

It is not easy to put on the new self . . . . The Holy Spirit who seeks to
dwell in our inmost being has a bitter struggle with the old self and his
lethargy and his fleshly inclinations. God is faithful; he will not let you

---

[8] Ibid., p. 21f.

be tempted beyond what you can bear. But when you are tempted, he will also provide a way out so that you can stand up under it. O weak human beings, remember the great fatherly love of your God.**

7

A BLUE COLLAR WORKER AMONG BLUE COLLAR WORKERS

After Paul Schneider passed his first theological examination, he again set his sights on the German working class that had to suffer especially hard from the poor, even oppressive, conditions following the First World War. Theoretical reflections on social conditions are certainly necessary and useful; but such reflections are praiseworthy only when action can be seen as the end result. Paul Schneider writes to Weilheim:

> As far as my immediate future is concerned, I first want to go to a mine near Dortmund to become familiar with the miners at work on the scene, which my body also enables me to do. I want to get to know their merits and shortcomings to possibly recognize in what corner of their heart religion has gone into hiding. I hope that I will learn to love them more and more.[1]

The industrial workers have always been the stepchildren of society; this was very apparent in the nineteenth century when industrial developments entered a new stage, and continued their tragic progression in the twentieth century. Church and state were linked together too closely in that era; the fears of the state were also the fears of the church. The specter of revolution cast its shadow; and leading industrial circles in Germany believed that the working class could instigate a revolution. The alliance between the throne and the altar forged in this era alienated the working class from the church for generations. Paul Schneider recognized the problems that had arisen in this context and

---

[1] *Prediger*, p. 25.

decided to take an "industrial internship" to be a blue-collar worker among blue-collar workers for a while.[2]

On May 2, 1922 he arrives in Dortmund-Aplerbeck at his uncle's home, who is the business manager of a steelworks there. He is at once introduced

---

[2] A speech that was given on September 1, 1919 by the Church Congress President R. Moeller in Dresden shows how closely the Protestant church was linked together with the throne: "The first German Protestant Church Congress is convening in a difficult, serious time. Our nation collapsed in a world war that was without parallel, after a more than four-year long heroic struggle against a whole world of enemies. The glory of the German empire, the dream of our fathers, the pride of every German is gone. The exalted bearer of German power, the ruler and the ruling dynasty whom we as the standard bearers of German greatness so dearly loved and protected, are gone with it. A terrible peace has put an end to the terrible war. A peace was imposed on us by the harsh cruelty of our enemies to bring us two things: an end with horror and a horror without end, to take from us virtually everything that could lift our spirits, to destroy our nation, if possible, politically, economically and spiritually, to take from it not only its military but its honor as well. The German people, plunged into radical change and a seemingly interminable upheaval of all public life by having to make immeasurable sacrifices of property and blood, and by suffering many years of hunger and starvation, lie shattered on the ground and are still bleeding from a thousand wounds. The Protestant church of the German Reformation has been drawn deeply into this collapse. The Protestant churches of our fatherland have maintained the closest connections to the public authorities of the state since the days of the Reformation. We can do no other than solemnly testify to what rich blessings have rained down on both of them—on the state and the church—and through both of them on the people and the fatherland as a result of the close connections between the state and the church. And we can do no other than to solemnly testify in deep anguish how the churches of our fatherland owe a deep debt of gratitude to their royal patrons, having maintained close ties with their lineage in many cases through a history of many hundreds of years. We know how this deeply felt sense of gratitude will live on unforgettably in the people of the Protestant church. On a large scale, the overthrow of the state constitutions has had far-reaching effects on the church constitutions. By losing a church government upheld by the ruler of the state, the churches have had their chief support taken from them. In this situation the established churches have been effected even more by the demand of the new authorities to separate the state from the church, and it is unmistakable that strong forces are also at work to implement this demand with the intention of seriously endangering the church" (quoted by H. W. Krummwiede, *Evangelische Kirche und Theologie in der Weimarer Republik* [Grundtexte zur Kirchen- und Theologie-geschichte] [Neukirchen-Vluyn, 1989], p. 18f.). The father of Paul Schneider could fully agree with this. But the son sets out to chart a new course that must lead in a different direction because he is compelled to register doubts about the traditional concept of the church. He seeks out those to whom the church had previously paid little attention.

by him into "high society" and experiences there nothing but a gaping void spiritually. He notes:

> And then comes dinner at Westermann's house with my uncle and his colleagues. A lone Catholic engineer shows some appreciation for religious questions; most of them are completely indifferent and do not participate in our discussion of the subject. Only Mr. R. and the director, who is a radical rationalist, do.**

From then on Paul Schneider avoids those circles and also does not accept the well-endowed position his uncle arranged for him. The diary note reads:

> Thursday afternoon. Knowing that I prefer miner's work, I cannot bring myself to follow my uncle's order to start that job. I reported to the plant manager that my purposes were poorly served there and that I wanted to work elsewhere.**

This remarkable entry follows:

> I came here to be a blue collar worker among blue collar workers. It was no surprise that Uncle R. immediately was pulled into high society. I heard statements that were hostile to the workers and I knew that I had lost my inhibitions. I saw the contrast between labor and management too sharply. I turned to Phönix in Hörde. I went through all the channels I could until I was promised work. I thought I would miss the main purpose of my project if I were seduced by the offer of well-paid work.**

The fact that this unaccustomed activity would bring problems for him is understandable. He notes:

> I have already been at Phönix for two weeks as the third man at the smelting furnace in the Martin works. The first few days, namely the first afternoon shifts, turned out to be really miserable for me. The second afternoon shift almost made me wilt. I think that now I have pretty well gotten used to the work.**

In his free time Paul Schneider seeks out conversations with his working companions. He got a room in a dormitory where only single workers live. He notes in his diary: "I came home at ten o'clock encouraged by all kinds of interesting conversations." He does not miss Sunday worship, and in spite of all the physical stress and strain he listens to God's voice in his heart so that he can give an account of himself.

> I imagined that I had made a sacrifice when I went to the single men's dormitory at Phönix to be among the workers; so I daily suffer defeats as I struggle with my selfishness, violating the law of love. Why did I have to leave my companions in Schwerte and go swimming in the Ruhr? Why haven't I seen my uncle for fourteen days? And whenever the devil of selfishness controls me, I am sick and indecisive. Then the others probably say: "Funny character!" It is as if I can be especially ugly and disgusting in my daily personal life after trying to build my life on great ideals. What counts now are my little everyday struggles to lead a life motivated more by love. May God help me to do that.**

Paul Schneider did not come to the blast furnace as an onlooker, as a spectator, but to get to know people who have to earn their daily bread under the most difficult conditions, people whom he missed in the Christian community of faith. In the midst of his work at the blast furnace he struggles to find the content and dimensions of his proclamation: "What should I preach?" He entrusts to his diary:

> Once again I am on the go. Although I am beginning to dread the thought of hiking all alone, I am driven again and again to do so, for no one cares to share my interests. I am disgusted by the loneliness, and disgusted by the company of human beings. I no longer have anything. Everything is a problem: capitalism and socialism, religion and life. I am left with nothing. I feel empty and completely drained of all my strength. My time on this job is coming to an end. I am supposed to preach again and work in my father's business. What should I preach? The gospel: all human beings becoming fully human, my views on private property, on socialism? How difficult it is for a rich man to enter the Kingdom of God! How about doing God's will? How about the prodigal son and his older brother and Jesus' words about saying,

"Lord, Lord?" Power from on high is necessary; I want to pray for it.**

Paul Schneider does not suppress the emotional devastation, but faces it in order to find acceptable answers that can give him the proper direction as he continues his journey. He leaves his "job" in Hörde with mixed feelings and returns to his father's manse. On September 7, 1922 he notes:

> I am sure that my close ties with some here will outlast our outward separation. I cannot even put into written words all the love that was shown to me there and one is doubly grateful for that in this rough industrial work environment. But it has strengthened my faith in our people and above all my faith in our blue-collar workers. Thus I would not like to have missed out on these three months in the single men's dormitory at any price.

As he said good-bye, his working companions said: "You are one of us, you should stay here!"

8

A NEW PHASE BEGINS

Before Paul Schneider continues his theological training, he becomes engaged to the pastor's daughter Margarete Dieterich from Weilheim near Tübingen. We read with great respect what his wife later writes about the beginning of their engagement: "More and more we offer each other a home, we can support each other pastorally."[1]

On October 31, 1922 the theology candidate Paul Schneider enters the seminary of his church in Soest. As the first of nine candidates he has to conduct the worship service. His sermon is based on the gospel from Luke 9:57–62 and deals with the seriousness of discipleship!

Paul Schneider feels really well in Soest and notes: "I am feeling the very beneficial effects of the order, tranquility and spiritual work I experienced during my stay at the convent; if only I could truly enjoy it as a gift with a clean conscience."**

We read further:

> And when I had to deal with Schlatter in Soest, I was at first disappointed, but during this semester I learned to appreciate him more and more. A change in my own theological views goes hand in hand with this. I think I have understood a little bit more and would rather call myself positive than liberal as far as the basic structure of my theology is concerned. The absolute importance of the divinity and redeeming power of Jesus Christ is being revealed to us as we become aware of our own sinfulness . . . . Nothing has become of my dissertation for my degree. I have again dozed away and squandered a week and am about to do it with a second one. What should I do? I cannot find a

---

[1] *Prediger*, p. 21.

way out. Whatever way you look at it: Be faithful, believe and trust.**

Soest, June 19, 1923
What is hardest of all for the human heart is humility. Only the one who gets totally free from the self has humility. We must learn to hate ourselves. The darkest hours of our lives lead us closest to God and we owe him the greatest debt of gratitude for them.**

Paul Schneider postpones his second theological examination, which causes trouble for the consistory in Koblenz, but the director of the seminary can handle it. "I postponed my examination . . . . No one can serve two masters. I think that I have a right to postpone it in the interests of an unhurried development in my life of faith and my spiritual life."**

Until the next date for his examination he engages the thought of theologians such as Friedrich Tholuck (1799–1877), who influenced the revivalist movement as a professor in Halle and Berlin. In his sermons he especially objected to the infiltration of theology by the alien philosophy of Idealism as well as to the rigidity of biblical proclamation as it was perpetrated by orthodoxy. Besides these very important sermons for him, sermons by Johannes Wichelhaus (1819–1858) fell into his hands in the Soest library. Wichelhaus had likewise taught in Halle. Coming from Rhenish revivalist circles, he took an unambiguous position on Holy Scripture and on the confessional documents of the church that led him to become isolated within his faculty.

In conjunction with his reading Paul Schneider entrusts to his diary: "Thank God who fills my days and who takes the tedium out of them . . . . No temptation has seized you except what is common to man. And God is faithful; he will not let you be tempted beyond what you can bear. But when you are tempted, he will also provide a way out so that you can stand up under it."**

This thirteenth verse from the tenth chapter of the first epistle to the Corinthians runs like a central thread through the further life of Paul Schneider. In spite of all his inner tensions he does not lose sight of the human beings who are affected by social and economic hardship. We read in his diary:

Because of the strong solidarity of our workers this suffering is spreading across the whole working class, welding them together even more firmly than before. It will transform Germany into a workers' state, and this will be the socially just state. It is clear who alone can give the strength that is needed to find this will to work and so this social state will have to be much more imbued with the strength of Christianity than the national community has been until now.**

On July 11, 1923 Paul Schneider finds these comforting words for his future father-in-law, who is suffering heavily from the hardship of his people:

> A dark shadow is spreading over the autumn of your life, as it is over all of our lives, the hardship of our fatherland, its emotional and psychological distress which has not yet allowed it to find its stabilizing anchor in the storms and waves breaking over our days.
>
> This is why the distress must rise even higher for the time being. Will the German Empire be broken by this crisis? It is a strange feeling today when one sees how the great prophets of the Old Testament faced the almost complete destruction of their people with such cold determination. May God's Kingdom be more important than anything else!
>
> Even the German nation is only his tool that he is preparing for his purposes as he always does. It can also be a temporal, transitory, conditional link on the way to the goal: "Since he will make his kingdom great and there will be no end to the peace on David's throne and in his Kingdom." No cruel fate of our fatherland, no matter how cruel it may seem to us, should ever be able to rob us of profound joy, the joy that is found in God although we do not see it. For what is visible is temporal, but what is invisible is eternal. And if the prophets of old, living in hope, did not become frightened even though they had not yet seen the salvation of their God, if they valued this hope more highly than fame and honor and the happiness of their people, why should we be frightened, for we are the ones to whom salvation has been given and for whom it is sealed. We are the ones who know that everything that is still to come is only the completion of salvation history's course! Certainly, we still live in this world and with this suffering people and also share its sufferings. But we have a commission and a calling from another world and our citizenship is there. And we know that in spite of everything this world will one day be victorious: Therefore, we will be cheerful in tribulation.[2]

---

[2] Ibid., p. 29. Paul Schneider had written this letter to his father-in-law, who suffered from the hardship of the fatherland just as his own father did, on the occasion of his 67th birthday. The letter ends: "Send my greetings to mother and the whole household. In grateful

Here we can clearly see the source emerging from which he drew his strength in the days of horror in order to survive everything: "But we have a commission and a calling from another world and our citizenship is there." Paul Schneider makes a further significant discovery after passing his second theological examination:

> My academic homework, "What are we to think of the concept of the facts of salvation?" made me answer this question in quite positive terms . . . . This homework helped me to clarify my own viewpoint. You know, I have to find my way to it from the liberal viewpoint. This practical, yet academic work was called: "Instruction in Religion and Morality." I was in my element there. I proposed two basic theses: Instruction in religion is not the same as instruction in morality and there is no instruction in religion without the teaching of the Law.[3]

After the examination we find Paul Schneider in Berlin. His fellow brother at the time Wilhelm Grundler reports:

> Paul Schneider is not a suitable candidate for later glorification, as simple and modest as he was. But it was precisely this simplicity that bound us together. He simply tried to speak the truth that had shone on him and to bear witness to what had become a reality for him in his own life before both friend and foe . . . . We both passed the second theological examination. While asking the question "What now?" we followed an invitation made by Pastor Eric Schnepel to go to Berlin to get involved in the city mission there, since at the time no associate pastoral positions were vacant. For half a Dutch guilder sent to us by Pastor Schnepel (it was the fall of 1923, in the midst of the inflation), we both traveled to Berlin, each to a different place that Pastor Schnepel assigned to us there within his staff, most of whom were men from Chrischona.

Paul Schneider reports from Berlin:

---

love, your son, Paul." Paul Schneider felt that he was a son in the house of his in-laws in the truest sense of the word.

[3] *Prediger*, p. 31.

It was not without reason that I got into Pastor Schnepel's circle of friends. His mission had freed itself financially from the city mission in an earlier time of hardship to ease the city mission's financial burden. Since then they expect to receive everything directly from the living Lord and no longer by way of any organization. In an external sense as well, they trust the Lord to provide for their daily bread. So each individual staff member is not tied to a specific salary . . . . Grappling with a piety whose claims go beyond anything found in traditional church doctrine was not so easy for me and forced me to once again play the role of the spiritually bankrupt Christian, yet in the end it could be chalked up as a good experience. Even if I did want to run away from this strange city of Berlin with its even stranger people at one time or another, God renewed my courage, as you prayed, and now I certainly do not want to leave here until I have gotten a handle on the questions I grappled with in Pastor Schnepel's circle. Here there are people who claim that they not only know Jesus and seek to follow his teaching, but possess him as the living power of their lives. He has set them free from sin so that it no longer has any control over them. They not only claim this, but they give the impression that they really have, in fact, totally surrendered their lives to Jesus, have loved only him alone and have really died to their own desires, ideas or feelings. They gave the impression of really being redeemed. They prove their Christianity by being willing to make great sacrifices and by radiating joy. In a quite child-like way they associate with the Savior as they would with a close friend who is really alive and who certainly hears all of their prayers. Here I must say to myself: You are not yet such a child of God. I feel as if I were ostracized by him, for so much unconfessed sin still separates me from him, so much clinging to my own desires, so much brazen insistence on my own ideas. Thus it has come about that in dealing with the subject of mission I have first turned into its object.[4]

He advises his future brother-in-law from Berlin: "Test the spirits! Many claim to be pious, but that is why it is also really instructive to immerse oneself here in the life of this circle."[5]

---

[4] *Prediger*, p. 32f.

[5] Ibid., p. 33.

In the summer of 1924 Paul Schneider is assigned to his sick father as a personal assistant pastor and ordained on January 30, 1925 in Hochelheim by superintendent Wieber who is responsible for the Rhenish Synod of Wetzlar. In his ordination service Paul Schneider preaches on Romans 1:16: "I am not ashamed of the gospel, because it is the power of God for the salvation of everyone who believes: first for the Jew, then for the Gentile."

The consistory in Koblenz entrusts the young pastor with the position of an assistant pastor in downtown Essen, which in many ways poses a challenge for him. Again he listens to his heart and entrusts these thoughts to his diary:

> *September 5, 1925, Essen; Weberstrasse 5*
> I have not made an entry in my diary for almost two years. Have I made progress in Christianity, in the art of living, in knowing God, in knowing the world of human beings? Have I used my time, or was I an unfaithful steward? . . . You alone, God, know the magnitude of my guilt. I turn to your grace and compassion; do not turn your face from me and show me the way I should go . . . . I have the loveliest girl imaginable and cannot bring her home. God, that is a just punishment! I am in the highest profession and can only practice it poorly, almost not at all . . . my life more and more resembles that of a sleepwalker.

During this time Paul Schneider goes through one of his most difficult spiritual crises. With an almost pedantic honesty toward himself he sifts through his relationship with God, whose Word he is to proclaim to human beings.

In Hochelheim he meets a father who is dying. Then on January 13, 1926 his father is called home. Soon Paul Schneider is given his second job as an assistant pastor.

> *March 13, on a Sunday morning*
> From Essen I am moved again to Rotthausen on February 1, 1926; up to now I have not been able to preach any sermon. My head is too weak and my conscience and my will are too irresolute. While I was still in Essen, I became familiar with Mazdaznan[6] and the reformed life. I preached the "pure blood" like a gospel and am losing my faith in God and Christ because of it . . . . What should I preach? . . . Until now

---

[6] The system of a lifestyle based on old Tiranian ideas.

I always thought that my weak head was to blame for my inability to perform the duties of ministry. And yet at the same time it was always the feeling that I wasn't fully behind the things I was supposed to say. This is very distressing to me as I prepare my sermons; it was also what kept me from using pious expressions when I made pastoral visits. The faith of the church is not my faith. I have lost all joyfulness in preparing and delivering my sermons. My prayer life was always very stunted and has now completely dried up . . . . I only say phrases, just for show, repeated hundreds of times. I simply lack the memory to perform my official duties as competently as my colleagues. Already I feel as if the church members with whom I associate have seen through my lack of truthfulness. I can no longer bear this breach of confidence.**

What is going on in the young pastor? Does he really feel incapable of assuming the pastoral office? Does he not set the bar of the demands he places on himself too high? Or must the reality of sin and grace first become stronger in the world of his experience?

Paul Schneider becomes more and more convinced of a direct encounter of all human beings with God. This makes him restless; here he must be truthful and must not remain silent about Christ. For Paul Schneider man experiences a new reality by faith, a new life is in store for him. This new reality is of overriding importance. But this also means that as one who proclaims this new reality, he must be steeped in it in order to fulfill his task honestly and with joy. On June 8, 1926 he notes:

The worm of death is sin, but thank God who in Christ has taken away death's power! . . . How true it is that my past is a document of my unbelief! From what great distress has my God rescued me, yet again and again I fail to understand that there is no point in trying to help the work of his hand, how great is the damage then. I am privileged to sing songs of praise to my God again. The Spirit from above is much stronger than all natural powers. Now we are also no longer servants of nature. God, all of life is drawn to you, and what does not come to you becomes sick. Wrote Hans a letter yesterday . . . and want to cheer up Gretel again today.**

He writes to Weilheim:

It will make you and especially father happy to know that I am glad to be a pastor, even in the big city. God is also giving me increasing strength to go with the increasing tasks. On Sunday I performed five official duties. This is to be my comfort and my confidence, as Wichern once exclaimed: "You, God, leave nothing unfinished and you have awakened my desire to serve you; you will also give me the strength to perform my tasks according to your grace and love for Jesus' sake.[7]

[7] *Prediger*, p. 36.

9

PASTOR OF HOCHELHEIM AND DORNHOLZHAUSEN

After the death of Pastor Gustav Adolf Schneider the sessions of the Protestant church of Hochelheim and Dornholzhausen in the Rhenish Synod unanimously elect his son Paul to be the pastor of the two congregations. Certainly various wishes expressed by the congregation are connected with this election. Yet he soon shows that as the son of his predecessor "he is prepared to go his own way for which he alone assumes responsibility."

Since the conditions set by the consistory to get married and have a family are met on assuming the pastorate, the long engagement is ended. In Weilheim his father-in-law performs the wedding ceremony, he chooses as their wedding verse: "Where you go I will go, and where you stay I will stay. Your people will be my people and your God my God" (Rt. 1:16). The tenor of his meditation is: "Be united, united in faith, love and hope."

On September 4, 1926 the superintendent of the Wetzlar Synod installs Paul Schneider in his office; he exhorts the young pastor: "Be strong and courageous, and do the work. Do not be afraid or discouraged, for the Lord God, my God is with you. He will not fail you or forsake you until all the work for the service of the temple of the Lord is finished" (1 Chr. 28:20). During the worship service Paul Schneider preaches on 1 Timothy 3:1: "Here is a trustworthy saying: If anyone sets his heart on being an overseer, he desires a noble task," and 2 Timothy 3:14–17: "But as for you, continue in what you have learned and have become convinced of, because you know those from whom you learned it, and how from infancy you have known the holy Scriptures, which are able to make you wise for salvation through faith in Christ Jesus. All Scripture is God-breathed and is useful for teaching, rebuking, correcting and training in righteousness, so that the man of God may be thoroughly equipped for every good work."

Paul Schneider knows from the beginning that he is responsible for all the members of both congregations. As grateful as he is on the one hand for the attendance of the "Evangelical Community," on the other hand he looks out for the others who move on the fringes of both congregations.

From 1931 a church newsletter is preserved which he had written while on vacation:

> My dear congregations of Hochelheim and Dornholzhausen, I want to send you my warmest greetings today from my vacation home, from the home of my childhood, Pferdsfeld, in the Kreuznach district. Our regional supplement in the "Kasseler Sonntagsblatt"[1] is called "The Church in Our Region" and our Rhenish Sunday newsletter also features a "regional corner."
>
> In these days I especially remember how good it is to cultivate memories of our home region, our local history and a love for our native land since I am living in the area where I was born and where I gained the first impressions of my childhood. The little village is nestled high in the meadows where the Hoxbach valley begins. From there one can see the powerfully ascending hills of the Soon Forest, the old, humble little homes, the nooks and crannies of the village. Some of the people are still the familiar old figures of my childhood, and the bubbling fountain is the same now as it was then. How wonderful it is that all this captivates the soul in a strong and good love, how great a blessing it is that both body and soul enjoy resting in the lap of one's hometown. But, my dear congregations, you should not think that I do not consider you as my home, especially since you have asked me to stay in my parental home in Hochelheim and at the place of my youth by choosing me as your pastor. You are now the home of my work, the home of my manhood and the home of my parish, which I as your pastor would like to help you develop into a truly cozy and warm church home for all of you with all the strength and love that are given to me. And precisely because you know that as your pastor I enjoy living among you and want to stay with you, you will surely now grant

---

[1] A Christian weekly periodical.

me the privilege of enjoying the hometown of my childhood during this vacation and gaining new strength here for my work.

On November 24, 1927 Paul Schneider opens his diary for the last time and notes:

> It has been almost a year and a half since I have entrusted anything to you, my little book. And now you call me to quiet reflection once again. I have become a husband, father and pastor. Yet how many walk on the wrong path in such an office!
>
> Yet in these days a great restlessness has come over me. Has my heart left everything to serve Jesus? Have the "soft arms" of which Kierkegaard writes been my undoing? Have I made the right decision to follow the path of self-denial and renunciation at decisive moments of my life? May I step before the congregation tomorrow with the joy of advent and the message of advent? If only the Spirit would burn more brightly in my heart! May God let me experience the abundance of his grace once again! Otto Carstens consoled me by saying that I have taken a big step forward since Berlin. I think my being here means new strength and blessing, as I have requested for myself. O God in heaven, let me not be robbed of everything again! Give me the gift of faith and peace! Living under constant strain, I must put a question mark behind all that I do and say. You, o God, can pour out your Spirit of love on me so that the question mark may turn into a joyous Yes. Amen!**

An awakening of the youth took place in the nineteenth century. The young generation was looking for new forms of communication that were suitable for it, for it could no longer identify with the social customs of the middle class of its time. So it set out to rediscover nature, poetry, the fine arts, and music. The *Wandervogel* (hikers) youth movement, whose individual chapters appeared in diverse forms, soon had a great influence on the social life of Germany. This new beginning gained an additional component in the industrial working class that was forming then. It is significant that the members of these diverse groups came from all levels of society and showed their solidarity within their groups in order to look for new paths to explore. Exceptions that prove the rule are found in the youth groups that were exclusively oriented toward party politics. This awakening of youth had a lasting effect that stretched far into the twentieth century and we cannot imagine the social life of the latter part of the nineteenth century up to the first third of the twentieth century without it.

The church administration had a hard time dealing with the concerns of youth. The establishment of church youth groups depended on the respective activity of the local pastors. The "Free Church Communities" became especially active; thus it is not surprising that a wide variety of groups shot up like mushrooms. It was regrettable that precisely in the "Christian" realm an unpleasant competitive mentality produced its deleterious effects.

It is important to know for our present day that in those days it was the Christian youth groups that early on made international contacts which proved their worth in later times.

Paul Schneider was always prepared to address the problems of young people. The reason why he was especially prepared to listen to them resulted from the experiences he had in working through his own questions and from the inner tensions he experienced. We find out from a letter he wrote how he saw Protestant youth work in contrast to the recipient:

> We have already been wrestling with the questions you raised for five years. The community movement (the Pietists) had a "churchly purpose" when in its men's and youth clubs it did nothing else but hold a Bible study except for its brass ensemble. The study was surely not poorly explained by Messenger Trippler[2] or was the trombone playing also supposed to fall under the category of "educational purposes" which has no place in these clubs? Of course, until now purely church songs were played. There was also a similar young women's association, only mixed choral singing took the place of the trombone playing. But these pure, unadulterated "church" structures were stuck in a pitiful stage of development, without any influence on the rest of the younger generation and, as I discovered, also without real Christian understanding or knowledge of Scripture. Affairs at an early age and occasionally gross moral lapses occurred with this kind of youth leadership that strongly stressed "only the Word." Then the girls came by themselves and wanted to me to serve them in the same way we ran our confirmation program, first reading something nice to nurture their emotional life. We assumed responsibility for the young women's

---

[2] A preacher with a special missionary commission within a Pietistic community of the established church or a free church community.

association and placed it under our leadership, not without occasional clashes with the older members. In addition, we looked after the other girls on open evenings until we had a retreat for young girls where we offered Bible study and a serious discussion of their questions along with singing and dancing as well. Its success motivated us to expand our ministry and establish a young girls' association where the Pietistic community girls and the other girls are together.

In a similar fashion we have united boys from the Pietistic community and others in a young men's association. In both groups I intentionally offer games and singing and other kinds of educational entertainment and work that is not directly biblical in addition to the devotional . . . . In my view the established church as such also has an educational task just as the parental home and the school does. And if we wanted to, we could characterize Christian education in the home and in school as church work. However, how much more does the church have educational work to do where the home and school largely fail! And could you as a local church pastor take the responsibility for gathering a group of born-again boys or five pious young women around the Bible who don't need anything else, and let all the other young people in your parish go or leave their education in the hands of today's educators, teachers, secular clubs and political parties? Then you would be just like our failing homes of today where parents no longer ask where and how long their children are hanging around outside. If you are serious about what you wrote, you are actually discounting all other methods that would enable us to reach the youth who have become strangers to us. I agree with you about this: Of course, a Christian association must be centered around the Bible, or around Jesus Christ and its goal must be to lead individuals into a living faith relationship with Christ.[3]

Paul Schneider also lets his colleague know that for him the sum total of the church's youth work cannot just be a youth bible study. Influenced by God's Word, he sees man in his totality, i.e., as a creature of God with both body and soul.

In this world the Word of God also has a body and truly does not only consist of anemic dialectics . . . . I claim my whole pastorate as

---

[3] A copy in the possession of the author.

a ministry of the Word, including administrative work and care for the physical well-being of the sick and the renewal of the church and planning and fundraising for the pre-school. The fact that preaching and bible study and the pastoral visit have to remain the soul of ministry is obvious.

A partnership such as a Christian association or club not only has a soul, but also needs a body. And the younger generation more than any other knows very well that it has a body. We do not hold the Catholic viewpoint that places a lesser value on the physical. We do not believe in an asceticism of the body, but the sanctification of the body. Jesus himself did not disdain the idea of binding his disciples to himself in the closest partnership imaginable. By doing so, he stressed the educational principle. Just as I reject the principle of isolated conversions practiced by the Pietistic community, I also reject isolated church activity, an isolated action of the Word . . . .[4]

---

[4] Ibid.

10

1933: THE YEAR OF CHANGES

As far as party politics is concerned, Paul Schneider and his wife sided with the "Christian-Social National Service" which originated in Württemberg. In a family newsletter he expresses this opinion:

> By the way, I am getting around in a much more lazy way. I'm riding my motorcycle in a yellow biker's suit. Then I am beyond recognition as a pastor and am greeted by the children and other enthusiastic followers of Hitler with the typical *"Heil Hitler"* shouts. We have not yet fallen victim to this modern popular movement—I am expressing myself cautiously so as not to bring any political divisions into the circle of our brothers and sisters—but much prefer to side with the home-grown Swabian Christian National Service. We have loyally and openly pledged our allegiance to Hindenburg in the elections, though it has made my position more difficult and brought a complaint that the district leader of the NDSAP made to our General Superintendent. However, we are not in agreement with Hindenburg's most recent actions.
>
> O how I lament the unfortunate partisan spirit that sins against the nation as a whole both here and there! Where are the men and women with discerning Christian consciences who get their standards for political action neither from National Socialism nor from Socialism, but from the gospel? National Socialism does not yet draw from this source; will it really be able to unite both poles and lead our nation toward moral and religious renewal which it so urgently needs?[1]

---

[1] The family newsletter stems from 1932. Hindenburg, Hitler and Thälmann were candidates in the election for President of the Reich held on April 10, 1932. Von Hindenburg

The synod has entrusted Paul Schneider with the care of the homeless and needy children in the Wetzlar church district. This task involved dealing with various problems. In Hochelheim there was a shelter for the homeless. If a couple with children was to be put up there, which occurred rather frequently at that time, Paul Schneider brought them to the manse. In this context he writes to his mother-in-law: "This is a saying so fitting for our day: real socialism does not begin in the street, but in the family."[2]

National Socialist propaganda liked to declare its takeover a "national uprising" which had been initiated by the German people themselves. Guided by political expediency, it stirred up nationalistic and patriotic emotions with all the means at its disposal. This tactic was hardly recognized. Even Paul Schneider wonders if it could not contribute something to rebuilding the fatherland. "If only we as a church could also make a positive contribution to the inner reconstruction of our nation, which we owe it as we perform the actual duties of our office."[3]

National Socialism had an easy job persuading the German people at that time. Unemployment was alarmingly high and the state's unemployment benefits were not sufficient for most of the unemployed to make ends meet. Charitable organizations established food distribution centers in the big cities and not a few took a daily warm meal there. Germany not only had to suffer from the effects of the lost war (1914/18) but was also affected by the world economic crisis to an especially great degree. This inevitably had serious consequences for its political and social life. The new political agitators got a productive "field of operation." The National Socialists promised "work and bread" and a new "German consciousness," meaning the termination of all international treaties. They propagated a merciless struggle against the Jews and against all who resisted them. The "newly awakened German consciousness" was dependent on each new National Socialist dictate.

---

garnered 53.95% of the votes cast, Hitler received 36.68% and Thalmann 10.13%. Also compare on this subject *Prediger*, p. 51.

[2] Ibid., 49. If the shelter was stretched beyond capacity, space also had to be occupied in the manse if there were complicated cases, which was frequently the case for couples with children.

[3] *Prediger*, p. 52.

Throughout the country one could soon read signs at the restaurants: "Today there will be a German evening and German dancing!" Paul Schneider remarks on this:

> Today there will be a German evening with German dancing. Is this a different kind of dancing from the usual kind? But one invites the great majority to slide shows and bible studies in vain. What have our Protestant churches become? And yet these are God's times! And somehow God has his work among us, we must cling to this and joyfully move forward in faith.[4]

On March 21, 1933 the final German Reichstag that was elected according to democratic rules convened for its first session in the old garrison church in Potsdam with great nationalistic pomp and circumstance. The freely elected representatives of the Communist Party and a large number of Social Democratic representatives were missing. They were prevented from taking their seats because they were either arrested or victimized by National Socialist terrorist actions. The incumbent Reich President von Hindenburg had appeared for this ceremony especially dressed in his old imperial field marshal's uniform. Nationalistic and patriotic excitement was decreed for the German Empire. We find out from the following session minutes what happened in Hochelheim:

> Meeting of the session on March 21, 1933
>
> At the urgent invitation of the Pastor all the members of the session immediately gather in the manse, and thus constitute a quorum.
>
> The situation is that at nine o'clock this morning the village rang its bell proclaiming that from noon to 12:30 p.m. the church bells should be rung without the pastor or session being aware of any edict or church announcement. At the same time a motion made by a National Socialist church member was sent to the chairman of the session, stating that the bells should be rung according to an announcement made by the leadership of the NSDAP.

---

[4] Ibid.

The chairman requests that the motion be denied without offending those participating in this national day. This request is made not only because the NSDAP and the municipal authorities are encroaching on the rights of the church, but also to make clear that we are not a state church. Anton Hartsmannshenn also condemns the encroachment of the municipal authorities, but speaks in favor of participating in the bell ringing because of the day's national significance.

The chairman makes his motion and a vote is taken. The rest of the members approve the bell ringing. The chairman maintains his position during the vote.

The whole session votes unanimously to inform the municipal authorities that in the future it will reject any similar encroachment on the rights of the church and that the right of determining the use of the bells is one of them (occurs by oral agreement of the pastor with the chairman of the village council).

The session is closed with the blessing of the Lord.

Signed,
Pastor Schneider, Hartmannshenn, Joh. Zorb,
H. Simon, F. Heintz

From now on the National Socialists kept an eye on the pastor of Hochelheim and Dornholzhausen who had already caught their attention before their takeover. They placed spies in his worship services to collect material against him. What is so terrible is that there were not a few at that time who willingly assumed such duties.

Let us remember a proclamation of the "German Protestant Church Committee" from March 1933 to get some sense of the drama in the "German Protestant Church," which was divided into 29 regional churches. Paul Schneider's behavior was, in part, influenced by the drama. Among other things the committee stated:

The Protestant Church, always deeply tied to the character and fortunes of German national traditions, has the calling to serve not individual groups within the nation, but the whole nation independent of the changing political situation. Its methods are the proclamation of the divine Word that has been entrusted to it, and the ministry of love to which it calls its members and which it offers without exception to all irrespective of their political stance. Therefore, the church has the right and duty to give pastoral admonitions that are addressed to all church members irrespective of their party:

1. The more hatred there is, the more we are to show love (Rm. 12:21).

2. The more lies there are, the more strictly we are to uphold the truth. Take the 9th commandment seriously.

3. The more selfish behavior there is, the more selfless devotion we are to have to what belongs to our neighbor. We are to be devoted to what is above all of us, the nation, the whole fatherland.[5]

Of course, the National Socialists did not like such ideas. They contradicted their views and ideas about national traditions. In the midst of the discussions that were carried on at that time a confidential pastoral letter written by the patriotic, nationalistic general superintendent Otto Dibelius became public, provoking vehement protests by the National Socialists. In this letter the general superintendent unfolded the task of the church after the elections of March 5, 1933:

There will be only a few among us who do not wholeheartedly rejoice in this turnaround. On the other hand, we must see whether our church has learned to be the church in the bitter school of one and a half decades. We must and will be united in the conviction that the gospel does not know the autonomous man, but the justified sinner, that it does not preach hate, but love, that not our national character, but the kingdom of God is the object of evangelical proclamation. We will be united in the conviction that the gospel stands in sharp contrast to every human ideology, be it National Socialist or socialist, liberal or conservative, that the gospel does not affirm, but judges the selfish desires of man and that only by submitting to the gospel can the rebuilding occur in which nation and state, tradition and freedom and all other human things gain their Christian legitimacy.[6]

---

[5] J. Gauger, *Gotthard-Briefe-Chronik der Kirchenwirren* (Elberfeld, 1934/35), p. 68.

[6] Ibid.

The fact that the National Socialists labeled such a statement as "high treason committed against the church," should not be surprising, for whenever criticism of their behavior and the foundations of their worldview was expressed, they offered a scathing response.

Christianity had brought the sanctity of Sunday to the nations and rooted it in them. It was a fixed part of the Decalogue that the Christian churches had to remember again and again. Paul Schneider is aware of this fact and makes the following decision with the session in Dornholzhausen:

Dornholzhausen, May 17, 1933

Meeting of the session:

Invited according to the church by-laws, the session gathers at the home of Johannes Olbricht. All four members were present. The meeting has a quorum and is opened with prayer.

On the agenda: A motion sent to the district synod regarding the district church's influence on Sunday sporting activities in our congregations. Referring to the section of the minutes submitted on May 15 from the Dornholzhausen congregation's book of minutes regarding the discussion about church youth work and the affirmative position of the representative body of the larger church about the following subject, the session sends the following motion to the district synod:

The district synod decides to make the following announcement public from the pulpits of the churches in the synod and to send it to the youth clubs, sport clubs and gymnastic associations, including the Hitler youth and SA and SS-units: For Protestant Christians our Sunday worship must be our top priority and will continue to be our main concern.

The worship life of our congregations is at risk of being seriously impaired and endangered by the hiking, gymnastic and sporting activities of the youth clubs and gymnastic associations, also by the newly created National Socialistic groups and organizations. These Sunday activities also harm the aforementioned groups and their own members . . . all who want to help in rebuilding our fatherland and in promoting the physical fitness of our young people should have a very strong interest in strengthening the life of the Christian churches in our homeland as well and especially in seeing that our youth are included in this.

This motion is approved unanimously and the chairman is authorized to pass it on.

The meeting is closed with the blessing of the Lord.

Signed,
Pastor Schneider, Jacobi, Vogt, Ruhl

This is certainly a praiseworthy decision that nevertheless shows how ignorant Paul Schneider and the elders were in assessing the balance of power at that time. The Nazi rulers always saw such a request as an attempt by the church to undermine their organizations and thus to attack its power. They countered this alleged attack with the power apparatus that had fallen into their hands.

They deliberately kept the relationship of the Nazi rulers to the Protestant Church obscure. Even before his takeover Hitler had a conversation in Königsberg, East Prussia with the military chaplain Ludwig Müller who was posted there. It is very probable that church organizational issues were discussed in this conversation. It was a time when the "German Christians" had enjoyed growing popularity. They took advantage of the favorable situation and tried to lay the groundwork for the guidelines that they passed on May 6, 1933 to achieve their plans for the Protestant Church. They read in part:

(6) We demand a change in the Church Convention (political clause) and a struggle against Marxism which is hostile to religion and the nation and against its Christian socialist trainbearers of every stripe . . . . We see our race, traditions and nation as a way of life given and entrusted to us by God and it is God's law that we ensure its survival. Therefore, we must take steps against the mixing of the races. For a long time our German foreign missions have been shouting to the German people on the basis of its experience: "Keep your race pure!" and tell us that faith in Christ does not destroy our race, but enhances and sanctifies it . . . . (8) We see a properly understood homeland

mission as living Christianity in action . . . . Mere pity is "charity" and becomes arrogant when it is coupled with a guilty conscience, making the nation soft. We know something about our Christian duty to love the helpless, but we also demand protection from those who are unfit and inferior. Our homeland mission must not in any way contribute to the degeneration of our people. Moreover, it must keep away from economic adventures and must not become stingy. (9) We see the Jewish mission as a grave danger for our national character. It is the gateway for foreign blood to enter our national body . . . . We reject the Jewish mission in Germany as long as the Jews possess our citizenship. As citizens they can conceal their race, thus there is a real danger of bastardization. The Holy Scriptures also have something to say about the wrath of love that fails. In particular, marriage between Germans and Jews must be forbidden."[7]

The "German Christians" and other groups within the Protestant Church loudly demanded that all 29 independent Protestant regional churches be merged into one national church. Their motivations and objectives in making this demand were different.

In April 1933 General Superintendent Zöllner issues an "appeal to gather the Lutherans":

> We need bishops but we do not need any church parliaments . . . . Our false adaptation to the democratic principle of the Weimar state must be dropped. The synod bodies must be working organs in the structure of the whole . . . . The confessional foundation and the freedom of our church to serve the people that was solemnly assured by the Chancellor must be preserved . . . there must be no imitation of state structures.[8]

The "Reformed Alliance" raises its voice at a meeting in Rheydt. In its declaration the "Protestant Church of the German nation" is affirmed if it is based on the confessions and is free of state interference. "Therefore, it is taken for granted that those of us who are Reformed can order and arrange our life according to the distinctive features of our tradition."[9]

---

[7] F. Wieneke, *Die Glaubensbewegung "Deutsche Christen"* (Soldin, 1933), p. 23.

[8] Gauger, p. 72.

[9] *Reformierte Kirchenzeitung* Nr. 17/1933.

The provincial church council of the Rhine province that speaks for the United Church, declares on April 28, 1933 that it does not consider any Union constitution except the existing one as a viable option and declares: "Far-reaching adaptations to other church bodies appear unproblematic within its framework, which would require us to keep our synod's constitution and reject the office of bishop."[10]

Emotional shockwaves rocked the Protestant church at that time. By proposing a constitutional reform in the Protestant Church, the President of the "Protestant Church Federation," D. Kapler, tried to save what could still be saved. Meanwhile, Hitler appointed military chaplain Ludwig Müller to be "the representative of the Protestant Church" and he immediately intervenes in this constitutional work. Baron von Pechmann from Munich, a member of the church committee for many years, leaves this body and tells the President of the committee:

> In the light of all that I have read after the end of our extraordinary meeting of the church committee, especially in the light of statements made by military chaplain Müller, my reservations about the new political course of our German Protestant church are growing even more serious than they were before. I now consider it impossible to fruitfully participate in any further work of the Church Federation.[11]

In a special letter to the Bavarian Synod von Pechmann gives the reason for his decision and writes:

> Today there are incomparably more important and more urgent things to do for the church than to get wrapped up in busy work on constitutional issues: "With intense soul-searching and single-mindedness we must struggle to gain the inner strength the church needs if it is to be a faithful church for the people and the state—something that has never been more important for both than it is today."[12]

---

[10] *Kreuzzeitung* (Berlin) Nr. 119/1933.

[11] Gauger, p. 74f.

[12] Ibid., p. 76.

The list of pronouncements could be continued. They all show how the church struggled to find the right balance for its proclamation so that it could do justice to the claims of the gospel of Jesus Christ. It was the tragedy of Protestantism that it could not display and could not live its diversity in unity. This is where its weakness could be found—a weakness that paralyzed it when it faced the National Socialist worldview. This became apparent at later synods with frightening clarity.

On May 13, 1933 the "Reformational Youth Movement" demanded the appointment of Pastor von Bodelschwingh to be the Reich bishop. On May 27, 1933 he received the approval of the great majority of the German Protestant regional churches. On May 29, 1933 he assumed office. The "German Christians" protested vehemently with the help of the NSDAP and published a declaration on May 27, 1933 in which it categorically stated: "We can not be shaken. Our course is set. For us there is only one solution: Military Chaplain Müller must become the Reich bishop." On June 24, 1933 Pastor Bodelschwingh resigned as the Reich bishop.

On July 23, 1933 elections took place to elect the church bodies in the German Protestant regional churches. On the evening before the election Hitler gave a speech over every German radio station, thus clearly offering election support for the "German Christians." A letter the DC national leader Hossenfelder delivered to all the district leaders of the National Socialist Workers' Party shows how the NSDAP intervened in this election alongside Hitler:

> To the District Leaders
> of the N.S.D.A.P.
>
> Dear Party Comrades!
>
> I would like to remind you of my letter from June 10, 1933 and the order issued by the chief of staff of our political organization, Dr. Ley:
>
> "Order Nr. 28/33: Military Chaplain Müller, the commissioner of the Führer for the Protestant Church, tells me that the Führer requests that the German Christians push the reactionary forces out of their last positions in the church. The German Christians will begin a four-week long battle. The NSDAP has to support this battle with all of its

resources without leading the battle itself. The district leaders will take the necessary steps on their own initiative.

Heil Hitler!
The Chief of Staff
of the Political Organization

Signed,

Dr. Ley[13]

The path was now clear for the German Christian military chaplain Ludwig Müller. German Protestantism had shown itself to be incapable of taking action. The tragedy of the "German Protestant Church" continued. From now on the individual congregations with their pastors were challenged to tell the state what belonged to the state, and to tell the church what belonged to its office in the state and in the world.

On the personal initiative of the Reich President von Hindenburg negotiations to achieve reconciliation within the Protestant Church took place before the church election. The product of these negotiations was the completion of a set of agreements that were signed on July 11, 1933 and ultimately called for a national church that had higher authority than the regional churches.

In July 1933 the "German Christians" organized a rally in Wetzlar at which Pastor Probst from Frankfurt/Main skillfully inspired his audience to support the goals of the "German Christians" with an emotional, patriotic speech. When he no longer seemed to toe the party line of the National Socialists because he took a patriotic, nationalistic stance and upheld the Reformational confessions, he was later arrested and after being released from detention, he was deported from Frankfurt/Main.[14]

---

[13] On the resignation of Bodelschwingh see K. Meier, *Der Evangelische Kirchenkampf,* vol. 1, p. 95f. and S. Gauger, p. 77f.; E. Beyreuther, *Die Geschichte des Kirchenkampfes in Dokumenten 1933/45* (Wuppertal, 1966), p. 62. A letter documenting the election support of the NSDAP for the "German Christians" is printed in K. Scholder, *Die Kirchen und das Dritte Reich,* vol. 1, after p. 448 in the picture section (document 61).

[14] On this complex of issues compare K. Meier, *Die Deutschen Christen* (Halle/S. and Göttingen, 1964), p. 22ff.; E. Röhm and J. Thierfelder, *Evangelische Kirche zwischen Kreuz und Hakenkreuz* (Stuttgart, 1981), p. 321f. On Probst compare M. Hoffmann, ed., *Dokumentation zum Kirchenkampf in Hessen und Nassau* (Darmstadt, 1974); M. Benad and

Paul Schneider, who attends the rally in Wetzlar, joins the "German Christians," having been impressed by the speech.

The "German Christians" distinguished themselves by a pure activism under their national leader, Pastor Joachim Hossenfelder. It wreaked its havoc by using the sensational term, "struggle": "The German Christians are the SA of Jesus Christ in the struggle to destroy physical, social and spiritual need."[15]

Before the National Socialists and other "folkish circles" disseminated their various neo-Germanic ideas, a new theological approach in Protestant theology took place in the twenties. The Luther renaissance and dialectical theology summoned it to reflect anew on the task of defining the position of theology and the church. In the midst of this new era that was dawning, questions were asked and answers were given that, if at first unconsciously, proved their worth in later coming to grips with the "folkish" worldview that campaigned under the battle cry of "all or nothing."

A new era in church art accompanied this new theological reflection. It discovered its place within the proclamation of the gospel. As a result many Protestant church choirs organized choral retreats at which they cultivated both the old and new songs of the church. The music's connection to Scripture always had top priority in all that was produced. Of course, at such choral retreats they also discussed the present church situation.[16]

At that time new ideas for the choral movement emanated from several centers in Germany. Lübeck was one of them. Bruno Grunsnick, director of the famous Lübeck choral group that found a home in St. Jacobi church, and the pastor there, Axel Werner Kuhl, were active patrons of this new era in church music. Their theological insights invariably led them into the Confessing Church. The choral retreats received both musical and theological inspiration from there. Although Lübeck's church government was dominated by the "German Christians," a strong group formed there that opposed the pseudo-religious posture of the brown rulers. Thus even before the constitution for the national church was completed, two Lübeck pastors, Erwin Schmidt and Julius

---

J. Telchow, eds., "Alles für Deutschland—Deutschland für Christus," *Evangelische Kirche in Frankfurt am Main 1929–1945* (Frankfurt/M., 1985), p. 402f.

[15] Gauger, p. 93.

[16] Certainly there were also supporters of the "German Christians" at such retreats, yet the number of those who took a critical attitude toward the German Christians or even rejected it was predominant. Compare also *Prediger*, p. 53.

Jensen, set out on April 20, 1933 for Berlin to find out from national leader Hossenfelder what the purpose and goal of the "German Christians" was. They put down in writing what they discussed at this talk:

> This faith movement does not have any theology or doctrine— "theology is nonsense; it stands between the people and the church." The confessional foundation remains; pastors are being told now "not to think, but to obey." "Whoever does not go along will be slammed into the wall." "Our goal is to revolutionize the church from below and create a church of the people." Just as Hitler gave the fatherland back to the worker, this movement of faith wants to bring Christ to the people. Hossenfelder denied that this was a kind of revivalist movement. Rather their concern was to "revolutionize the church through the organizational inclusion of the people." All of this would be modeled on the NSDAP. We do not need a new organizational beginning; "we have the outstanding party apparatus."
>
> "Primary elections for all church bodies are scheduled to take place on October 31, 1933. It is to be expected that the propaganda apparatus of the party will be available for this purpose. Newspapers and church newsletters that take a position against the German Christians would be prohibited."
>
> In response to our follow-up question of whether Hossenfelder wanted to equate the oppositional church press with the Marxist press that is hostile to the state, he answered: "I am not saying that, but we can not accept the opposition's griping against us." In this way the German Christians plan to take over the church.
>
> In this context Hossenfelder used these words: "The boss (he meant the Chancellor) does not want to get involved; but we will get him involved when he sees that the church members are behind the German Christians!"
>
> In further similar remarks Hossenfelder's plan became crystal clear: By revolutionizing church members he intends to give the state cause for advocating its case against church authorities that have the people behind them.[17]

---

[17] K. F. Reimers, *Lübeck im Kirchenkampf des Dritten Reiches* (Göttingen, 1965), p. 32; K. Meier, *Der Evangelische Kirchenkampf*, vol. 1, p. 65.

The experiences of these Lübeck pastors were the topic of conversation at choral retreats across Germany. Paul Schneider participates in a choral retreat in August 1933 at which the controversy in the Protestant church is discussed. On the Sunday following his return he makes the following statement in front of his congregation: "I intend to be and remain a simple Protestant Christian and to spare myself the label 'German,' for that goes without saying."[18]

The end of the twenties had not only been politically unsettling, but especially filled with social hardships and tensions that became more and more unbearable in the years to come. Paul Schneider does not live as a privileged spectator on the fringes of these events. From the vantage point of his mission as a pastor he wants to assume responsibility for helping to shape his era. His job as a Christian is to help lessen social and political tensions; passing on the gospel of Jesus Christ is his obligation as a pastor. He feels the tensions of his era and they get under his skin. He cannot uncritically accept what presents itself as the salvation of the nation. He openly expresses what he thinks and reaps not only misunderstanding, but open hostility.

N.S.D.A.P. District leadership
Wetzlar, June 15, 1933

Superintendent Wieber
Garbenheim

The following incident was reported to me on June 11 from Dornholzhausen. "In his sermon today Pastor Schneider took the liberty of committing several gaffes which are bound to provoke strong anger in all thoughtful National Socialists. It was one long concerted attack against the "German Christians." The Arian and heroic ideal was condemned outright. It seems about time to set the ethical demands of the "German Christian" faith movement against such narrow-minded representatives of a church that leaves people cold. People such as our Pastor Schneider are well on the way to nipping the crop of National Socialism in the bud.

I feel called to take a position against this in public, but I must tell you that my heart bleeds when I see how dark forces are at work to destroy

---

[18] Compare on this subject *Prediger*, p. 53.

what the best people in our nation are trying to achieve for the glory
of Germany.

Please take note of what I have just described. I ask that you would take
steps to remedy the situation.

Heil Hitler
The district leadership of Wetzlar

Signed,
Grillo

For people today it is surely difficult to imagine what the overall situation
was like at that time. On the one hand, a movement committed to reflect anew
on the foundations of the church sought to gain a hearing for itself; on the other
hand, the neo-paganism promoted by the state surged against the walls of the
church. The "new song" also emerges in this era. Siegbert Stehmann wrote the
landmark treatise called "Striking the Right Balance."[19] "The choral as a form
of prayer, a response to God's Word, as a form of praise, and thanksgiving in
ultimate simplicity also requires ultimate mastery. If the spiritual song is to
be a symbol of this right balance, it needs cautious lips and devoutly timid
hands." Rudolf Alexander Schroeder had written the song that Hans Friedrich
Micheelsen put to music in 1938. Since then it has had a fixed place in the
hymnal: "O Christian people, rejoice today and every hour. You have hardly
begun the struggle and you have already overcome. The fool asks: Where is
your God who daily thinks up ways to jeer and mock you? Withstand the
onslaught, rejoicing; soon the wall will reveal the finger that slays him."[20]

The text of this song that was written during the lifetime of Paul Schneider
found its equivalent in his life. Looking at the macabre, imperious behavior of
the powerful, Jochen Klepper wrote his sonnet that was not allowed to become
public: "The new king will only rise up if he lies at your feet as a penitent. He
does not insist on his rights, only on forgiveness, and without fanfare his day
dawns. Lord, when the new kings return, there will nowhere be an outcry or

---

[19] Reproduced in R. Wentorf, *Siegbert Stehmann. Ein Dichter in der Bewährung*
(Giessen und Basel, 1965), p. 45f.

[20] R. A. Schröder, *Gesammelte Werke*, vol. 1 (Berlin and Frankfurt/M., 1952), p. 923;
see also *Evangelisches Kirchengesangbuch*, Nr. 225.

pushing and shoving. Only bells will ring, and the pious will introduce their king with prayers. Only he who sees the cross has even remotely understood holiness in earthly judgment.[21] If kings did not find your Golgotha, they did not find their thrones."

The parishes were obligated in those days to pass on extracts from their church books for the purpose of "genealogical research." Paul Schneider, who knows about the background of such an order, frequently writes under the extracts: "You, Aryan, don't forget your first parents!" When the Giessen Wingolf demands "proof of his Aryan ancestry," he leaves this fraternity. He considers such a request from a Christian fraternity to be absurd.[22] A friend of Paul Schneider writes: "No one whom I know or whose story I have heard, has fought this fight for our church more simply and unpretentiously, and yet more sincerely and relentlessly than my friend and brother Paul Schneider."[23]

The political situation in Germany was so intricate that even foreign diplomats who were accredited in Berlin often assessed the situation falsely. Such false assessments did not remain without consequences and too often only enhanced the National Socialists' claim to power. Even the German resistance later had its difficulties with similar errors spread by foreign diplomats who did not describe the true German reality.

The "ethical and moral sense of the Germanic race" written into the party platform of the NSDAP was used by the regime to measure the "Jewish-Marxist spirit in and outside of us." Now it had entered the church through the "German Christians" and was causing considerable anxiety and confusion in it. Paul Schneider rejects the party platform in public and is grateful for the establishment of the Pastors' Emergency League. Through the work of this league Pastor Martin Niemöller from Berlin points the way for the church to

---

[21] J. Klepper, *Ziel der Zeit* (Witten und Berlin, 1962), p. 39.

[22] Compare on this subject *Prediger*, p. 53. For Paul Schneider man is simply God's creation. The Old Testament is the book that binds Judaism and Christianity together. Jesus, born as a Jew, is the Savior of all humanity. With the proof of Aryan ancestry the population was to be subjected to a kind of class division. The proof of German citizenship was planned as a further measure. Here the German was considered more worthy than a Polish or Russian citizen, for example, and ultimately more worthy than persons who are citizens of other states. Paul Schneider sent a clear signal at that time by refusing to submit a "proof of Aryan ancestry" to Wingolf and by pointing out that man is a creature of God.

[23] *Prediger*, p. 53.

help "non-Aryan" pastors. In a circular letter from September 1933 written in Berlin we read:

> Church "leaders" and authorities have failed to confront the "German Christians." A nasty timidity has arisen among many serious-minded brothers in the pastorate. Because of this distressing situation we have started an "emergency league of pastors" who have committed themselves only to the Holy Scriptures and to the confessions of the Reformation and to the best of their ability take an interest in alleviating the hardship of those brothers who must suffer because of it.[24]

The declaration of commitment that every member of the emergency league had to sign, read:

> I commit myself to perform the duties of my office as a servant of the Word solely by committing myself to the Holy Scriptures and to the confessions of the Reformation as the correct interpretation of the Holy Scriptures. I commit myself to protest against any violation of such a confessional stance with unreserved dedication. I know that I am responsible to the best of my ability for those who are persecuted for the sake of such a confessional stance. Having made such a commitment, I testify that a violation of this confessional stance has occurred with the application of the Aryan paragraph within the framework of the church.[25]

This was an unusually courageous step. Nevertheless, we must ask ourselves whether Martin Niemöller and his colleagues had already seen through the whole spectrum of claims the National Socialist had made to assume total power. A few weeks after the pastors' emergency league was established, on October 15, 1933, Hitler received the following telegram:

> In this crucial hour for our people and fatherland we salute our leader. We are grateful for the manly deed and the clear word that preserved

---

[24] Compare H. Hermelink, *Kirche im Kampf* . . . (Tübingen und Stuttgart, 1950), p. 48f. and K. Meier, *Der Evangelische Kirchenkampf,* vol. 1, p. 120, note 458. Compare also E. Röhm and J. Thierfelder, *Evangelische Kirche zwischen Kreuz und Hakenkreuz*, p. 53.

[25] Ibid.

Germany's honor. In the name of more than 2,500 Protestant pastors who do not belong to the faith movement of the German Christians, we pledge our faithful allegiance and intercessory remembrance.

Harnisch, Berlin; Messows, Steglitz; Müller, Dahlem; Niemöller, Dahlem; Röricht, Dahlem[26]

Pastor Harnisch had initiated the telegram as the Emergency League's representative for public relations. In this telegram Germany's withdrawal from the League of Nations was praised as a "manly deed." Harnisch also had an interview in the propaganda ministry and asked that the telegram be officially disseminated. When he found no support for his concern, he complained in the interior ministry and gave the following reason: "To show foreign countries the unity of our nation and to take action against attempts to portray our struggle within the church as a struggle against Hitler, as the 'German Christians' try to do time and again."

Appealing to Romans 13 he further wrote to the ministry:

And if Paul could speak in this way, the one who stood under the authority of the government that nailed his Lord Jesus Christ to the cross, how much more joyfully may we pledge our allegiance to our Führer Adolf Hitler who clearly and deliberately makes Christian moral laws the rule of his actions. Therefore, I maintain that we love our fatherland more than the "German Christians" do . . . . I declare, irrespective of whether we are Protestant Christians or "German Christians," (that we) stand behind our Führer Adolf Hitler with our prayers and with our work in unshakable loyalty.[27]

This commentary could be heard on February 20, 1934 in a program deliberately orchestrated by Bavarian Radio:

One thing is unmistakably clear for all Protestant groups, whether "German Christians" or "Pastors' Emergency League" or "Young

---

[26] *Junge Kirche I* (1933), p. 252. Compare also the discussion about this telegram in F. Baumgartel, *Wider die Kirchenkampf-Legende* (Neuendettelsau, 1958).

[27] K. Meier, *Der Evangelische Kirchenkampf*, vol. 1, p. 562; K. Scholder, *Die Kirchen und das dritte Reich*, vol. 1, p. 847.

Reformers," of course, for Pastor Niemöller as well: their struggle for Protestantism never casts doubt on their loyalty and unswerving solidarity with the Third Reich. They are all united in their devotion to Hitler and the Third Reich.[28]

The mixing of national and National Socialist views, as in the case of the Pastors' Emergency League, caused much irritation within the Confessing Church as time went on and suppressed a compelling discussion of the issue. In fact, it even prevented them from actually grappling with the worldview of National Socialism which was so hostile to the church and humanity. Although Paul Schneider had always mistrusted the National Socialists, at first he fell for their patriotic, nationalistic emphasis and joined the "German Christians" for only a few weeks until he had recognized their dishonest game.

Through this servile behavior, as demonstrated by the example of the Pastors' Emergency League, such organizations focused only on their own interests. All others, the maltreated Communists, Social Democrats, Jews, gypsies, Jehovah's Witnesses, courageous Christians and national patriots were left lying on the side of the road and the robbers pounced on them.

Of course, in the early stages of the "Third Reich" it was difficult for those who had not dealt with the publications of the National Socialists to see through their machinations. On the one hand, they propagated their "neo-Germanic, German world view" as the new, irrefutable foundation for an orderly community life in the Third Reich. On the other hand, SA storm troopers were ordered into local worship services in 1933 with their flags and standards. Then the flag bearers and standard bearers had to stand beside the altar, standing at attention with a tight strap under their chin. We must also remember the mass weddings of SA and SS members.

It was a time of great obfuscation that enabled them to better achieve their real plans behind such a camouflage. On January 29, 1934 Paul Schneider writes on the basis of the experiences he had made with the National Socialists:

---

[28] Compare also the telegram send by prelate Kaas to Hitler: "Sincere congratulations and best wishes today. Be assured of our single-minded cooperation in the great work of creating a Germany that is internally strong and socially pacified and externally free," reprinted in E. Matthias and R. Morsey, eds., *Das Ende der Parteien 1933. Darstellungen und Dokumente* (Düsseldorf, 1955), p. 369.

I do not think that our Protestant church will be able to avoid a conflict with the Nazi state. It is not even advisable to postpone it since we owe God our Christian obedience.[29]

---

[29] *Prediger,* p. 55.

11

THE CONFLICT BEGINS

At the beginning of his study of Protestant theology in 1919 at the University of Giessen the student Paul Schneider notes in his diary: "We are to be servants and leaders of the nation, not its masters."

This statement had an influence on his relationship to his neighbors and at the same time encouraged his vigilant behavior. The National Socialists talked a lot about serving Germany, but in fact they geared all their activities to expanding and maintaining their power. They claimed the people needed to be "reeducated" and needed to practice Nazi thought and behavior patterns. One could find out from the Nazi press what these looked like. The "*Völkische Beobachter*" reported:

> Chief of staff Röhm is campaigning against sanctimoniousness. The chief of staff of the SA Röhm has issued an appeal that is targeted at sanctimonious persons. The fact that this has gone haywire in recent times is undeniable. For instance, the most nonsensical regulations are being demanded for swimsuits and behavior at public swimming pools. The German woman is being prohibited from using powder or smoking in restaurants. In the big cities all places of entertainment that are somehow out of line with middle-class values are to be eradicated. All of this is supposedly happening because they feel a holy responsibility for the well being of the people.
>
> Recently there were reports that even SA and SS leaders and troops were appointing themselves as judges of others' morals and harassing females in swimming pools, restaurants or in the street. It must be clearly stated that the German revolution was not won by philistines, sanctimonious persons and moralists, but by revolutionary fighters. These men alone will also safeguard it.

The task of the SA is not to keep an eye on the clothing, facial care or chastity of others, but to lift up Germany through its free and revolutionary fighting spirit. Therefore, he forbids all the leaders and troops of the SA and SS to continue their activities in this area or to lower themselves to be accomplices of eccentric moral aesthetes.[1]

First and foremost, the denominational youth associations active outside of the Nazi movement were the intended targets of this appeal. They were to model themselves on the "National Socialist fighters" as they prepared for their immanent takeover by the Hitler Youth, the SA or the SS. The appeal was inscrutable for many and thus caused confusion; in a very subtle form it was designed to make fun of those who did not model themselves on the "revolutionary fighters." Paul Schneider cannot keep quiet about such nonsense as a responsible shepherd of his congregation. Following the worship service he makes the following statement which he then makes public in the glass-fronted notice board of the congregation:

Hochelheim, October 8, 1933

In the newspapers an appeal made by chief of staff Röhm was published, titled "Against Sanctimoniousness." This man in his high position who lays claim to being heard by the National Socialist youth, especially by the SA, speaks out against the validity of moral principles and against an advocacy of them in our national life in such a way that one can only protest most sharply against the spirit and content of this appeal from the standpoint of Protestant faith. If chief of staff Röhm thinks that the development of our people and the task of the SA have nothing to do with morality and chastity, and when he speaks of these things as being done by "eccentric moralists," he is mistaken and has not done our nation any favor by issuing this appeal.

Pastor Schneider

This act stirred up the demons that would no longer let go of Paul Schneider. A few days after this article is published, he feels challenged to register another

---

[1] *Völkischer Beobachter,* edition of September 1933.

protest. He cannot leave the statement of a Hitler youth leader unchallenged, for he had made the claim that he was the leader of all German youth.

To explain the situation at that time, allow me to make the following remark. The "Protestant Youth Movement" with the youth associations that had merged in it was one of the strongest groups (if not the strongest) within the German youth movement. The National Socialists had dissolved the political parties and their youth organizations immediately following their takeover and forbidden them from carrying on any further activities. Some of them went underground. The Nazi rulers did not succeed in silencing the Communist and Social Democratic youth groups in spite of the fact that both groups were persecuted and spied on. At first the denominational youth associations were untouched by the prohibition because the authority of their respective churches covered them. The Nazi rulers followed a very shrewd path in dealing with them. The Reich youth leader, Baldur von Schirach, who was personally appointed by Hitler, allowed the Protestant young men to continue to wear their olive green outfit and to have pennants, banners and signs with them. On October 13, 1933 the following text was made public at a conference with the leaders of the church youth clubs that convened in the interior ministry:

> There was agreement that the associations affiliated with the Reich youth leadership stand alongside of one another in full equality. The German youth movement has these great pillars: The Hitler youth, the Protestant youth, the Catholic youth, the sporting youth and the professional youth. As the standard bearer of the National Socialist youth movement the Hitler youth have been given the privilege of holding a special place within the overall youth movement. There was also agreement that a friendly relationship should link together the associations that are recognized by the Reich leadership and that are placed under its authority.[2]

Paul Schneider kept this agreement. He even implemented it before it was made public and reminded others of it when he took a position on the appeal made by Gross, the Nazi youth leader from Limburg an der Lahn:

---

[2] Compare S. Gauger, p. 124; K. Meier, *Der evangelische Kirchenkampf,* vol. 1, p. 146ff.; E. Röhm and J. Thierfelder, *Evangelische Kirche zwischen Kreuz und Hakenkreuz,* p. 44ff.

Hochelheim, October 11, 1933

The appeal made public by Nazi youth leader Gross, Limburg, promoting the recruiting month of the Hitler Youth, is targeted in a one-sided fashion at denominational youth work and conflicts with the spirit and content of the agreements made by the Protestant Youth Organization with the leadership of the Hitler Youth.

The appeal contains the incorrect assertion that Protestant youth may no longer march or play scouting games. How is that compatible with the conscientiousness and truthfulness with which such an appeal should have been written? Up to the present day scouting games and marching are permitted and cultivated by our denominational youth, and not just since yesterday.

Furthermore, we are helping Adolf Hitler in his work of rebuilding the German nation at least as much as the Hitler youth and we will not allow them to surpass us in our love for the fatherland.

We are in a denominational youth association because we know that we are not only German, but also Christian young people. As such we would like to take seriously our calling to help each other in following our Savior Jesus Christ and living according to his Word: Seek first the Kingdom of God and his righteousness. Then we will also be good Germans.

The Hitler Youth as such are not able by themselves to provide a clear Protestant, Christian character education. We did not set up the prohibition of dual membership. We would like to live in peace and friendship with the Hitler Youth. This has been made more difficult for us since the Hitler youth posted such intolerant appeals containing these false assertions.

Sieg Heil!
Pastor Schneider

The Hitler Youth and the "National Socialist German Workers' Party" did not remotely think of permitting the denominational youth groups to have their own independent existence. Just two months after the conference in the

Reich interior ministry on October 13, 1933 the Reich youth leader held a typical speech in Braunschweig, in which he remarked:

> It has recently been said of us that we are an anti-Christian movement. It is even said that I am a committed pagan. Yet the National Socialist movement has furnished more visible proof than the Christian parties that we have cast in our lot with the Lord in heaven. These parties that have vanished are now trying again to bring the poison of dissension into our youth under the guise of one youth organization or another. And I will resist that. I solemnly declare in front of the German public that I stand on the foundation of Christianity; but that I will suppress any attempt to bring denominational conflicts into the Hitler youth. . . . We claim that all other youth organizations in Germany no longer have any right to exist. These organizations must disappear.[3]

On December 31, 1933 Dr. Erich Stange, the director of the Protestant Youth Organization, was forbidden to continue his work in the Reich leadership council that was supposed to coordinate youth work in Germany even though he had only been appointed to the council on June 22, 1933. He received the following telegram: "Effective immediately, I am removing you from your office in the youth leadership circle. I have moved that you be immediately expelled from the National Socialist German Workers' Party in summary proceedings."[4]

However, Dr. Stange was at no time a member of the NSDAP and could thus not be expelled. In this context it made youth leaders wonder what was going on when they found out that two Protestant youth leaders were arrested at the same time in Frankfurt am Main to prevent them from holding youth meetings. The brown rulers had already decided to crush all the denominational youth work in Germany. The fact that the "German Christians" helped them to do this must not be left unsaid.

The National Socialists were always intent on proving to their superiors that they were loyal, ready for duty and devoted. The local group leader of the NSDAP reports to the district leadership on the events in Hochelheim:

---

[3] Gauger, p. 125.

[4] Ibid., p. 126.

Hochelheim, October 11, 1933
NSDAP, Base Hochelheim
To: NSDAP District leadership Wetzlar

Concerning: Notices on the signboard of the church in Hochelheim posted by Pastor Schneider.

With reference to the telephone conversation I just had with comrade Petry, I am sending you copies of the two protests against the appeals made by the chief of staff of the SA and Gross, the leader of the Hitler Youth, which were made public by Pastor Schneider.

Yesterday it was reported to me that Pastor Schneider had posted the protest against chief of staff Röhm on the aforementioned signboard. When I wanted to see for myself this morning, I also found the protest against Gross. I then sent SA group leader Alfred Jung from here with a letter to Pastor Schneider (I have enclosed a copy of it) with the request that he give Jung the two protest notes. However, Pastor Schneider refused to grant my request. I then tried to call the district leadership but did not get an answer. District leader Grillo could also not be reached by phone. (It was in the period between noon and one o'clock.) I didn't want to act on my own authority, but wanted to first receive instructions from there.

Since I could assume that Pastor Schneider might remove and destroy the two protest notes, but on the other hand, in my opinion the protest notes had to disappear immediately so as not to cause any further public disturbance, I had the locked box taken down and brought to my home after informing Pastor Schneider through SA group leader Jung. After consulting with comrade Petry, I then opened the box by force and took out both protest notes. The box was not damaged since I only had to loosen a few wooden screws. I had the box delivered to Pastor Schneider since it was the property of the congregation.

Heil Hitler
Mehl, local group leader
3 copies

The following letter reached Paul Schneider the day before:

Hochelheim, October 10, 1933
NSDAP
Base Hochelheim
Pastor Schneider, Hochelheim

On the signboard of the congregation you made public two protest notes concerning chief of staff Röhm and the Hitler youth whose contents are likely to stir up unrest and cause misunderstandings among the populace. I therefore ask you to immediately remove them from the signboard and hand them over to the bearer of this letter.

In the future I ask you to submit documents of a political nature to me before you make them public.

Heil Hitler!
Mehl, local group leader

The first call of the local group leader from Hochelheim was made to the Nazi district leadership on October 11, 1933 between noon and one o'clock, which initially was not successful. A notification of the district administration in Wetzlar triggered the activities.

Just a few hours later the representative of the district administration called the consistory in Koblenz; we take the following excerpt from the record made there:

> Assessor Engfer informed me in this conversation that the NSDAP was asking to immediately take Pastor Schneider into preventive detention. The district administration asks that Pastor Schneider be given some time off until this matter is settled so that in the future the authority of Pastor Schneider in his congregation is not undermined by the possibility of further detention.
>
> A call is requested by 4:30 p.m. in the office of the district administration; Wetzlar Nr.2046, after 4:40 p.m. Assessor Engfer: Wetzlar Nr. 2411.

The unrest among the party functionaries that the "troublemaker" in the Hochelheim manse had stirred up could no longer be contained. At 4:45 p.m.

a new call was made to stress the importance of the first one. We read from the documents of the consistory:

> After Mr. Rudorff had notified me (on the next page), the representative from the district administration called me again at 4:45 p.m. He gave me the following information in addition to what had been communicated up to now. The demand to take Pastor Schneider into preventive detention was made by the district leadership. They felt it was necessary to avert personal danger that threatened Pastor Schneider because of agitation in the populace. If the consistory was not immediately able to order the suspension, the preventive detention could not be avoided. After this conversation I promised the suspension. At 5:10 p.m. I contacted Superintendent Wieber-Garbenheim by phone. He had already heard about the matter. As many different people have repeatedly said to him, Pastor Schneider has good intentions, but is very incautious and tactless. I gave Superintendent Wieber the order to immediately grant him his immediate suspension either by phone or by a personal visit in order to avert the preventive detention and to order him to come for a personal discussion on Friday, the 13th of this month. Superintendent Wieber was thoroughly aware of the importance of this matter, and promised to immediately carry out my order.

> Siebert

After the phone conversations the bureaucrats in the state, in the Nazi party and in the consistory took action. As already mentioned, the district leadership of the NSDAP had turned to the district administration for help.

> Wetzlar, October 12, 1933

> NSDAP
> District Organization
> To the District Administration Wetzlar

> Enclosed I am sending you a report of an incident in Hochelheim. Pastor Schneider was using a signboard there to take action against the NSDAP and against chief of staff Röhm. Furthermore, you can see from this incident that the local group leader removed this

appeal. I ask you to call Landjäger's[5] attention to the fact that he is to immediately prohibit the use of this signboard in the future and take Pastor Schneider into preventive detention. This individual belongs in a concentration camp and not in the pulpit. He read the same appeal from the pulpit during his sermon.

Heil Hitler!
District Organization of the NSDAP

Memorandum of the district administration: "Very urgent!" I discussed the matter by phone with Siebert, a member of the consistory in Koblenz, who promised me to suspend Pastor Schneider on the same day until this matter is settled.

The next higher party level, the regional organization of the NSDAP in Frankfurt/Main was also notified. This letter contains some remarkable sentences just as the letter above does.

Wetzlar,
Oct. 12, 1933

NSDAP
District Organization in Wetzlar

To the Regional Organization
in Hessen-Nassau-South, Frankfurt/Main

Following through on the telephone conversation of this morning I am sending you as requested the copy of the letter posted by Pastor Schneider, Hochelheim, on the public sign board of the congregation. I would like to add the remark that Pastor Schneider read the same letters from the pulpit as well.

Moreover, Pastor Schneider is one of the few pastors in this area who opposes the NSDAP.

---

[5] The police officer on duty.

Heil Hitler!
District Organization

These letters went through all the political channels until they were delivered to the consistory. What is so provocative about this is that the National Socialists could afford to get involved in such escapades only a few months after taking power. None of the politically active groups at that time kept them from doing this. The German nationalistic circles that had helped National Socialism take power and acted friendly to the churches watched without taking any action.

The following correspondence between the consistory and the district administration shows how quickly and thoroughly such "serious" cases were handled. On October 10, 1933 the Protestant Church of the Rhineland was given a bishop for the first time in its history although a considerable number of Reformed congregations in it rejected the office of bishop on the basis of their confessional stance. Dr. Heinrich Oberheid, a leading "German Christian" who was installed as bishop on this day[6] had to deal with the "recalcitrant" pastor from Hochelheim as his first "official business." After he had spoken to Paul Schneider, he sent the district administrator the following letter:

Koblenz, October 13, 1933

The bishop of the Protestant bishopric Cologne-Aachen
To the district administrator in Wetzlar

Your honor informed the Protestant consistory yesterday that Pastor Schneider from Hochelheim, in the district of Wetzlar, posted on the sign board of the congregation a public notice about the appeal of chief of staff Röhm and that the district organization of the NSDAP was demanding Pastor Schneider's preventive detention because of the agitation of the populace. They believed the preventive detention was necessary to avert personal danger. Your honor wants to refrain from carrying out the preventive detention if the consistory immediately orders the suspension of Pastor Schneider. After that the consistory

---

[6] Compare on this subject G. van Norden, ed., *Kirchenkampf im Rheinland. Die Entstehung der Bekennenden Kirche und die Theologische Erklärung von Barmen 1934*, vol. 76, *Schriftenreihe des Vereins für Rheinische Kirchengeschichte* (Pulheim, 1984), p. 69.

issued the suspension and Pastor Schneider was ordered to appear for a discussion this morning.

In the discussion I made clear to Pastor Schneider that the public notice was a forceful act of political interference even if Pastor Schneider thought he had to act because he felt a serious concern for the congregation entrusted to him. I strongly reprimanded him for his offense. Pastor Schneider willingly accepted my accusations that also extended to other clashes with members of the congregation. He made the following statement:

"Having been informed by my church superiors that the meaning and purpose of chief of staff Röhm's appeal to the SA and SS against sanctimoniousness was of a different nature than I assumed in my protest of the 8th of this month, I regret that I made this protest and hereby withdraw it."

Pastor Schneider will announce this statement in the same way he made his protest public.

On the basis of this discussion I am confident that Pastor Schneider will find the right attitude toward the measures of the state and party from now on. I ask you to refrain from further considering the preventive detention. If your honor could let the Protestant consistory have a corresponding notification, it would then be possible to rescind the suspension.

The Nazi district administrator in Wetzlar answered the bishop without delay:

Wetzlar, October 14, 1933

The District Administrator
Phone Number 8746

To the bishop of the bishopric Cologne-Aachen
in Koblenz

In response to his letter of October 13, 1933:

After consulting the district organization of the NSDAP and personally observing the mood in the parish I do not consider it feasible to withdraw the suspension of Pastor Schneider until the matter is fully clarified. I do not think we can consider the matter to be settled merely by posting his statement of revocation on the signboard. The relationship between the pastor and the local group leaders in both congregations of his parish has become too tense in recent weeks for this to be the case. Pastor Schneider has created the impression by his attitude that he does not fully stand with us in support of our modern state. A lot of petitions about him have been submitted to the district organization of the NSDAP. If he now fills his office such a short time after the incident with his appeal against chief of staff Röhm, I fear there could be incidents that are harmful to the reputation of the church. Therefore, I consider it necessary that you on your part clarify through your own observations whether it is possible for the pastor to stay in Hochelheim. I would consider it appropriate if this could happen by sending a representative to the scene. I personally believe that this matter can hardly be resolved in any other way than by transferring Pastor Schneider. Today I told him this myself and ask you to take the appropriate steps from there as soon as possible. In my opinion the suspension that has been decreed cannot be rescinded.

(Signed) for,
Engfer

There was no longer any talk of imposing the "preventive detention." By approving the immediate rescinding of the suspension, the Nazi district administrator feared he would lose face, for he combined the functions of district administrator and district leader of the NSDAP. Thus it becomes clear what a shrewd game was being played. So he hid behind the alleged "unrest" in the populace which in fact was never there. Such behavior was typical for powerful Nazi officials who wanted to document their power by applying such pressure.

In the meantime, the superintendent of the Wetzlar synod reported to the consistory:

Garbenheim, October 14, 1933
The Superintendent's office

Diary Nr. 1000

I report the following action to the Protestant consistory in Koblenz in response to the decree of October 13, 1933 II 7342:

Following the telephone conversation of consistory member Siebert with me I immediately called the post office in Hochelheim with instructions to call Pastor Schneider to the telephone. After some time I was given the answer that he was in Dollar. I then drove there immediately and met him in the manse at Dollar. I revealed to him the mission given to me by consistory member Siebert and in the presence of Pastor Heider I told him that his action was wrong and called his attention to the fact that Röhm's appeal was certainly not to be understood in the way he understood it and that the way he protested against Röhm was by no means the right one.

I then immediately authorized Pastor Hardt in Klein-Rechtenbach to administer the pastorate of Hochelheim-Dornholzhausen during the suspension of Pastor Schneider and arranged what was temporarily needed to hold the worship services.

Wieber,
Superintendent

Whoever wants to even remotely understand Paul Schneider's feelings when he took this initiative, must consider the overall scheme of contemporary events. It is important to know that Paul Schneider lived in a church environment that was strongly characterized by groups that had withdrawn to the stands, watching the action from the sidelines and responding only to orders. Only a few faced up to the issues of the time and were willing, if necessary, to take an opposing position. The National Socialists among them were intoxicated by their power and understood themselves as masters over time and space.

We read in a later sermon by Paul Schneider:

The ministry of retribution in the world is equivalent to the ministry of comfort in the hearts of disciples. The non-believing world does not receive the gift of the Holy Spirit, but it must certainly sense how its sin is found guilty of violating divine justice and how they are convicted of the judgment that has been pronounced over them. Since our life is still bound up with the powers of this era, since the church of Christ is still struggling and still being persecuted by the powers of this world, since each individual is still tempted by the power and desires of this world, this convicting penalty of the Holy Spirit must help liberate our song of faith and turn it into a new song that rises up to the Holy Spirit free from anxiety and fear and that even now gives us a share in his glory. This penalty must keep us from being drawn into the sin and judgment of this world . . . . This is the liberating work of the Holy Spirit in our day, that he clearly exposes this sin, that the world is again revealed as the world in (Rosenberg's) myth of the twentieth century and in the unquestioning faith Nazi ideology places in German superiority. The Holy Spirit is clearly showing us how divided opinions are on the issue of who Christ is.[7]

After enduring difficult inner struggles Paul Schneider pointed to Christ again and again as the irrevocable foundation of Christian faith from the beginning of his pastoral ministry and advocates this even more clearly during the time of conflict with National Socialism. It is neither dogmatism, nor fanaticism that has a formative influence on his pastoral activity, but his recognition that each individual can be lost for eternity, a concern that extends even to the horror of the concentration camp.

The consistory sent two representatives to Hochelheim and Dornzholz-hausen. Here are their reports:

> Travel report, concerning the complaint against Pastor Schneider in Hochelheim in the Synod of Wetzlar.
>
> On the 19th of this month, Pastor Wolfrum from Oldenbach and I negotiated on behalf of the bishop in the case of Pastor Schneider first with the district administrator in Wetzlar, who is simultaneously the district leader of the NSDAP. The district administrator expressed his opinion that according to the reports made by the deputy district leader Haus, Pastor Schneider demonstrated by his statements and actions that he does not affirm National Socialism and that as a result he must be transferred in his opinion as soon as possible. The

---

[7] P. Schneider, ". . . und sollst mein Prediger bleiben," *Predigten* (Giessen und Basel, 1966), p. 43.

district administrator could not provide specific information on what charges could be brought against Pastor Schneider except the matter of chief of staff Röhm's edict. He merely handed over to us the enclosed correspondence and asked that we return it after making copies. The district administrator objected to the idea of rescinding the suspension. Then the deputy district leader Haus was called in and reported that according to the reports made to him by the local group leaders in Hochelheim and Dornholzhausen Pastor Schneider had made critical statements about the national state and National Socialism in various sermons. He showed a letter from the local group leader Mehl that, however, only contained general remarks and did not document quotations from a sermon. In other respects as well all of the deputy district leader's remarks were of a more general nature. What he said was more or less that Pastor Schneider supported the idea of maintaining the local chapter of the Young German Order in Hochelheim, that on one Sunday he publicly announced his resignation from the religious movement of the "German Christians" from the pulpit in Dornholzhausen and that his appeal concerning the edict of chief of staff Röhm was read from the pulpit in Dornholzhausen. The local group leaders of the NSDAP were so upset that they could barely be kept from issuing a public appeal asking that the populace no longer attend the worship services of Pastor Schneider.

Moreover, the district administrator and the deputy district leader pointed out the enclosed letter written by Pastor Schneider concerning Nazi youth leader Gross in Limburg. I expressed my opinion to the district administrator that in view of the present legal situation a transfer would be difficult and from the viewpoint of the church could only be initiated if serious, specific offenses were present. A judgment on rescinding the suspension could only be made when the material could be examined by us that was in the possession of the local group leader and that was based on the information provided by the deputy district leader.

We then immediately drove to Hochelheim and discussed the matter with Pastor Schneider there. Pastor Schneider denied that he took a negative attitude toward the national state. Pastor Schneider did not write down the sermon from June 11 of this year that was attacked by the local group leader, so the contested sections could not be determined. He admits that he read his appeal concerning the edict of the chief of staff from the pulpit in Dornholzhausen. He explains the fact that he publicly announced his resignation from the religious movement of the "German Christians" by saying that he had also announced his entry into the group at a church gathering and thus felt obligated to inform the congregation of his position on this issue of church politics.

With reference to his letter concerning Nazi youth leader Gross he pointed out that the relationship between the Hitler youth and the Protestant clubs has not yet been clarified, citing various detrimental effects on the Protestant youth of Hochelheim to justify his attitude. He rebuffed the charge that he had not participated in the harvest festival and commented that he had the children learn poems, but the local group leaders of the NSDAP prevented him from having the children recite the poems. However, he did participate in the harvest festival in Dornholzhausen.

The elders and session members unanimously decided to issue a declaration of support for Pastor Schneider and sent it to the district leadership (a copy is enclosed). A similar declaration of support was also supposed to be drafted in Hochelheim; however, since the teacher Wagner warned the people that they could inconvenience themselves by doing so, the declaration has not yet been made. According to Pastor Schneider they will soon make up for this delay. As evidence of his position on the national state Pastor Schneider pointed out that on May 1 he took part in the parade and also later participated in the midsummer celebrations of the party. In contrast he cited the irreconcilability of the opposing side. The local group leader in Hochelheim posted a public notice and had it announced by ringing the village bells. He stated that whoever says anything against him (the local group leader) in connection with the suspension of the pastor will be strictly punished. The police officer added the comment: "Now we'll get him out of here." Pastor Schneider mentioned in this context that the personalities of the local group leaders, especially the local group leader Mehl in Hochelheim, are not impeccable in many respects, mainly in the area of ethics. Furthermore, they had interfered in his pastoral work several times.

Following this discussion with Pastor Schneider Pastor Wolfrum spoke to the two local group leaders Mehl and Reuter. Pastor Wolfrum will report on the results of this consultation.

Only two elders could appear from the session in Hochelheim. Both of them clearly spoke out in favor of Pastor Schneider and his remaining in the congregation and declared that the other elders were also of the same opinion. Third parties were partly responsible for causing the difficulties with the local group leaders by telling them all kinds of untruths about Pastor Schneider.

The overall impression of Pastor Schneider that was later confirmed by Superintendent Hepp of the Braunfels Synod was that he is a somewhat stubborn and headstrong person who cannot easily be dissuaded from advocating his views. Consequently, this will also give rise to further difficulties in the future. However, he realizes that in many cases he acted at least in an unwise manner and promised to fully restrain himself with regard to politics from now on.

He is willing to accept a transfer from Hochelheim, but asked us to delay such a measure so that he would not have to leave bearing the stigma of inadequate nationalism.

Dr. Jung,
October 20, 1933

The second representative of the bishop, Pastor Wolfrum, who was a member of the NSDAP, wrote the following report:

On behalf of the bishop I took part in the negotiations which consistory member Dr. Jung conducted in the case of Pastor Schneider with the district administrator in Wetzlar as well as with the pastor himself in Hochelheim. In Hochelheim I then negotiated with both local group leaders of the NSDAP on the Schneider case in the home of local group leader Mehl in Hochelheim. The two local group leaders at first claimed that Pastor Schneider was unacceptable for them and that a pastoral ministry in Hochelheim was no longer an option for the pastor. I then spoke to both persons as a party member and asked them about the personal qualities of Pastor Schneider and found out that no objections of any significance were being made to Pastor Schneider with regard to his character. The only charges that are being made against Pastor Schneider are that he is not consistent and that he often acts overzealously and that above all he has not yet found the necessary proper relationship to the NSDAP. Furthermore, it has been said that he often gets involved in personal affairs and does more of a bad than a good job. I made clear to them that not much would be gained by transferring Pastor Schneider. After establishing the fact that they could find no objection to Pastor Schneider as a pastor and as a Christian, it merely came down to inducing him to cooperate more loyally with the NSDAP in the future, especially since he expressed his willingness to do so both orally and in writing. The two local group leaders agreed that Pastor Schneider could remain in the pastorate and could continue his ministry in Hochelheim. Only they demanded certain assurances. It was agreed that Pastor Schneider should express his willingness to loyally work with and cooperate with the local leaders of the NSDAP at an evening social event that will take place shortly at the church. Furthermore, it should be recommended to Pastor Schneider to desist from making any remarks following the sermon which in any way deal with political things (such as the edict of the chief of staff or his position on the Hitler Youth). Furthermore, he should refrain from personally interfering in local politics and disputes. The local group leader promised on the other hand to ensure that the Hitler youth would be urged to attend the worship service and church events. He would also welcome the idea of the pastor serving the Hitler youth by giving lectures or doing similar things. Following this discussion I shared the opinions of the local group leaders with brother Schneider and asked him to be considerate of these opinions and in the future adjust his behavior accordingly. It is my conviction that with a measure of good will a truly fruitful collaboration with the congregation is possible; if Pastor Schneider maintains the necessary restraint, the case should be settled. Pastor Schneider's suspension can thus immediately be rescinded.

Pastor R. Wolfrum

The following letter, bearing the date when the actions against Paul Schneider reached their climax, contains statements that were also an object of discussion between Pastor Wolfrum and the local group leaders. Unfortunately, it can no longer be clarified if the letter was written on October 12 or 13, or if there is a typographical error.

Hochelheim, October 12, 1933

Mr. Johannes Mehl, Local Group Leader,

I can understand your actions concerning the church signboard from your viewpoint and from the perspective of your official capacity. In order to avoid a misunderstanding between us as much as possible, I would like to tell you that my protest against Röhm's appeal was a matter of conscience, since other church authorities were making no protest. According to Luther it is not advisable to do or fail to do something against your conscience. No courtesy shown toward the state can release us from this calling. Indeed, acting according to one's conscience must always be in the true interests of the state. You know that I have a loyal attitude toward the state today and am committed to working with you in a positive way and would like to be even more committed to doing so if I am given the opportunity.

Second, I considered it to be my solemn duty to publicly stand up for my boys considering the continual pressure that is being exerted on them and the numerous false reports that are also being spread in Hochelheim. As long as our group exists, I consider it my duty to place myself in front of them, even if we are only two persons. I cannot act on my own authority in the way you said. My hands are tied by the decrees of the official church and the Reich bishop, who has strictly forbidden that any group be dissolved. But if you want to help pave the way for a better agreement on our youth work in the future, then I ask you to temporarily refrain from taking any action that is targeted at our church group in particular since we have the official recognition of the state and church . . . .

I am fully convinced that on their own strength alone the Hitler Youth, and the state youth movement as such, cannot perform the task of raising our children to be Protest Christians, instilling in them Christian character and thus enabling them to be truly German men and women. Rather, it can do this only in closest association with the gifts and strengths of the church, which are given to it by the Holy Spirit through the Word of God and through living faith in Christ. This association, though, cannot be limited to occasional participation in the worship service.

I would greatly rejoice if I would receive an occasional invitation to attend an evening with the Hitler Youth, let's say, a church-based evening where we could discuss questions of life, and learn songs from the choral movement since some of these songs have already been introduced into the Hitler Youth, where we could let God's Word speak to us in a way that is suitable for our young people, but where we can also innocently and gladly socialize in a Christian atmosphere. Until now I have deeply deplored the fact that there was such little need for this in our village life. I would be glad if National Socialism would bring about a change here and would also create more opportunities for such activities in our village, which would certainly be a blessing to us and of great benefit to our village. Of course, then I would refrain from promoting our church group, but seek to fully serve the Hitler Youth. In this way you can help us achieve peace on your part. The present unfriendly tension would be eliminated and the looming alienation of our young people from the church would be avoided. At the same time this would be a right preparation for a possible merger of the denominational youth into the Hitler Youth at a later date. I would conceive of this in such a way that the former group would remain united in a loose form in order to especially serve the church and community.

With warm regards,
Pastor Schneider

This incident shows in a frightfully clear way that Paul Schneider, the German Christian pastor Wolfrum and even the local group leaders of the NSDAP in Hochelheim and Dornholzhausen simply did not see through the true intentions of the Nazi rulers.

They should have known that the cooperation between the Hitler youth and the Christian congregation implied here would have signified a complete reversal of the Nazi party's way of thinking and strategy. Then the great majority of its pronouncements up to then would have been meaningless. Yet such a request contradicted the National Socialists' self-understanding.

From time to time party offices issued official decrees meant to create the impression that the National Socialist state and the National Socialist German Workers' Party took a neutral stance on the groups in conflict with each other in Protestant church politics. These decrees caused considerable confusion and ill feelings among a large number of German Christians. These radical "German Christians" were annoyed, in their opinion, at the too gentle approach of party and state authorities toward those who appealed to the independence of the church on confessional issues. They wanted to radically get rid of the Scriptures of the Old Testament and of the Apostle Paul that were recognized in the church as authoritative.

A clear historical proof of such a German Christian way of thinking was the "Sports Palace Rally," which has entered church history as the "Sports Palace scandal" of November 13, 1933. At this rally the head of the German Christians in Berlin, Dr. Reinhold Krause, demanded that the church should distance itself from the Old Testament and the Jewish ideas contained in the New Testament.[8]

In Hochelheim the plotting and scheming against Paul Schneider continued. He never received an answer to his letter addressed to the local group leader Mehl. The declaration of the Dornholzhausen session mentioned in the report of consistory member Dr. Jung in response to the district leadership reads as follows:

Dornholzhausen, October 19, 1933*

To the District Leadership of the NSDAP

The undersigned session members and representatives of the two churches feel compelled to reject as untrue the following accusations

---

[8] Compare on this subject G. Gauger, p. 109; K. Meier, *Die Deutschen Christen*, p. 31. Looking at the "Sports Palace Rally," the order of the Reich interior ministry from November 30, 1933 is instructive of the propaganda game the Nazi rulers were playing. Compare S. Gauger, p. 116: "Within the German Protestant Church discussions are presently ongoing which have as their aim a clarification of the overall situation in the church. The Chancellor has made the express decision not to intervene in this controversy from the outside because it is an intra-church matter. In particular, any police intervention such as preventive detention, or confiscation of property among other things should not be undertaken." In July 1933 a German Christian statement came from Hamburg: "The view of Christianity advocated here, especially our view of a newly conceived true Christian ethos, is no longer centered 'only in the cross' as it has been traditionally. In our era the impression is growing stronger, as we can conclude from various indications, that the customary way this orientation has been affirmed has robbed the gospel of its validity in a terrible way and that the religious roots of our Protestant Church's inadequate missionary strength can be found here. If we could recover these roots, we could create a new reality. We are psychologically using up all of our strength to recognize the cross as a judgment on all of humanity, and as a result we lack the power to believe the gospel" (O. Langmann, *Deutsche Christenheit* in *Zeitwende, Juli-Ausgabe* [Hamburg, 1933], p. 68).

against Pastor Schneider, Hochelheim. First, that he does not take a loyal approach to the present state and second, that Pastor Schneider has caused a disturbance among the populace through his actions so that his administration of the pastoral office and his ability to serve with the blessing of the congregation is called into question.

Sincerely yours and most respectfully,
The session
The larger representative body of the two churches
Four elders
The larger representation
Ten members of the larger body

(This document is a reproduction of a handwritten copy that only contains the number and not the names of the elders and the members of the larger representative body.)

After the investigations by the consistory were concluded and the discussion had come to an end, the consistory in Koblenz made this decision:

Protestant Consistory
of the Rhine Province II 7383 II

1. The committee has decided to rescind the suspension of Pastor Schneider in Hochelheim and at the proper time transfer him to another pastorate. Pastor Schneider has already been informed that the suspension has been rescinded.

The district administrator in Wetzlar is informed of the decision of the consistory in writing:

Protestant Consistory of the Rhine Province

Koblenz, October 21, 1933
II 7383 I

To the District Administrator
Wetzlar

Concerning: Pastor Schneider in Hochelheim

Since on the basis of the local negotiations of our representatives with the local group leaders of the NDSAP in Hochelheim and Dornholzhausen they agreed that Pastor Schneider could remain in his office and resume his ministry in Hochelheim, dropping their complaint against him, the Protestant consistory has rescinded the suspension imposed on him, of which we inform you with reference to our discussion of the 19th of this month.

We have disclosed to Pastor Schneider what the requirements of his future behavior will be and cherish the hope that in keeping with his promise he will avoid everything that could be seen as a lack of agreement with the new state authorities. Nevertheless, as we now share with you confidentially, we are holding out the prospect of later transferring Pastor Schneider to another pastorate at an opportune time, taking church requirements into account. We are sending back the documents concerning the behavior of Pastor Schneider that you kindly turned over to us.

Consistory member Dr. Jung, who kept the correspondence, informs Paul Schneider:

Protestant Consistory
of the Rhine Province

Koblenz, October 21, 1933
II 7383 II

To Pastor Schneider, Reverend in Hochelheim
Also to the Superintendent in Garbenheim

On the basis of the results of the discussions our representatives had on the 19th of the month in the matter of the complaint against you we hereby rescind the suspension imposed on you, effective immediately. We use this occasion to impress on you again that you have to exercise complete restraint in the area of national politics and that any ill-considered action that could even remotely give rise to misunderstandings or suspicions must be refrained from. We urge you, both in your personal interest as well as in the interests of your ministry to willingly follow the advice given to you by Pastor Wolfrum on our instructions. He asked you to loyally work together with the local leaders of the NSDAP and to take into account the requirements of the present time. It is expected of you as it is of every clergyman to serve the present state in honest collaboration and make it your duty to work together fruitfully with all the members of your congregation in a way that fits the given circumstances. We will keep an eye on you so that you adjust your future behavior accordingly and trust that without further measures on our part and in keeping with your promise, you will avoid everything that could be seen as a lack of agreement with the new state authorities and could lead to new difficulties.

Jung

The personal file of Paul Schneider remains in the business cycle of the consistory. On December 15, 1933 it again lies on the desk of a lawyer who informs the personnel department head that he could only deal with the prospective transfer in January 1934. The memorandum is marked "resubmit after one month" and is confirmed with the initials "Ha" for "Hasenkamp."

In a letter to his mother-in-law from October 26, 1933 Paul Schneider expresses his opinion on the recent events:

On October 8, in Dornholzhausen eight days earlier, I had protested against Röhm's appeal to combat "sanctimoniousness" from the pulpit and on the church sign board. As I had suspected, I was, of course, reported. To protect me from arrest, the consistory quickly suspended me. We were enjoying our time with the choral group in Dollar when the superintendent drove up in his car. I was ordered to appear in Koblenz the next day, before a consistory member and our new bishop Dr. Heinrich Oberheid (a leading German Christian). I had to be instructed that Röhm's appeal was mainly targeted at the unjustified actions of SA and SS men against third persons and that I must not start a fight about such an important matter as an individual in a hierarchical church . . . . I allowed myself to be persuaded—or should I say, seduced?—to publicly retract my protest. But the district leadership was not yet satisfied. For a long time now I have been slandered there as politically unreliable, and the Nazi local group leaders as well as the district leadership had evidently come to an agreement that I should at least be transferred. The consistory could not rescind the suspension because of the resistance from Wetzlar. I naturally did not agree to such a transfer without further proof. Two representatives of the consistory came; they were first with me and then with the local group leaders. In the meantime considerable unrest and rebellion against the local group leaders had awakened in both congregations . . . . So they were glad to soften their tone in the end. Last Sunday I preached again on Romans 1:16 (I am not ashamed of the gospel, because it is the power of God for the salvation of everyone who believes: first for the Jew, then for the Gentile.)

As mentioned, Dr. Heinrich Oberheid was appointed to the newly created office of bishop of the "Protestant Church of the Rhine Province" on September 30, 1933 and was supposed to reorganize the Rhenish church in a way that suited the "German Christians." The following is reported about his installation:[9]

> After assuming office Oberheid sent greetings to the Rhenish congregations in which he explained that just as the National Socialist revolution had created a new order out of chaotic confusion in the life of the state, a new order has also been created in the life of the church.
>
> This work of unification was not brought about by the church relying on its own strength, but was borne "by the National Socialist movement under our leader Adolf Hitler." This is why the church today salutes "the National Socialist movement, the Führer and Chancellor Adolf Hitler and the wise old Reich president von Hindenburg with the deepest gratitude." The living God has "given us the Führer . . . . To Him we give praise, honor and thanks in the church!"

Following this political tribute he instructed the pastors that at all times the church has only one mission: to proclaim Jesus Christ, the Crucified and Risen One.

> But this unchanging mission takes place in "the given orders of this world . . . in the always changing reality." Since the National Socialist

---

[9] G. van Norden, ed., *Kirchenkampf im Rheinland*, p. 69.

revolution has created a new reality in the German people, a new order has begun in the church, a bitter struggle that has opened severe wounds on both sides. But this struggle is now over with the unification of the Protestant Church under the leadership of the Reich bishop. Now it is a matter of "extending our hands to one another in sincerity to begin this new work we share together so that the full gospel may be purely preached.

What did the Crucified and Risen One, Jesus of Nazareth, mean to a National Socialist "bishop"? As we have mentioned, on November 13, 1933, the "German Christians" in conjunction with their "bishops" launched an attack on the still existing structures in the church that were committed to the confessions. The "German Christians" showed their true face at that large rally in the Berlin Sports Palace, but they would not let themselves be swayed by the great exodus that began afterwards.

12

AGAINST A COMMUNION TRADITION NOT BASED ON THE CONFESSIONS

As a candidate of theology at the seminary in Soest Paul Schneider studied under Adolf Schlatter who made this statement on the Lord's Supper in his dogmatics:

> The historical connection to Jesus is just as indispensable for the Lord's Supper as it is for baptism. We have not yet described it adequately when we use the idea that Jesus instituted it: Because Jesus instituted it, and he commanded it, the church observes this celebration . . . . But in giving us the Lord's Supper, he not only gave us the form of the sacrament, but its content as well . . . . Therefore, we only achieve a believer's celebration of the Lord's Supper that transcends the dispute over it in the church when we grow in our understanding of what Jesus said and accomplished with his Lord's Supper.[1]

In his congregations Paul Schneider aims to institute a celebration of the Lord's Supper where a profession of faith in Jesus Christ and in his office as Savior has its unshakable place. He is always aware of what Paul had written to the church in Corinth: "For I received from the Lord what I also passed on to you. The Lord Jesus, on the night he was betrayed, took bread, and when he had given thanks, he broke it and said, 'This is my body, which is for you; do this in remembrance of me.' In the same way, after supper he took the cup, saying, 'This cup is the new covenant in my blood; do this, whenever you drink it, in remembrance of me.'" For whenever you eat this bread and drink this cup, you

---

[1] A. Schlatter, *Das christliche Dogma* (Tübingen, 1911), p. 468.

proclaim the Lord's death until he comes. Therefore, whoever eats the bread or drinks the cup of the Lord in an unworthy manner will be guilty of sinning against the body and blood of the Lord. A man ought to examine himself before he eats of the bread and drinks the cup. For anyone who eats and drinks without recognizing the body of the Lord eats and drinks judgment on himself. That is why many among you are weak and sick, and a number of you have fallen asleep. But if we judged ourselves, we would not come under judgment. When we are judged by the Lord, we are being disciplined so that we will not be condemned with the world."[2]

In Paul Schneider's view, the believer, i.e., the communicant, must take these statements seriously. The pastor has the duty to make the profound seriousness of Holy Communion the object of biblical proclamation and draw out its full, comprehensive significance for the communicant. He has to be vigilant so that the personal relationship of the communicants to the content of Holy Communion is not lost in the traditional rhythm of habit. Paul Schneider must inevitably break with this tradition because this is obviously the case in Hochelheim and Dornholzhausen.

In a letter from January 29, 1934 we read:

> At Christmas I could not announce and hold the young peoples' communion service based on an old tradition after having done so for seven years. Sports and Hitler Youth have finished this worship tradition among our young people—it was sheer mockery to observe how they all crowded into this Advent communion just to fulfill an obligation to God and the church in this way. So now I have shattered the straitjacket of this tradition. I called for a celebration to declare our faith in Christ, followed by voluntary communion.

The session does not understand the concern of the Pastor and reacts to "his unauthorized act" with the following petition:

Hochelheim,
December 19, 1933

To Pastor Schneider!

---

[2] 1 Cor. 11:23–32 (NIV)

Unless there is a decree of the church authorities, we, the undersigned elders, reject this arrangement you have made and insist on holding the Advent worship service on Wednesday and the communion service for our young people on the first holiday, following the order we have established. We ask that you immediately announce this by ringing the bells. Otherwise we will call a meeting this evening.

Hartmannshenn
Johannes Kraus
Heinrich Merte
Friedrich Schuster
Friedrich Schieferstein
Anton Zorb

A return to the Reformational heritage of German Protestantism took place in the midst of the euphoria of a "thousand year Reich" engendered by the National Socialists and by the propagation of a Germanic-nationalistic worldview that served as a substitute for Christian faith. This worldview was to be imposed on the German people in cooperation with the "German Christians." The confessions of the Protestant Church based on the Bible served as the foundation on which the conflict with the anti-God forces of the "Germanic-National Socialist ideology" could be waged. On the issue of the Lord's Supper Paul Schneider is already practicing one response to this conflict that the church found as it turned its heart and mind back to its confession of faith. He explains the reason for his concern to the superintendent:

Hochelheim, December 21, 1933

Dear Superintendent!

I would like to inform you of a change in our communion tradition. I believe I will have to answer to my own conscience for it. I should begin by mentioning that in the seven years I have been here the rigid tradition of these communion services has been my greatest burden, for I have seen numerous people appear at the table of the Lord who otherwise do not need the church and God's Word. Performing this duty has offended my conscience because this tradition has to a large degree suppressed truthfulness and honesty. As a result I could no longer enjoy any blessing from this celebration of the Lord's Supper. I had to call a stop to this unworthy and unrepentant observance of communion at this service, or rather, the members had to be freed from the straitjacket of this tradition.

A previous pastor from Hochelheim (Rochel) said in the church even in those days: There is no word more hypocritical than the "Yes" of confession at Holy Communion. I never found that my democratically elected session, led by Mr. Hartsmannshenn, had a sufficient understanding of my pangs of conscience, although some members of the congregation did understand my concern.

Soon the time had arrived for our youth Christmas communion service. Sunday after Sunday I had witnessed the gaping void in the church pews where the boys were assigned to sit. Instead, the boys were at sports events or the Hitler Youth was holding its meetings. I saw in this practice nothing but contempt for the church, God's Word and Sunday worship. I couldn't let this go unchallenged (see the petition of the session in Dornholzhausen to the synod from May 17, 1933). How often did I admonish the young people with earnestness and severity but also with love and kindness at their communion service! Now their gross failure to understand that regular church attendance is a prerequisite for participating in the Lord's Supper was no longer acceptable. I could not decide to announce and celebrate Christmas communion in the usual way. This is now compounded by the ecclesiastical situation, the brazen attempts to spread false doctrine and worldliness in our church. This is also present in our congregations in a subtle form. I could not ignore the request made by the church weekly "Sunday Greetings," also reprinted in the most recent issue of the "Pastors' Weekly,"[3] to begin clean up operations at the scene of church devastation without delay, gathering members into confessional communities of faith and Christian life.

Therefore, on the third Sunday of Advent, I called on the congregation to observe the third mid-week Advent service of the week last Wednesday as a confessional worship service, and invited them to a

---

[3] The "Sonntagsgruss" is a church weekly newspaper; the "Pfarrerblatt" is the official organ of the German pastoral associations.

voluntary celebration of communion following the service, which was to bear the character of an Advent and confessional celebration.

At the same time I canceled the previous Christmas communion for our youth, citing the reasons I laid out to you above, and invited the youth who had a need for Christmas communion to attend the Wednesday evening service. I alone assumed responsibility for what I did because I could only expect the session to hamper and not to promote this new approach. Afterwards I asked the session for its consent. I did not get it, but the session, which is making itself too dependent on the leading village criers, raised an objection both to the evening service that was to have a confessional character and be linked to communion as well as to the canceling of the traditional youth communion service. After that I called a congregational meeting with a discussion of the general and local situation of the communion tradition. Many men and young people showed up. I introduced the discussion and justified this new arrangement by stressing the need for honesty and by explaining the necessary requirements for a blessed observance of communion. I found opposition as well as agreement. The forest keeper supposedly explained to the lumbermen in the forest: The pastor is right. He is a member of the larger representative body of the two congregations. A Pietistic community man who sells calendars in the village has supported the change that has been made and speaks in favor of it in the homes of his customers.

Several defenders of a serious and more profound view of the Lord's Supper also spoke up at the meeting. Then when the word "herd of sheep" slipped out of my mouth as I was urgently exhorting them to attend the confessional worship services in comparison to the mass communion services, those of ill will used it to protest and walked out. The great majority remained in the hall, and we went back and forth, having a fruitful discussion of church and Christian issues. I was delighted by the evening, the good turnout of men and their interest in it. At 12:30 a.m. I went home with the last ones there.

We then held our evening worship service as announced in the presence of the whole session. The turnout was much better than at the last Advent worship service. Under the Advent wreath with its burning candles we held a reverent, blessed communion service in which not all who were in the church participated. The number of communicants did not coincide with the "Pietistic community." Not all the members of the Pietistic community were there, and other church members were also there. The communicants registered by handing in slips of paper with their names on them. I was glad that it went like this, that we have turned the evening worship service and communion into a true declaration of faith in Christ. I was glad that a breakthrough had taken place there, that we were able to get beyond the rigid communion tradition that had become a bad habit, a tradition that no longer allowed the purpose and significance of observing the Lord's Supper to become clear.

I could not do it any other way. The beginning has now been made. I can no longer go back. Dear superintendent, I ask for your kind understanding or even approval of my actions. We want to become the church in this momentous time when violent storms are perhaps immanent. I would also like to add that by taking this action that was informed by my conscience, I am in agreement with many voices today who are calling for the reform of our church and congregations, including Johannes Graber: "How Should our Church be Governed?" and "A New Church in the New State" by the pastors of the Tecklenburg Synod.[4]

Training courses for young mothers and a homeland missions week are being planned for the week after Christmas, so it does not seem as if I merely want to tear down. This tearing down is only intended to make way for the healthy reform and rebuilding of the church. I am praying that God may give his blessing to these efforts.

Congratulations and best wishes for a blessed Christmas to you and to your dear wife and family.

Respectfully yours,
Pastor Schneider

---

[4] Compare W. Niemöller, *Bekennende Kirche in Westfalen* (Bielefeld, 1952), p. 47.

Four elders from Hochelheim who refuse to be satisfied with the reform of the communion service directly contact the consistory in Koblenz. The personal file of Paul Schneider had been resubmitted through the official channels anyway.

With their petition the four elders add another complaint to the ones already filed by the Nazi district leadership, which does not come at an inopportune time for the consistory that had promised the Nazi district administrator that it would transfer Paul Schneider.

Hochelheim, December 28, 1933

Concerning: The report of the elders to the Protestant Consistory in Koblenz

The undersigned elders feel obligated to inform the consistory of the change in church procedures in the Hochelheim congregation made by Pastor Schneider.

On Sunday, December 17, Pastor Schneider announced after his sermon that the final Advent worship service on Wednesday, the 20th, would be a confessional communion service and that the communion service for our youth scheduled for the first holiday would be dropped. He explained that many of our young people only attend the worship service when there is communion, thus partaking of it unworthily.

The undersigned elders could only come out against this as the enclosed note to Pastor Schneider shows. In response to our action Pastor Schneider invited the whole congregation to a meeting at the restaurant of Wilhelm Jung by ringing the village bells (at 8:30 p. m.). The session was invited to a meeting an hour earlier (at 7:30 p. m .in the pastor's office) by the sexton.

After Pastor Schneider informed the session of his plan, we proposed that we should temporarily stay with the old order, since no explanation of the change had preceded his actions. Furthermore, we told Pastor Schneider that he should admonish the young people in love but with all the earnestness of the precious Word of God (almost all of them showed up for the communion service together), and if better attendance at the worship services could not be expected, expel them from the next youth communion service that coincides with Pentecost. If this measure should not suffice, then drop the whole celebration. The session affirmed this proposal unanimously.

Pastor Schneider did not accept it, but explained that he was acting on the basis of his convictions, come what may.

Without asking us to participate in the public meeting, Pastor Schneider, the chairman, left his office and left the elders standing there. When he did not return after a considerable amount of time, one of the elders thought the pastor might already be at the meeting. We had hardly entered the meeting room when Pastor Schneider opened with his lecture that proceeded without discussion. He then announced the change in communion and the crowd shouted at him. Pastor Schneider then said that none of the new elders could assume the office of church treasurer and those in attendance also called this remark despicable. Here we must add that since the election of the elders only one meeting of the session has taken place, where the church's statement of accounts was examined. Following this, Pastor Schneider announced that he had allowed the now honorary elder Johannes Zorb to remain in the office of deacon and we did not object. When the Pastor requested that one of the new elders should assume the office of treasurer, we asked him to temporarily retain this office that he had already held for years. In our opinion this would not be any great burden for him.

From this it can be seen that the cause of this problem is not found in the refusal of the elders to cooperate or in their ignorance. Instead, we can see that Pastor Schneider does not respect his new elders because he did not invite us for a consultation, but only invited us to examine the church accounts. He has not yet even appointed a deputy chairman or had one elected.

Very few of those present partook of the Lord's Supper while the others sitting there were infuriated because the pastor postponed the benediction until after the Lord's Supper had ended whereas the non-communicants are usually dismissed with the blessing. This shows us that the membership did not recognize the value of the confessional communion service. To show the stubborn character of our pastor, we must mention that he explained to an elder in response to his remark that he, the elder, could not be responsible for dropping the communion service, "Then you should resign from the office of elder."

We do not have to specially mention what indignation such incidents cause in our congregation. We, the undersigned, declare that under such circumstances it seems impossible for us to work with him and ask that you remedy the situation as soon as possible.

The elders
With a German salute!
Hartmannshenn
Anton Zorb
Friedrich Schieferstein I
Heinrich Merte

In response to the accusations Paul Schneider goes through the proper channels and writes to the consistory:

Hochelheim, January 12, 1934

Superintendent Wieber, Garbenheim

To the Consistory II 8847

Concerning the change in our communion tradition, the letter of Mr. Harmannshenn and my statement on this, may I ask you to pass on my letter from December 21 on this issue to the consistory. I am again enclosing a copy of this letter, and ask that you would return the copy when you no longer need it.

I would like to express my opinion on your letter from December 23, 1933 on this issue. I have been well aware of the regulations of our book of order. But certainly convention and tradition do not have to be an unalterable right in the opinion of the book of order. In a Protestant congregation we must have the right to break a tradition that has obviously become a bad habit that no longer allows God's claim and demand to become clear, according to a higher right to act on the basis of a conscience captive to God and committed to the Scriptures.

Contrary to his statements in his complaint, even Mr. Hartmannshenn will not be able to deny that I tried to do this in an orderly way through the session. He knows exactly how I failed in my attempts to implement at least an imperfect church discipline for the publicly offensive and impenitent sinners in Hochelheim.

That is why I contest the right of Mr. Hartmannshenn and the session led by him to raise an objection when I wanted to gain recognition for the sanctity of the communion service, for the possibility of serious self-examination for all communicants, which the Scriptures admonish us to do, and for communion as a voluntary act of declaring our faith in the Lord. The Christian community and the proper understanding of Holy Communion must be destroyed when irreconcilable neighbors, members involved in lawsuits, and members who have been guilty of gross immorality and are known for it, are admitted to Holy Communion without the session's objection and without repentance. Since then I had tried to put a stop to the worst of it through pastoral admonition, but I saw the session and especially Mr. Hartmannshenn put a spoke in my wheel. This man has no right to talk about the "stubborn character" of his pastor. Rather the completely unspiritual and arrogant way he sabotaged our church's program of pastoral care for the sick that I started shows who has the stubborn character (see my detailed report to the consistory about this).

As our superintendent writes, Judas figures have certainly been around longer than yesterday and we cannot create any community of saints on earth. But knowing the spirit of the Scriptures, the way in which Jesus celebrated the Last Supper with his disciples and identified the traitor, knowing the admonition of the Apostle to examine oneself, something only the believer is able to do, I cannot accept that holy communion is there for the masses of people in the established church who have hardly any or little contact with the Christian church and the divine Word. It is impossible in these circumstances for Holy Communion to appear in all its glory and sanctity as the highest celebration of the Christian church, as our fellowship meal with the risen Lord. I think that it is not even possible to speak here of a Judas because the village tradition completely suppresses the voluntary nature of every confession of faith and undercuts an awareness of the serious responsibility it entails. At the most our families could be guilty of raising even more Judases by following a tradition of celebrating the Lord's Supper that is contrary to Scripture, and our Savior surely does not want that.

I would like to make an additional comment on the tradition of celebrating the Lord's Supper without registration on the day when confession is made preceding communion. This tradition did not always exist. Only in 1899 under Pastor Fröhlich were the communicant lists done away with. Confession on Saturday was probably discontinued at the same time. My efforts to reintroduce confession on the day preceding the service likewise met with a lack of understanding and rejection in the session. So there was, in fact, no opportunity for me to point out the significance and the seriousness of the communion service to those who hardly ever participate in the life of the church or no longer do so.

Another distressing situation was the large number of communicants. From 150 to 200 village residents came to the communion service in three, and more recently, four age groups, each group twice a year. This naturally resulted in a very lengthy communion service with confession (one hour to an hour and fifteen minutes), following the preaching service. This was obviously a great emotional burden for the communicants who were not accustomed to the worship service. This also made it impossible—and this too is usual—to use the actual communion liturgy with the songs of praise. Thus the joyous, festive character of the communion service had to be suppressed.[5]

Now I would like to introduce a new order and discipline into our communion services with my session, in such a way that the congregation would be given an opportunity to partake of the Lord's Supper on one Sunday each month. The division based on age groups would be dropped. Confession would take place on the Saturday evening before communion. Registration with one's name would be requested so that a pastoral visit is possible and so that I can keep track of who is attending the communion service. Only in this way can the issue of confession be taken seriously again. Only in this way can their willingness to improve their lives and follow Jesus, their hunger

---

[5] Compare with Noetel, *A Commentary on the Rhenish-Westphalian Book of Order*, p. 93, and note 3, on working toward shortening the communion service.

and thirst for God's righteousness and their joy in fellowshipping with the Lord be the decisive reason for partaking of Holy Communion. Only then will the blessing and the rich grace of this celebration be displayed.

I ask the superintendent and the consistory to influence the session along these lines. The session is more likely to remember its duties of church governance and discipline if it sees that church authorities as well desire and approve of such governance and discipline compared to secular disorder and rebellion.

I would also like to comment on the issues mentioned in the report and on the complaint made by Mr. Hartmannshenn or better, the session. The report contains incorrect and incomplete statements that create a false impression.

1. Sitting around the round table both on the sofa and in the chair, I did not leave my elders standing after the discussion in my office, but was the first person to leave my office in the manse in order to go to the meeting. During the one-hour discussion I sought in vain to convince the gentlemen of my motives and asked them to support me. After it was over, I left just because it was time and I did not want to make people wait at the congregational meeting. Mr. Hartmannshenn should be ashamed of responding to my kindness in making my office, living room and furniture available to church boards for their meetings by making such accusations.

2. For information on how the meeting went I refer to my report to the Superintendent on December 21. Mr. Hartmannshenn forgets to mention that several persons voiced their opinions, expressing their appreciation and support for me and saying that I was right. The one who "shouted at" me the most is the accountant Reitz, who only appears twice a year in church for Holy Communion, balances his books on Sunday mornings as he himself admits and sees customers in his office. He got worked up about the holy traditions and customs of the villagers and justified his right to receive the Lord's Supper by saying that as a member of the civic community, which after all pays for the church, he is also helping to pay for the bread and wine. Of course, his argument gave everybody at the meeting a good laugh. It is

sad that an elder appeals to such "shouting" from the congregation to make his case against the pastor.

3. On the issue of an elder assuming the office of church treasurer I must state that I repeatedly offered this office to Mr. Hartmannshenn who is well suited for this job because of his handwriting and his other business qualifications, but he has always refused my offer. In this context I said that whoever has something to say in the congregation must also be willing to do something. We are still paying our sexton for collecting our house offerings of 3 RM per member because the elders are not willing to assume this duty. They are already leaving unpleasant things completely unfinished.

4. However, on the issue of the number of meetings we have held, they are correct. But Mr. Hartmannshenn fails to mention that I have to arrange all of our business matters with the village mayor and the office of Rechtenbach and all of our decisions in the session and the larger representative body have only limited value because the town council virtually has the final word. Thus we have already wasted too much time discussing church business. The church's representative body does not want to be responsible for the least amount of additional church money. Up to now they have denied all support to my youth work and childrens' worship service and I have always been dependent on my own initiative. When I am planning something in the congregation, I honestly confess that I am afraid to ask the church board, knowing that they might put a spoke in my wheel. (Take for instance the pre-school and pastoral care for the sick. They were also up in arms about the introduction of the new hymnal after the decision had already been made. The session, too, would have preferred to cancel it.) So in this era of the democratically elected church board I have actually depended much more on my self-supporting clubs to do the work of the church. I have appreciated their active participation in the ministry of this church and have spent my time supervising them. We have held many unfruitful and unedifying session meetings in the past. *Ceterum censo*: Our church's electoral law is in need of reform.

5. On the issue of our confessional worship service with the celebration of the Lord's Supper that went better than expected, see my report to the superintendent from December 21.

I would like to mention that the people who think in terms of the Bible's view of the church, who have a good knowledge of the Christian faith, together with wide sections of the congregation, are indignant at the arrogant behavior of Mr. Hartmannshenn and that one elder has disassociated himself from the action of the other elders, has not signed the petition, was not invited to the elders' discussions on this issue and has fully backed me up. Most of the congregation is in agreement with a new order for Holy Communion.

I would finally like to say that the worship life and church life of our congregation does not appear to be disrupted, worship services and the women's organization are better attended than previously, a parenting course for young mothers will be fully booked in the coming week and we are joyfully looking forward to a home missions week scheduled for the middle of February. I am convinced that our congregational life will turn out fine without intervention from the outside.

Pastor Schneider

In contrast to Paul Schneider the sessions of Hochelheim and Dornholzhausen had different views on what the church is.

1. In Paul Schneider's view, the church is an institution founded and commissioned by Jesus Christ, who works in the world by means of his Word and the sacraments instituted by him in order to say to human beings: "We have a mission and a calling from another world and our citizenship is there."[6] Man is responsible to make the most of his life in this world for the short time he is here, so he can and must never be the measure, for then there is always the danger that he will lose his citizenship in the other world. The Christian church and individual Christians in it live in a personal relationship to their risen Christ, which is of overriding importance. What counts is maintaining this relationship and not losing it (compare 1 Cor. 11:17–34).

2. For the majority of elders the church is an institution that should influence the ethical and social behavior of human beings and serve our personal edification. It has to nurture and preserve the structures that have become traditions.

---

[6] A letter to his father-in-law.

Paul Schneider tried again and again to make clear to the congregation that all behavioral patterns tied to a tradition the congregation appeals to, must always be open to scrutiny and must even be called into question by the Word of God and by the confessions of he church that have emerged from it. In doing so, our declaration of faith in Jesus Christ as the living Lord always has to be the foundation of faith and thus of life in the church.

Ideas such as the ones Paul Schneider develops in his letter to the superintendent were seriously discussed at a time when the confessional communities that were forming then began to reflect on their Reformational heritage; thus Paul Schneider did not stand alone. It was inevitable that a separation would occur from those who had distanced themselves from the confessions of the church and devoted themselves to a liberalism that was contrary to Scripture and in which man sets the standards.

The immanent transfer of the pastor creates renewed unrest in the two congregations. His opponents in the NSDAP, now in league with the elders who had turned to the consistory for help as they filed their complaint, try to gain the support of the congregation. For the "Protestant Ladies' Aid" of Hochelheim this state of affairs is unbearable, so it writes to the consistory:

Hochelheim, January 13, 1934

To the Protestant Consistory, Koblenz

Concerning: Our Pastor Schneider in Hochelheim

Since the rumor that our Pastor Schneider will be transferred from here has again been spreading through our village in recent days and we have heard that a petition has already been sent to the consistory from here, we feel motivated to get to the bottom of this matter because we do not know what reasons there could be for this. In our view this rumor can be attributed to the personal disputes of a few men from our village who want to forcibly disrupt the peace we have enjoyed in our church life until now. For when a pastor proclaims the Word of God faithfully and with a sincere heart, there will always be people who cannot bear the truth, especially when sin is called by its name. This is the way it was at the time of our Lord Jesus and also at the time of John the Baptist. We can only testify on his behalf, for he is really a truth-loving, faithful and righteous pastor and not a stupid boy as he is being called by his chief opponents whose reports are perhaps already in circulation.

They are also accusing him of not being a genuine National Socialist. We must reject this allegation and maintain that the opposite is true. For when our old Reich president wanted to call his troops together in 1918, our pastor was the only citizen of Hochelheim who felt it was his duty to join the battle and rescue the fatherland.[7]

He also acts according to the Word of the Apostle Paul in 1 Timothy 2:1–7, both in the church, in our clubs and in his private life. And he is the first of many who have made the campaign slogan of our Führer and Chancellor his own: The public interest takes priority over personal interest. The ones who can confirm this best are our brothers from the country roads as well as the poor among our congregation and the one yoked with us.

Several men are forcibly seeking to find misunderstandings and points of friction, only to manufacture reasons for transferring our pastor.

We are asking our consistory to especially listen to us in this matter since we in the Protestant Ladies' Aid have been working with the pastor and his wife for about seven years. Every time we meet in the manse we spend our time under the Word of God, in prayer and discussing the work of our organization. With a clear conscience we can report only good things about him, the increase in our club's membership from fifteen to 60 proves it. Since our pastor is also a human being and perhaps there are differences of opinion now and then, we must always seek the way of peace out of respect for the church and our religion, which, however, is no longer possible because of a few men who would like get our pastor out of here. They are accusing him among other things of having changed the way we have always served communion. This is true. As a faithful pastor he could not act differently because our former tradition had been linked to serious abuses that his conscience could not longer bear.

---

[7] Here the letter writers are mistaken. The student Paul Schneider was a part of this mission at the request of the government in Thuringia at that time.

We the undersigned ask and want our pastor to remain active in his ministry here and continue to work here as he has until now. Therefore, we urgently ask the consistory to reject any further motions made by the session since there is no reason to transfer him. If we were to collect signatures for him in the whole congregation, we would hope to find two-thirds of all our members who would speak out in favor of our pastor remaining in the congregation.

The Ladies Aid of Hochelheim
with 60 members

Many women support this petition by signing it. We cannot list them all here for reasons of space. However, what is striking about the letter from the Ladies' Aid is how at that time a "nationalistic, patriotic" attitude was equated with National Socialism. As we reported, in 1920 (not in 1918) Paul Schneider took part in a military mission in Thuringia as a student in Marburg and as the pastor's son in Hochelheim. We encounter a false interpretation of the term National Socialism in the next petition as well. The developing folkish movement from which National Socialism emerged did not play any role at all around 1920.

The "Evangelical Community" in Hochelheim has found out about the courageous petition of the "Protestant Ladies' Aid" before it wrote to the consistory:

Hochelheim, January 12, 1934

The Evangelical Community of Hochelheim joins the petition of the Ladies' Aid. As we found out on the evening of January 11 by elder Hartmannshenn, the session made a report to the consistory. We are informed about the Lord's Supper, since we were present when the pastor announced it after his sermon. We are firmly convinced that Pastor Schneider postponed the youth communion service not to gain an external position of power, but from an inner conviction since few young people sit under God's Word in the Sunday worship services except when the youth communion service is offered. Our pastor had given our young people the opportunity to attend the communion service at the last mid-week Advent service. Only Mr. Hartmannshenn, his wife and daughter sought to stir up the worshippers, as a woman from the congregation who sat next to them told us. Otherwise, everything was very peaceful in church. We hereby declare that elder Hartmannshenn is a member of our community and we have already asked him more than once to give up his eldership so that peace and order can be restored to our church, for he has assumed an external position of power in the church which is not in the Spirit of Jesus Christ. We hereby assure the consistory that Mr. Hartmannshenn is an opponent of the pastor's proposals almost every time a motion is made at session meetings. We kindly ask the consistory not to transfer Pastor Schneider because of such petitions. We are firmly convinced that Pastor Schneider has been conscientiously and faithfully administering his office. We hereby declare that Pastor Schneider is a dedicated Christian and National Socialist and he is respected and loved by most of the members in Hochelheim as well as in our yoked congregation of Dornholzhausen.

With a German salute!
Karl Hepp
Konrad Schus
Anton Weller
Wilhelm Schuster

P.S. As we have found out from reliable sources, Mr. Hartmannshenn went into the homes where our young people live and told them that they should not attend the communion service on the evening in question. Here is clear proof why so few young people participated.

It should and must also be mentioned that the party offices of the NSDAP foment the unrest kindled by a few elders in Hochelheim under the leadership of Hartmannshenn.

The petitions of the "Protestant Ladies' Aid" and of the "Evangelical Community" sent to the consistory meet with the full approval of the session in Dornholzhausen. All the elders personally sign the petition. Now the sole decision rests with the consistory in Koblenz, which processes the petitions on January 17, 1934 and adds the following note on the margin:

Nr. 658 K. Jan. 17, 1934

Pastor Schneider is being transferred.

It is desirable that Pastor Schneider soon goes to another pastorate. For the time being he is trying to go to Monschau: Therefore, nothing is to be initiated. So file it away.

Jung Jan. 17, Hasenkamp Jan. 17.

The wife of Paul Schneider comments on his "trying to go to Monschau":

> At the beginning of January Paul is asked to give a trial sermon in Monschau. Since Paul was in conflict with his Hochelheim session because of "his Scriptural understanding of the Lord's Supper and the issue of confession that must be taken seriously," the consistory insisted that Paul seek a pastorate elsewhere after receiving the session's complaint. But he still felt committed and leaving would have seemed like desertion to him. So after the trial sermon he withdraws his candidacy.[8]

For the consistory his transfer was settled, only they lacked the legal grounds since even then no pastor could be easily transferred to another pastorate against his will. The initiative for the forced transfer came from the district leader (district administrator) of the NSDAP who knew the plans of the consistory "in confidence."

It was not Paul Schneider's nature to let unjust behavior go unchallenged. Thus his situation is shaping up to be more and more difficult. The "powerful" do everything they can to muzzle their adversary, the pastor of Hochelheim and Dornholzhausen who is true to the confessions.

---

[8] *Prediger*, p. 55.

13

THE PASTOR IS NOT SILENT

The propagandists of the NSDAP continued with great intensity what the chief of staff of the SA Ernst Röhm had started in September 1933 with his appeal against "sanctimonious behavior." In the process the power apparatus of the state protected the behavior of their own Nazi VIPs. The pertinent literature provides information on this. In the following chapter I will show what difficulties Paul Schneider runs into again when he expresses his opinion on this "new" sense of morality in a sermon.

Morality and everything connected with it should comply with the pertinent "requirements" of the Nazi state. Therefore, it was necessary for the new rulers to start a process of rethinking, and reeducation—for the Nazi agitators a welcome opportunity to label the church adversaries they feared as "moralists," "bedroom sleuths," and "pious old maids," making them the laughing-stock of the public.

We know today only too well what this "new morality" looked like: Good-looking young Jewish girls and Polish girls were enticed, or to put it more honestly, ordered into brothels, having been given threadbare and false promises. When they had followed the orders given to them for a while, they were handed over to the concentration camps where they were classified as people who were "unworthy to live," as candidates for death, along with others: communists, Social Democrats, national patriots, gypsies, Jews and courageous Christians. The "master race" wanted to rule, therefore, the ones stigmatized by them were not permitted to stay alive.

Mass killings of those suffering from so-called hereditary diseases and the campaign to "Give the Führer a child!" were a part of this "new morality." The partner who possessed the race certificates demanded by the SS could be made an official member of the party. Only the child was important; he or she was to be given a National Socialist upbringing. After the birth of the child the respective partners were free to go their own way. These facts should not be ignored when we read the essay of the Reich propaganda minister Goebbels, whom Paul Schneider opposed.

"More Morality, but Less Moral Hypocrisy"
January 27, 1934

Every revolution has its atrocious deeds, so does ours. This is not bad in itself, but most of the time they even themselves out or are evened out again by time. What is crucial is that those who are responsible keep a watchful eye on it and do not remain silent for fear of the public when speaking out would be appropriate. It is quite natural that the historic, large-scale upheaval that accompanies any revolution brings large amounts of refuse to the surface along with the tremendous values it also produces.

It gets dangerous when the refuse is left lying there, hardens and then inhibits and restricts the healthy, organic development of the revolution.

Today it is about time we bring a few of these atrocious deeds into the bright light of public attention and mercilessly scrutinize them, subjecting them to the critical examination they deserve.

This seems even more necessary because otherwise a dangerous situation would be created where the style of our revolution and its way of life would slowly degenerate over time and convey to posterity an image of our being and intentions that in no way corresponds to our National Socialist convictions and world view. In our public life the great moral principles of our national life have not only been defined and laid down through public regulation, but beyond that a nonsensical situation has often developed where the authorities dictate in detail to the private individual the moral code of his purely personal views.

This leads over time to a moralistic snooping that is anything but National Socialist.

Unnatural people who either have been through life or do not deserve to have a life ahead of them are dealing in morality in the name of our revolution. This kind of morality often does not have much to do with true morality. It sets up ethical laws that could perhaps regulate the community life of a nunnery if need be, but that are misguided in a state with a modern culture.

This is moral hypocrisy instead of morality and those who advocate it have taken leave of their senses.

But they should at least not go before the public and appeal to us; for we want to have nothing to do with their stuffy view of life.

An example: an advertising poster for a soap company is supposed to be put up in a rather large central-German city; the poster shows a fresh, charming girl holding a box of detergent in her hand. A judge of public morals who unfortunately has the right to make a decision on this poster forbids it from being displayed, explaining that it violates the moral sense of the populace, especially since the woman portrayed on the poster is holding the box of detergent in a place "that could not be described in greater detail for reasons of decency."

Who is moral here? The censor who assumes that the emanations of his filthy imagination can also be found in other people, or the German people and the National Socialist movement who are rightfully indignant at such an embarrassing action and reject it? On closer inspection it turns out that this brilliant individual discovered his heart for National Socialism only three months after our takeover, which did not prevent him from issuing his prohibition in the name of National Socialism.

This is going too far! This bunch of moral censors does not even stop at the purely private realm. More than anything else they would like to appoint chastity commissions in town and country. They would have the job of monitoring the marriage and love life of Smith and Jones. As it says in the well-known operetta, they would not abolish kissing because that is a much too popular activity; but they would still transform National Socialist Germany into a wasteland of stuffiness and sanctimonious behavior if they could, in which informing against neighbors, snooping in bedrooms and blackmail would be nothing unusual.

These same moralizers frequently approach their superiors in government with their request to ban movies, plays, operas and operettas because female dancers and theatrical stars etc. appear in them, who supposedly represent the worst endangerment of public safety. If we would give in to their demands, then we would soon see only old maids and pious hypocrites of the male or female gender striding across the silver screen or across the stage. The theaters would be empty because the audience in general does not hope to find in them what they are looking for in the churches and houses of prayer.

Therefore, may they spare us this hypocritical behavior that does not represent any genuine strong view of life nor any genuine, honest morality. It is mainly just the resistance of those who have gotten less than their fair share in life against life itself. They will not repeal eternal life and its laws, but at most force it to recede behind a wide screen of despicable hypocrisy and false prudery.

The German woman does not go out alone, she does not sit alone in a restaurant, she does not go on a Sunday afternoon drive with a boy or even an SA-man without a chaperone, she does not smoke, she does not drink, she does not get dressed up or use makeup, in short, she does everything to put the German man with his evil desires in his place. This is about how the little hypocritical moralist imagines the German woman. And woe to such a poor female creature who is at her wit's end with all these decency laws if she has the misfortune of violating one of them out of ignorance or a sinful desire. It goes without saying that the German woman does not wear a bob cut, only Jewish girls and other despicable creatures do that.

These moralizers do not have the faintest idea that with their arrogant behavior they are deeply offending and humiliating millions of German women who are uprightly and honestly doing their duty in life and on the job, who are good companions for their men and sacrificial mothers for their children. They do not have the faintest idea that they are embarrassing and compromising National Socialism in the whole world, that they have come thirty years too late and that we have to call them to order because they are beginning to be annoying. There are good and bad, diligent and lazy, decent and less decent women with and without a bob cut; whether or not they powder their nose is always a sign of their inner worth, and when they smoke a cigarette once in a while in a family or party setting, they do not have to be rejected and banished from society.

In any case, those who take such a hostile attitude toward them or like all real men are indebted to them for an unending amount of happiness, relaxation and domestic peace but do not want to admit it in their stuffy arrogance should not set themselves up as the judge of their morals.

It is not National Socialist to enjoy life; on the contrary, we must always only think of the dark side of human existence, pessimism and human hate are the best teachers in our earthly vale of tears. Therefore, a true National Socialist does nothing to make this pitiful life more beautiful. Primitivism and a modest lifestyle are the only values of character. If you have one clean collar and one dirty on, then put on the dirty one to demonstratively express your hatred of the damned bourgeois lifestyle. Whoever owns a good and a bad suit, put on the bad one especially for festive occasions; for then you will be showing the people around you how revolutionary your attitude is; joy and laughing in themselves are taboo because the people should have nothing to laugh about. Do we live in a state run by priests or in the age of life-affirming National Socialism?

We are beyond suspicion of supporting tedious pomp and pageantry or enervating luxury. The Führer and many of his closest advisors do not drink or smoke and do not indulge in epicurean pleasures; but those who would like to kill any joy or optimism in a nation of 60 million people are despicable, apart from the fact that their foolish actions only bring poverty and unhappiness to countless human beings.

For every need that is given up makes new people unemployed; when people no longer drive their cars, then the automobile plants are shut down, when no one wears any new suits, then weavers and tailors no longer have anything to do, if people no longer go the movie theaters or to theaters, then hundreds of thousands of stage and film industry employees will be forced to go on public welfare.

Taking the joy of living from a nation means making it unfit for its struggle for daily bread. Whoever does that sins against the rebuilding of our nation and embarrasses the National Socialist state before the whole world.

A pathetic impoverishment of our public life would be the result, and we are taking a stand against it.

We do not want to eliminate joy, but let as many as possible, all if possible, share in it. This is why we are leading the people to go to the theatre, this is why we are also giving the worker the opportunity to get dressed up for festive occasions, this is why we are imparting strength through joy, this is why we are casting off the agents of a prudish hypocrisy and will not tolerate their continued attempts to spoil the joy of our people by their incessant lecturing that harasses them. Our people need that joy to handle the trouble, anxiety and deprivations of everyday life, for they are decent and good people who have every reason to get the strength they need to master their struggle for survival by consciously affirming life anew.

Therefore: More affirmation of life and less sanctimonious behavior!
More morality, but less moral hypocrisy![1]

For the sake of honesty we must say that the articles of Goebbels and Röhm met with criticism from the "German Christians" as well, nevertheless they did not speak up and thus remained committed to the Nazi rulers. As early as August 4, 1933 the "representative of the Führer for the German Protestant Church" was elected by the Old Prussian church senate to be President of the Supreme Protestant Church Council with the official designation of "regional bishop." On September 5, 1933 a Bishop's Law was promulgated for the realm of the "Old Prussian Protestant Church" by which the "regional bishop" could definitely be installed.

Paul Schneider follows these events very vigilantly and with others asks himself the question of whether it is good to keep silent about these hidden attacks of the Reich propaganda minister. Likewise, he wonders with others what is gained for the proclamation of the church by introducing a "regional bishop" into the Protestant Church of the Rhine province at this time, especially since the "German Christians" were more energetically demanding a "Reich bishop" who was to bring the regional churches into line and thus make them subservient to the Nazi state.

On September 27, 1933 the military chaplain Ludwig Müller had reached his goal. He was unanimously elected to be the "Reich bishop" by all of the German Protestant church leaders in the small Elbe metropolis of Wittenberg that had such historical significance for Protestantism, where the Reformation began. This Wittenberg of the Reformation had been very cleverly selected to be the site of this inglorious spectacle. This election was preceded by a more than embarrassing diplomatic, tactical maneuver orchestrated by individual regional church leaders, i.e., even by regional Lutheran bishops, which weighed heavily on the overall situation in the church. Following these developments the churchmen who courageously affirmed the confessions only slowly joined forces. The following years showed how difficult an uncompromising declaration of faith was in the Nazi state.

Immediately after he was installed in his office Müller began to force the regional churches to conform in order to put them under his commanding authority.

---

[1] Reprinted in "Wetterleuchten" (Munich, 1939), p. 383–385.

At the apex of their power the "German Christians," who liked to operate with the term "home missions," organized the previously mentioned, notorious "Sports Palace Rally" in Berlin on November 13, 1933 at which they unmasked themselves by openly expressing and showing what kind of people they were, and experienced an obvious disaster in the process. The German Christian Reich bishop was not impressed by that and issued the "Decree Concerning the Restoration of Orderly Conditions in the German Protestant Church" of January 4, 1934. This decree has entered church history as the "Edict to Muzzle Freedom of Speech." He decreed in it:

> The political struggles are destroying peace and order in the church; they are disrupting the necessary solidarity of the Protestant Church with the National Socialist state and are endangering both the proclamation of the gospel as well as the newly acquired bond with the people. Therefore, to safeguard the constitution of the German Protestant Church and to restore orderly conditions, reserving the right to take further measures, I am ordering in a responsible exercise of the office of leader granted to me by the constitution on the basis of Article 6, Section 1 of the Constitution of the German Protestant Church:

> 1. The worship service serves exclusively to proclaim the pure gospel. The misuse of the worship service for the purpose of promoting political conflicts in the church, irrespective of its form, has to stop. The opening as well as the use of our houses of God and other rooms for political rallies of any kind is forbidden.

> 2. Church office holders who publicly attack the church government or its measures or by disseminating written materials, especially in the form of brochures, fliers or circular letters, are guilty of violating the official duties that are incumbent on them. The filing of petitions through the prescribed channels remains unaffected.

> 3. A formal disciplinary procedure with the goal of removing the offender from office is to be immediately initiated against church office holders who violate the rules of number 1 and 2. During this procedure they will be temporarily relieved of their duties. For the duration of the temporary removal from office his income will be cut by at least

a third under the reservation of further regulations to be added to the disciplinary laws.

4. The law concerning the legal situation of clergymen and officials of the regional churches from November 16, 1933 and the provisional church law concerning the legal situation of clergymen and officials of the regional churches from December 8, 1933 and the church law concerning the settlement of political disputes in the church from December 8, 1933 are repealed.

5. This decree becomes effective on the day it is promulgated.[2]

This decree triggered a storm of indignation in the whole "German Protestant Church." Paul Schneider as well cannot remain silent about these events.

The local group leader of the NSDAP who had informants report to him on the sermons and announcements in the worship services which Paul Schneider held, informed the district leadership in Wetzlar:

NSDAP
Base Dornholzhausen, January 29, 1934
District Leadership of the NSDAP
Wetzlar

Pastor Schneider, Hochelheim, again unleashed outrageous statements against the government and its men in yesterday's worship service.

He protested against the article by propaganda minister Dr. Goebbel's "More Morality, but Less Moral Hypocrisy" and declared that he could not approve of it as a Protestant pastor.

Furthermore, he registered a protest against the decree of the Reich bishop concerning church business, and explains that there were already several pastors who objected to it and he would join them. Moreover, he stated: Certain people have sneaked into the government as a wolf sneaks into a sheep pen.

---

[2] Gauger, p. 130.

Finally, he admitted that he should not dare to make these statements, but his conscience would not give him any peace of mind.

I would also like to remark that Schneider wants to travel to Koblenz tomorrow to speak to his church superiors; it would be good if they were informed about the inflammatory sermon he gave yesterday.

Heil Hitler!
Germer

P.S. He called Rosenberg's book *The Myth of the 20th Century* paganism.

The Nazi district administrator Grillo immediately reacted and alluding to his "authority," he informed the consistory:

The District Administrator
Wetzlar, January 29, 1934

To the Protestant Consistory for the Rhine Province in Koblenz

Enclosed please find the copy of a petition of Dornholzhausen's local group leader of the NSDAP from the 29th of this month. According to a report I received at that same time from Hochelheim Pastor Schneider is said to have made the same remarks there as he did in Dornholzhausen. Referring to the phone conversation of my deputy Engfer with Secretary Wagner I ask you to hear what Pastor Schneider has to say about this matter if he should go to see you tomorrow. Furthermore, I urgently request that you immediately suspend him, since otherwise I would see myself compelled to take Pastor Schneider into preventive detention based on present circumstances. I would be grateful if you would notify me by telephone of what you have initiated.

Signed,

Grillo

Certified:
(Signature)
District Secretary

With this turn of events the avalanche started to roll again, which no one could stop under those conditions. Once a pastor had attracted the attention of the brown rulers, he could hardly elude their grasp in the future.

The discussion between Paul Schneider and the consistory in Koblenz was set for January 30, 1934 the first anniversary of the National Socialists' seizure of power. As he had agreed, Paul Schneider writes on the day after the interview:

Hochelheim, Jan. 31, 1934

To the Protestant Consistory of the Rhine Province in Koblenz

Referencing my discussion yesterday with consistory member Euler, I am taking the liberty to directly send you the original manuscript of my sermon from last Sunday and, because of the careless handwriting, a copy as well.

Apart from the special remarks on the margin I would like to explain that the statement of the pastors from the Emergency League led me to preach a thematic sermon and deal with the text thematically. I read the statement as one of our announcements and affirmed what it said. In general I tend not to bring church politics or political things into my preaching.

I think it was wrong to mention the name of Dr. Goebbels. The fact that I took a position on a similar appeal in spite of the previous matter with Röhm can be explained by the concern I felt about how such remarks must affect National Socialists who are not morally strong anyway, such as those in leading and subordinate positions in Hochelheim. After the Röhm appeal sincere older colleagues told me what a negative effect it has had on the morals of the big cities (such as Frankfurt and Berlin). So I regretted having withdrawn my protest for the reasons presented to me by the consistory. A bit of personal insincerity remained as a thorn in my flesh, prodding me to get it off my chest in this way.

Nevertheless, I regret having taken Dr. Goebbels' essay to heart more then it deserved and having followed an obstinate or unrighteous path in reacting to it.

Since I have agreed to the suspension suggested to me by the consistory in an act of good will, I ask that you would allow me to discuss with District Administrator Grillo, who threatened to arrest me immediately, whether there are grounds for such an action in the statements I made and then to decide with him on the legitimacy of his threat. However, at the same time I ask for the opportunity to provide information at an appropriate time on how deeply concerned pastors are about the effects of such misleading appeals and edicts on their congregations. Such appeals as those made by chief of staff Röhm and Reich minister Goebbels naturally carry weight with our National Socialist members and can be especially misleading for them.

I admit that I let myself get carried way by the stridency of my statements on church politics in front of my congregation. I express my regret about this and I do apologize.

Pastor Schneider

When difficulties occur Paul Schneider looks first in himself for the reasons that lead to conflict. He does not talk around the matter, but is always willing to assume responsibility for it. He is still trying to see the consistory in Koblenz as the spiritual leadership of the Protestant Church of the Rhine Province. As a visible sign of this he expects them to offer him benevolent counsel.

Paul Schneider is slowly maturing on the road to martyrdom. From October 1933 on he is constantly threatened by "preventive detention"—a National Socialist term used to camouflage police terror! (In German the term is literally "protective detention.") For who was supposed to be protected? The Nazi rulers were not so benevolent that they would protect their critics! The preventive detention was merely an instrument the National Socialist state used to muzzle its critics and opponents.

The sermon he submitted is as follows:

"Christ's Stormy Boat Ride and Jesus' Glory"

Dear congregation! By now it has surely not escaped the attention of any thinking and attentive Christian that we in our Protestant church are being challenged to fight, to bear witness and declare our faith and that we can not simply enjoy the fruits others have picked for us. Rather we have to struggle for the soul of our people with the church of Christ, with the true Protestant Church. To be sure, many are still sleeping and have not yet recognized that the hour has come to rise up. They think that although everything around us has become different, everything should stay the same in the church, or they even want the church to fully submit to the ruling political power. They think the church should organize its life from a political standpoint as the "German Christians" do.

Of course, they must underpin this practice with the false teaching that the message of the church is not the gospel, the good news of Jesus Christ, the Savior of sinners and the Kingdom of God alone, but our national character and traditions plus the gospel. They are in fact breaking with the living God and his Christ by placing blood and race and the history of the nation as sources of revelation alongside God's Word, alongside God's will revealed to us in the Word of Scripture alone, alongside Jesus as the only mediator between God and man. The struggle in our church has erupted over this issue and there can be no peace until the traitors of pure doctrine and those who have forced their way into the sheep pen as wolves have vacated their bishops' chairs and representatives' seats or until the confessing Christians have left this false church. (Explanatory marginal notes handwritten by Paul Schneider: I mean with the help of political power and methods.) But they are still in power and would like to muzzle those who resist them. Or they would like to put them out of action with the help of the ruling political power by casting suspicion on them as reactionaries and enemies of the fatherland, which they are not. The little ship of Christ's church is sailing in a storm.

All of this has not come out of the blue, only since yesterday; it has not come without our complicity. Disorder and a lack of discipline have been permitted to spread throughout the Protestant Church for a long time now. No fence separated the holy from the unholy ones, who did not really want to know anything about God's Word and did not want to belong to God. (Note by Paul Schneider: I am especially thinking of the communion tradition in our congregation as a tradition of our village.) We tolerated the teaching of Balaam, of liberalism among us, which praised the goodness and freedom of man, reduced the redemptive work of the Savior and God's glory and dissolved the seriousness of eternity into a foggy notion (the repercussions of liberal preaching are very palpable in Hochelheim). We do not hate the works of the Nicolaitians enough! The letters of Revelation warn us about the works of those who are morally lax, greedy, disreputable, and despise the Lord's Day. We have had communion fellowship with obvious and unrepentant sinners. We auction off the forgiveness of sins, the holy possession of Christ's church, as if it were a mass-produced article that anyone could have for a penny. (Note by Paul Schneider: the practice of confession in our public communion services.) And now the storm tide has swept over our church, and its little ship is swamped by ruinous and corrupting waves, and we need to scoop them out.

Christ's church is sailing along on the ocean of multi-national life; our German Protestant Church is sailing on the waters of our German national life. With gratitude to God we Protestant Christians accepted what seemed healthy to us in the turnaround of our nation's destiny—the will to achieve political unity, restore our national honor and work together in a socially-minded national community where even the poorest and least sons and daughters of the nation are loved and honored. We gladly joined in the holidays and supported the steps pointing in that direction. But we cannot close our eyes to the towering waves we see rolling in and inundating our people in the third Reich. Those who are getting together in the German religious movement under the leadership of influential National Socialist men, including Rosenberg, who is the editor of the *"Völkischer Beobachter,"* are advocating sheer paganism, thus there can be no agreement with them from the standpoint of Christian faith. We can and do not want to believe what the great Rhenish-Westphalian newspaper writes. It claims that the ideas in Rosenberg's book *The Myth of the 20th Century* are already or will become the worldview of National Socialist Germany. Let us not say: This does not concern us at all, for the German religious movement appears in public making the claim that it is the religion of all Germans. We openly say that we as Protestant Christians cannot agree with all the statements and speeches made by many of the leading men in the new Germany. The charge of sanctimonious behavior does not bother us; we also do not question the existence of both "morality and moral hypocrisy," but we have God's clear commandment against whoring and adultery that Luther interprets for us in our Small Catechism: "We are to live modestly and chastely in all our words and works." Only a truthful and disciplined attitude, as the Bible show us, is consistent with this teaching, and gives the woman greater honor. It is not compatible with the freedoms Dr. Goebbels now wants to grant to the German woman. (Note: examine chief of staff Röhm's edict on sanctimonious behavior.) We know the joy that is based on a deeper foundation and that has given hundreds and thousands of believers the strength to make sacrifices for the fatherland. The activities of *Fasching* (the Mardi Gras type of carnival celebration before Lent) are foreign to Protestant Christianity; it does not want to have anything to do with it based on the Word of Scripture: "Nor should there be obscenity, foolish talk or coarse joking, which are out of place, but rather thanksgiving" (Eph. 5:4 NIV). Our faith is our greatest joy.

We would also like to know as Protestant parents that our children are clearly being raised in our Protestant faith and are being taught that faith. We would like to know that those who teach in the spirit of national religion are leaving them alone. (Note: In the circle of the Pastors' Emergency League the rumor is making the rounds that Rosenberg's book is recommended for purchase in school libraries.) We want Sunday to be the day for church and we especially want Sunday morning to be fully reserved for the worship life of our youth as well. We want the state to remain in its political realm and not to encroach on the realm of faith and the worldview determined by it. We want the state to be humble enough to be able to listen to God's Word coming to it through the ministry of the church. We appeal to Hitler's word that he needs the strength of Christianity to build up the life of the people. We are willing to do so, but in the freedom that obeys God alone.

Now you are being challenged to declare your faith and to bear witness, dear Protestant church, dear Protestant Christian. So now do not be mute dogs, for the Savior says: "Only those who confesses me before men are the ones I will confess before my Father in heaven." You Christians in your churches: now you are threatened on all sides by the waves that are rising against you from the church, from the people and the state. And we are anxious; we are frightened. We are like the disciples on the lake. We cry out: "Lord, help us, we are drowning."

We do not see that the poor, defenseless little ship of the church is to be preserved in the midst of the powers and forces of this world. But then we remember that the Lord is with us in this ship of the church, that this church has the promise. Whether or not a Rosenberg writes about the myth of the twentieth century, we have the promise: "The gates of Hades will not overcome it" (Mt. 16:18). It only seems as if our Lord is sleeping and does not care about our hardship. Soon he will wake up, for the storms are only sweeping across his church and the life of the Christian so that *his* glory may be revealed, so that his strong and powerful arm may be visible to us and even the world must confess in amazement: "What kind of man is this? Even the winds and the waves obey him." (Mt. 8:27 NIV) Therefore, he guides the ship of his church safely through the crashing waves of the nations of this world. But we must be ashamed of our little faith or lack of faith, our fear of man and fear of the world. Or will not the one who himself overcame the world on the cross not stand by us and comfort us? Will the Lord, who established his church on earth, abandon and neglect it in this moment? O, let us renounce all our lack of energy and tiredness, all of our cowardly, lethargic fears! The Lord walks to you and gets in the ship, the lake turns calm, and you may be peaceful and secure.

This is the way it is with all the storms that strike you who are Christians. You must suffer these storms for Jesus' sake and because you want to follow him. Then you shall know: "He, the Lord is with me; he lets me wake him up. When the force of the waves threatens to engulf the little ship of your heart in the dark of the night, you will stretch out your hand. Watch over me, o keeper in the night!" Where is the storm? Yes, it is less around you than in you, in your heart.

Then, like Peter, you see the tempest coming toward you in your heart, you are afraid and begin to sink. But even then the Lord extends his saving hand to you and holds you tight to strengthen your weak faith. But what is it that you alone must do to experience Jesus' glory in the storm, in the storm swirling around the church, in the storm swirling around your Christian life? You should believe, trust and rely on the wondrous power of the Lord in whom you want to believe. But if you do not believe, then do not say that you are a Christian, then you are only a nominal Christian, an intellectual Christian or a hypocritical Christian. "Our faith is the anchor of our heart," Luther says. Whoever does not want to live by faith and confess his Lord, will perish, and lose his soul. Even if he gained the whole world, he will be condemned with the faithless world. "I would rather believe unto death" than have the cowardly, refined life of this earth with the world. The Bible does not say that God will allow us to live out our life on this poor, little earth under all circumstances, and allow no harm to befall our money and possessions, our body and life, our wife and child. Rather such distress must at times come upon Christians; but the Lord will bring the little ship of his church safely through the surging waves of world events and the waves will subside when he gives the command. He calms the storm in your heart as the words of the song you women like to sing put it: "Even if I do not know the way, you know it well. That quiets the soul and makes it peaceful. You know where the wind blows so violently, and you command it to be still and you never come late. Therefore, I calmly wait, your Word is without deceit; you know the way for me, that is enough." The Baltic martyrs could go to their deaths confidently and cheerfully with the peace of this song in their hearts. The Lord is guiding the little ship of his church, the ship of your Christian life, not toward a temporal, but toward an eternal destination. This is our great hope, our joy. Do we not want to crowd even more closely together in the ship of Christ's church, even more closely than here in these pews, in the bond of faith that unites our hearts? Do we not want to rejoice that this ship is given to us? See, it is not just a story of old, our gospel is a story of today, of the living Lord and his church, just as you have been singing this song in the village from earlier times: "O church of Christ, noble ship, how glorious is your course, many a reef surely threatens you in the storm, many a wave surges up. But God is with you, so be confident, the Lord is leading you to your destination. However much the sea surges and rages, when he gives the command, it is still!" O, Jesus, hear my plea, scatter the enemies' hordes, let all the world see it, our God is with us. Lead your children evermore toward the safe haven and let your flock be one, rejoicing in blessed peace!

Amen!

The pulpit announcement of the "Confessing Church" follows the sermon, which was read from many pulpits in Germany:

Before God and this Christian congregation we raise our voice in protest against the decree issued by the Reich bishop and accuse him of seriously threatening the use of force against those who for the sake of their conscience and for the sake of their congregations can not remain silent about the present emergency in the church and of again putting into effect laws that are contrary to our confessions, laws that he himself had repealed for the sake of peace in the church. Even in our relationship to the Reich bishop we must act according to the Word: "We must obey God more than men!"

This sermon is an appeal and a request to take faith in Jesus Christ seriously. What Paul Schneider later testified to in Buchenwald can be heard loudly and clearly there. The pulpit announcement illustrates the serious situation in which the German Protestant Church found itself at that time and what method the German Christian Reich bishop used to bring the entire German Protestant Church under his commanding authority. Police action taken against his critics served to support his and the "German Christians'" display of power. As I said earlier, their goal was to force all 29 Protestant regional churches to conform to the party line.

The following incident shows what capers were possible at that time to achieve this plan under the cover of "restoring order to the church": By way of decree the regional bishop transferred his authority to the national bishop Ludwig Müller:

> 1. March 2. On the basis of the (null and void) decree of January 26th national bishop Müller decrees as the regional bishop of the Old Prussian Union Church: "I transfer my authority to the German Protestant Church."

Following this decree, on March 2, the ministry of spiritual life passed the following church law about the leadership of the Protestant church of the Old Prussian Union:

> 1. The German Protestant Church assumes the leadership of the Protestant Church of the Old Prussian Union through its organs under the leadership of the national Reich bishop who also serves as the regional bishop.

> 2. In abolishing the institution of the General Synod, the Regional Synod replaces the German Protestant National Synod. This Regional Synod consists of the elected Old Prussian members of the National

Synod. The national bishop is authorized to increase the number of members by additionally appointing 30 new members.[3]

Apart from a few travel days, Paul Schneider is present in the worship service of his congregation Sunday after Sunday during his suspension. Pastor Harth from Klein-Rechtenbach is administering the pastorate of Hochelheim and Dornholzhausen as his deputy.

Pastor Schneider receives a letter from the consistory signed by four consistory members in response to his petition from January 31, 1934:

Koblenz, February 15, 1934
Protestant Consistory of the Rhine Province, Nr. 1317

To Pastor Schneider, Hochelheim, from the superintendent in Garbenheim

On January 30, 1934, after the district administrator of Wetzlar had demanded your immediate suspension and expeditious transfer, threatening you with preventive detention because of your sermon on January 28, 1934, our case workers disclosed to you during the discussion in this office building that you had to consider yourself as suspended until further notice and that you had to be transferred to another pastorate as soon as possible.

From the exact copy of your sermon that you submitted to us we see that you sharply criticized several leaders of the present state by naming their names. Certain other statements that were viewed by your accusers as an attack on state dignitaries were actually targeted at the "German Christians" and at the supreme leaders of our church as is clear from the text of the sermon.

We will refrain from taking disciplinary measures against you since our case workers have already pointedly shown you your offenses in the oral discussion and you yourself admitted in your petition of January 31, 1934 that you let yourself get carried away by making utterances on

---

[3] Compare on this subject S. Gauger, p. 150.

church politics that were much too harsh and since you expressed your desire to apologize.

In the meantime your transition to another pastorate must be brought about as soon as possible.

Around Easter the pastorate of Dickenschied/Womrath in the district of Simmern will be vacant because the pastorate of Ellern-Morschbach is to be given to the present pastor R. Christmann. As soon as we receive the approval of the Supreme Protestant Church Council to fill the pastorate of Dickenschied/Womrath, we will inform the congregation that we have chosen you as the prospective candidate for this position. The superintendent of the Simmern district will notify you of the Sunday on which the congregation desires to listen to a sermon by you. We ask you to inform us within a week of your willingness to assume this pastorate.

After eight days the personal file had to be submitted again to the appropriate caseworker. After Pastor Schneider had declared his willingness to assume the pastorate, the file on Hochelheim-Dornholzhausen was closed. Mrs. Schneider reports:

In spite of his second suspension he felt obligated to stay for the sake of those in the congregation who stood faithfully behind him. But on February 19, 1934 the official letter with his transfer to Dickenscheid arrived. He was no longer allowed to perform any ministerial duties until the move at the end of April. This was a difficult trial for Paul, standing and living within the congregation and yet having to turn over preaching and teaching to others.[4]

Paul Schneider notes under March 1, 1934:

My Hochelheim session did not support me, and amid so many sympathetic members in both congregations there are only a very few who want to stick out their neck for their pastor.[5]

---

[4] *Prediger*, p. 56.

[5] Ibid.

Although the district leader of the NSDAP as the district administrator got the consistory to agree to the transfer of the pastor and thus had achieved the goal he had set from the beginning, the NSDAP does not let Paul Schneider out of their sight.

The official party organ of the NSDAP, the *"Völkische Beobachter,"* from time to time put its party members in the right mood to join the looming conflict with the confessional pastors:

> When offended pastors stir up the members of their congregation against their superiors in church and state from a wrongly understood sense of duty, then they clearly prove that they are not really concerned about the salvation of their parishioners' souls and the internal peace of the church. They must tolerate the suspicion that they are involved in reactionary circles and are being used as their tools and that they want to sabotage the National Socialist government's work of rebuilding Germany by way of the churches and by endangering the peace of the church. But saboteurs must be put out of action even if they play their reprehensible game in the guise of God's servants.[6]

The NSDAP determined the measure of all things; it decreed what had to be defined as reprehensible and what not. They saw in everything that opposed them the given of reactionary behavior that had to be combated.

When we take an overview of Paul Schneider's journey through life, it becomes clear how the leaders of the National Socialists satisfied their personal resentments against the Christian churches by using the NSDAP's instruments of power.

In retrospect, allow me to remind you of two statements made by Paul Schneider. This statement of his was recorded in the minutes of the session of the Protestant congregation in Hochelheim, whose chairman was Paul Schneider: "The message of the church cannot be proclaimed loudly and clearly enough to the National Socialist awakening of our people."

We take the other statement from the letter we have already quoted:[7] "I do not believe that our Protestant Church will be able to avoid a conflict with the

---

[6] S. Gauger, p. 136.

[7] *Prediger*, p. 55.

Nazi state. I do not think it is even advisable to postpone it any longer if we are to render to God the Christian obedience we owe him."

These are two momentous statements! Momentous because they make clear how isolated Paul Schneider was as a lonely voice in the surging waters of a euphoric, diabolical time. An additional factor was that the "legal" church authorities bowed to the all-controlling party, whereas the men of the "Confessing Church" had to look forward to even more difficult trials, without having any other support than the gospel.

14

A FORCED TRANSFER TO DICKENSCHIED AND WOMRATH

Dickenschied was not an unknown parish for Paul Schneider. After all, it was not located far from the village where he was born, Pferdsfeld. He still clearly remembered how as a young boy he used to hike to Dickenschied to see his Uncle Walther who was the pastor there at that time. When he assumed the pastorate, the book of minutes his uncle had used to record the motions of the session was still in use. Paul Schneider writes of his new beginning:

> The family rode quite comfortably, others would say like gypsies, with the rest of the furniture, sitting in a sofa and chairs, with a rear view, covering the 120 miles from Hochelheim to Dickenschied in the moving van. Like a sheep dog I myself accompanied the van with my motorcycle. The fully gathered congregation with the President in front gave us a warm reception in the churchyard.
>
> My installation was celebrated in the yoked congregation of Womrath on May 8, 1934 in the most beautiful and friendly way with festive greens and church banners. The superintendent Ernst Gillmann, Simmern, had chosen as the text of his address Jeremiah 15:19–21:
>
> "Therefore this is what the Lord says: 'If you repent, I will restore you that you may serve me; if you utter worthy, not worthless words, you will be my spokesman. Let this people turn to you, but you must not turn to them. I will make you a wall to this people, a fortified wall of bronze; they will fight against you but will not overcome you, for I am with you to rescue and save you,' declares the Lord. 'I will save you from the hands of the wicked and redeem you from the grasp of the cruel'" (NIV).

I gave my inaugural sermon on 2 Peter 1:19: "And we have the word of the prophets made more certain, and you will do well to pay attention to it, as to a light shining in a dark place, until the day dawns and the morning star rises in your hearts."

The assumption that Paul Schneider could pursue his ministerial duties in peace in the seclusion of the Hunsrück would be a misapprehension. This would be to forget that it was the Nazi district leadership in conjunction with the consistory in Koblenz dominated by the "German Christians" that orchestrated this forced transfer. Thus Paul Schneider is marked by the National Socialists when he arrives in Dickenschied.

Conscious of their power, the National Socialist functionaries from time to time dropped their masks when they wanted to display their total claim to leadership. The NSDAP was a hierarchically structured and tightly managed organization that could vary considerably in the way it treated people for the purpose of achieving its goals. When examining the statements made by the Nazi rulers, the reader is well advised to always keep their goals in mind so that you will not be the victim of erroneous ideas as so many were in those days.

The *"Völkische Beobachter"* reported on April 28, 1934 that Nazi leader Alfred Rosenberg, responsible for educating the party on its worldview in his capacity as the national leader of the NSDAP for ideological instruction, had said at a rally of "The League of Struggle for German Culture" in Königsberg:

We have declared that we are protecting the denominations both as a movement and as the state. Every faith is respected; its office holders are protected. But we are not here to be the secular arm of a denomination, also not to be the guardian angel for a part of this denomination, not even when it believes it is especially sympathetic to National Socialism.

Our opponents should be clear about one thing: We are no longer fighting for dogmas; this struggle has ended. A new struggle for character values has begun. So we reject the idea of burdening German youth with inferiority complexes from an early age. We do not want to evoke in it an awareness of its sinfulness, but values of its character. If we had always held a list of our sins in front of us during the struggle, we would never have been victorious.[1]

---

[1] S. Gauger, p. 188.

At the national convention of the "League of Struggle for German Culture" Rosenberg went on to explain:

> It is our duty to anchor the National Socialist world view in the people so that it shapes the character of the new Germany. I think that in this struggle for the correct worldview times will be hard. I think that the next ten years will result in many heated debates. But I also know that National Socialism will be victorious in this battle.[2]

Rosenberg was right. From its own self-understanding National Socialism could not tolerate Christian groups modeling themselves on National Socialism, no matter how watered down their views may have been. So it is all the more incomprehensible that the "German Christians" who believed they were building on the foundation of Reformational Christianity ignored this state of affairs (except the radical "German Christians" of a Thuringian character).

Paul Schneider had seen through the behavior of the Nazi rulers and at first still hoped that the consistory would recognize the seriousness of the situation. Today we can not imagine what a severe disappointment it was for him when he was forced to recognize that the Protestant consistory in Koblenz had entered into an alliance with the National Socialists.

His disappointment grew day by day because the consistory did not want to recognize that the functionaries of the NSDAP wanted all or nothing and would allow only a very limited time for the proclamation of the gospel of Jesus Christ in Germany. As is now well known, it was to be replaced by a "Germanic religiosity" which they called the "National Socialist worldview." Thus it is not surprising that even in the Hunsrück region he soon clashed with a functionary of the NSDAP.

---

[2] Ibid.

15

THE MOMENTOUS CLASH

This is how Paul Schneider reports on the confrontation with the district leader of the NSDAP in the neighboring community of Gemünden, where he had filled the pulpit while the pastor was on vacation:

Dickenschied, June 12, 1934

Dear Superintendent!

I want to inform you of a clash I had yesterday during the burial of an eighteen year-old Hitler boy and member of the labor service, Karl Moog from Gemünden. All of the Hitler Youth and the League of German Girls as well as a unit of the labor service and a SA-unit were called in to form an honor guard.

After the liturgical blessing of the body at the graveside, the unit leader (deputy) of the labor service camp ("fate gathered him to his fathers"), representatives of the Hitler Youth and then the district leader of the NSDAP, Nadig from Gemünden, all spoke. He said among other things that Karl Moog had now crossed over into the storm of Horst Wessel. I had not yet said the benediction and could not bless him into the storm of Horst Wessel. So then I said: "I do not know if there is a storm of Horst Wessel in eternity, but may the Lord God bless your departure from time and your entry into eternity. Let us go now in peace to the house of the Lord and remember the deceased before God and his holy Word."

After that the district leader again stepped forward and said: "Comrade Karl Moog, you have crossed over into the storm of Horst Wessel." And then I said: "I protest. This is a church ceremony, and as a Protestant pastor I am responsible for the pure teaching of the Holy Scriptures."

Then I left the cemetery with the Gemünden church president at the head of the procession and we walked to the church.

Only civilians showed up there, one man was in uniform, and finally a number of girls from the League of German Girls pushed their way in. The mass of the remaining uniformed persons including the school children had obviously been ordered to walk past the church although some of them stayed in the restaurants of Gemünden for quite a while longer.

Dear superintendent, I ask you to take the steps that seem appropriate to you in order to protect the dignity and purity of our church funerals.

With friendly greetings
Pastor Schneider

The matter was not finished for Paul Schneider. He wrote a letter to the district leader, but we do not know whether these lines fell directly into his hands as a result of Paul Schneider's arrest.

Dickenschied, June 13, 1934

Dear District Leader!

I would like to write you a few lines about the incident that occurred yesterday at the cemetery after I sought in vain to speak to you yesterday. I ask you to understand my actions there.

I am personally sorry that this clash occurred, but I acted this way because I was in a predicament. The committal service at the cemetery is also a strictly church ceremony, opened in the name of the triune God and closed with the blessing and the invitation to go to the house of God. It is not acceptable that anyone can say what he wants there. I may assume that you have an appreciation for this proper church order. Perhaps you could miss how in a Protestant church ceremony the living God was replaced by "fate" that had called the boy away, but the introduction of the heavenly storm that, by the way, was concocted by the former bishop Hossenfelder, forced the pastor to object, for he performs the ceremony and is responsible for its confessional character as an act of the church. I did this in its mildest form, which was intended to cause the least sensation. The repeated occurrence of the word "fate" forced me to register this protest.

In a Protestant church ceremony God's voice has to be clearly heard from the Holy Scriptures. Our church people are liberalized enough, so it is no longer appropriate to allow any opinion to be expressed in the church. There can no longer be any place for this because especially at a church funeral the seriousness of eternity does not tolerate being measured by human standards. Therefore, not everyone who does his duty in the Hitler youth or the SA fairly well can be beatified. I will certainly accept the earthly storm of Horst Wessel, but that does not mean by a long shot that God will allow him to march straight into eternal salvation. That is perhaps "German faith," but it is not biblically based Christian faith that takes seriously the full reality of sin that is so deeply rooted in the heart and life of man.

Moreover, I appeal to your appreciation for order and discipline. I am not permitted to appear at a party meeting of the NSDAP and say what I want. At best laying a wreath with a simple eulogy would be compatible with a church ceremony at the cemetery, but not a long speech with faith-like statements, especially when the consent of the pastor officiating at the funeral had not been obtained in advance.

I am probably giving you only a superfluous assurance here, but it was not a political reaction that led me to do what I did at the cemetery, and you will surely believe an upright German man and Christian when he appeals to his pastoral conscience that is captive to God. By the way, it would also be a pleasure for me if we could continue to talk about the matter itself and the realities of faith behind it.

With a German salute!
Pastor Schneider

National Socialism wanted to introduce its worldview to the German people openly but it also did so surreptitiously because it knew it was incompatible with a biblically based Christian faith. Its national "faith" was not permitted to know anything about the "full reality of sin so deeply rooted in the heart and life of man" because it alone felt chosen to set the standard and did not tolerate any critical discussion. The incompatibility of Christian and pseudo-Christian thinking becomes conspicuously clear when the statements of Rosenberg in Königsberg on the one hand are compared with the statements of Paul Schneider on the other hand.

The response of the district leader was the arrest of Paul Schneider, who supposedly had to be protected from the "seething national soul" by the decree of "preventive detention." But the following letter provides information on what the actual situation was.

Simmern, June 14, 1934

The Superintendent
No. 269/34
including two enclosed letters
Registered Letter

To the Protestant Consistory in Koblenz

I hereby confirm the Protestant Consistory's decision in the matter of the preventive detention of Pastor Schneider, Dickenschied, given over the phone by Siebert, a member of the Consistory. He stated that the consistory cannot and does not want to do anything in this matter. But I am enclosing copies of two letters, one sent to me and the other to the district leader, so that the consistory can at least put an account written by the accused Pastor Schneider in its files later. These letters were both written before the preventive detention and without Pastor Schneider knowing that it would be imposed. Brother Christmann was in Womrath and Dickenschied today and informed us that the anger being expressed by the populace is extraordinarily intense. However, to rule out any misunderstanding, it is not targeted at Pastor Schneider.

2 enclosed letters!
E. Gillmann, Superintendent

The superintendent's letter with the enclosed letters without a doubt clarified who was to be "protected" at that time. The consistory, not wanting to stand up for Paul Schneider, also received another petition.

> To the Protestant Consistory in Koblenz
>
> We hereby submit to the consistory of the Rhine province the copy of a letter that we wrote yesterday to the provincial governor because of the arrest of our beloved Pastor Schneider.
>
> Womrath, June 15, 1934
>
> To the Provincial Governor in Koblenz
>
> Our Pastor Schneider, Dickenschied, was arrested on the 13th of this month as a result of an incident during a funeral.
>
> We are of the opinion that at the graveside of Karl Moog, Gemünden, our pastor as a servant of the Word of God could not say anything other than what the clear text of Scripture proclaims. In our opinion he did not in the least offend the state or its Führer, therefore we are standing up for our pastor and request his release.

The signatures of 43 out of 48 families followed. The session in Dickenschied joined the petition from Womrath with its own separate petition. Its closing section reads:

> We are using this opportunity to ask you to intercede with the relevant authorities on behalf of Pastor Schneider who has the confidence of the whole congregation, so that he is released from detention and can again perform the duties of his ministry. The whole Hunsrück is indignant and angry about the arrest.
>
> In the name of the whole congregation
> The session of Dickenschied
> Klos, Müller, Diener, Jakoby

The consistory commented on the two petitions in this way: "We are aware of the petitions from the Gestapo in Koblenz. File."

The Hunsrück pastors' brotherhood, of which Paul Schneider was a member, did not remain inactive at that time. Among other things, they clarify the events in their petition. We read:

> We, the undersigned pastors, declare our full solidarity with our colleague Schneider. We are of the conviction that in the framework of a church burial citing the "heavenly storm of Horst Wessel" is inappropriate in view of the seriousness of death. Everything that is said and done at a church burial must be measured by the sole norm of God's Word. But the Word of God, the Holy Scriptures of the Old and New Testament, does not know any "heavenly storm of Horst Wessel," but only a judgment awaiting this fallen world enslaved to sin and death, and an eternal life in which the Christian may have confidence through true faith in his Savior Jesus Christ. To be sure, we think that the Christian has to do his duty wherever he is placed, all the more so in a political formation such as the Hitler Youth, but we know that we can by no means be saved by fulfilling this duty—not even by doing one's duty in the Hitler Youth. Rather, we believe and confess that we are saved by faith alone in the grace revealed by Jesus Christ. The idea of the "heavenly storm of Horst Wessel," which, by the way, seems to have been brought up by the former Bishop Hossenfelder, contradicts the inner essence of the gospel as the Reformers have taught us to recognize it anew.
>
> Any reasonable person can easily see that Pastor Schneider's rejection of the expression mentioned above can by no means signify a personal denigration, disparagement or dishonoring of the deceased.
>
> Furthermore, it is clear that this rejection represents anything but a denigration or disparagement of our modern state or the National Socialist movement although it was apparently viewed as such. Otherwise, the preventive detention of our colleague Schneider would certainly not have occurred. We know that the protest of our brother Schneider was determined only by the gospel. This is why he had to oppose those unacceptable statements within a church funeral. What motivates us as well is nothing other than our concern to keep Christian faith and morals pure. It is incomprehensible how the behavior of our

colleague Schneider that was motivated by religious and Christian concerns could be misinterpreted as a political action against our modern state which he recognizes just as we do. It is completely incomprehensible why he has been detained and not yet been released on account of a thoroughly justifiable resistance to anti-Christian false teachings within the framework of a church service.

Not only we, but also the lay people, especially in the congregations of Dickenschied and Womrath, have been deeply angered by this arrest. The anger that led to this arrest is slight compared to the shockwaves sent through the communities of the Hunsrück as a result of the arrest. The congregations of Dickenschied and Womrath understand this measure against their pastor as little as we do. They see their pulpits are vacant. The Word of God is no longer being preached. Pastoral care has ceased. Another preventive detention could simply not be justified in view of this shockwave that has swept through our Hunsrück populace.

Therefore, we issue a heartfelt and urgent appeal to all relevant authorities to restore our colleague Schneider to his ministry and quickly provide for his rehabilitation.

Simmern (Hunsrück), June 18, 1934 Langensiepen-Guldenroth
Deuchert-Buchenbeuren Finsterbusch-Castellaun
Disselnkotter-Sensweiler Rolffs-Bell
Lutze-Cleinich Ringhardtz-Dill
Oberlinger-Thalfang Langensiepen, retired pastor
Reif-Veldenz Petry-Wischweiler
Storkebaum-Irmenach

Paul Schneider writes to the Gestapo after his release from detention which occurred immediately afterwards:

Dickenschied, June 21, 1934

To the Gestapo office in Koblenz
through the district administrator

As I already expressed to inspector Schmidt upon my release from preventive detention yesterday when he made his disclosure to me, I vehemently object to the belated judgment of the incident at the cemetery in Gemünden on June 12 as a "statement that was hostile to the state." It is this false assessment of the incident that led to my preventive detention. The dignity of my office compels me to lodge this protest.

The presence of the many uniformed men and women, whom I had to regard in this case as hearers of the church's message, made it all the more my confessional duty to stand up for the pure doctrine of the faith.

Therefore, I cannot allow you to put the stamp of "hostility to the state" on the teaching discipline I exercised in a mild form. I know that on this issue I am in agreement with many who were present there in uniform. This is why I cannot promise, as you suggest, to refrain from making similar statements "that are hostile to the state" in the future if the duty of my office and of declaring the Christian faith calls me to do so.

However, to avoid such incidents in the future, which, of course, could damage the image of the party in the eyes of our populace that holds to the Bible and our confessions, it would be advisable if the ordinances of the Protestant Church as well as the teaching and image of the church would by sincerely respected by the party and its organizations.

Pastor Schneider

A few weeks later Pastor Schneider writes in a letter as one who was affected by the machinations of the National Socialists and targeted by them:

Moreover, we must learn to endure these tensions by trusting in God and always give ourselves the opportunity to recover from the tension that is in the air today, not in our congregations, but in general. We must know that the church of Christ is actually returning to its normal condition by having this tense relationship to the world. But may the Lord make us, his little flock, prepared for the hour of decision when it is necessary to not deny his name.

The general "church climate" ordered by the National Socialists changed constantly and caused the confusion they intended. I think the following incident will illustrate this—its repercussions could be felt even in Dickenschied and Womrath.

The "National Synod" convened in Wittenberg on August 9, 1934 where the legalization of the German Christian leadership of the "German Protestant Church" under the leadership of Reich bishop Ludwig Müller was first on the agenda. The Reich administrator August Jäger commented on the new procedural rules at the synod. He explained:

> Previously battles were fought at such meetings. Obstructionist tactics could be brought to bear. We do not need that in the third Reich. The procedural rules simply regulate the essentials and I do not have to bother with further explanations.[1]

At this synod the machinations of the "German Christians" became only too clear. They did not shy away from flagrantly breaking the law in order to secure the autocratic rule of the national bishop. This incident is taken from a whole host of events that the Christian church in Germany was worried about at that time and that had an influence on the behavior of Paul Schneider. The Swedish theology professor Andreas Nygren aptly described the ecclesiastical situation in Germany in May of 1934 before a group of pastors from Stockholm:

> The church struggle is aimed at Christianity itself. A new religion of race has begun. What is so dangerous is that the present church regime does not have the slightest appreciation for what is at stake in this struggle. It thinks it can maintain the position of Christianity and does not notice that it has lapsed into a new religion of race. But there are men in the German church—and fortunately there are not just a few— who understand what is on the line and who understand that what this new religion has to offer human beings is nothing but idolatry from a Christian standpoint. They are creating for themselves a new God in their own image, in the image of the "German man." The Christians who see this are being forced to fight because they are faithful to the gospel; by fighting they are being drawn into a tragic conflict, for there is so much in the new state that they joyously affirm with all their heart.

---

[1] Compare on this subject S. Gauger, p. 273ff.

But by combating this new pagan spirit that has penetrated the church and has claimed its leadership, they are labeled as enemies of the state by this church regime that has no understanding of it. Now it has come to the point where the present church government is fighting those who do not want to give up their Christian faith with drastic measures and the Gestapo is resorting to dismissals and suspensions. . . . We Protestant Christians of a related people have seen with distress and concern that the German church government has sullied the Christian name by proceeding in such a way. With profound sympathy we stand by these hard-pressed Christians in their heroic and sacrificial struggle, in which they are fighting for the Christianity of the Protestant persuasion in Germany and in the world.[2]

Professor Nygren had correctly described the situation of the "German Protestant Church" at that time. It was incomprehensible for the whole ecumenical movement and it was totally unjustifiable that a Protestant church in the land of the Reformation could model itself so closely on such an obviously anti-Christian, worldly form of church government. In August of 1934 Paul Schneider writes:

I wish I could have a peaceful new year in my life as I celebrate my birthday! Of course, now we must declare our disobedience to the National Synod and its laws next Sunday on the instructions of the Confessing Church. I must say that I am very glad to do it, for there can be no honest peace for the church of Christ with these false practices, though we need God to have mercy on us not just outwardly, on our wives and children, but also inwardly. We must pray that he will cleanse us and humble us and equip us anew for his ministry and for our task of bearing witness. We should not throw away our confidence in him, for it has great promise. The world continues to be the world, and our era is certainly not more pious and more Christian than other eras were. But God wants to renew his church in this dangerous time, and in a different way than the German Christians think.[3]

---

[2] S. Gauger, p. 192.

[3] *Prediger*, p. 71f.

The pulpit announcement, by which Paul Schneider associates himself anew with the disobedient members of the Confessing Church, reads:

> On August 9, 1934 a meeting convened under the name of a national synod made decisions, passed laws and declared legal what had been illegal until now. This so-called national synod, its actions and decisions are invalid according to ecclesiastical and secular law. Whoever follows them violates the constitution and the law of the church. We refuse to accept it and call on the congregations and churches to not be guilty of violating the constitution and the law. By continuing to act against the best interests of the church, the national church government, especially the national bishop appointed to protect the constitution of the German Protestant Church, is responsible for the fact that the situation in our German Protestant Church has deteriorated this far. The national church government despises the most basic principles of law and justice. It puts the proclamation of the gospel under the will of fallible human beings who are determined to seize power. It is devoid of the brotherly love demanded by the Holy Scriptures. It thereby abandons the foundation of the Reformational church that is built on the gospel. Those who violate the law and constitution they are supposed to protect have forfeited the right to demand obedience. Those who are called to lead the church, but who time and again abandon the foundations of Christian teachings and action, place themselves outside of the church. Therefore, we declare to the churches, the congregations and their members, being responsible to God: Obedience rendered to this church government is disobedience to God. Nevertheless, God's solid foundation stands firm, sealed with this inscription: "The Lord knows those who are his"; and "Everyone who confesses the name of the Lord must turn away from wickedness" (2 Tm. 2:19).[4]

For Paul Schneider the free synods and their organs constitute the actual government of the church and no longer the consistory in Koblenz that is not guided by the Holy Scriptures and the Reformational confession. In this context the statements of the free synods that distance themselves from the state-controlled national church government are important. The Synod of Dahlem declares on October 20, 1934, among other things:

---

[4] H. Hermelink, *Kirche im Kampf*, ibid., p. 120f.

> We call on the Christian congregations, their pastors and elders not to accept any directives from the previous national church government and its agencies and withdraw from any collaboration with those who want to continue to be obedient to this church government.
>
> We call on them to adhere to the orders of the Confessing Synod of the German Protestant Church and the organs recognized by it.[5]

Paul Schneider agrees with this summons from an inner conviction to which he remained faithful until his death in the concentration camp. He was able to smuggle a letter out of the Gestapo prison dated November 24, 1937 in which he repeats the remarkable sentence from March 1935: "Make the congregations as independent as possible!" For Paul Schneider the church is manifested where human beings come together under the Word of the Holy Scriptures and administer the sacraments scripturally as a church that believes in Jesus Christ. Thus he is grateful for every link with like-minded believers and for every expression of solidarity in the faith. He knows how to distinguish between spiritual and worldly authorities. Compromises between the two authorities are not permissible for him and have no place in his thinking. He draws the lines of separation sharply. Thus he inevitably resists when the secular authority demands something from him that prevents him from exercising his spiritual ministry. When he judges a certain action to be correct, he goes his own way, even if it means he is isolated in the circle of his colleagues. He reports in a letter about a "preventive detention" the Gestapo imposed on him because of his refusal to sign a statement in which he would have been obligated not to read the declaration of the Old Prussian Confessional Synod from March 5, 1935:

> Make the congregations as independent as possible . . . . We would have much to write to you about us. You have heard about the 500 pastors arrested in Prussia over the past week. They refused to certify by their signature that they would allow the state to prohibit the declaration issued by the Old Prussian Confessing Synod on March 5, 1935 that was to be announced to the members of the church.
>
> The state wanted to thereby curb the confessional character and the impact of this church witness that illuminates the situation like a flash

---

[5] Compare on this subject S. Gauger, p. 379; H. Hermelink, *Kirche im Kampf,* ibid, p. 72f.

of lightning. It did not turn out well. Many pastors were arrested. They are all temporarily free again. I sat in the prison of Kirchberg from Sunday evening through the National Day of Mourning until Tuesday morning. Unfortunately I was the only pastor from the whole Hunsrück, but it was good that one person saved the honor of the Hunsrück. The brothers had allowed themselves to get caught by surprise and were forced to sign. Afterwards they deeply regretted what they had done, and in the meantime they have all withdrawn their signatures, at least those who belonged to the Pastors' Emergency League. Gretel had to put up with another house search on Saturday, and I have been deprived of a great number of papers and books they took from me. They met with very limited success when they tried to take the copies of the declaration out of circulation that I had previously distributed in the villages. The congregations remained faithful again . . . .

The declaration read:

In agreement with the declaration of the provisional leadership of the German Protestant Church in Nr. 4 of its announcements from February 21, 1935 the Confessing Synod of the Protestant Church of the Old Prussian Union in its meeting at Dahlem on March 5, 1935 addressed the following word to the congregations:

The second Confessing Synod of the Protestant Church of the Old Prussian Union that convened in Berlin-Dahlem on March 4 and 5, 1935 likewise accepted the responsibility of addressing a word to the congregations that was targeted at the new pagan religion.

We see our people threatened by a deadly danger.

This danger consists of a new religion.

At the command of its Lord the church has to watch carefully to ensure that our nation gives Christ the honor he deserves as the judge of the world. The church knows that it will be called to account by God if the German people turn away from Christ without being warned.

I. The first commandment is: I am the Lord your God. You shall have no other gods beside me.

We obey this commandment believing in Jesus Christ, the Lord who was crucified and raised for us. The new religion is a rebellion against the first commandment.

1. The racist, folkish worldview becomes a myth in it. Blood and race, national character, traditions, honor and freedom become an idol in it.

2. The belief in the "eternal Germany" demanded by this religion replaces faith in the eternal kingdom of our Lord and Savior Jesus Christ.

3. This delusive faith makes its god for itself in the image and nature of man. Man honors, justifies and redeems himself in it. Such idolatry has nothing to do with positive Christianity. It is anti-Christianity.

II. Obedient to our church's mission, we have to testify before our state and people in view of the temptation and danger of this religion:

1. The state has its sovereignty and authority by God's commandment and gracious order. God alone establishes and limits all human authority.

Whoever makes blood and race and nation the creator and lord of the state's authority in the place of God undermines the state.

2. Earthly law fails to recognize its heavenly judge and keeper, and the state itself loses its authority when it allows itself to be clothed with the dignity of an eternal kingdom and turns its authority into the highest and ultimate authority in all areas of life.

3. Therefore, it cannot submit to the claim of total authority that the new religion ascribes to the state, for it binds the conscience. Committed to the Word of God, it is obligated to bear witness to the exclusive rule of Jesus Christ before the state and the people. He alone has the power to bind and loose the conscience. All authority in heaven and on earth is given to him.

III. According to the command of its Lord the church has to preach the gospel of the grace and glory of Jesus Christ to all peoples.

a. Therefore, it must not allow itself to be pushed out of the world's public realm into a corner of private piety where it would be disobedient to its mission in self-sufficiency. It must also not cease to proclaim the Word to the authorities, for Christ commissioned the church to proclaim it.

Number 2 of this declaration calls on the church to resist the secularization of the church's traditions (the desacralization of Sunday, the dechristianization of its festivals), Number 3 calls on the church to instruct and educate the younger generation in a way that is based on Scripture. Then it continues:

> IV. The church prays that God's name may be hallowed among us, that his kingdom may come to us and that his gracious will may be done in our people and state as well. Therefore, the church must watch carefully to ensure that the intercession and thanksgiving for all authority commanded by God's Word takes place in truth and does not become a religious transfiguration and consecration of earthly powers and events.
>
> The oath finds its boundary in the truth that only God's Word binds us unconditionally.
>
> Bound by God's Word, the church calls on its members to willingly offer its obedience, commitment and sacrifices to the nation and state. But it warns the German people against entrusting itself to an idolatry by which we bring down God's wrath and judgment on us.
>
> We should fear, love and trust God above all things.[6]

---

[6] H. Hermelink, *Kirche im Kampf,* p. 250.

16

AGAINST THE GLORIFICATION
OF THE STATE

Paul Schneider continued his journey in an uncompromising fashion, a journey that was defined solely by his commitment to Jesus Christ. He simply could not glorify the state at that time. For this reason he rejected any cultic honoring of Hitler. His refusal to do so was interpreted as hostility to the state and it led to interrogations. Unfortunately, the records of these interrogations are no longer available in Dickenschied and Kirchberg. Did an interested party destroy them?

The consistory that had meanwhile moved from Koblenz to Düsseldorf receives a complaint about Paul Schneider on October 17, 1935 from the temporary provincial governor of the Rhine province. Two weeks later a further more detailed complaint on the part of the provincial governor follows:

Provincial Governor
I a I Nr. 1001
To the Protestant Consistory of the Rhine Province in Düsseldorf

Concerning: Pastor Schneider in Dickenschied

There is reason to call your attention to the following incident: The Protestant pastor Paul Robert Schneider, born on August 29, 1897 in Pferdsfeld, the district of Kreuznach, presently in Dickenschied Nr. 58, the district of Simmern, has repeatedly refused to use the Nazi salute at the beginning and end of the confirmation class which he holds in the elementary school in Dickenschied.

When the mayor interrogated him about this on October 9, 1935, he made the following statement:

"Just as we do not begin and end the worship service with the Nazi salute, I must reject the practice of beginning or ending religious instruction with the Nazi salute, as some of my colleagues also do." After that the district school administrator tried to persuade Pastor Schneider in a personal conversation that the use of the Nazi salute must be required. Pastor Schneider, however, could not be persuaded, rather he declared that he had to stick with the statement he made on October 9 and added that they were making the German people into a people of hypocrites and helots by making the salute mandatory. He upheld his refusal to use it even when the district administrator explained that good wishes for our head of state are contained in the salute "*Heil Hitler*" and that as a result, one is fulfilling a truly Christian duty when one uses the salute.

If Pastor Schneider has revealed his hostile attitude toward the state by his conduct, I must add that he appeared as an enemy of the new state as early as 1934. I am referring here to the incident at the burial of the Hitler youth Moog on June 12, 1934 that led to the preventive detention of Pastor Schneider. The subject matter of a Sunday sermon he gave at the beginning of September is typical of Pastor Schneider's convictions. He came to speak of the "chosen people," the Jews, and remarked that we must try to teach the Jews Christianity.

Furthermore, Pastor Schneider tried to make fun of the German Christians in his sermon by explaining that the pastors of the German Christians appeared for worship services in their tuxedos and opened their worship services with the Nazi salute. Moreover, the abridged Lord's Prayer was prayed and military march songs were sung. At the conclusion of his sermon Pastor Schneider pointed out that at the end of the worship service they would take a collection for a Jewish mission in Germany, and recommended that the churchgoers eagerly participate in the collection. The investigations into this matter have not yet been concluded.

In spite of all this I consider Pastor Schneider a definite enemy of our state on the basis of the other charges that have been clearly shown to be true. Taking this situation into account, I ask that you seriously consider whether it seems advisable to remove Pastor Schneider from his office.

I have likewise filed a report with the national and Prussian minister for church affairs.

Signed, Turner
Certified: Bode
Office Clerk

The letter of the temporary provincial governor of the Rhine province that arrived at the consistory office two weeks before the more detailed one printed here is passed on by the case worker responsible for Paul Schneider, Hasenkamp, a member of the consistory, to Superintendent Ernst Gillmann who is asked to explain his position on the matter.

Protestant Consistory Düsseldorf
October 24, 1935
Nr. 12261
To Superintendent Gillmann in Simmern

The provincial governor of the Rhine province has sent us the following information about Pastor Schneider in Dickenschied. We ask you to return it to us after you have examined it.

We took notice of this information with deep regret. We ask you to arrange a discussion with Pastor Schneider as soon as possible and persuade him to change his behavior. You may want to confront him with the fact that his refusal to use the Nazi salute in front of the school children not only brings him, the individual pastor, new political hostility, but that he seriously damages the image of all clergymen by such conduct. He also does the "Confessing Church," of which he is a member, a bad favor. For he arouses the suspicion that it tends to support reactionary politics and that it can considered an enemy of the state. Although the Confessing congregation has repeatedly rejected this charge with painful indignation, his conduct adds fuel to the fire.

If the instruction of the children were only a matter of a religious ceremony such as the childrens' worship service which takes place in the church itself, the patriotic salute would be neither expected nor appropriate. But the pastor is dependent on a classroom of the local school for his confirmation instruction in Dickenschied; thus he is a guest of a state institution. Every teacher entering the classroom is obligated to give the Nazi salute. The pastor who gives instruction in the classroom can and must not exclude himself from this custom if he does not want to lose the respect of the children and if he does not want to incur the state's displeasure. Saluting the Führer of the German nation should also not be difficult for him for inner reasons. After all, on every Sunday he calls down God's salvation and blessing on the head of state in prayer. Therefore, instead of foregoing the salute in front of the children, he should rather make clear to them in what profound sense a believer can and should verbalize this salute that expresses our desire for the well being of our head of state. For the sake of our clergy's image and for this innermost reason we would welcome your success in persuading Pastor Schneider to change his point of view when he hears your objections. We expect a report about this as soon as possible.

The provincial governor of the Rhine province received the following answer to his letter from October 10, 1935 (received by the consistory on October 17, 1935)—Document 1835, concerning Pastor Schneider in Dickenschied, the district of Simmern:

We have immediately authorized the superintendent of the district synod in Simmern to persuade Pastor Schneider to change his behavior in a personal discussion with the pastor in Dickenschied. We deeply regret that the pastor is failing to give the Nazi salute, which the children hear and expect at the beginning of every class, when he gives his confirmation instruction in a state classroom in front of the children. Pastor Schneider is not at all aware of the magnitude of his misconduct due to his theological stubbornness that we have often had to note with regret. We hope that he will listen to the serious objections we have obligated the superintendent to raise.

Paul Schneider's attitude is quite obvious from the response of the superintendent Ernst Gillmann:

The Superintendent Simmern
November 9, 1935
Telephone 484
Nr. 360/35 II

To the Protestant Consistory in Düsseldorf

I hereby inform you that I attempted to talk with Pastor Schneider, Dickenschied, but I did not succeed. Pastor Schneider shared the following information with me in a letter dated November 8, 1935:

Copy:

> Superintendent Gillmann, Simmern
>
> In response to your request of November 2 for a talk with you concerning the Nazi salute in my confirmation class that you addressed to me as authorized by the consistory, I must reply to you that I am not prepared to have such a talk.
>
> I have explained my position twice to the provincial governor, the first time recorded by the mayor in Kirchberg, the other time orally and in writing by the district school administrator. I recognize that the state is now seeking to contact me via the church in the matter of my confirmation class. But my higher church authority is not the consistory, but the Protestant Confessing Synod in the Rhineland and the Rhenish Brotherhood Council that represents it. This Rhenish Brotherhood Council has already approved my stance on this issue and informed me that it is not appropriate to begin the class with a salute that is an expression of a political movement because confirmation is a part of the proclamation of the Word.

Should the provincial governor still not understand and approve my stance, I suggest that he speak to my higher church authority, the Rhenish Brotherhood Council.

Signed,
Pastor Schneider

In spite of my failure to have this talk I urgently recommend that you do not take any measures against Pastor Schneider because he has made a decision of faith based on his conscience, which does not allow us to draw any conclusions about his political views. Schneider is an old soldier and a very honest, honorable man the state can count on in any situation. He sees confirmation classes as, for example, the Catholics see communion classes, as part of the preaching office.

Pastor E. Gillmann

In view of Paul Schneider's clear response, which causes confusion in the consistory, it turns to the highest administrative office in Berlin for assistance, sending a petition to cover itself:

Protestant Consistory Düsseldorf, November 18, 1935
Nr. 13284

Concerning: Pastor Schneider's refusal to use the Nazi salute in his confirmation class (Dickenschied, in the district of Simmern)

Without an edict
Report made by consistory member Hasenkamp

Pastor Schneider has refused to directly report to us because he considers the Rhenish Brotherhood Council as his church authority. In his response to the superintendent he holds the view that confirmation classes must be seen as an official duty of his religion which must not be introduced with a salute coming from the political sphere. He advocates this view in agreement with the Brotherhood Council that informed him that "it is not appropriate to begin the class with a salute that is an expression of a political movement because confirmation is a part of the proclamation of the Word."

As we know, the Nazi salute has not yet established itself in church instruction that is given in church buildings. This has not caused any trouble elsewhere. But in this case, where the pastor is a guest in a state school building, his conduct had to seem offensive to the school children. He should consider this and avoid the problem.

A clarification by a higher authority seems to be urgently called for since the provincial governor is expressly accusing Pastor Schneider of an attitude that is hostile to the state because of his refusal to use the salute and is asking us to seriously consider removing Scheider from the pastorate in connection with a few other less significant incidents. On the other hand, since many pastors think and act like Schneider, new lawsuits could easily emerge from this which would endanger the reorganization of the relationship between church and state on the basis of the appeal made by the national and regional church committee. We therefore ask you to consider whether you should make a request to the regional church committee, asking them to issue a directive as to how the issue of using the Nazi salute in confirmation classes should be handled.

The National Socialist "blood-and-soil-ideology" was supposed to slowly creep into the people's consciousness and replace Christianity. The activists of this liquidation could not only be found among the National Socialists, but especially among the radical "German Christians" and the so-called "believers in God," who recorded the abbreviation "ggl." (believers in God) in their personal documents instead of a denominational affiliation.

Although Paul Schneider was strongly moved by the events in church and state, he lovingly cared for his family. Thus he writes to his mother-in-law:

Dickenschied, December 19, 1935

Dear mother!

The great and precious Christmas holiday gives me another welcome opportunity to lay at your feet my feelings of childlike love and gratitude. We certainly have so many reasons to feel this way when we consider how faithfully you think of us in letters, give us craft items you have made and send us packages. I always wonder where you get the strength and also the money for all your faithful acts of caring, and not only for us. There is something to the proverb about the mother who would rather support ten children than . . . .

We are glad to still hear about new trips you take, and about the visits you receive. Then we know that your old vigor and strength are unbroken. We are also glad that you are accompanying our church odyssey with such concern and good advise, but also with understanding and trust. We know that it must not be very easy for you in the intact Württemberg regional church to always understand our journey, resistance and struggle.

The situation is serious enough since one must certainly say that the obfuscation created by the church committees has not been without success and many are about to fall for the empty peace slogans that are intended to deprive us of the insights of the Confessing Synods of Barmen and Dahlem. God will surely strengthen and keep together those who wholeheartedly cling to him and do not accept any other commitment for the church than to obey the Word of God. We are now holding confirmation classes in the manse and have been passing out the commitment cards of the Confessing church for the past two weeks, though they are only slowly being picked up. But it is good that way . . . .

Although Paul Schneider lives far from the centers of the events, he alertly observes everything that is taking place in the realm of the church, church politics and general politics. He studies every declaration of the "Confessing Church" very thoroughly before he passes them on to the congregation. The following letter shows how much he is affected by the events.

Dickenschied, February 14, 1936

Dear Ludwig!

Your greetings from Thale made me very happy. I also thought of you often by name via your admirable mother. I think I remember that you had a wife and two children. In the meantime you probably have more . . . .

Your card reached me in the Hunsrück, my old childhood home where I was given a new pastorate. This came about in the following way: by the providence of God and the confusion of man. It was a political move initiated by the state, arising from the trouble I had in the congregation. But it was probably the right move, and I have found faithful congregations here with whom we have already shared many joys and sorrows, and two arrests, among other things. They are solidly on the side of the Confessing movement. We have been up here for two years now.

We have already had so many experiences, and how many more are still to come! For it is obvious that the question of the church is not solved and cannot be solved by the church committees.

Indeed, who would have thought during the war that we would soon have to fight an even more important battle for the gospel at home! If we were true soldiers out there for the Kaiser's honor and the fatherland's defense, now more than ever we also want to be truly brave soldiers of our Lord Christ and prevail in this holy war as well, of which this is true: "For whoever did not fight will also not wear the crown of eternal life."

And if we risked our lives out there, why should we not also cheerfully risk them for an even greater prize, especially since we know that we are also doing our people and fatherland the most necessary and most important favor by engaging in this faith struggle and church struggle. How vivid and real is our ancient foe who seeks to work us woe; his craft and pow'r are great, as Luther sings! This struggle for the Christian worldview, the Christian faith and the Christian church will certainly affect you profoundly enough as a pastor's son. And what Christian could be uninvolved here . . . .

At the suggestion of the highest administrative office in Berlin the national church committee called together to "pacify" the controversies within the church had to deal with the question of the Nazi salute in confirmation classes. It issued the following guidelines:

I. The Nazi salute in church vestments

> The clergyman in principle uses the Nazi salute in church vestments as well. However, the following restrictions apply:

> 1. For the duration of a church ceremony (congregational worship service or official duty) the clergyman in his vestments does not salute individual persons or flags and other such things, but only the congregation gathered for worship in the form called for by the liturgy ("The Lord be with you" etc.), where this is customary, possibly in conjunction with the raising of the right arm or both arms for a blessing.

> 2. The worship service in self-contained spaces (church, funeral home etc.) begins when the clergyman enters the place of the ceremony (during funerals, for example, at the graveside) and ends when he leaves the place or the location of the ceremony.

> 3. The rule made in number 1 and 2 also applies when the congregation marches in a closed procession to church ceremonies where the clergyman is participating in his vestments (funeral procession, the dedication of a church building or cemetery).

II. The salute in confirmation classes

> The requirement of using the Nazi salute in confirmation classes will be regulated according to the existing rules for school classes.

Berlin, September 1, 1936
The National Church Committee
Dr. Mahrenholz
For Duplication

The National Church Committee was guided by the following considerations in laying down the principles described above:

A particular church salute does not exist in the Protestant church. It merely knows the fixed liturgical form of greeting between the clergyman and whole gathered congregation. The personal greeting of the clergyman in his vestments is a secondary matter.

The usual forms of personal salute used by clergymen in their vestments are of a non-church origin. Rather, they are borrowed from secular customs:

The salute made by the right hand touching the beret is copied from military tradition. One must realize that the clergyman's robe cannot, in principle, be spoken of as a uniform. If a binding rule has been established for military chaplains in this regard, it is due to their special position within the framework of the armed forces.

The salute by taking off the beret originates in a civilian custom.

We conclude from this that the present forms of greeting used by clergymen in their vestments come from the state or social environment. If the Nazi salute, made by raising the right arm while saying *"Heil"* to the Führer, has become official and generally prevalent during national songs and in front of the flags of the Third Reich as well as in personal interactions, it seems self-evident after what has been said that the Protestant clergyman uses this salute in his vestments as well.

We must take into consideration the fact that for those of us who are Christians the Nazi salute with the spoken or unspoken good wishes linked to it signifies a prayer for God's blessing on the Führer and the Third Reich.

There continues to be no room for a personal greeting during the clergyman's immediate performance of his duties in the worship service or during ceremonial acts.

For the ecclesiastical reasons explained above and in view of the children trained to follow this order by the school, it is necessary to also begin and end confirmation classes with the *"Heil Hitler"* salute. As usual, a song and a prayer will frame the instruction itself.

Mahrenholz

Such announcements betray only too clearly the line the national church committee was actually following. The "progress report of the Prussian Secret Police" for the administrative district of Erfurt from February 3, 1936 shows how the Gestapo assessed this committee:

The active part of the Confessing Church is under the leadership of Pastor Niemöller from Berlin and Pastor Müller from Dahlem. They are determined to sharply resist the pacification attempts of the National Church Committee as they have until now . . . . The second part of the Confessing Church under the leadership of Bishop Marahrens has given up its oppositional stance toward the National Church Committee and is willing to bring about a final and real pacification of the situation in the Protestant Church. This switch by Bishop Marahrens has provoked great indignation among the fanatical supporters of the Confessing Church. They are accusing him of having abandoned the mission of the Confessing Church.

Beyond this simple statement of fact, we cannot further examine here what motivated Bishop Marahrens and Professor Chr. Mahrenholz to take such a stance. After the Second World War Dr. Mahrenholz was appointed to be a member of the highest administrative office of the Protestant Church and the abbot of Amelungsborn. It is obvious that on the basis of his experiences Paul Schneider was not in favor of these pacification attempts made under National Socialist auspices:

We must all first become somewhat accustomed to the state of war, but then we can learn not to see anything strange or unusual in it. Jesus says: I have not come to bring peace, but the sword. And we as Christians cannot love our people and fatherland without putting Jesus in first place, and if we don't do that, we aren't doing our people and state the favor we owe them. Instead we are allowing it to sink into idolatry.[1]

The *"Heil Hitler"* salute demanded of Christians was idolatry for Paul Schneider. It had nothing to do with wishing people well as they tried to make him believe. He never saluted a Swastika. When the situation heats up on the issue of the salute in his confirmation classes, Paul Schneider informs the Brotherhood Council of the Rhenish Confessing Synod:

4. I am not giving religious instruction in school. I have caused no offense in my capacity as synod youth pastor for the Confessing

---

[1] *Prediger*, p. 73.

Church. The police expelled me with my confirmation class from the school hall that is located on church property where we have the right to hold church events. They did so because I did not introduce the Nazi salute into my church classes in the school building. The question is whether and how we should fulfill the obligation we assumed when we made our decision and how we can avail ourselves of our rights that are contractually established. The school hall is available to us for Bible study as usual.

Pastor Schneider

17

A COURAGEOUS DECLARATION

On the occasion of the election ordered by the Nazi administration in 1936 in which the voters could only vote "Yes," it demanded that citizens put flags on houses and churches and ring the bells. After his sermon Paul Schneider makes the following statement:

I owe the Evangelical and Reformed congregation the following explanation:

The forced participation of the church in today's Reichstag election by ringing the bells and showing the flags compels me to abandon the low profile I have kept until now. The church can either give the state a divine blessing for its plans and actions or confront the state with a divine warning when its plans, decisions and actions are obviously directed against God's will and Word. However, showing the flags and ringing the bells can too easily be understood as giving a blessing. But the church cannot give the state this blessing at the moment. This Reichstag election is clearly not only linked to the demand that we give the Führer our vote and approve the foreign policy of the Führer, but also that we approve the worldview policy of National Socialism that will profoundly affect the whole destiny of the nation. Yet this policy is setting itself ever more clearly in opposition to biblical Christianity. But Germany's destiny will be decided not by the troops at the Rhine, but by the position of the German people on the Word of God.

Therefore, this question of worldviews is more important than any other. But right up to the present day the life of the Confessing Church has been kept more and more from freely developing its mission of proclaiming the Word of God to all our German compatriots. Rather the German people and its youth have been led in the direction of becoming even more alienated from the church of Christ and the teaching of the Holy Scriptures and thus of turning away from God and rebelling against him. An unchristian, non-denominational German school is to be pushed through by force in place of our present denominational schools. Not the slightest promise has been made by the responsible men in the state and in the party that anything will be different in these things. This is why the church of Christ can not sanction the course the Third Reich is taking in these most important of all questions, it cannot give the election of the new one party-Reichstag the divine blessing. Rather its duty is to announce to the Führer and the government the divine warning and God's judgment if they do not refrain from implementing the policy of de-christianizing public life and removing the influence of the Christian denominations from it. However, you, dear Protestant congregation, wake up and bravely defend your most holy possessions of faith, testify to the honor and majesty of the living God, the Father of our Lord Jesus Christ compared to the false gods and idols of this passing world.[1]

This courageous and open word that illuminated the situation in those dark days shows at the same time what a human being can do when his conscience is fully captive to God. The believing church was engaged in a battle, as Nygren said, "against the religion of race that was planting itself in the hearts" of so many Germans. The National Socialists wanted to impose its worldview, its political religion on the people with all the means at its disposal. Each affirmative vote for its political decisions was in its mind a declaration of agreement with its worldview demands. From the standpoint of his conscience Paul Schneider had no other choice: he had to resist!

The "highest administrative office of the Protestant Church" in Berlin was completely different. With the consent of the regional church committees and all the provincial church committees of the Old Prussian Union it issued an order that the confirmation ceremonies that traditionally took place on Palm Sunday had to be postponed because of the Reichstag election that had been ordered by the National Socialist regime.

---

[1] Ibid., p. 78.

The election of March 19, 1936 is of crucial significance for the life and future of our people . . . . We ask all participants to joyfully make this sacrifice and thus prove that German Protestant Christianity wholeheartedly stands up for the nation and its Führer, for the future of our fatherland and for peace with honor.

Paul Schneider's wife reports how it went for them on Election Day and in the days after it:

Against all expectations we had peace from the party on election day itself although they did put some pressure on us. However, on the Sunday after that, on Easter morning, the front of our house was adorned with large letters and much red paint! "He did not vote, is this his fatherland?? People, what do you say??!!" Now, the German people could hardly take a stand on this case, but the congregation did so all the more thoroughly. In spite of it being Easter morning they came with scrubbing brushes and joyfully tackled the job of removing the paint! Afterwards Paul thanked them for this help during the worship service.[2]

The Old Prussian Brotherhood Council of the "Confessing Church" decided on April 30, 1936 to carry out a general visitation of the congregations in the whole area of the regional church in the period from May 17 to June 15, 1936. It issued the following statement to the congregations:

On the day of the visitation we will greet the congregations in the name of the Confessing Church of the Old Prussian Union. May the grace of God and the peace of Christ be with you in the midst of the storms during this eventful time!

Our struggle to achieve the exclusive rule of the pure gospel in the Protestant Church of Germany has been going on for three years. We do not know when the struggle will end. We only know one thing— that the church of Christ can never stop fighting to ensure that no alien fire burns on the altar of the church and that its proclamation and its life is determined by nothing but the Word of God.

---

[2] Ibid., p. 79.

We wage this struggle with the daily prayer that God's Spirit will sanctify us so that we can gain the strength, love and discipline we need. We wage it with profound gratitude for many glorious evidences of loyalty to the faith that the Lord has produced through his Word and his Spirit in our congregations. We wage it with the certainty that the Lord of the church will bring this struggle to a good conclusion in spite of all the mistakes of human beings.

In a time of great distress Dr. Martin Luther wrote from the fortress of Coburg to Melanchthon: "If Christ were not with us, with whom else would he be? If we were not the church or not a part of the church, with whom else would the church be? If God's Word were not with us, with whom else would it be? Therefore: If God is for us, who could be against us?"

We accept this word of evangelical hope and trust with humility and confidence. With this word we call on the congregations to pray for new faithfulness and new assurance of faith. Do not allow anyone to move the goal: Christ alone is Lord! Whoever perseveres to the end will be saved!

The Brotherhood Council of the Protestant Church
of the Old Prussian Union
Müller[3]

Paul Schneider participates in this visitation together with Professor Dehn, Superintendent Neumann (Beeskow) and pastors Andler (Buckow), Buismann (Sellin), Harthausen (Guben), Hintzsche (Silkerode), Iskraut (Frankfurt/O.), Klingbeil (Essen), von Rabenau (Berlin) and two elders: Kreuch (Erfurt) and Papst (Schoitzsch). It is an exciting time to be together and proves to be a blessing for all who participated. It also leaves a lasting impression on the congregations that were visited. Wilhelm Niemöller remembers:

All of (the visitors) were in my house once or several times. We got along magnificently and besides the fruitful work we did, we had many delightful hours to develop a bond with the brothers. This is especially

---

[3] Compare W. Niemöller, *Aus dem Leben eines Bekenntnispfarrers* (1961), p. 167ff.

true of Buismann and Hintzsche who lived in our home, and of Paul Schneider the martyr of Buchenwald, who could be recruited to speak to my Ladies' Aid for an hour and made a huge impression on us. The word of the Apostle: "May the brotherly love among you be heartfelt" was beautifully fulfilled in those days.[4]

---

[4] Ibid.

18

A CRUCIAL PULPIT ANNOUNCEMENT

Paul Schneider was deeply grateful for every word of guidance that he was able to pass on to his congregations. Thus he writes on September 2, 1936 to a friend who was a teacher in Wetzlar:

> On August 23rd we had to read the announcement of the provisional church government and the Brotherhood Council; it made my soul happy, it was a great liberation that our church government found this word and dared to announce it. By doing so, we were permitted to pierce through the patchy fog of deceit and lies the Nazi regime uses to camouflage the worldview situation and confuse our poor Christian people. The sun breaking through again after rain clouds and an endangered harvest was for me a sign that God was kindly declaring his support for this word.[1]

The pulpit announcement read:

Dear brothers and sisters!

The German people are facing a decision of the utmost historical significance. What is at stake is whether the Christian faith should retain its right to live in Germany or not.

The gospel of Jesus Christ is being combated today in our country with a forceful, systematic effort that is without parallel. This is being done

---

[1] *Prediger*, p. 81; compare also M. Greschat, ed., *Zwischen Widerspruch und Widerstand* (1987).

not only by those who reject any faith in God, but also by those who do not want to deny God, but who think they can reject the revelation of the one true, living God in Jesus Christ.

The state's and the party's instruments of power are being continually used against the gospel of Jesus Christ and against all who declare their faith in him. It is hard for us to say this.

The Protestant Church knows of its solidarity with our people and its obligation to the temporal authorities through the Word of God. Every Sunday in our Protestant worship services we intercede for the Führer and the fatherland. Three years ago millions of Protestant Germans ardently welcomed the new beginning in the life of our people. They did so all the more joyfully when the government said in its first proclamation on February 1, 1933 that it would "firmly protect Christianity as the basis of our whole morality."

For Protestant Christians it is a virtually incomprehensible idea that organs of the state in our German fatherland are opposing the gospel of Jesus Christ. But it is happening nonetheless.

We have kept silent about this for a long time. We have been told that it is only the actions of a few individuals who have to be called to order. We have waited. We have raised objections. We have also presented to the Führer and Chancellor in writing what is weighing on the heart and conscience of Protestant Christians. As early as April 10, 1935 the provisional leadership of the German Protestant Church, the national Brotherhood Council and the church governments linked to the provisional leadership and the brotherhood councils in the name of the whole Confessing Church in Germany addressed a letter to the Führer and Chancellor. It sounds like a cry made in deep distress when this letter begins like this: "It has come to the point in the German nation that the honor of German citizens is being trampled in the dust because they are Christians. The indignity of being mocked and ridiculed has provoked the anger of the Christian people in Germany. In the press, in lecture halls and at the theater as well as at mass events their character and reliability are being called into question in every way because of their faith in Jesus Christ. Those who are determined to faithfully uphold the gospel are especially subject to this suspicion. All attempts to bring about change here have been in vain, especially since almost every opportunity to mount a public defense is being taken away from us to an increasing extent."

This year the present provisional leadership and the council of the German Protestant Church sent the Führer and Chancellor a memorandum in which all of the distress and concern of the Protestant population becomes apparent. The memorandum has been backed up point by point with an extensive body of evidence. With great conscientiousness this memorandum and its contents were kept secret from the public, and even from the members of the Confessing Church, to give the Führer of the Reich the opportunity to carefully examine it and at the same time to prevent the memorandum from being misused in public. The memorandum was published in the foreign press and thus became known in Germany against our will and without the Confessing Church being responsible for it.

We are now forced to publicly stand by this word. We must now testify to the church what motivates us as we look at our people and our church. It is necessary for the Christian church to freely and publicly counter attacks on the gospel without fearing any human beings. It is necessary for it to open its members' eyes, above all, to open the eyes of its young people to the danger we all face. We are speaking with this obligation in mind. Whatever may come of our testimony, we commend it to the One who has called us into his service. He has commanded it and he will prevail!

Even the leading men of the state are attacking the truth of the gospel in public. We remind you of the speech by the national leader Dr. Ley on May 1, 1936, which was disseminated by radio and by the whole German press. The Protestant Church is not permitted to counter such attacks with the same wide publicity.

In their training camps they often teach the worldview of Rosenberg's myth, which glorifies man and robs God of his honor. In certain places they openly proclaim that this worldview is incompatible with the Christian faith and that it is destined to replace the Christian faith. Even those Christians who are honestly willing to serve their

nation have to be fought; this is what was said in a training camp for
students:

"When the party program speaks of 'positive Christianity,' what
it in fact means is not Christianity, but a positive religiosity. They
could not express that view right away. For a doctor cannot tell the
sick person the full truth." National leader Derichsweiler expressly
confirmed these explanations. They have become familiar to hundreds
of thousands. They have never been officially contradicted. When
this ideology claims total authority over the German people, it puts
numerous Protestant men and women in a moral dilemma. The church
is being increasingly pushed back into the four walls of the church
in all of its activities under the motto of "removing the influence of
denominations from public life." In the land of Martin Luther it is
being denied the opportunity to bear witness to the gospel in public
gatherings. For instance, although preaching and pastoral care are
offered in the armed forces, they are largely not tolerated in the camps.
Protestant schools are being combated. Pastoral care for the coming
generation is being made virtually impossible. They are continually
hurling abuse at the Christian faith in the written materials of the
Hitler Youth, in newspapers and magazines such as the "Black Corps,"
yet their scurrilous attacks are not worth repeating. Whoever rebels
against this battle being waged against the Christian faith must expect
to be labeled as an enemy of the state. The Protestant Christian often
finds that state authorities will not listen when in good conscience he
must oppose things that are against God's clear command, such as the
mass gatherings at which children took an oath of loyalty to the Führer
on April 20, 1936.

Finally, the genuine moral commitments of the people are undermined
when their conscience is oppressed, exacerbated by constant spying,
growing hypocrisy and a servile attitude. It is profoundly painful for us
to say all of this. We are willing to sacrifice our possessions and blood
to the state and our German people, but we do not want to be told
before the judgment seat of God: When the gospel of Jesus Christ was
fought against in Germany, you remained silent and you abandoned
your children to an alien spirit without resistance.

In view of what is happening today in our midst, we testify to the eternal truth of God before the whole German nation.

The Lord our God is a holy God and cannot be mocked. He has revealed himself in his Son Jesus Christ, the Crucified and Risen One. There is no god besides this one who is the Father of our Lord Jesus Christ. His Word has eternal validity and saving power for all. He demands and creates faith as well as our obedience, leading us to entrust our whole lives to the grace of God.

The German people have also encountered the salvation of God in Jesus Christ- in no one else but in HIM! He says: "What good is it for a man to gain the whole world, yet forfeit his soul?" (Mk. 8:26 NIV) No external ascent, no economic upswing, no social uplift will make up for what is forfeited in the soul of a nation.

"Righteousness exalts a nation, but sin is a disgrace to any people" (Pr. 14:34 NIV). This is the eternal truth.

Christians owe government obedience as long as it does not require what is against the commandments of God. Christians owe the government resistance when it demands what is against the gospel.

The church has been commissioned to proclaim the Word of the living God to all people, not just to those who come together to worship God in our congregations.

Christ says: "What is whispered in your ear, proclaim from the roofs!" (Mt. 10:27 NIV) "Go into all the world and preach the good news to all creation" (Mk. 16:15). The church is committed to this Word. We appeal to the government of the German nation.

The national government has clearly promised that it intends to firmly protect Christianity as the basis of all its morality. The word that was spoken before the German Reichstag on March 21, 1933 is just as clear: "The rights of the church continue to exist, its position will not be changed!"

Protection for the gospel cannot mean that the gospel must be protected by human powers. The gospel is protected by a higher power! But it must mean that the disparagement of the gospel must be kept away from the public life of the German nation and that the faith of our youth to which the church bears witness must not be systematically destroyed. In the name of the living God we demand this from all who hold office in Germany.

We must have the right to publicly and freely proclaim to the German people the faith of its fathers. The continual spying on the work of the church must stop. The prohibitions of church gatherings in public spaces must be dropped. The chains shackling the church press and the church's charitable activities must be broken. Above all, state agencies must stop continually interfering in the internal life of the church. They are causing the destruction of the Protestant Church by their teaching and actions. They are making it impossible for many Protestant Christians to attend the worship service by scheduling marches, parades, rallies and other events on Sunday mornings of all times, and this must stop. We must demand that German young people are not so completely preoccupied by their political and sports activities that Christian family life suffers damage as a result and that there is no longer any place for the church to take care of its youth.

In all this the church's right to exist in this world is at stake. We ask all government authorities in the German nation to seriously consider the fact that they must give an account to the living God for all that they do. We implore them from now on to do nothing and permit nothing that is against the commandments of God and against the freedom of conscience that is anchored in God!

We turn to the whole Protestant church in Germany. True to the admonitions of the gospel, we ask you: Do not allow yourselves to become bitter toward the state and nation when you have to suffer for the sake of your conscience!

The Protestant Christian owes loyalty to his state and to his people always and under all circumstances. When the Christian resists a command that is against God's Word and in doing so calls his government back to obedience to God, he is being faithful then as well.

We ask all Protestant Christians to take an interest in the coming generation and to preserve its respect for the gospel that has given the German people strength and support in a history that spans a thousand years.

We call on all Protestant Christians to firmly and openly confess the gospel of Jesus Christ. In this hour of decision Jesus Christ wants to have upright confessors and resolute disciples. Now this word is true: "Whoever acknowledges me before men, I will also acknowledge him before my Father in heaven" (Mt. 10:32). We call on the servants of the church to bear witness to the gospel of Jesus Christ without compromise and without fearing men. Many pastors and laymen and women have suffered in these years because of their faith. Some of them have been in prison and in a concentration camp or have had to endure deportations among other things. We do not know what is still in store for us. But whatever comes—we are committed to obey our heavenly Father! Let us do what is necessary for us to do and let us joyously live our faith so that human beings who only fear God and nothing else in the world are the best servants of their nation.

We raise our hands to God, the Father and the Son and the Holy Spirit:

Take care of our nation and have mercy on it! Let your truth remain with us! Help it to be victorious! Amen.

The Brotherhood Council of the Confessing Synod of the German Protestant Church

Koch, Asmussen, D. Dürr, v. Arnim-Kröchlendorff, Müller (Heiligenstadt), Tramsen, L. Steil, Martin Richter, Hans Iwand, von Soden, Hesse, Middendorf, Berger, von Thadden, Remé, Niemöller, Jacobi, Kloppenburg, Humburg, W. Pressel

The Provisional Leadership of the German Protestant Church Müller, P. Albertz, Forck, Fricke, Böhm[2]

---

[2] K. D. Schmidt, *Dokumente des Kirchenkampfes* II/2 (1965), p. 984.

In the days when this declaration was made the conflict between Christianity and the pseudo-religious National Socialist worldview had flared up with unparalleled intensity. The SS-leader Heydrich saw the church as the second main enemy of the state after the Jews. The Nazi leader Dr. Ley and Reich propaganda minister Dr. Goebbels believe "in Adolf Hitler alone" and "in Germany that alone is able to save." The SS-leader Schulz who resided in Pomerania often closed his speeches with: "For the kingdom and the power are ours, for we have the strong armed forces, and the glory, for we are again a respected nation, forever. *Heil Hitler!*"

In the aforementioned declaration we find statements that Paul Schneider had openly made at an earlier time and for which the NSDAP charged him with disloyalty before the consistory. At the height of the controversy between the Confessing Church and the National Socialist worldview a statement made by "Bishop" Heinrich Oberheid on April 26, 1936 at a district meeting of the "German Christians" in Jena is typical:

> The New Testament can not be considered as an appendage of the Old Testament. It is crass to read the message of the New Testament through the eyes of the Old Testament. Luther pushed aside a centuries-old tradition and broke through to the Scriptures. We have continued the search for 400 years and have broken through to the Savior. This intellectual work spanning 400 years must not be suppressed. We have broken through to the Savior, for he is the Word of God and not the whole Bible. We will remove the Old Testament, and we will also critically examine the New Testament. The Jew named Paul cannot be a standard, just as any confessions from the past cannot be either. We will demand that many, many verses from the New Testament appear before the judgment seat as well.[3]

The National Socialists single-mindedly worked for a decision on the church problem that would be to their liking. In so doing, the unrest they had sown in the church was a successful way to achieve their goal.

Two groups had formed within the National Socialist political hierarchy. To be sure, they went different ways, but they had the same goals—they both wanted to liquidate the church:

---

[3] Ibid., II/I, p. 621.

1. The group around the national minister of church affairs Hanns Kerl followed a course leading to a centralized state church so that the Protestant church could be subordinated to the authority of the Nazi state.

2. Another group that had come together around Himmler and Rosenberg and which Bormann also joined, worked for the immediate, complete isolation of the church so that it could be eliminated by way of state decrees.

Such intentions or similar ones could not remain unrecognized among the people, because what the "top leaders" thought and did, found its corresponding expression on the lower party level among the party comrades who faithfully followed the party line. These people wanted to prove their devotion to the state so that they could also share in the power of the state.

Paul Schneider, who fully supports the declaration of the Brotherhood Council of the Confessing Church—not from a passion for church politics, but from a sense of pastoral responsibility for his congregation—very soon gets into a situation where it is necessary to resist the unchristian spirit that is so hostile to the confessions and is now invading the church.

19

GROWING UNREST IN WOMRATH

A farmer from Womrath, a member of the NSDAP and "German Christian," wants to break up the confessional unity of the Dickenschied and Womrath congregations so that the "German Christians" could gain acceptance in the villages. Pastor Wippermann from Kreuznach who is a part of the extreme right wing of the "German Christians" is responsible for this.

In this context it is important to know that the Protestant congregations in the Hunsrück region were firmly established communities of faith upheld by the confessions of the Reformation in which the sessions carried special weight. It was the intention of the "German Christians" to cast doubt on the authority of these sessions guided by the confessions in order to loosen the ties that bound them to their traditional commitments and responsibilities. They sought opportunities to do this that the members of the NSDAP provided for them. As a result the farmer from Womrath writes to Paul Schneider and does not shy away from making allegations:

Dear Pastor,

Since you want to expel me from the congregation because I am a bad member, as you yourself said to me, and since I am still the father of my son, I can no longer send my son to your confirmation class. It is against my conscience and my honor as a father. I thus ask you to give me a certificate so that I can send my son to another pastor's confirmation class.

Heil Hitler!
Ernst Scherer

Paul Schneider answers the letter in February 1937:

Dear Mr. Scherer!

I must inform you of the following facts in response to your two requests that I issue a certificate for your son Hermann to change confirmation classes.

My last visit to your home on the occasion of the illness of your daughter Hilde and the talk I had with you and your wife was a pastoral matter I sought to deal with personally as your pastor. I cannot expel you from the congregation, as you write. I expressly told you that. The session can also not expel you. But it can and must take you under church discipline if you persist in taking this stance.

The session expressly decided on April 16, 1936 within the framework of the present Rhenish-Westphalian church order to take fathers under discipline who send their children to a confirmation class other than the legal one or who keep their children away from the congregation's confirmation class.

A certificate of dismissal for your son Hermann could only be issued by us if you can indicate and prove that you are sending your son to another Confessing Church confirmation class . . . . This is not your intention since you contest the legality of the Confessing Church. We no longer have any direct church relationships with churches that have a different alignment, so we cannot issue any certificates of transfer.

Moreover, since you took my pastoral visit in your home as an opportunity to keep your son away from our church's confirmation class, we would be putting ourselves in the wrong and reinforcing your contemptuous attitude toward the life of our church that is upsetting the whole congregation if we issued you a certificate of transfer.

As your pastor I ask you to immediately send your child to the legal confirmation class. Otherwise you will force me to hand this case and the issue of your whole conduct over to the session which will then discuss the possibility of further church discipline.

With warm regards,
Pastor Schneider

Before we continue to follow the events in Womrath, we should deal with the issue of church discipline.

John Calvin, whose theological statements have had a formative influence on the congregations of Dickenschied and Womrath, writes:

> But there are people who out of sheer hatred for church discipline find even the name offensive. They should know the following truth: If no community, if not even a house in which only a few persons live together can be kept in the proper condition without discipline, then such discipline is much more necessary in the church whose condition must be ordered as properly as possible. Just as the doctrine of Christ that brings salvation is the soul of the church, discipline in the church takes the place of the sinews: It ensures that the members of the body, each in its place, remain connected to one another. Therefore, those who desire that discipline should be abolished or prevent its restoration are undoubtedly seeking the complete dissolution of the church, whether they do it intentionally or from a lack of reflection. For what will happen if each person may do what he likes? But this is precisely what must occur if the preaching of doctrine is not combined with personal admonitions, rebukes, and other aids of this nature that support the instruction and do not allow it to remain without effect. Discipline is thus like a rein by which all those who defiantly rebel against Christ's teaching are to be held back and restrained. Or it is like a spur to spur on those who are not very willing to follow Christ's teaching. But at times it is also somewhat like a fatherly rod with which those who have committed serious wrongs are to be gently chastised in harmony with the meekness of Christ's Spirit. Because we already see in an incipient form a terrible devastation descending on the church that can be attributed to the fact that no care or consideration was expended on keeping the people within reasonable bounds, the distressing situation itself tells us loudly and clearly that a remedy is necessary. But the only remedy is what Christ has decreed and what has been in use among the pious.[1]

---

[1] J. Calvin, *Institutio* IV/12.

Likewise, Martin Luther had to deal with the question of "church discipline"; he comes to the following conclusion:

> Christ has instituted this outward excommunication. Matthew 18:15 states: "If your brother sins against you, go and show him his fault, just between the two of you. If he listens to you, you have won your brother over. But if he will not listen, take one or two others along so that "every matter may be established by the testimony of two or three witnesses." If he refuses to listen to them, tell it to the church; and if he refuses to listen even to the church, treat him as you would a pagan or a tax-collector.
>
> This is how the excommunication should be handled: First, we should seek neither vengeance nor our own benefit. This is a harmful practice that is now occurring everywhere. Rather, we should seek the improvement of our neighbor . . . for excommunication can be nothing other than a kind, motherly scourge, aimed at the body and temporal possessions, by which no one is pushed into hell, but rather pulled out and compelled to leave damnation and enter into salvation . . . . But the tyrant cannot use it without causing horrible damage, for he sees in it nothing less than a tool of violence and fear to gain profit for himself, for they reverse the excommunication and its work and turn the medicine into a poison.[2]

Paul Schneider understood church discipline or discipline toward repentance as a "motherly scourge," as Luther said, to keep one's neighbor from eternal death. It was their concern for their neighbor that motivated Paul Schneider and the sessions to reflect on discipline toward repentance.

These ideas from the Reformation flowed into the Rhenish-Westphalian book of order from 1923 in section VI. This book of order was binding church law during the time of Paul Schneider's ministry:

> 51: It is decided, 1) that members of the congregation with an offensive or dissolute walk who have not been persuaded to lead a better life through pastoral care, who expressly reject and mock the Christian faith and cause offense in the Christian congregation, should be earnestly and kindly admonished by the session or the pastor in the name of

---

[2] M. Luther, *Ein Sermon vom Bann* (Munich), vol. 1, p. 399ff.

the session; 2) that those who continue in a notoriously dissolute and offensive walk or continue to express a decided unbelief as described above, in spite of the admonitions that had been issued, thus continually violating the Christian sense of the congregation as well as the honor of the Christian fellowship, should be excluded from partaking of holy communion and from the right to be godparents by the session until they have made the promise to lead a better life and have demonstrated that they have reformed their Christian walk. Recourse to the board of the district synod remains open to the excommunicated member.

The Heidelberg Catechism was and is to the present day the confessional document of the Dickenschied and Womrath congregations. The Protestant church members who grew up there are familiar with it and know questions 81 through 85 of the catechism:

> *Question 81. Who are to come to the Lord's table?*
> A. Those who are displeased with themselves because of their sins, but who nevertheless trust that their sins are pardoned and that their continuing weakness is covered by the suffering and death of Christ, and who also desire more and more to strengthen their faith and to lead a better life. Hypocrites and those who are unrepentant, however, eat and drink judgment on themselves. (1 Cor. 10:19–22; 11:26–32)

> *Question 82. Are those to be admitted to the Lord's Supper who show by what they say and do that they are unbelieving and ungodly?*
> A. No, that would dishonor God's covenant and bring down God's anger upon the entire congregation. Therefore, according to the instruction of Christ and his apostles, the Christian church is duty-bound to exclude such people, by the official use of the keys of the kingdom, until they reform their lives. (1 Cor. 11:17–22; Ps. 50:14–16; Is. 1:11–17)

> *Question 83. What are the keys of the kingdom?*
> A. The preaching of the holy gospel and Christian discipline toward repentance. Both preaching and discipline open the kingdom of heaven to believers and close it to unbelievers. (Mt. 16:19; Jn. 20:22–23)

> *Question 84. How does preaching the gospel open and close the kingdom of heaven?*

A. According to the command of Christ: The kingdom of heaven is opened by proclaiming and publicly declaring to all believers, each and every one, that, as often as they accept the gospel promise in true faith, God, because of what Christ has done, truly forgives all their sins. The kingdom of heaven is closed, however, by proclaiming and publicly declaring to unbelievers and hypocrites that, as long as they do not repent, the anger of God and eternal condemnation rest on them. God's judgment, both in this life and in the life to come, is based on this gospel testimony. (Mt. 16:19; Jn. 3:31–36, 20:21–23)

Question 85. How is the kingdom of heaven closed and opened by Christian discipline?

A. According to the command of Christ: Those who, though called Christians, profess unchristian teachings or live unchristian lives, and after repeated and loving counsel refuse to abandon their errors and wickedness, and after being reported to the church, that is, to its officers, fail to respond also to their admonition—such persons the officers exclude from the Christian fellowship by withholding the sacraments from them, and God himself excludes them from the kingdom of Christ. Such persons, if they promise and show real improvement, are received again as members of Christ and of his church. (Mt. 18:15–20; I Cor. 5:3–5, 11–13; 2 Thess. 3:14–15; Lk. 15:20–24; 2 Cor. 2:6–11)

During the church struggle Dietrich Bonhoeffer also expressed his opinion on "church discipline":

Church discipline is the necessary visible consequence of the proper use of the keys of the Kingdom within the congregation. The New Testament church knows a number of steps in exercising discipline. The origin of all discipline is the preaching of the Word based on both keys. But this proclamation is not limited to the worship service. Rather, the office holder who knows how to conduct himself in the household of God (1 Tm. 3:15) is never released from his commission. "Preach the Word; be prepared in season and out of season; correct, rebuke and encourage—with great patience and careful instruction" (2 Tm. 4:2 NIV). The office holder who uses the keys of the kingdom should exercise discipline as one who gives pastoral care in his dealings with his congregation. This is part of his office, it is the beginning of church discipline . . . . For example, if a brother openly falls into sin of word or deed, the congregation must have the strength to initiate the actual church disciplinary process against him. This consists of three parts: The congregation must have the strength to separate itself from the sinner. "Have nothing to do with him" (1 Tm. 5:14); "keep away from them" (Rm. 16:17 NIV); "with such a man do not even eat" (Lord's Supper, 1 Cor. 5:11); "have nothing to do with them" (2 Tm. 3:5; 1 Tm. 6:5 NIV); "in the name of the Lord Jesus Christ, we command you, brothers, to keep away from every brother who is idle and does not live according to the teaching you received from us" (2 Thess. 3:6). This conduct of the congregation is there "in order that he may feel ashamed" (2 Thess. 3:14) and to win him back in this way . . . . The sinner still remains our brother and thus experiences the punishment and admonition of the congregation. It is compassionate brotherliness that makes the congregation exercise discipline . . . ."[3]

Church discipline was thus not an invention of the sessions of Dickenschied and Womrath, but a component of the order of a church that is committed to Jesus Christ. Paul Schneider participated in the Rhenish-Westphalian Church Day "Under the Word" on March 18, 1934 with several of his elders. It assigned the theme "Discipline in the Church and its Promise" as a commissioned work for further clarification. Paul Schneider later went through the published work with great care and considered the pros and cons of church discipline that were openly unfolded in this work.

In this work we read:

1. Forgiveness should be preached to the people, peace must rule in the congregation, the bonds of love must not be severed, in short, peace and calm is the first duty of its members! How is the church supposed to have the task of excommunicating certain individuals when it has the duty of preaching forgiveness to the people? How could the church be so uncompassionate, so unfaithful to this mission of the church that it should dare to erect a wall of separation between itself and those whom it considers blatant sinners? For should not the church open its doors wide, not asking whether they are Jews or pagans, sinners or righteous ones? Does it not make its own proclamation unpersuasive when it expels one person from its fellowship but not the other? For the

---

[3] D. Bonhoeffer, *Gesammelte Schriften*, vol. III, p. 374.

church is called to proclaim salvation to all people. Does not church discipline violate the authentic love that is demanded of us?

2. A second objection is raised from the concern that the church falls into a Pharisaism that denies its essence when it passes judgment on the Christian walk of another. Does not the church set itself up as judge over a matter that only God can judge? Is it not seizing a duty that is forbidden to it: Do not judge, or you too will be judged? Must not the church grope in uncertainty and darkness, make its way by faith and not by sight, waiting patiently for the day of Jesus when the Lord will make the separation between the pure and the impure, separating the wheat from the chaff, something we cannot and must not do? ... Is not church discipline to be rejected for the simple reason that it can be wrong? . . . How do we poor, miserable and fallible human beings know what thoughts God has about the sinner? How are we supposed to know that we are acting not from error and delusion, but in obedience, how is the church that claims to be a church of justified sinners supposed to exercise discipline . . . .

3. And finally, the objection can be made: Church discipline is impossible today. The church of the Reformation has become an established church. To be sure, it still has a confession in which the exercise of church discipline is constantly demanded, but the validity of this confession has necessarily lost something of its power . . . . This is certainly a serious reservation, what can be said against it? Nothing else will be helpful except briefly reflecting on the nature of church discipline . . . .

> 1) Church discipline is necessary for the sake of the truth and certainty of the forgiveness of sins. We must refute the objection to church discipline that claims God is love and the church has to preach forgiveness. Precisely when the church preaches forgiveness, its preaching must make certain that it also preaches the binding of sin for the person who is not willing to repent. Precisely because God's love for human beings is real, it must become clear that this love is given to us when we repent, when we change our mind. It is not love when the church leaves him in doubt about whether he can really believe his sins are forgiven when his brother who has something against him or against whom he has something, also

partakes of the Lord's Supper. It is not love when the church keeps human beings in a state of uncertainty about whether a believer can really be blessed only by living in obedience to the Holy Scriptures . . . . The church that does not know any discipline cheats its members and the world out of the certainty and the seriousness of the forgiveness of sins . . . . By what right does one hold back the certainty of forgiveness in the church of the Reformation? By what right does one dispense with the claim in word and deed that it is serious here? Can the idea of God's Word proclaimed as an uncertain Word that is only possibly reliable be harmonized with any kind of "humane approach?" What love of what God does one mean, what forgiveness of what sins, if one no longer wants to know and believe that the church is commissioned to use the keys of the kingdom, retaining and forgiving sin? And it has to exercise this authority in spite of the danger that it might be abused, which in fact should not be underestimated. What kind of love is it that would mislead a person to think that he had not disturbed the congregation, that he had not given offense to the congregation by his walk . . . .

2) Church discipline is indispensable in a true church from another vantage point as well. God sought to glorify himself by sending his Son into this world so that he would choose a church for himself through which he is honored. What happens in the church of Christ, what goes on in the fellowship of those who hear and proclaim the Word of God is not unimportant, is not something that is of concern only to human beings; rather it is of concern to the living God. If the church of Christ is dishonored, he is dishonored. How can the church exercise discipline? This is not the real question. Another, more important question has priority: How can the church tolerate the fact that it and thus the glory of its Lord is dishonored by blatant sins and by the offense that its own members cause? A church that does not know that it should not only believe the holy church of the third article, but to the best of its ability be the holy church because it is holy, relinquishes the right to approach the world with the proclamation of the forgiveness of sins because it no longer knows about the seriousness of sin and the holiness of God's wrath. For the sake of the truth the church must exclude the impenitent sinner from its fellowship. For the sake of love it must

not leave the question of sins without an answer, otherwise it makes itself uncertain of forgiveness.

3) This question remains: How does the modern church with all its present defects and shortcomings get the right to exercise church discipline in individual cases? Can we, who are fallible human beings, who know our weaknesses and passions only too well, take the risk of using church discipline again . . . ? In response to this question we must first and above all say: The church has this commission from the Lord! We must say to all those who are so afraid of reintroducing church discipline, who time and again question the church about its authority with such a suspicious passion: By what right and by what authority do you consider the words of Matthew 18:15ff to be binding? Who gives you the right to declare that you want to postpone your obedience to Matthew 18:15ff to more convenient times because you think you have special insight into the difficulties and dangers of church discipline? By what right do you simply want to let everything the Reformers said about church discipline go by the board? The church has been commissioned to preach the whole Word of God, and Matthew 18 is truly a part of it. The church has to be guided by these words in its life and in its walk.[4]

A document described later in this book will show that Paul Schneider took seriously the statements of the New Testament on this issue and had to ultimately pay for this seriousness with his life in the Buchenwald concentration camp. The conflict with the consistory in Düsseldorf led by the German Christians in league with the Gestapo on the one side and Paul Schneider with his sessions of Dickenschied and Womrath on the other side shows how he struggled to win each individual member of his congregation.

---

[4] H. Hellbardt, *Die Zucht der Kirche . . . 1935*, p. 23f and E. Röhm and J. Thierfelder, *Evangelische Kirche zwischen Kreuz und Hakenkreuz* (1981), p. 54f. The Church Day did not run without problems. "The local difficulties became especially clear when participating in the Church Day in Dortmund on March 18. All the participants came too late because the steering mechanisms of the buses were sabotaged" (W. Oehme, *Märtyrer der evangelischen Christenheit 1933–1945* [1985], p. 162).

20

A SERIOUS CONFLICT IN THE OFFING

This statute was written in the book of order on November 6, 1923 and was still in effect during the ministry of Paul Schneider: "The issuing of a certificate of transfer is left to the judgment of the pastor" (75, in section 1).

As long as the farmer Ernst Scherer from Womrath is a member of the Protestant Church of Dickenschied and Womrath that placed itself under the authority of the Confessing Synod, the session in office and the incumbent pastor are responsible for him. Therefore, Paul Schneider visits the family of Ernst Scherer just as he visits every other family in the congregation. Such visits often suffered from a tension-filled atmosphere during this time of turmoil in church politics and the reason was that Ernst Scherer tried to put Paul Schneider in a tricky situation when they talked.

Ernst Scherer had turned to the German Christian pastor of Gemünden for help in this matter. He contacted his German-Christian colleague about the aforementioned statement found in the book of order. Pastor Karl Wippermann in Kreuznach immediately turned to the highest administrative office in Berlin-Charlottenburg that was dominated by the "German Christians." This office consulted with the consistory in Düsseldorf, and it received this answer:

> To the Highest Administrative Office of
> the Protestant Church
> Berlin-Charlottenburg
>
> Concerning: the complaint of Pastor Wippermann, Kreuznach
>
> Decree of March 9, 1937-E.O. III/798/37

Enclosed you will find the documents sent to us with the decree mentioned above. Pastor Schneider in Dickenschied, who is of a strange psychological disposition and also a very zealous supporter of the confessing front, has given rise to complaints made by various party offices and state organs.

The consistory has frequently dealt with him on account of such complaints. In 1934 he had to be transferred because of political difficulties. However, a sufficient reason to take disciplinary action has not presented itself until now.

Contrary to the statements made in the complaint of Pastor Wippermann, the provincial church committee has had no reason up to now and, above all, no legal opportunity to take action against Pastor Schneider.

As far as the present complaint is concerned, we disapprove of Pastor Schneider's action in refusing to issue the applicant a certificate of discharge which is contrary to the Rhenish-Westphalian book of order.[1] Likewise, we disapprove of the reasons he cited for threatening disciplinary action in the letter of January 12, 1937 to Scherer and then for later taking such action.

Scherer similarly turned to the consistory for help with his letter of February 14, 1937 and asked that we issue the certificate of discharge. This was given to him by order of the consistory on March 1, 1937 after completing a consultation. The actual object of the complaint is thus taken care of. We will now turn our constant attention to the behavior of Pastor Schneider.

Kaphahn Sp. (March 16)

---

[1] Here is a clear offense on the part of the consistory against the church law that was then in effect. Also notice their remark about his "strange psychological disposition" (E. Röhm, *Sterben für den Frieden* [1985], p. 230ff.). Here too decisive straightforwardness is interpreted as being psychologically deviant, a popular method in those days of running down one's opponents.

Based on our present level of knowledge Pastor Wippermann and his colleague in Gemünden must be classified as part of the Thuringian wing of the "German Christians." They played an inglorious role in the background.

The church attorneys in the Düsseldorf consistory apply German Christian standards to the book of order then in effect and thus contradict the intention and spirit of this church order. The farmer from Womrath launches a number of serious attacks against Paul Schneider when he submits his petition to the consistory:

> The pastor of our congregation, Pastor Schneider, Dickenschied, who has already become known far beyond the Hunsrück as a devious opponent of our new state leadership, has thwarted and destroyed the internal peace of our congregational life in a way that is outrageous. The great majority of his sermons are filled with concealed and nasty attacks against National Socialism and the government . . . . He is driving our youth into a moral conflict between a Jewish-Christian doctrine of religion and the political worldview . . . . In his opinion only those who have a green membership card of the Brotherhood Council Church are considered to be "genuine Christians" . . . . Moreover, after having become familiar with his quite eccentric medieval views and even having had to witness his pursuit of dubious goals with a fanatical zeal . . . .

We later find these statements used as the reason why a deportation order banning Paul Schneider from staying in the Rhine Province was seen by the Gestapo as absolutely necessary.

After receiving the "certificate of discharge" from the consistory, Ernst Scherer sends his son to the pastor of the "German Christians" of the Thuringian persuasion and thus testifies that what is at stake is not faith in Jesus Christ and the Word of God, as it is delivered to us in the Old and New Testaments, but the interests of his party, which he saw best represented by a Thuringian "German Christian."

The following report shows how difficult and dangerous it was to carry on conversations with National Socialists. It also proves that Scherer's written statements had fallen into the hands of the Gestapo. In the later Koblenz "preventive detention" Paul Schneider writes down the following reconstruction of these events:

My pastoral concern is to admonish Ernst Scherer to give up his reserved attitude toward the church that he has had for a long time now. Ernst Scherer immediately used my allegedly hostile attitude toward the state and the Confessing Church's alleged hostility toward it as an excuse for his negative attitude toward the church. He also alleged that I stirred up hatred against the government, of which he could have heard very little . . . . I tried to make clear to Ernst Scherer that the Confessing Church's allegedly hostile attitude toward the state had its basis in certain tensions and differences of opinion. I mentioned to him the example of the Nazi student leader Derichsweiler and also the training manuals for the Hitler Youth and said that a truly Christian church naturally has the duty to declare its faith and take a stand against such unchristian endeavors based on God's Word.

Then Ernst Scherer drew the person of Hitler into the debate. Wasn't Hitler a Christian? I no longer know what I literally answered, but I am certain that I did not answer his question in the affirmative! It is possible that to shed light on Scherer's question I pointed out the conclusion of Hitler's speech at Hindenburg's burial in Tannenberg. It is possible that we also got on the subject of Valhalla from the Gemünden funeral for the Hitler Youth member Karl Moog, which Scherer brought up. It is clear that both the storm of Horst Wessel as well as Valhalla are not fitting terms and images for our Christian hope of eternity. In order to clarify this for Scherer I told him the anecdote about Valhalla that a foreign newspaper (I think the *Times*) is said to have reported, which I could just as well have made up at that moment.

What was important to me was that I wanted to convince Scherer that the fate of the Christian church could not simply be placed in the hands of the state and party in blind trust and that a Christian church can only be a confessing one when it is willing to oppose such plans and endeavors of a hostile state, especially since a worldview that is different from the Christian one is prevalent in the party.

Ernst Scherer hardly showed any appreciation for this point of view considering his reserved attitude toward the church that has continued for a long time. It is possible that he later wanted to turn our conversation against me politically and distort what I said, even though it was carried on in a relatively friendly and peaceful way.

Since the conversation during the first of my three visits in his home was carried on in a relatively friendly and peaceful way, it is simply unthinkable that I would have used the term "brown crowd" in this nasty or disparaging way when Ernst Scherer brought up the Gemünden burial. This is why I thought at first that I could deny having used the expression. Only because I was introduced to the context of Scherer's statements in the police prison in Koblenz on October 19, 1937, do I think that I should not hold onto my denial of having used the expression although I myself cannot remember using the term. One should deny something only when one is firmly convinced that it was not so. It may be that I said I wanted to bear witness to the seriousness of death and eternity before the whole brown crowd on the occasion given to me. But by "crowd" I basically meant "gathering." I deny that I used this term in the disparaging or nasty way it was interpreted and I deny that I used it frequently. I do not by any means consider it proven that I even used the expression. The subject of the Hitler Youth and the confirmation classes must have been brought up during a later visit.

21

AGAINST AN UNCHRISTIAN
CHRISTMAS CELEBRATION

On January 24, 1937 Paul Schneider gives a sermon on Luke 2:2ff, in which he addresses the issue of Christian education and explains it by making three points: "1. Christian education is suitable for children. 2. Christian education can take place only in what is God's, that is, in the church of Christ. 3. Christian education can only be a total education encompassing the whole life of the child, or it is not a Christian education."

In the course of this sermon Paul Schneider mentions that a daily newspaper published an article according to which Christmas must be considered a Germanic ancestral inheritance and no longer a Christian celebration. Here is the newspaper article:

> Belated Christmas mail from the Womrath Switzerland. On Saturday evening before the fourth Sunday in Advent the girls' work camp, the choral society and the school children jointly put on a nativity play under the direction of teacher Sturm. Modeled on the Oberufer nativity play and the "German nativity play" by Lienhard, it was specially put together for our situation. It was made even more beautiful by the addition of several men's, women's and mixed choirs and many folk Christmas songs.
>
> By way of introduction teacher Sturm briefly pointed out that the German Christmas celebration is undoubtedly the most beautiful and the most heartfelt one in the whole world and that the features that make it so dear and precious to us were not brought into the country when it was christianized, but stem from our Germanic ancestors as part of our German nature. We modern men and women who are often lacking in instinct have lost a sixth sense that was characteristic of our

ancestors to a high degree: a close connection with the warp and woof of nature and emerging from that, a sure instinct for the unwritten laws of life as well as a lively imagination vividly bringing to life the forces working behind the mere life and events of nature. It would be a blessing for our people if we could regain this nature of our ancestors.

The subsequent reading of Selma Lagerloff's first Christ legend led us deeper into these ideas and ended with these words: "What is necessary is that we have eyes that can see God's glory." After the nativity play Santa Claus' helper Knecht Ruprecht showed up, surprising the children and giving them gifts of gingerbread men and coloring books. Afterwards everyone stayed together in the school hall to celebrate for a few more hours under the burning candles of the Advent wreath and sat at tables festively adorned with candelabras and greens, enjoying cake and coffee. The Christmas songs we sang together and the Christmas poems recited by the children awakened a sense of community and an Advent frame of mind. "And when it is most beautiful, then we should break camp and go home, then the experience lingers in us most beautifully and most purely." This is how the final speech admonished us, helping us to collect our thoughts and finishing with these words: "We are carrying a light into the darkness of the night."

The National Socialists tried to popularize an idea of Christmas that was shaped by their political view of religion. In those days Hans Baumann published his song "Exalted Night of Shining Stars," that along with others was to replace the old Christmas songs. Paul Schneider expresses this opinion in his sermon:[1]

> I have listened carefully to what could recently be read about the characteristics of a Christmas celebration in the belated Christmas mail from Womrath, and I hope you have listened as well. There we read in the retelling of the "Christian teacher's" speech "that the features that make Christmas so dear and precious to us have not come to us at all through Germany's Christianization." To put it more clearly, Christmas has nothing to do with Christianity, but "originates with our Germanic ancestors as part of our own German nature." I can only advise and admonish us to realize that a Christmas celebration

---

[1] The copy of this sermon is in the possession of the author.

that fits this description and that the Hunsrück newspaper wrote about on January 4, could no longer be seen as a Christian celebration of Christmas. It intentionally no longer wants to have any thing to do with the church and for this reason we want to keep our children away from such celebrations and similar ones as well. Wanting to do Christian education without the Christian congregation and church is a bad joke. Christian education takes place only in the Christian church. "Do you not know that I must be in my Father's house?"[2]

A report in the announcements of the National Federation of German Protestant Schools from December 1936 that was illegally mimeographed as a manuscript shows that Paul Schneider did not stand alone with such ideas.

Christmas has arrived again in German lands. This year as well much has been said and written about it. We do not want to increase the number of these often-noncommittal observations by adding another one. It is our concern to address a clear word to the circle of our friends and co-workers, a word in a clear cause, in our cause—the biblical, Christian education of our young people in our homes, schools and churches. Especially today this means that we must put a special, renewed emphasis on the Christian school, or, to put it bluntly, on "the school and the Bible." It will become apparent in our nation—perhaps very soon many will recognize—who still wants this school or who is willing to assume partial responsibility for its counterpart that believes in German superiority.

Hardly any other time of the year is as suitable as the Christmas season to reveal to us the various frontlines in the battle of worldviews and faiths. However, no other season forces us to so seriously examine our own position as the final days of another passing year.

Precisely during these weeks it could again be clearly noticed that the "German Christmas" and the "German School" run along the same lines. We should be grateful for every further clarification of the matter! More and more we should accept the fact, i.e., very soberly expect and adjust to the fact that today large sections of our nation no longer want to know anything about our Christian celebration of Christmas. Instead, they would like to reanimate the customs and

---

[2] Reproduced in P. Schneider, ". . . und sollst mein Prediger bleiben" (1966), p. 123ff.

traditions of our pagan ancestors or in any case give priority to the celebration of the folkish rebirth as well as the triumph of the folkish efforts to pull together to address the economic emergency within the framework of the Nazi winter relief organization. As valuable as these things may be in themselves, they no longer have anything in common with the Christian celebration of Christmas. Therefore, one thing should become clear to us: We should not expect anything from a Christian school where people celebrate "German Christmas" like this or in similar ways. If we consider the issue of the schools in connection with the issue of Christmas in our time, we will notice with alarm how empty all their promises about the Christian character of such "German schools" have already become.

Thus, if we are about to trade in a Christian celebration of Christmas for a German Christmas replacement, the worst thing about it is that very many Christians are not even aware of this development. And this state of affairs leads us to serious self-examination in this Christmas season. What have we ourselves made of Christmas . . . ? Again, we have become aware of this problem over the issue of our schools. The opponents of the Christian school in many locations have launched a surprise attack precisely under the protection of the festive Advent and Christmas season. When we tried to appeal for a vigorous counterattack, we received this annoyed, dismissive response in many congregations: Our time is so monopolized by Christmas celebrations that we could not possibly deal with the school issue at this time.

We remember a similar response by the Württemberg church leadership that early this year felt it had to reject determined advocacy for the Christian school by pointing out the serious nature of Holy Week. The sad consequences for Württemberg that resulted from this rejection are very familiar to our friends . . . .

Paul Schneider does not understand by the term "church" an organization created by human beings for human beings that has to deal with religious, philosophical, ethical and moral questions under the influence of the spirit of the times. For him the church of Jesus Christ exists where people, addressed by the Holy Spirit, are willing to live as disciples of Jesus and openly express this in a declaration of faith. Therefore, church for Paul Schneider can never be an institution managed on the basis of general political principles and practices which have this bias today and another tomorrow.

In Paul Schneider's view the church must not build up any outward power structure or be modeled on such a structure. Wherever it has done this in the course of its history, it has erred; it has failed. The members who are united in the church by their faith in the one Lord should act like salt in the world so that through the message of the gospel the conscience of man is sharpened and he may open his eyes wide to see the Kingdom of God.

Paul Schneider did not orchestrate political conflicts in the church, but prevented politics from entering the church. If he championed Protestant confessional schools, it was because he could not tolerate the idea that young people who had received the pledge of being children of God through holy baptism should be kept from practicing the Christian faith by powerful political groups seeking to impose their worldview.

We can see from the following letter how seriously the sessions of Dickenschied and Womrath took the school issue.

The session of the Evangelical-Reformed
Church of Dickenschied

Dickenschied, Feb. 15, 1937

To the Provincial Governor in Koblenz
as the supreme school authority in the Rhine Province
through the school administrator in Simmern

Concerning: the Protestant School and teacher Kunz in Dickenschied

The joint session of the Protestant congregations of Dickenschied and Womrath sent the school administrator in Simmern a number of complaints about the religious instruction in the Protestant schools of the two churches. It has become known that the district school administrator visited both schools and also examined the religious instruction. We are dependent on the statements of the children for determining what observations he made. He has not deigned to answer us up to now.

Moreover, the Protestant character of the school in Dickenschied has been further removed by dropping Protestant school prayer and by replacing it with something quite different. Furthermore, teacher

Kunz tries to clearly display his contempt for the congregational life of our Protestant Church and to offend the Christian and church-minded people of our community, which is the great majority.

When the congregation had to gain by force its contractually guaranteed right to use the Protestant school hall on February 11 after the key was supposedly not available, the congregation gave vent to its displeasure with its teacher in angry scenes, a teacher who still calls himself Protestant. All of a sudden he was quickly able to come over when the congregation was still in the school hall.[3]

With few exceptions the joint congregation is expecting the session to deal with the issue of our school and teaching emergency . . . .

If the Protestant congregation should no longer find any understanding of its Protestant school interests from the school authorities, such unresponsiveness would not only be deplorable, but also not in the interests of the cooperation needed between the church and the school, i.e., between the parents and the school. It would also not be in the interests of true peace and the national community that has never been an unimportant matter for the Protestant Church. Then a Protestant congregation would be compelled even more to confront the teacher of its children who is acting against evangelical doctrine, the evangelical spirit and the Protestant churches by means of the church discipline given to it and to point out to the parents their right and their duty to give their children a Christian education, a duty given to them by God.

The Protestant Church of Dickenschied is willing and determined to stick with its Protestant church school for which it respectfully but emphatically requests a truly evangelical teacher.

The session of the Evangelical-Reformed
Church of Dickenschied

---

[3] The school property belonged to the Protestant congregation.

Alfred Rosenberg, since January of 1934 the "Representative of the Führer for the Supervision of Worldview Training for the Party and its Groups and Associations," said at a "Conference on National Culture" in 1938:

> It is fully clear to me, and I think this also represents the Führer's view, that the Catholic Church and along with it the Protestant Confessing Church must disappear from the life of our nation in their present form. Our curriculum in all the categories of our schools has already been structured in terms of an anti-Christian, anti-Jewish bias, ensuring that the coming generation will be kept away from the swindle in black garb.[4]

Hitler was a nihilist in religion. In 1942 he declared in front of his generals in his East Prussian bunker without provoking the slightest hint of contradiction from them: "I am not of the opinion that something must remain just because it once existed." Looking at Christianity, he further said: "The time in which we live is a witness to the phenomenon that this thing is collapsing. It could still take another 100 or 200 years. I am sorry that like Moses I can see the Promised Land only from a distance."[5]

Paul Schneider recognized the hypocrisy and brutality of National Socialism and drew his conclusions from this, which he confirms again and again by the stance he takes on it. He speaks up for the rights of parents, for according to Psalm 127:3 children are a gift of God, for whom the parents are responsible to God.

The National Socialists were unceasing in their efforts to banish the biblical message from public life. Thus Pastor Karl Steinbauer was charged with high treason before a military court in August 1944 because of statements he made in a sermon he had given as a soldier during a sick leave in the Christmas season of 1943. In most of these cases such a trial ended in a death sentence. When questioned during the trial he reported to the military court:

> On May 1, 1937 Dr. Ley ridiculed the biblical message of repentance and grace in his appeal. After that I refused to put up flags in the church because I could not display flags in the place where I had been

---

[4] Compare S. Gauger, p. 188 on this subject.

[5] H. Picker, *Hitlers Tischgespräche im Führerhauptquartier* (1963), p. 115.

commissioned to proclaim this message that had been ridiculed by Dr.
Ley, on a day when the biblical message was clearly being mocked. The
detailed explanation of my refusal to ring the bells and display the flags
ultimately resulted in my second preventive detention, a repercussion
from earlier conflicts. At that time they told me I would soon be put
on trial. I was interrogated, but the trial was never held. After a year in
detention I was again released without any reason being given.

The military judge asked me for the reason why I was admitted to
the Sachsenhausen concentration camp. The occasion for my arrest, I
continued, was a sermon I gave based on the text about the murder of
the children in Bethlehem, pointing out the spiritual endangerment of
our youth in the present day. In this sermon I openly told about how
the leader of the League of German Girls called all the higher-ranking
leaders of the *BdM* to the highland camp and explained the following
point there: "It is necessary that I have complete clarity in my leadership
corps. Christianity and National Socialism are like fire and water and
are incompatible. We not only reject political Catholicism, but also
the Protestant faith and every form of Christianity. Therefore, I must
demand a clear decision from each of you, though you must not say
anything about it publicly under any circumstances. Otherwise that
would cause too much unrest among the old people. We must leave
them alone until they die. But the young generation must be clearly
trained to turn away from Christianity. Therefore, I ask you: What are
you deciding for, for National Socialism or for Christianity? Whoever
decides for Christianity is a traitor." Three girls declared themselves
as Christians and were expelled from the camp in disgrace. In my
sermon I publicly and honestly called attention to these dangerous,
dreadful machinations because I could not assume the responsibility
for the youth of our congregation alone, knowing about these things.
Therefore, I called on all who have been appointed by God to raise our
youth—parents, godparents, and teachers—to share this responsibility.
At least no one could say that I had not told them about it.

Eight days after giving the sermon, on Sunday, January 15, 1939,
it may have been about three o'clock in the morning, ten to fifteen
drunken SA men forced their way into the manse, smashed down the
front door and smashed in the windows and got me out of bed. I was

taken to prison and from there sent to the concentration camp after several weeks.[6]

One member of the court had demanded the death penalty, but after a difficult trial Karl Steinbauer was acquitted.

---

[6] K. Steinbauer, *Die Predigt vor dem Kriegsgericht*, 1963, p. 15.

22

THE SESSIONS ARE NOT SILENT

The elders of the Evangelical and Reformed congregations of Dickenschied and Womrath knew that they were responsible to uphold the Heidelberg Catechism, with which they had grown up. Buoyed by this responsibility, they followed contemporary events with their pastor.

The political situation of the church in Germany was worsening. The agitators of the "National Socialist Workers' Party" traveled throughout Germany to prepare what was to happen in the future according to the will of the Führer. The disparagement of the Christian church in favor of a "religiosity suitable for the Nordic race" played a special role in their campaign.

In Dickenschied and Womrath the sessions resorted to self-help. They considered silence irresponsible and pitiful. They knew of the profound seriousness of Ezekiel 3:17–19:

> Son of man, I have made you a watchman for the house of Israel; so hear the word I speak and give them warning from me. When I say to a wicked man, "You will surely die," and you do not warn him or speak out to dissuade him from his evil ways in order to save his life, that wicked man will die for his sin, and I will hold you accountable for his blood. But if you do warn the wicked man and he does not turn from his wickedness or from his evil ways, he will die for his sin; but you will have saved yourself. (NIV)

The sessions of the two congregations felt compelled to follow a path that was not unusual in the Hunsrück because of constant attacks made by several National Socialists who were members of the congregation. Their purpose was to preserve their confessional stance and admonish individual members of the congregation who had followed the wrong path. The book of order that was in force at the time gave the sessions the grounds for taking action, as mentioned above. We print here the most important sections of this book of order:

On Church Discipline:

109: (1) The pastor has the right and the obligation to admonish his congregation to lead a Christian life not only in his public lectures and to warn them of prevalent vices and unchristian principles, but also to practice special pastoral care and to ask, admonish, warn and comfort each individual member of the congregation.

(2) The elders as well have the right and the obligation to promote Christian order and a pious Christian walk of the members by request and admonition.

(3) In particular, the session is responsible for: a) handling church discipline in the congregation within the legal limits . . . .

110: Concerning the exercise of church discipline, regardless of the general ecclesiastical statutes (the church law from July 30, 1880), the following decisions 205–207 of the 4. Westphalian Provincial Synod in 51 remain in effect.

(1) A depraved and obviously godless walk as well as the express rejection and mocking of the Christian faith in specific written or oral declarations or public actions are subject to church discipline after previous attempts to deal with the situation pastorally have failed. The persons concerned are to be emphatically admonished by the pastor upon authorization of the session. It is left to the discretion of the session to repeat this admonition and to point out the following stage of church discipline.

(2) If these admonitions remain fruitless, the pastor upon authorization of the session forbids the person admonished in vain from partaking of holy communion and from being a godparent until the session has made a decision to allow the excommunicated member to partake of holy communion after the offense has been dealt with.

(3) An appeal to the board of the district synod can be made regarding both the legality of the session's admonitions as well as the excommunications decreed by the session mentioned under number 2 or its refusal to readmit the person to the Lord's table or to allow the person to assume the responsibility of being a godparent.

To make the context clear, a further section of the book of order must be added:

> 51: It is decided:
>
> 1. that members of the congregation who are leading offensive or depraved lives, after the situation has not improved through pastoral care, as well as those who expressly reject and mock the Christian faith as well as those who give offense to the Christian congregation, should be earnestly and kindly admonished by the session or by the pastor in the name of the session;
>
> 2. that those who in spite of the admonitions that have been made continue their notoriously depraved and offensive lifestyle or the expression of definite unbelief described above, thus continually violating the Christian sense of the congregation as well as the honor of the Christian fellowship, should be excluded from partaking of holy communion and from the right to be a godparent by the session until they have made the promise to live a better life and demonstrate that they are living a better life. Recourse to the board of the district synod remains open to the excommunicated members.

The sessions have not made the decisions they had to make easy for themselves. They have considered all viewpoints they were obligated to consider, as sessions are required by the book of order. Their purpose was to preserve their confessional stance in conjunction with the salvation of the persons concerned. If it often may have been difficult in the course of church history to discern the spirits, everything could be clearly recognized during the era of National Socialism.

The sessions had to deal with the curriculum of the Protestant schools in Dickenschied and Womrath that was contrary to the confessions. What was taught there no longer had anything in common with a Christian school; it was nothing but the dissemination of the new Germanic worldview with its National Socialist bias. There was also the behavior of two farmers who unreservedly supported the course the National Socialists followed in school politics. They wanted to make allowance for the ideas of National Socialism in the villages. Paul Schneider was inevitably a thorn in their side. They did not leave the church, but tried to influence the life of the congregation with the help of the NSDAP and the "German Christians" operating from Kreuznach.

So the sessions decided to write the following letter to those concerned:

Protestant Parish of Dickenschied
Dickenschied, March 12, 1937
Kirchberg (Hunsrück) country

Mr. . . .

The session announced Christian discipline for you from the pulpit of the church for the first time on February 28 and on the past Sunday for the second time. We had earlier announced this to you with our summons for you to attend the meeting of the session.

According to this decision you will be excluded from the church of Christ by the congregation and forbidden to partake of the sacraments and you will be excluded from the Kingdom of Christ by God himself until you promise to live a better life and truly demonstrate that you are living a better life (Heidelberg Catechism question 85 and its biblical grounds).

You are familiar with the reasons. An additional factor is that you have despised the discipline of the congregation and participated in a drive to collect signatures that is intended to make room in the congregation for the proclamation of a pastor who is a part of the Thuringian German Christians and is acting on their orders. In so doing, you have tried to gain entry into our congregation for a sect whose ideology was called a false teaching that is outside the church of Christ by the chairman of the former national church committee Dr. Zollner who made this judgment in a theological report.

The congregation is summoned and urged to break off Christian and church fellowship with you, however to treat you kindly in all necessary interactions, just as Christian discipline does not seek your ruin and damnation, but your repentance, hoping to win you back as part of the congregation.

You retain the right to hear the proclamation of the Word and receive pastoral care in the congregation. You have to continue to pay your church contributions as a member of the congregation, which you outwardly still are.

If you still do not listen to the congregation, the discipline goes into effect with the third proclamation. May God prepare your heart to receive his truth and mercy and may you recognize his holy Christian church on earth apart from which no salvation and eternal blessedness can be found.

In the name of the session,
Pastor Schneider

The third proclamation of the discipline never occurred. From the outset Paul Schneider was willing to carry out this discipline only if the core of the congregation could publicly identify with the decision of the session and the persons concerned continued to support the "neo-paganism" advocated by a radical "German Christian."

Church discipline has nothing to do with personal discrimination; it is an old custom in the church that was practiced often in the Upper Rhine region. Today it still has its fixed place in the young churches.

It must be taken into consideration that the Christian faith makes certain rules necessary in the life of the congregation whose violation jeopardizes the salvation of the individual as well as of the whole congregation. The penetration of a Thuringian "German Christian" into Dickenschied and Womrath with his proclamation that suited the interests of the brown rulers would have inevitably led to serious harm in the congregation.

Paul Schneider knows his Bible; he and his session are not only covered by the book of order then in effect and the statements of the Reformers, but by Holy Scripture itself (compare Mt. 18:15–18, 16:18f; Jn. 20:23; or in Paul's writings, 1 Cor. 6:9–10 and Gal. 5:19).

Paul Schneider is not an "innovator," but wants to put a stop to this new false teaching together with his sessions, reflecting on the traditions of the Reformed confession developed from Holy Scripture. In doing so, he is acting true to the insight gained in Barmen: "Listen to the brothers!"

The reaction to the announcement in Dickenschied is spectacular; the session could not expect anything different. The Nazi press speaks of it being "genuinely Jesuit and genuinely Jewish."

Before the first announcement of the church discipline Paul Schneider gave the following speech to the congregation:

Dear members of the congregation! For the first time in its history the session has felt compelled to use a tool, public church discipline, that has long been neglected in our church. In three cases in which this happened it was a question of a public offense that was given to the church of Jesus Christ and that could easily cause greater harm in the church if it were not placed under the punitive discipline of the congregation according to the instruction of our Lord Jesus (Mt. 18:15–20) and according to the confession of our Reformed church (Heidelberg Catechism question 83ff).

This church discipline of the congregation is carried out under the authority of Christ and in response to his command and his promise. Christ says: "Whatever you bind on earth will be bound in heaven and whatever you loose on earth will be loosed in heaven." "But earnestly remember that what he promises is certain: if you perform the ministry of the keys, I will also perform it; indeed, if you do it, it shall be done. What you bind and loose shall be bound and loosed, without any binding and loosing on my part. It is a single work, yours and mine, so if you do your work, mine is already done. So we have to retain sin or forgive it." The congregation's church discipline is not carried out in anger or hatred, but in love. The Reformers praised church discipline as the precious tool given by God to practice real love for a person by holding his sins before him and especially by driving him to repentance through its earnest entreaties. Luther says: "Church excommunication is thus a loving and motherly scourge of the church, imposed on the body and physical things."

Thus it is both our concern for the congregation and our love seeking the betterment of the unrepentant sinner that make the church discipline of the congregation inevitable. If one were to object that hostility is stirred up and the congregation is divided and torn apart by church discipline, we must not pay such great heed to a false unity and a false peace that will not stand amid the world's attack on the church and the congregation. There is no true unity and peace without truth.

1. This is rather the destruction of the church—when public offense is given to it with impunity, when the congregation, Christian parents and the place where their children receive instruction are torn apart by the way this happens and a chasm is cemented between the school and the Christian congregation; when a different way of celebrating the holy Christmas holiday is introduced and praised.

2. This is the destruction of the congregation—when there are several who keep their children away from confirmation classes and the children's worship service. This is the destruction of the congregation—when the Word and Sacrament and the admonition and discipline of the congregation are despised and the session appointed to lead them, the pastor and the elders of the congregation are mocked and scolded without providing any evidence for such attacks.

3. This is finally the destruction of the congregation—when one goes from house to house, seducing the members of the congregation to sign a petition demanding that the preaching of another Thuringian German Christian should be allowed in our congregation, even though he stands on an unbiblical and non-church foundation in the expert opinion of General Superintendent Zöllner from the national church committee.

Truly, where all this can happen in a congregation, it is time for the Christian congregation to remember the right and duty of Christian discipline toward repentance, if it does not want to deserve the accusation that it is itself to blame for the destruction and secularization of its Christian congregational life.

Whoever is annoyed at church discipline certainly has the right to be annoyed; but he proves that he is not standing on the confessions of our forefathers and that he does not love a disciplined church that lives by the Word of God alone and obeys its Lord Jesus Christ alone. Christian discipline does not seek the ruin of the sinner whom it excludes from the Christian and church fellowship, but his betterment. Thus, says Calvin, "even if church discipline does not allow us to visit in the homes of the excommunicated persons or to have close contact with them, we should nevertheless endeavor to turn them back to God so that they may bear better fruit and call them back into the fellowship and unity of the church." This is what the Apostle teaches in 2 Thessalonians 2:15: "Do not consider them enemies, but punish them as brothers."

So those who are under Christian discipline retain the right to hear the proclamation of the Word and to receive pastoral care in the congregation, even if they are forbidden to use the sacraments and their church rights have been suspended.

May God use the revival of serious church discipline to bless our congregation and those concerned and to save their souls.

The national church committee that was appointed by the minister for church affairs ("to pacify the situation within the Protestant Church") had invited leading theology professors to discuss the question of how the "Thuringian German Christians" related to the first article of the constitution of the "German Protestant Church."

> Article 1: The inviolable foundation of the German Protestant Church is the gospel of Jesus Christ, as it is proclaimed in the Holy Scriptures and came to light anew in the confessions of the Reformation. The authority the church requires for its mission is determined and limited thereby.[1]

For Paul Schneider this article carries decisive weight in the conflict with the "German Christians," for it confirmed his own thinking and action. This is why it is more than understandable that he welcomes the report put together on the occasion of the discussion mentioned above.

> 1. Our call to relate our faith in Christ to the political task given to us as Germans is understood by the Thuringian German Christians in a way that is not in harmony with the gospel of Jesus Christ as it is proclaimed in the Holy Scriptures and interpreted in the confessions of the Reformation.

> 2. First of all, this can be seen in their wrong understanding of the nature of the church. The church must never be equated with the nation as a community that has arisen from natural and historical forces. To be sure, it enters into every nation in a particular historical form, but as the church it remains distinct from all nations and independent of them. No historical nation, not even as a Christian nation, has the mission that is given to the church.

> 3. The false equation of national and salvation history corresponds to the false equation of the nation and the church. For the recognition that God deals with all peoples just as he deals with the German people in their history as a nation, is falsified into a exhibit of historical philosophy that turns German history into salvation history, namely

---

[1] H. Hermelink, *Kirche im Kampf* (1950), p. 44.

into the history of a nation that brings salvation to the whole world, also suffering the fate of the Savior based on his mission to bring salvation. Contrary to the New Testament and the confession of the church, the history of Christ and German history, Christ's significance as the Redeemer and the political significance of the German nation are confused here in an unbearable way. A historical nation takes the place of the church of Christ.

4. This is linked to the false view of the nature of the Christian faith. Christian faith is not an unquestioning trust that understands the task set by the historical situation as a divine command. It is also not the strength of mind needed to devote oneself to such a task. Rather Christian faith has its object in God's revelation in Jesus Christ.

5. But Jesus Christ is misunderstood if he is viewed as the "guarantee" of an unquestioning trust that is already present without him. The cross of Christ is misunderstood when its fundamental difference from all human suffering and sacrifice is not emphasized.

6. The false alternative of "life" versus theology rests on that misunderstanding of faith defined as the strength of mind needed to devote oneself to tasks within this world. If Christian faith is the saving faith awakened by the Word of proclamation, it contains as such quite specific insights into God, the world and man that can be clarified and substantiated in theological reflection. With the task of proclaiming the Word the church is inevitably given the task of continually fighting for the truth and thus for doctrinal unity. By fundamentally contesting the binding nature of Christian doctrine the unity of the church is abolished because the essence of the church is found in its common confession of faith. The diversity of doctrinal formulations must be endured, but must not lead to an attitude that minimizes the importance of theological work, for this diversity is, in fact, a sign that this task of fighting for the truth and the unity of doctrine is really being tackled.

7. Finally, the Thuringian German Christians' idea of a German "national church" inevitably follows from its false starting point. This idea shows its fanatical character by asserting that its fulfillment is not expected by the truth of the gospel of Jesus Christ, as Luther proclaimed

it, achieving a new breakthrough in the Christian churches, above all in the Roman church as well, but by abandoning its doctrines that divide and going back to "its unity of mind in the spirit of Jesus" (circular letter of the Thuringian regional church council from June 4, 1936) or to the message of the Kingdom of God.[2]

Although the national church committee was not an organ of the Confessing Church, with this report it made a contribution to clarifying the issues facing the church at that time and defining the different positions in the church struggle in contrast to its statement on the church's duty to use the Nazi salute. Thus Paul Schneider finds himself in good company even outside the Confessing Church with his argumentation against the "Thuringian German Christians."

On the last Sunday before Lent in 1937 Paul Schneider gives a sermon on Luke 18:31–43. No one could imagine that it was to be his last sermon in his regular pastoral ministry.

Dear members of the congregation!

Today we walk again through a new gate, through the entrance gate of the holy Lenten season where our precious Lord and Savior would also like to take us to himself and speak to us: "See, we are going up to Jerusalem!" He is waiting for us to really take seriously what we have sung: "Let us go with Jesus, following his example." May he then take us to himself on the road to his passion, on the road to suffering, to the holy cross? Or are we perhaps a part of the crowd of whom it is said: "From then on—when he spoke of his suffering and death—many of his disciples left him?" The truth that our crucified Lord would like to take us along up to the place of the cross, down into the depths of suffering, should have gradually become clear to each person who sincerely loves the Lord Christ.

But it is his great mercy that we are allowed to gather again around his cross at the beginning of this Lenten season. Our comfort and our confidence is that he will show us and prepare us by his Word how to go up the path with him. And right now in our first gospel at the gate of his passion the Lord shows us so much glorious and comforting truth, so much light and grace, that it may accompany us like an encouraging

---

[2] K. D. Schmidt, *Dokumente des Kirchenkampfes* II/2 (1965), p. 825f.

signpost in front of the gate of his passion: the truth that the path to glory is through suffering and the path to the crown is through the cross. This path must be recognized by faith and the signpost must be accepted by faith.

When Jesus speaks to his disciples about his path through suffering and death to the resurrection, by first being humiliated and mocked and spit upon, by being handed over to the pagans and flogged and being put to death and then being raised to life on the third day, the disciples cannot comprehend it. They did not think and they did not understand that this could be the path their dear Lord and Master would take because God was so obviously with him when he performed signs and wonders and healings. And although their Lord and Master had also pointed out to them the testimony of Scripture that everything the prophets said about the Son of Man had to be fulfilled in this way, they simply could not grasp it. It was far too much in conflict with all their reasoning. How were the disciples supposed to be able to comprehend this! He was to be sacrificed to the pagans, subjected to the worst kind of humiliation, and killed, and yet the story was still supposed to have a glorious outcome! Because the reason of the disciples could not grasp the word of their Master about holy suffering and death on the cross, this word and this path of the Savior through suffering to glory must be combined with faith that can grasp such a word. But the path of the Master is the path of his disciples and his church just as the apostles also learned and experienced after that. The disciples and the church as well can only go through suffering to glory and through the cross to the crown.

This is why Jesus put this beatitude at the gate of the Sermon on the Mount. All the beatitudes have their power and significance only when we consider them together with this one: "Blessed are those who are persecuted because of righteousness, for theirs is the kingdom of heaven" and: "Blessed are you when people insult you, persecute you and falsely say all kinds of evil against you because of me" and again: "Whoever follows me must deny himself and take up his cross!"

And over all this is the promise that our faith is the victory that has overcome the world, and that we are to live, rule and triumph with Christ if we have suffered with him and have died with him.

All this is against our natural feelings and against our reason, just as the words of Jesus were for his disciples then. Natural man sees in the cross and the way of the cross only the collapse of all human strength and the complete end of the way. Without faith no one can be willing to go the way of the cross and thus also has no part in the glory of the victory, no part in the wondrous power of God.

How foolish it is when people ask today with regard to the church struggle: Will there not soon be peace and good order for the church again? Will the church soon manage to get through the hard times? I think we will manage to get through it! Those who are favorably inclined toward the church think so; they are already horrified at the humble beginnings of the struggle and suffering into which God has led us, and think it could not possibly continue like this, and by thinking this way, they exclude themselves from the path of suffering. But the others, the enemies of the church, are now fully convinced that our cause, the cause of Jesus Christ, is over and done with, that now only a handful of fighting pastors are left and so they have no hesitation in leaving the church to its own devices, awaiting the end that is inexorably approaching. Both of them, our friends and our enemies, cannot see that the Protestant church's way of death is precisely the way of Jesus, the way of the cross, the way to life. A glance at Russia should teach us a lesson; every outwardly organized church has been crushed there, the pastors have disappeared, the church buildings are destroyed except for a few.

And yet the church of Jesus Christ lives there more than ever and perhaps even more vitally than our churches in Germany. It lives there under the holy cross of persecution in those who gather in the homes, moving here and there, it lives in the modest lay priests who proclaim the Word and willingly take upon themselves the penalties imposed on them. Why should the way of the church in Germany not also lead through even much greater suffering and dying, through utter defeat on the surface to the victory of glory? And do not be deceived: You too can have a share in Jesus' glory and victory in no other way than by taking up the holy cross for Jesus' sake and going the way of suffering and death with him. To do that, you need faith that knows of the power and victory of the cross. Such faith is truly a hidden, quiet strength, but for that reason it is not inactive and lethargic, but is confirmed in the heartfelt struggle of prayer.

The blind man on the road to Jericho heard about Jesus who was in the process of going up to Jerusalem; and he believes in Jesus and waits for him. When he passes by, he lets out his cry, and does not let others hold him back, those who want to persuade him that the Savior was not there for his needs and his misery. But when he stands in front of Jesus, he boldly and with strong faith dares to make his request: Lord, would you please restore my sight! And Jesus rewards him for it: Your faith has helped you! The world is blind to the way of Jesus and his disciples: the way that leads through suffering to glory; and we are also blind to it by nature. Our eyes are closed so that we do not see the hidden and coming glory on the path of suffering. We are like the blind man, disheartened, despairing, desperate in his distress and suffering, blind to the glory of the cross. We are like the pagans who know nothing of Jesus, who sit on the path as beggars and wait until Jesus passes by; in the midst of our old Christianity we likewise sit in this blindness to the crucified Jesus' glory, blind to the glory of the way of the cross. We would much rather choose gladness and joy than the humiliation of Christ.

What if we would go to our Lord with this urgent, heartfelt request: Lord, would you please open our eyes of faith to see the glory of your cross so that we may be made happy, content and rich by this sight that comes through faith, so that we no longer have to sit as beggars on the path of this world and no longer have to live by the joy and pleasure it takes in begging. The world does not want to let you go to Jesus so that you cannot follow him. It wants to break the strength of your sole desire right at the beginning of the passion journey by enticing you to embrace its desires. It is the expression of servile unbelief when we think we have to make merry with the world once more before the beginning of the Lenten season as if the world can compensate us for what we have to forfeit under the cross. The disciple who seeks first to make up for his losses by indulging in worldly pleasures is not making an evangelical, inward, heartfelt choice to follow the way of the cross. "Do not love the world . . . !" The Mardi Gras events and carnival activities did not arise on Protestant soil, and truly evangelical Christians do not have anything in common with them, not even when such carnival amusements are organized by "Strength Through Joy."[3] Instead, quietly focusing on our inner readiness and on truly celebrating his resurrection during Sunday worship, let us come before our Lord Jesus, and in faith ask him to give us sight to see the glory of his journey to the cross! "But rejoice that you participate in the

---

[3] A National Socialist organization whose purpose was to arrange vacation and holiday activities.

sufferings of Christ, so that you may be overjoyed when his glory is revealed" (1 Pt. 4:13 NIV). "Let us, then, go to him outside the camp, bearing the disgrace he bore" (Hb. 13:13). In this way he will meet us in the blind man sitting by the roadside and speak to us: Receive your sight, your faith has healed you.

Thus, in our Lord's discipleship of the cross God has given us a way that leads through suffering to glory. Is it not in the end the most beautiful and best way through this life on earth? Is it not the way we avoid being trapped in the beggar's life of this world, but have the privilege of being rich, blessed children of our generous heavenly Father? By following this way, we are no longer dependent on the insipid, trivial and poisonous pleasures of the world, but are privileged to gain the joy of the Lord everywhere. The disciples who were kept from understanding the words of their Lord nevertheless followed him, and their way of obedient discipleship issued in the exquisite joy of Pentecost. The blind beggar whose sight was restored and who could simultaneously see Jesus' glory also followed him and praised God. "When all the people saw it, they also praised God." How else ought we to step through the gate of suffering, how else ought we to walk with Jesus than by giving God the honor and glory as well? The Lord who goes ahead of us at the cross will strengthen us and keep us from evil. He will preserve our life if we lose it here for his sake, and give us eternal life. He will allow us to see his glory, here and there. For his way leads through suffering to glory. May we believe this according to his Word; therefore, may we ask him for faith according to his promise, may we thank him for it with joy in our hearts. Amen![4]

In this sermon Paul Schneider allows the congregation to share in what he believes. He shows the source of his strength and says unmistakably that he will never surrender to the powers of this world when the honor of Jesus Christ is at stake. Here the congregation experiences how New Testament statements and their uncompromising logic can impact a human life.

As a result of a car accident for which he was not responsible he must stay in bed for several weeks. The letter he wrote to his congregation from his sickbed has been preserved for us:

---

[4] P. Schneider, ". . . und sollst mein Prediger bleiben" (1966), p. 133ff.

The Church Newsletter of the Parish
Dickenschied-Womrath

Our verse of the week: We have not received the spirit of the world but the Spirit who is from God, that we may understand what God has freely given us (1 Cor. 2:12 NIV).

On the occasion of holy Pentecost this first church newsletter goes out to the homes as a supplement to our preaching and Sunday weeklies. At the same time it is a heartfelt Pentecost greeting from your pastor after a long interim period of six weeks caused by my accident in which the contact between the pastorate and the congregation could only be loose.

This interim period must surely have had its purpose and blessing for the congregation as well. If I may view my sickness as a vacation from my official duties, in a way the congregation has also had a vacation from their local pastor and has had the opportunity to hear the gospel from a different preacher. This must have made some of you even more certain of the way we are going with our congregational life. You have again recognized from the preaching of other servants of the Word how living and powerful the Word of God really is. You have recognized it as the sharp, double-edged sword that does not leave us alone in our own peaceful and satisfied world, but calls us to repentance so that we can truly believe in Christ as the One who saves us from our sins.

But at the same time you must also have recognized the Word of God from the preaching of other witnesses. It is the bright, sharp weapon against the spirit of the times and the unbelieving and unrepentant world that would like to walk over the Lord Jesus Christ and his church as if they did not exist. Then the world could organize life solely according to earthly, human standards and objectives. That is why we ought to journey through this age and this world as a congregation that boldly and resolutely confesses its Lord! Others must certainly have heard the Word of the gospel more eagerly and receptively from other preachers—the Word of God's judgment and the Word of God's grace lavished on us in Jesus Christ. How I wish from the bottom of my heart that such gospel preaching did not harden their heart, but led to faith and the salvation of their souls. It was certainly a time of God's special purposes for the congregation, for he has given us this interim period in which he has led many other pastors to visit the congregation and fill the pulpit in my stead.

Therefore, our congregation also wants to warmly thank those pastors who so gladly filled in for me in brotherly love. Even if it has been a time of loose contact between the pastor and the congregation from Easter to Pentecost, I sincerely rejoice in the personal concern of so many members who visited me in Simmern and at first in Dickenschied as well. The congregation has provided the ministry of comfort for its pastor according to the words of Jesus: "I was sick and you visited me." The compassion of the congregation has been a great comfort to me as well as a source of great refreshment on my journey through ministry that has not always been easy for me. I would like to sincerely thank you again here for this support. Last but not least, I am also grateful for our precious youth from both congregations who came to me in such large numbers—boys and girls, confirmands and school children. I was especially glad to see this response because it is a sign of the strong bond that endures between our young people and the Christian congregation in our village. May God continue to preserve this bond!

In spite of all the difficulties and all that we have missed, our congregation and its pastor can look back on this time that has gone by as a time of blessing. Even when God leads us on the paths of judgment, it is always salutary and good for the church of God, for "in all things God is working for the good of those who love him." May God lead us by his Holy Spirit more and more into all truth and into a personal knowledge of his grace and holiness and his effusive love for us in Christ Jesus, our Lord, according to His Pentecostal promise.

"This is the covenant I will make with the house of Israel after that time," declares the Lord. "I will put my law in their minds and write it on their hearts. I will be their God, and they will be my people. No longer will a man teach his neighbor, or a man his brother, saying, "Know the Lord," because they will all know me, from the least of them to the greatest," declares the Lord. "For I will forgive their wickedness and will remember their sins no more." (Jeremiah 31:33–34 NIV)

23

THE GESTAPO INTERVENES

Paul Schneider's wife reports:

On May 28 Paul is finally freed from his cast. The leg now had to be given radiation treatment and massaged; there was no time left for him. I call him home, since there is an especially tragic death in the congregation. On May 30 he holds the funeral service in the church. On May 31st he is arrested by officials of the Gestapo in his study and taken to Koblenz for an "interrogation." We who were at home remain without news until we find out from the superintendent and the provincial governor that Paul is in preventive detention in Koblenz. There is great dismay in the village, no one can imagine why he was arrested. Both of our congregations send four farmers to Koblenz to see the Gestapo. They are told when inquiring about the reasons for the arrest of their pastor: 1. They can read about the reasons in the newspaper; 2. Pastor Schneider is stirring up the whole Hunsrück against the state; 3. Since they were in no organizations whatsoever,[1] their statements would not even be considered.[2]

Superintendent Gillmann reports to the consistory:

To Simmern, June 2, 1937
the Protestant Consistory
Telephone Number 484 in Düsseldorf.

---

[1] They meant National Socialist groups.

[2] *Prediger*, p. 100.

In response to my telephone conversation with senior official Spiess concerning the arrest of Pastor Schneider in Dickenschied I inform you that I spoke with two offices of the Gestapo in Koblenz yesterday morning as soon as I received notification of the incident and I received the following information:

1. Schneider is in "preventive detention" in Koblenz.

2. They could not give me any further information; but I could request information in writing.

3. There is no reason to be concerned. Schneider had a serious accident and was in the local hospital for weeks. A doctor is available.

4. In response to my question of what I should tell Mrs. Schneider, I was given the answer that the matter of maintaining the detention would be decided in Berlin. That was not the responsibility of the Gestapo in Koblenz.

This information basically seems to coincide with the information given to Dr. Spiess, with one exception, "Mrs. Schneider has been notified." Not yet.

The agitation in the congregations is great
E. Gillmann

Then the congregations speak up:

The sessions of the yoked congregations
of Dickenschied and Womrath

Dickenschied, June 8, 1937
To the Council of the Protestant Confessing Synod
in the Rhineland
Wuppertal-Barmen

With reference to the report of Mrs. Schneider about the arrest of her husband we ask the Rhenish Council to file a complaint at the ministry of church affairs.

1. Pastor Schneider has always advocated the necessity of Christian discipline—even in his previous congregation—and has actually exercised it. He sharpened our conscience, persuading us that we should expand our church discipline. The announcement of church discipline to be imposed on three members of the congregation that was made in Womrath happened in response to our decision—which can be read in our book of minutes. We assume full responsibility for this decision.

2. The Gestapo in Koblenz gave our envoys a poor reception. After the Gestapo had collected their personal details, they were asked what organizations they belonged to. When they said "none," they were then told that their statements would not even be considered. It is painful for us to have to discover that the value of individuals in organizations carries greater weight then the word of those who can only cite their spotless reputation to establish the credibility of their words.

3. In response to their question about the reasons for the preventive detention of Pastor Schneider our envoys were referred to the newspaper. It is new to us that a corporation of public law—let alone the family of the one arrested—finds out the reasons for the arrest of one of its officials through the public press and is patronized by the arresting authority with a reference to a press notice.

4. Since the Gestapo in Koblenz has expressly referred to this news report in the press, we hold them responsible for its content. Then the following facts must be stated: It is not true that Pastor Schneider has called for the boycott of any person from the pulpit. In the letter written to the three members of the congregation on whom discipline was imposed, it expressly says: "The congregation is summoned and urged to break off Christian and church fellowship with them, but to treat them kindly in all necessary things, just as Christian discipline does not seek their ruin and damnation, but their repentance and hopes to win them back as members of the church." An improper judgment of the reasons that motivated the session to exercise the discipline is present in the expressions "in an irresponsible manner" and "for trivial reasons."

5. It was explained to our envoys in Koblenz that it is not permissible to publicly reprimand a farmer from the pulpit. In response to this we declare that we will not be deterred by such attempts of the secular authorities to interfere in the exercise of Christian discipline and that we will be guided in such questions by God's Word alone.

The session in Womrath writes a separate letter that is sent to all Brotherhood Councils and sessions of the Confessing Church in the Rhineland by the Protestant Confessing Synod:

Protestant Confessing Synod Essen, June 18, 1937
in the Rhineland

We hereby pass on the following word from the session of Womrath/ Hunsrück:

To the Brotherhood Councils and sessions of the Confessing Church in the Rhineland.

Dear Brothers!

Various daily newspapers have carried the following notice about the arrest of our Pastor Schneider (see the intercessory prayer list):

"Taken into preventive detention. Pastor Schneider from Dickenschied (Hunsrück) was taken into preventive detention by the Gestapo because he irresponsibly called for a boycott against a farmer for trivial reasons from the pulpit" (National Weekly Nr. 128 from June 5 and 6, 1937).

We sent our envoys to the Gestapo in Koblenz to inquire about the reasons for the arrest of our pastor.

They were rudely turned away and told that they could read what the reasons were in the National Weekly.

We know the news item in the newspaper could only refer to a case of church discipline in our congregation. Three men from our congregation are charged with having despised God's Word and sacrament in the congregation. In addition to this, one of them, the teacher of our village locked the congregation out of the school hall. Then on December 19, 1936 he held a Christmas celebration in the school that according to a news report "made the Christian theme take second place to the Germanic one. He called the Germanic theme the one that actually makes Christmas so precious and valuable to us. A farmer kept his son away from the children's worship service by force; another did not send his son to our church's confirmation class.

Pastor Schneider frequently visited all three men in response to these incidents. Since they could not be persuaded to repent of their evil ways, they were summoned to a meeting of the session on February 22, 1937. When no one responded to the summons and the teacher responded by writing an obscene letter, the session decided to impose church discipline on the three members. The decision was announced twice in the church.

The session asks you to announce this state of affairs in your churches in a manner that you deem appropriate.

Womrath near Kirchberg (Hunsrück), June 16, 1937
The session
Of the Protestant Church
The deputy chairman:
Pastor Langensiepen

The Elders
Auler, Fuchs, Scherer
(The fourth position on the session is temporarily unoccupied.)

The letters of Paul Schneider from prison, some of them legal, the most important ones illegal, give an eloquent testimony to his firm, inner stance. In the meantime the Rhenish Brotherhood Council makes an effort to support him. Mrs. Schneider receives the following letter:

The Council of the Protestant Confessing Synod in the Rhineland
The President
Wupperal-Barmen, June 18, 1937
Heinr.-Janssenstr. 16, Tel. 54235
Postal Checking Account Essen 37681

To Mrs. Schneider
Dickenschied, the district of Simmern

Dear Mrs. Schneider!

After trying in vain to speak to your husband in prison, I wrote (again) yesterday to the head of the Gestapo office in Koblenz and presented a few requests to him: That he let me or brother Langensiepen see your husband, that he allow you a visit, and that they turn over to him his Bible and hymnal etc. I asked yesterday whether he could have the privilege of theological literature being sent to him.

We want to see what will come of this. If you hear something from your husband, I would be grateful for the news.

With warm regards,
Your, Humburg

Pastor Fritz Langensiepen writes:

To do justice to Paul Schneider, every portrayal of him must give special emphasis to his main concern, the renewal of church discipline. A case of church discipline has landed him in the concentration camp. In my opinion, this point has not been discussed in sufficient detail in all that has been written and said about him until now.

There was a separate department for church affairs in the main security office of the SS in Berlin. The events in Dickenschied and Womrath were so weird for the Gestapo that it gave them its special attention. It must be noted that there was no case in the "German Protestant Church" that paralleled the Dickenschied and Womrath events. Paul Schneider always openly declared the truth of the gospel to the Nazi regime and was willing to accept the consequences. His resistance was demanded by the gospel and he endured it from a sense of Christian responsibility.

The Council of the Protestant Confessing Synod in the Rhineland continues to stand up for Paul Schneider.

The Council of
the Protestant Confessing Synod
in the Rhineland
The President Wuppertal-Barmen
June 26, 1937
Heinr.-Janssenstr. 16, Tel.: 54235
Postal Checking Account Essen 37681

To Mrs. Schneider
Dickenschied
The district of Simmern

Dear Mrs. Schneider!

I would like to once again write a few words to you. It almost seems to me as if the case of your husband is the most difficult one here in the Rhineland; he is obviously being treated more harshly than the others have been treated. What hurts me the most is that he evidently still does not have his Bible. As soon as something changes in this matter, please notify me of it. If you should get new evidence that your husband still does not have his Bible, I ask that you would write to me about that as well, and as soon as possible, so that I can do something about this matter. I am grateful for any news that you have.

I have written to the minister of justice about your husband, but he probably does not have much influence on the proceedings of the Gestapo. Let us cling to the Word of Scripture found in Psalm 12:6: "He will bring help to the one who longs for it."

With warm regards,
Your, Humburg[3]

---

[3] Paul Schneider was allowed to have a Bible in his prison cell, but no paper to write down his thoughts. He wrote them on the margin of the respective Bible verse. For example, Ex. 2:2: "Disobedient in faith to the King's command"; 1 Sam. 8:6–7: "So Germany has requested one man and rejected his man Jesus. The king is succeeded by the tyrant"; 1 Sam. 13:12: "Here God is made to serve men; the state must not become the church"; Neh. 9:36–37: "This is God's discipline, but he does not set any foreign Lord over the souls. But it is better to be enslaved in God's discipline than to be free in godlessness"; Es. 4:14a:

A renewed attempt of the Council follows a few days later:

The Council of the Protestant Confessing Synod
in the Rhineland
The President Wuppertal-Barmen July 3, 1937
Heinr.-Janssenstr. 16, Tel: 54235
Postal Checking Account Essen 37681

To Mrs. Schneider
Dickenschied, the district of Simmern

Dear Mrs. Schneider!

I have just telegraphed the national leader of the SS, Himmler, and requested that he make things easier for your husband. We must see what other things we can still do, but you may know that in the whole province many praying hands are being lifted up for you and your husband and your children. "And even if it lasts into the night and even into the morning, my heart shall not despair of God's power nor be anxious."

With warmest regards!
Your, Humburg

The Council of the Protestant Confessing Synod
in the Rhineland
The President Wuppertal-Barmen July 7, 1937
Heinr.-Janssenstr. 16, Tel. 54235
Postal Checking Account Essen 37681

Dear Mrs. Schneider!

"Shout it from all the pulpits!"; Es. 6:16b: "If I die opposing the king's command, then I die" (heavily underlined); Is. 6:13: "For the sake of the gift of God's calling, Lord! There is such a remnant of the Protestant Church in Germany as well"; Mt. 16:10: "Christian discipline is not eliminated from the church; exclusion from holy communion was correct"; Mt. 18:15–27: "Church discipline and prayer are linked together because of God's unlimited willingness to forgive."

When we were together yesterday, the Council, the Brotherhood Council and the representatives of the Rhenish Confessing Synod, it deeply moved all of us to hear the news I had to share about your husband. The only thing left to us is prayer. Peter was kept in prison, but the church prayed to God for him without ceasing, Acts 12:5.

Do not lose heart. Thousands of children of God in our Rhenish province remember your husband and children daily. We mention this case in every worship service. The more we become aware of our powerlessness to help, humanly speaking, our faith in the Lord who performs miracles perseveres all the more.

With warmest regards!
Your, Humburg

To the annoyance of the Gestapo Paul Schneider remains a pastor even in prison. He is not allowed to get any mail because of a pastoral conversation he has with an SS-man who was imprisoned with him. At the same time the report that Mrs. Schneider sent to the Brotherhood Council and that was circulated to the confessing congregations in mimeographed form falls into the hands of the Gestapo, which confiscates her typewriter and does not allow her to get any mail.[4]

---

[4] *Prediger*, p. 103.

24

THE DEPORTATION

For a while the Gestapo hardly pays any attention to Paul Schneider in prison. Then it focuses on him again and gathers material against him during extensive interrogations. But ultimately, it is very unsure of itself in spite of its display of power. Paul Schneider's "offenses" are not sufficient for a longer period of preventive detention, and the regular courts have not yet completely fallen in line with the Gestapo. So it releases Paul Schneider without a trial or verdict, but with an order: deportation from the Rhine province and thus from Dickenschied and Womrath.

Guarded by the Gestapo, Paul Schneider is taken by car from Koblenz to Wiesbaden, a city that is not a part of the Rhine province. Here it releases him on July 24, 1937. On July 25, 1937 Mrs. Schneider receives the following news from Womrath: "I am in Womrath! Although I was deported from the Rhineland, I will preach there today. If you have the heart, come over."[1]

Then he is once again in the pulpits of his congregations. A day later his friend Fritz Langensiepen persuades him to take a vacation in Baden-Baden. The pastor of the city mission there, Ipach and his wife, are willing to let Paul and his wife live at the Christian hospice during their vacation without registering at the police station. They do it fully aware of the risk. First, Paul Schneider drives there alone; his wife follows a few days later after she has taken care of family business. On the fourth day after his detention has been lifted Paul Schneider reports to the Rhenish President of the Brotherhood Council:

---

[1] *Prediger*, p. 108.

Baden-Baden, July 27, 1937

Dear Brother Humburg!

After taking your call yesterday morning before we set out on our trip, I would like to sincerely thank you again from here and report what can be said about my release from prison.

I have three letters from you here in front of me, letters you wrote to my wife to comfort and strengthen her. I can see from them how hard you tried to make my lot easier and change my situation. Certainly all these steps and requests and visits were not in vain and helped to finally secure my release. They will also continue to help me on my way now. Above all, the many hands lifted up in prayer gave me strength to endure in prison and are a help to me now that I am free; they are surely part of the reason why the weeks of detention on the whole turned out to be a time of confident joy for me and why I led the worship services in my congregations the day before yesterday.

They even wanted to visit me themselves. How annoying and depressing it is when they had to return home without having achieved anything. And yet once again it was not in vain because it expressed the Confessing Church's pledge of allegiance to the cause it represents and showed its solidarity. You know how hard they tried to isolate me and deal with my case in hermetic isolation from the congregation and the church. But this isolation led the church and congregation to take an even greater interest in my case. So God always brings good out of what men intend for evil.

Therefore, God did not allow me to remain without my Bible for the whole time even if it was their will to keep it from me. It comforted me and strengthened me, took me to task and showed me the way. The detention became a spiritual retreat for me, for which I am very grateful to God and which I would not want to do without.

On Saturday, July 24, I was released from prison. At the same time I was deported from the Rhineland and threatened with new punishment in case I acted against their orders. I pointed out that in the eight weeks of my preventive detention they did not even make the attempt to convict me of an unrighteous or rebellious action. When they revealed to me that I was about to be deported, I told them this proves that the preventive detention and the order to arrest me were an injustice and an untruth in view of the reasons they cited and on the basis of the well-known Hindenburg-paragraph.[2] They were clearly targeting the Confessing Church and thus persecuting the church of Jesus Christ. I ripped up the arrest warrant before the eyes of the inspector who was probably questioning me as a representative of the chief. I further explained that, of course, I could also not recognize and accept the deportation. I told him that my superintendent assigned me to these congregations before God. Now they wanted to tear me away from them, and I had to obey God more than men. I rejected all the inspector's attempts to persuade me to accept my deportation. It became clear to me that their goal was to transfer me. He then had minutes taken of the hearing, dictating on his own initiative what parts of my statement seemed important or appropriate to write down. He also probably wrote down several corrections I made. I immediately pointed out that I would not sign the minutes. Nevertheless, he dictated in the first person like a witness giving evidence even when I pointed out again that I would not sign it. I gave several reasons for my refusal. Not all the contents of our hearing were put in the minutes, especially not the introduction and the tearing up of the arrest warrant. This was the main reason why I rejected the deportation. The second reason I gave was that all the minutes of previous statements I had made only resulted in more severe punishment because I openly assumed responsibility! Only this second reason was put in the minutes because the expression punishment was changed into responsibility. This was also not corrected when I pointed out that this was not the same thing and I wanted to be responsible for my actions and statements. I also pointed out again the other reason for my refusal to sign that was not put in the minutes. Two witnesses who were present signed the minutes instead of me. On the other hand, at the insistence of the inspector, I did sign a document after the hearing was over, stating that I did not intend to file any claims against the state on account of my leg that had not fully healed during the time

---

[2] A legal paragraph "For the Protection of the People and State" (*National Law Gazette*, Part 1, Berlin, February 28, 1933, Nr. 17, p. 83). Hitler persuaded Hindenburg to issue it under false pretenses.

of my preventive detention, since I had expressed no urgency in asking
to see a doctor.

In spite of my refusal to accept the deportation, I was forced to accept
the deportation order on receipt. It ordered my deportation from the
Rhine province on the grounds that I had endangered the public safety
and order in the Rhine province and my behavior shows that I did
not want to fit into the National Socialist state. In case I entered the
Rhineland, they threatened to levy a fine of 150 M, or to sentence me
to one day of prison for each 10 M; in addition, preventive detention
could be imposed 48 hours after a place of residence had been accepted
and 48 hours before giving it up. If I remember correctly, I was supposed
to report to the appropriate administrative district office. I no longer
possess the deportation order. At ten o'clock in the morning I was put
in a car and under the cover of two men besides the driver. I was taken
to Wiesbaden, crossing the boundary of the Rhineland. I had refused
to indicate a place where I wanted to be taken, in accordance with my
refusal on principle to recognize the deportation. In Wiesbaden I was
detained in the car for a long time while the officer authorized to carry
out my deportation notified some authorities there. I felt like I was
being watched in the city until I got to the railroad station. I then took
the next train to Simmern and in the evening I went by car to my yoked
congregation. On Sunday I led worship as usual in both congregations.
On Monday I went on vacation at the urging of my friends.

Regarding the preventive detention, I must still add that we
were supposed to be under the prison rules, as we were told. The
accommodations were clean but it was evident that we did not have
any rights. We could apply for permission to write, to provide our own
food and other things, which could then be granted or refused. In the
third week they withdrew my permission to write. I had to assume
they did this because they thought I was too loud in my cell (singing)
and from my cell window where in the evenings I sought spiritual
communication with a fellow prisoner according to the Word of God.
In any case, having called me to account for this, they promised to
withdraw every privilege I had, and shortly after this they did forbid
me from writing and receiving any mail. Thus of all the mail that had
been arriving from the beginning I was given only one letter from my
wife during the third week of detention, a package with baptismal cake

on the occasion of my child's baptism on June 13 and the necessary packages of linen and underwear. On the last day before my release I was able to acknowledge receipt of my Bible.

In other respects I cannot complain about the treatment I received. I ask you to make use of the preceding report in a way that seems suitable or necessary to you.

Dear brother Humburg, may God continue to give you the necessary strength and health for your difficult and responsible position. The address on the envelope will be a nice greeting for you just as the one who wrote it is a person through whom I can keep in close contact with you.

Your, Paul Schneider

President Humburg answers immediately:

D. Paul Humburg
Pastor of the Reformed Church of Barmen-Gemarke
Tel. 54235
Postal Checking Account Essen 23955

Wuppertal-Barmen, August 8, 1937
Heinrich-Janssenstrasse 16

Dear Brother Schneider!

I sincerely thank you for your report, which I passed on to the Rhenish Council. I do not want to address the details of the past—in writing.

Your case is continually on my mind. Today I would only like to make the following points. It seems important to me that your matter is dealt with clearly and accurately.

You have not recognized the deportation order and can do nothing other than return to your congregation. But please, brother Schneider, not too quickly and not on your own! It must not be a personal matter of yours; rather, it must be a matter for the church government. And it must not simply be a violation of the Gestapo's order. Instead, you or we must file a petition through an attorney (for instance, Dr. Holstein in Berlin) at the ministry of justice, asking that regular proceedings are initiated against you and a verdict is pronounced. Otherwise, you could not be kept from returning home to resume your ministry. . . . Therefore, I ask you to immediately get in touch with brother Schlingensiepen, who is now representing the president: either through my daughter Irmgard and Mrs. Schlingensiepen or better through a cover address: School Principal Hillebrandt, Virchowerstrasse 34 (please treat confidentially!), Barmen.

I assume that you are not aware of any blame and that in your judgment the action you took to impose church discipline is the only cause of your arrest and deportation. Otherwise, you would have reported everything to Schlingensiepen. At any rate, I ask you not to return until this preliminary work is done. You should decide to stay there longer, perhaps the whole month of August, for such matters do not go quickly.

This is only my opinion. I do not know whether the other brothers judge it differently. I have just written to Schlingensiepen along these lines and to Langensiepen (in shorthand through my son Waldemar, who is with him). From here I can do nothing but just express my opinion. May the Lord lead us correctly! I have just received the news that Müller from Dahlem and Niesel have been arrested again. We are still facing some tough struggles, this is all the more reason why we want to do everything we can to ensure that the legitimacy of our position is evident to any court and that in any case God's children can stand behind us in prayer.

I send my warmest greetings to you and your dear wife and brother Disselnkotter!

Your, Humburg

This letter shows their insecurity in dealing with those in power at that time. It gives the impression that President Humburg doubted that Paul Schneider was really arrested only on the basis of an action taken exclusively within the church.

President Humburg was right when he writes: "It must not be a personal matter of yours, rather it must be a matter of the church government." This statement raises the question of why the church government did not take action on its own in this matter and bring in a lawyer. Paul Schneider understood by church government the "Protestant Confessing Synod in the Rhineland," i.e., the Brotherhood Council as its executive organ. He expects guidance from it.

It becomes clear from his views on church government that he did not intend to take independent action, but that he recognizes the authority of a church government. We must remember time and again that for Paul Schneider a legitimate church authority must always be built on the foundation of the undivided Holy Scriptures and the confessions of our forefathers in the faith. Making concessions on the issue of this Scriptural and confessional foundation implies that signs of disintegration are already present in the church. Thus any concessions on this essential question must be rejected at the first sign of compromise.

A few days after receiving the letter from President Humburg he writes to his friend:

On vacation, August 8, 1937

Dear Fritz!

Your pictures today and Hilde's letter brought us and our precious children great joy on this Sunday. We sincerely thank you for taking the trouble to send them to us. We have never seen such beautiful pictures of our little group. Dear friends here as well, especially Irmgard Humburg, shared our joy.

I also thank you for the cute card from Hilde's friend and little Fritz's lines in response to my letter. I was still lashing out in it. I had no choice but to give that up. I hope that the church government does its job *properly*.

President Humburg wrote to me in a way that is similar to the excerpt I have enclosed today. He evidently fears to some small degree that I may not be fully innocent and could have perhaps given the state a legitimate reason to arrest and deport me. I immediately wrote to brother Schlingensiepen that the matter of church discipline was evidently the ultimate reason for my arrest and deportation, but I have a clear conscience regarding all the previous reasons I may have given the party and state to take such action. I also hope that the others as well as the church have a clear conscience. In listing the reasons, I forgot to mention that I did not participate in the recent political election and did not use the Nazi salute in my confirmation classes. When you get a chance, you can supplement that list. I also have a clear conscience about these points and have made the decisions I am facing here with my conscience captive to the Word of God. I am prepared to give detailed reasons for this stance if it is requested.

I also made the decision about refusing the deportation order and returning to my congregation after serious examination and prayer and, in principle, I have already acted on it. But I gratefully welcome the church leadership's decision to make my return to the congregations its cause and think it is correct. 1. This will be beneficial to us as we impose the church discipline and 2. it will bolster the resistance mounted against the deportation by the pastors and congregations. The church leadership has already made fundamental decisions in both matters along the lines of my action. I also think it would be good if the church government would have in its hands the declaration of the congregation's will in the form of the session's motion and the signatures of the members to back up its claim against the state. In Womrath this collection of signatures (110–120 out of not quite 280 souls) was taken too hastily on the Tuesday or Wednesday after July 25 and was confiscated by the police (perhaps not a bad thing!). In Dickenschied 100 signatures, out of approximately 180 souls, had already been given by the time my wife had departed to join me here.

I first want to fully submit to President Humburg's urgent request not to undertake anything on my own. But then I would like to respond to his request by urgently making my own request. For the sake of the cause, I intend to ask him to make a *quick* decision on my return or on the date of the return so that the intervening period can only be interpreted as vacation time . . . . We will see what God says about this and what new blows will be dealt to our Confessing Church. They have clearly sworn to destroy our church. But God is our confident hope and strength. He will not abandon us and will wonderfully allow us to sense his power and goodness if only we believe and stay the course he has shown us.

With warm regards to you and yours,
From Your grateful Paul

The fact that in spite of all these assurances Paul Schneider still remains alone is not least the tragedy of the Confessing Church; his courageous stand for the cause of the church, and his willingness to suffer the ultimate mental and physical consequences, were something new for it as well. Or had the gospel become powerless in the church because it was institutionalized in an organization? He unofficially writes to his wife from his later imprisonment from which he was no longer permitted to return home:

> However, although I was not so aware of it, I now consider the deportation I refused to accept, which was ordered by the state without legal grounds and is now to be enforced by means of the concentration camp, to be extraordinarily important for the relationship between church and state and for the internal and external freedom of the church which must be asserted for the sake of the gospel. I actually understand less and less how they put up with this attempt to strip the church of its freedom by merely protesting with words, especially since we still function as a corporation of public law. Hopefully the church leadership, which until now has not wanted to speak on my behalf, will realize the importance of the cause and will still find the words to do so. Or should I as the smallest and most insignificant pastor in the Hunsrück have to bear witness to the state alone as to what is right? It is almost expecting too much of the state to think they would take that seriously as a decision of the church. Why has the leadership remained silent for three months since I refused to accept my deportation? I had written to it, clearly stating that I thought it was right for the leadership to make my return their cause, a return that I had decided by myself and for myself. It seems to me that decisions for the church of the future will be made not by the church and its leadership, but by the individual congregations. This is why all the clever church politicians who do not fight and stand up for the gospel at their posts in the local congregation are miscalculating. Seen from here, my struggle to maintain the inextricable bond between pastor and congregation is (in

my view) undoubtedly right and vitally essential for the future course of the church.

The Gestapo pursues Paul Schneider by issuing this "wanted" circular:

Gestapo Düsseldorf
July 29, 1937
II B/8, 10/F.W. Otto

To the branch offices

The district administrators of the districts
Krefeld, Neuss and Viersen
and their political administrative offices

Concerning: actions taken against clergymen

A ban from speaking in the whole territory of the Reich has been imposed on the Protestant pastor Friedrich Wilhem Otto, born September 19, 1900 in Lichau in Samland, living in Berlin W 30, Nollendorfstrasse 14/15.

Pastor Paul Robert Schneider (from Dickenschied, the district of Simmern), born August 29, 1897, in the district of Kreuznach, has been banned from staying in the Rhine province.

The Protestant pastor Friedrich Middendorf from Schuttorf, born February 2, 1883 in Emden was banned from staying in the governmental district of Düsseldorf with the circular decree of May 20, 1937-IIb/80, 10 Middendorf. The ban has been rescinded. However, the ban from speaking in the whole territory of the Reich continues.

Additional information for the district administrators:

1. Overprints for the mayors are enclosed.
2. The dossier concerning Paul Schneider's ban from speaking is found in his personal file, as is the dossier concerning the rescinding of Pastor Middendorf's ban from staying in the governmental district of Düsseldorf.

3. Put one copy each of this circular decree in the dossier of Paul Robert Schneider and Middendorf.

4. The utilization of the archives in the cases of Schneider and Middendorf occurs in the dossiers concerned.

5. II F, personal card and search card: Start a file on Pastor Friedrich Wilhelm Otto's ban from speaking. For personal information, see telex.

6. File the personal card of F.W. Otto

(Two signatures)

The consistory in Düsseldorf reports to Berlin:

Protestant Consistory
6940 Düsseldorf, July 28, 1937

To the Highest Administrative Office of the Protestant Church in Berlin-Charlottenburg

Concerning: the arrest of Pastor Schneider in Dickenschied
Decree from June 21, 1937, E.O. III2524/37

Correspondent: Consistory member Hasenkamp

In a postscript to our report Nr. 68 from June 8, 1937 we report that the Gestapo office in Koblenz did not respond to our written inquiry about the reasons for the arrest of Pastor Schneider. On July 27 our caseworker, consistory member Hasenkamp, heard the following information from the superintendent there who was on a business trip that took him through Simmern. In keeping with a tradition in his congregation of imposing firm church discipline, Pastor Schneider had announced from the pulpit in the name of the session that a member of the congregation named Scherer had to be admonished because his child had not been sent regularly to the confirmation class.

In case no improvement could be seen, the session would be forced to exclude this father from Holy Communion. Evidently the individual concerned complained about it, and his complaint gave rise to the arrest. Pastor Schneider sat in the Koblenz prison for almost two months. Then

he was released from detention on the morning of July 24 without a
trial having taken place and was then deported to Wiesbaden, with a
deportation order banning him from staying in the Rhineland. Today
we are inquiring again at the Gestapo office in Koblenz as to why the
pastor was arrested and has now been deported.

Ha(senkamp) July 30

The consistory reminds the Gestapo of the first petition it had already
submitted by writing a second letter:

Consistory
6840/III Düsseldorf, July 28, 1937

To the Gestapo office in Koblenz
The Regional Board

Concerning: The arrest and deportation of Pastor Schneider in
Dickenschied, the district of Simmern

We have been notified that Pastor Schneider from Dickenschied was
released from his detention on July 24, 1937 and was simultaneously
deported from the area of the Rhine province. With reference to our
letter of June 8, Nr. 6840, we again urgently request information on
the reasons that led first to the arrest and then to the deportation of the
pastor. Those of us on the church's supervisory board have an urgent
interest in finding out the reasons that led to such drastic measures
being taken against a clergyman under our supervision. Therefore, we
request that you inform us of this.

Ha(senkamp) July 30

The Gestapo is not in any hurry to answer and makes the "German
Christians" in the consistory wait. However, whether the Gestapo office in
Koblenz was authorized to give such information, or whether it first had to
receive instructions from the Reich security main office of the SS in Berlin
located at Prince Albrecht Street 8, can no longer be clarified today. But one
thing ought to be undisputed: Paul Schneider had a particularly relentless

opponent among the National Socialists' important figures, who possessed far-reaching connections within the party as a comrade of the NSDAP and on the basis of his position as a party officeholder.

The deportation from the Rhineland hangs like a Damocles sword over these vacation days in Baden-Baden that the pastor's family from Dickenschied enjoyed in the truest sense of the word. Their actual concern is focused on the two congregations in the Hunsrück.

Bernhard Heinrich Forck, a pastor in Hamburg and at the same time a member of the provisional church leadership of the German Protestant Church, writes from Berlin to the pastor's family from Dickenschied and Womrath staying in Baden-Baden:

The Provisional Leadership of
the German Protestant Church
Berlin-Dahlem, August 18, 1937
Friedberg Street 11
Pastor Schneider and his wife, temporarily in Baden-Baden,
Taborhöhe

Dear Brother Schneider!

We received your letter yesterday and thank you for the lines you wrote. Of course, we continue to maintain our commitment to you and all our hard-pressed brothers by way of intercessory prayer. Your case especially moves us. In general the brothers have decided to follow the deportation order. But we well understand that the seriousness of the ordination vows leads the brother in ministry to be loyal to his congregation. Nevertheless, the Gestapo has the power in its hands and will also use it. This is a serious decision you are facing. Therefore, it is proper that the Rhenish Council has asked you to await the decision of the church leadership. If the church leadership instructs you to remain in your congregation, you have to obey, regardless of what follows from this. If the church leadership advises you to follow the deportation order, you will also have to follow this advice and must allow the church leadership to take care of the congregation. May God the Lord be with you and rest his blessing on you and yours! May he also bless your congregation in this time of distress! We always want to keep in mind our primary goal, praying that the cause of our Lord and his church may always be furthered and not hindered. But we may also ask the Lord to overlook our weakness and sin and in spite of everything to bless the church and to allow an abundance of fruit and wondrous blessing to result from the suffering of this time.

With warm regards,
In faithfulness,
On behalf of the Provisional Leadership of the German Protestant Church
Forck
Pastor Böhm, to whom you wrote your letter, has already been in detention for two weeks!

A restrained joy settles over the vacation in Baden-Baden, as the available pictures show us. It was more than an act of brotherly kindness for Pastor Ippach and his family to arrange this vacation for his colleague who had been deported from the Rhineland, making it possible for him to be together with his wife and then covering their illegal stay.

During this time the deputy president of the Protestant Confessing Synod in the Rhineland visits Paul Schneider and his wife. Mrs. Ippach wrote down the course of the conversation from memory in a letter to Mrs. Schneider after the war was over:

As the representative of the President, Pastor Schlingensiepen, asked your husband: "Is it your intention to return to your congregation after this vacation although the pulpit ban has been imposed on you by the Gestapo?"

Your husband answered: "I am committed to my congregation and in church matters do not accept any order from the Gestapo." Then Schlingensiepen said in so many words: "And if we as a Brotherhood Council urgently advise you not to return to your pulpit again, what would you do then?" His answer: "I would not like to take any position on that today, I will act according to my conscience" and hinted that he was determined to go back to his congregation. Then Pastor Schlingensiepen said to you: "What do you think about this—are you fully aware of the dangerous consequences the return of your husband to his congregation could have for him?" Your answer: "I can not hold my husband back if he sees it as his calling to go back to his pulpit; dangers lurk everywhere for him."

What is expressed here is rooted in the obedience of faith and tolerates no diplomatic compromise, not even when martyrdom is in the air. It must be added that Paul Schneider moves exclusively in the spiritual, church realm and does not take one step out of it. He never personally offended any of his opponents, and also took no regard for any disadvantages or harm that could come to him. His opponents as well as his "Christian" critics did not have enough decency and experience in life to recognize that Paul Schneider acted exclusively on the basis of his responsibility for the faith and his loyalty to the faith.

In those days it was not unusual for clergymen who had come into conflict with the state authorities to be banished from their congregations and regional churches. They were then subject to compulsory registration with the police and also had to endure many different handicaps. If a ban on speaking in the whole territory of the Reich had not been decreed, then they had the opportunity to pursue pastoral ministry at their place of residence.

The Rhenish Council tries to arrange a meeting of all pastors affected by deportation orders. They expect from such a conference not only an exchange of experiences they have had in dealing with the power of the state, but also a jointly coordinated attempt to take action against the National Socialist tyranny. Paul Schneider is given hope of such a meeting of brothers, but then it does not come about.

September 4, 1937

Dear Brother Schneider!

Due to the recent obstruction of the provisional leadership's work nothing will probably come of the meeting for the time being. I tried almost daily to arrange such a meeting, but am not getting any response. Now I can not make you wait any longer for news of this event, especially since I do not know whether you have the freedom to wait for an indefinite time. We commend you to God and his grace.

It was a great joy for me to be with you and your dear wife.

Faithfully thinking of you,
Your, Schlingensiepen

This momentous letter showing the sheer helplessness and insecurity of the Confessing Church reaches Paul Schneider in Eschbach near Usingen (Taunus). He had filled the pulpit there for his longstanding friend and colleague Emil Weber who was on vacation. At this point we may ask the question of what would have happened if the Rhenish Council had stood behind Paul Schneider.

President Humburg writes to Eschbach:

The Council of the Protestant Confessing Synod
in the Rhineland
The President Wuppertal-Barmen, September 17, 1937
Heinr.-Janssenstr. 16, Tel. 54235
Postal Checking Account Essen 37681

Pastor Schneider
Eschbach
near Usingen in Taunus

Dear Brother Schneider!

You have not heard anything from me for a while. I ask that you not interpret this to mean that we are no longer preoccupied with your case. It is still our concern to arrange a meeting of the brothers who have experienced the same kinds of things as you have as soon as possible so that we can agree on a consistent way of handling these cases. I sincerely ask you and urge you not to lose patience. It is naturally hard for you to think that your congregation is not being given pastoral care. But you must simply bear this.

As soon as anything is clarified and can be said, you will receive news from us.

Warmest regards,
From Your
Humburg

After more than eight weeks the Gestapo is prepared to respond to the consistory, and refers to its second letter:

Gestapo
Headquarters in Koblenz
Koblenz, September 24, 1937
im Vogelsang I
Tel. Nr. 2291
Case Nr. II B 355/37

Concerning: The arrest and deportation of Pastor Schneider from Dickenschied, the district of Simmern

Dossier: The letter there from June 2, 1937 Nr. 6840 III

To the Protestant Consistory of the Rhine Province in Düsseldorf
Inselstrasse 10

Pastor Schneider is a fanatical supporter of the Confessing Church who has used every opportunity to agitate against the National Socialist state. Therefore, several criminal proceedings are pending against him at the special court in Cologne. He is charged with violating the Treachery Act and violating paragraph 30a of the State Code of Law.

His preventive detention was temporarily necessary because he had announced "Christian discipline" against two national comrades from the pulpit. One of the individuals subject to discipline was a supporter of the German Christians. Pastor Schneider was taken into custody on May 31, 1937 because of this action that is reminiscent of medieval conditions as well as because of his disparagement of a national comrade from the pulpit. He was released from preventive detention on July 24, 1937.

On the basis of the decree issued by the Reich President on February 28, 1933 he was banned from staying in the Rhine province because his conduct endangered the public safety and order and ran counter to the interests of the National Socialist state. He also evaded this last order issued by the state by preaching in the church in Dickenschied in spite of the ban imposed on July 25, 1937 and then departing for an unknown destination.

Moreover, he was given the task of reporting his new place of residence to the local police station within 48 hours. He has also failed to do this until now. Do you know the place where Pastor Schneider is staying at the present time?

In proxy:
Signed Dr. Albath
Certified: Steil
Chancellery Clerks

The reasons for his arrest were openly expressed by the state in this letter. The Gestapo located in the Reich Security Main Office at the SS headquarters in Berlin spoke even more clearly. It documents how the Nazi state observed events within the church and wanted to put the church under its jurisdiction so that it could judge whether the church's decisions were right or wrong. Thus it did not take the church seriously, either as an institution, i.e., as a corporation of public law, or as a fellowship of believers. The Gestapo punished Paul Schneider by putting him in prison and deporting him because he refused to issue a certificate valid only in the realm of the church and because he announced that a member was being excluded from communion on the basis of purely ecclesiastical considerations. Paul Schneider, but not one church institution, openly declared the illegality and wrongfulness of such intervention by the state authorities:

So I explained that the deportation order they had just revealed to me proved that the preventive detention and the arrest warrant for this detention were an injustice and an untruth on the basis of the reasons cited and on the basis of the well-known Hindenburg paragraph. These measures were clearly targeted at the Confessing Church and thus persecuted the Church of Jesus Christ.

The highest Administrative Office of the Protestant Church makes the statements of the state authorities public by sending copies to the consistory:

The Administrative Office of the Protestant Church
Berlin-Charlottenburg, September 25, 1937
Jebensstrasse
Telephone: 315331
E.O.III 3625/37

Copy!
The Reich and Prussian minister for Church Affairs
I 15757/37
Berlin, W.8, August 17, 1937

Copy!
Gestapo
Gestapo office
B.-Nr. II B 2-873/37E

Berlin, SW 11, July 27, 1937

Concerning: Pastor Paul Schneider, Dickenschied, in the district of Simmern
File: UR-letter of July 8, 1937-G I 14599/37
Enclosures 4

Pastor Paul Schneider was taken into preventive detention on May 31, 1937 by order of the Führer for the following reasons:

The farmer Ernst Scherer in Womrath, in the district of Simmern, asked Pastor Schneider for a certificate of transfer to allow his son to participate in the confirmation class of another pastor because he did not want his son to be educated in the confessional front's way of thinking. Pastor Schneider responded to Scherer by saying that he could not issue the certificate since only the Confessing Church's instruction was legitimate and Scherer would have to be taken under church discipline if he continued to refuse to send his son to the confirmation class. Furthermore, Schneider had the farmer Scherer summoned to answer to the session and threatened him again with church discipline on this occasion in case he would not heed the summons. Since Scherer did not appear, Schneider announced two times from the pulpit that Christian discipline would be imposed and notified Scherer:

"You will, therefore, be excluded from the church of Christ by the congregation, prohibiting you from partaking of the sacraments, and from Christ's Kingdom by God himself until you promise and demonstrate that you are truly living a better life (Heidelberg Catechism, Question 85 and its biblical reasons).

"After this Christian discipline for you takes effect, the congregation is urged to break off Christian and church fellowship with you, but to treat you kindly in all necessary things, just as Christian discipline does not seek your ruin and your damnation, but repentance, and hopes to win you back as a member of the congregation. You retain the right to pastoral care and the proclamation of the Word in the congregation. As a member of the congregation, which you still are externally, you have to continue to pay your church contributions.

"If you still do not want to listen to the congregation, church discipline takes effect with the third announcement."

In the meantime, Pastor Schneider has been released from preventive detention and deported from the Rhine province.

On instruction Signed

(signature)

To the Reich and Prussian minister
for Church Affairs, Berlin W8

I am sending the above copy in reference to your letter of June 21, 1937-E.O.III 25/24/37-please give this document your kind attention.

On instruction Signed (Albrecht)

To the Administrative Office, Berlin-Charlottenburg 2

We are sending a copy to the Protestant Consistory subsequent to E.O. 2524/37 of June 21 of this year with reference to the report of August 2 of this year-Nr. 6840 III-please give this document your kind attention and make appropriate comments.

For the President
Signed, Freitag
Certified, Fiebig
Supreme Secretary of the Chancellery

The headquarters of the Gestapo exactly reproduces the letter written to Ernst Scherer in Womrath without comment and thus confirms that a purely internal church matter is at issue in this incident. In this context we must ask the question of why the headquarters of the Gestapo exclusively stresses the church discipline and does not mention the charges we know from the letter of the Gestapo office in Koblenz.

Aware of its unchecked position of power in the Nazi state, the Gestapo was in the habit of expecting those who came in contact with it to obey without objection. The Confessing Church had brought itself to declare its faith in the theological, verbal realm and took a strong position. In an open confrontation with the Nazi state, as it could be seen in the Hunsrück, the leadership seemed helpless, surprised, insecure and impotent, as we have shown elsewhere.

While the correspondence between Düsseldorf and Berlin is going back and forth, Paul Schneider is in a Hessian pulpit in Eschbach in the Taunus. During this time a collection of signatures in favor of Paul Schneider is being organized and confiscated by the police. The voice of the people must not be heard. Pastor Wippermann, Kreuznach, probably stayed in close touch with the power centers of the Nazi state as a zealous and radical advocate of National Socialist thought and reacted to any activity of the Protestant congregations in Dickenschied and especially in Womrath on behalf of Paul Schneider. For the headquarters of the Gestapo undoubtedly gained possession of the previously mentioned letter written to Ernst Scherer by the session in Womrath through him.

The session finds the present situation of the congregation without a pastor to be unbearable. It is willing to assume a share of the responsibility and informs its pastor:

Womrath, September 19, 1937

Dear Pastor Schneider!

Since the Gestapo in Koblenz has already taken you away from us since May 31st of this year and they could not prove that you were guilty of any offenses what would warrant punishment (. . .).

We see in this only a slanderous report to the police that should actually have been punishable by law. Since you have now been released from prison for a while and your deportation is not yet rescinded, we as members of the session of this congregation can no longer bear the present situation because the confirmands have not received any religious instruction since your departure and Christian instruction for our young people has been stopped. There is also a lack of pastoral care for the sick in both congregations. Holy communion has already been skipped twice. All members in good standing urgently desire your quick return so that you can again perform the duties of your office in God's name. Therefore, the session requests your quick return and asks you politely to pass this urgent request on to a higher state authority if at all possible; for we can no longer assume responsibility for the congregation in your absence.

The session of the congregation in Womrath,
Fuchs, Scherer, Auler

A letter of the session from Dickenschied had a similar text. Paul Schneider receives the following notification from the Confessing Synod of the Rhineland:

Protestant Confessing Synod in the Rhineland
Düsseldorf, September 28, 1937
Copernicus Street 9
Telephone: 10181 (in the evening) 17225

Dear Brother Schneider!

Since brother Humburg is presently absent, the Council has authorized me to answer your letter addressed to the president, referring to the decision of the Augsburg Confessing Synod. We would like to have this word expressly bear witness to you for your journey.

In the struggle of the Confessing Church for the freedom to proclaim the gospel, there have been an increasing number of cases in which pastors are being prohibited from publicly exercising their office in various ways. This represents a serious trial for them and for their congregations. So they are asking for a word of guidance from the church because both they and all of us are under orders from the Lord of the church who commands us to spread his message, using every single opportunity given to us. Although the decisions that must be made here are first being presented to these individuals, it is becoming clearer than ever that the whole church is being called to assume responsibility for these incidents. The synod expressly affirms this responsibility as its own.

Under the present circumstances it is not possible to give the pastors and congregations concerned a generally applicable, binding directive for their conduct because in spite of the large number of the same or similar incidents it can not be said in general when the specific point is reached at which the Scriptural word comes into effect: "We must obey God more then men." We cannot relieve the individual conscience of its responsibility to make this decision.

But sharing a common responsibility, we know that we must all submit to the same guidance of the Word and Spirit of God with the brothers and congregations involved. Therefore, we ask them to consider that our own human fears or hopes, or any threats or enticements they receive must not have a decisive influence on their decision, and ask them to commend themselves in all such temptations to God and the Word of his grace.

We have been commissioned to proclaim God's Word; that makes the responsibility so great. But at the same time God's Word also desires to carry us with its power amid the loneliness of the final, personal decision. We should be assured of the justifying grace and guidance of our Lord in the obedience of faith. Whoever relies on them in his decision does what is right.

He should know that in doing so he is in fellowship with the Confessing Church that upholds him with its prayers as a member of the one body of Jesus Christ and serves him with its brotherly counsel. We thus point out to all who are being tested that pastoral conversations can help to strengthen his faith and be an aid to his conscience. The church, the Brotherhood Council and our church leadership have to prove successful in their mission and bear witness that the Confessing Church is willing to assume its responsibility.

"God is faithful; he will not let you be tempted beyond what you can bear. But when you are tempted, he will also provide a way out so that you can stand up under it" (1 Cor. 10:13 NIV).

Dear brother Schneider! It does not seem to us as if a meeting of those who have been deported could come about in the foreseeable future. Therefore, we are not in a position to ask you to delay your plan by appealing to this prospective conference. What you can do on your part "to fulfill all righteousness" seems good and right to us as well.

It is clear to us that we cannot say "no" to your decision. But it is just as clear to us that if you decide to say "yes" it cannot be a question of following instructions given by a church government, rather it can only be a question of the assurance of obedience to the command of the Lord himself. This is why nothing can either be commanded or forbidden here.

Dear brother Schneider, we commend you to God and his Word of grace in the certainty that each of us stands or falls with his Lord. "For none of us lives to himself alone and none of us dies to himself alone. If we live, we live to the Lord; and if we die, we die to the Lord. So, whether we live or die, we belong to the Lord" (Rm. 14:7–8 NIV).

With warmest brotherly regards
in the name of the Council and authorized by it,
Your,
Signed, Beckmann

Paul Schneider personally underlined the sentences that were important to him shortly afterwards in a Gestapo cell in Koblenz. He writes to his wife that the Augsburg sentences "beat around the bush too much," for he himself expects clear instructions from a synod; he thus puts his hope in the next church meeting.[3]

Even in the most difficult situations Paul Schneider never held back his opinion. His dialogue partner, whether an opponent or friend, could recognize without difficulty that he was always honest and meant what he said.

There were only a very few lawyers in Germany at that time who stood up for those persecuted by the Gestapo. Dr. Horst Holstein was one of those courageous attorneys who were willing to assist those who were detained.

Attorney and Notary
Dr. Horst Holstein Berlin W 8, September 25, 1937
Maurerstrasse 18
Pastor Schneider, Dickenschied/ Rhineland

Dear Pastor!

You probably know that Pastor Danicke from Strausberg has been held here in investigative detention for eight weeks, first in Potsdam and

---

[3] The Augsburg Confessing Synod made a number of decisions in which differences of opinion between the confessions caused harm to the Protestant Church. When Probst Gruber spoke up for the "non-Aryans," i.e., for Christians of Jewish descent, he hoped for the support of the Confessing Church. A remark he made shows what a difficult time the Confessing Church had in dealing with the Nazi authorities even in 1939: "By the time most of the non-Aryan pastors who had been arrested were released from the concentration camps early in 1939, I was able to get a good impression of the harassment that they and the other prisoners had to endure in the camps. I was of the opinion that we should not remain silent about it. So I tried to get the church authorities interested in it. I informed the Confessing Church at the meetings of the Prussian and Berlin Brotherhood Council, but their hands were tied. Then I contacted the manager of the Lutheran Bishops' Conference, Martin Gauger. He gave me the opportunity to report on my investigations at a meeting of Lutheran church leaders. I described to the gathered bishops how the concentration camp inmates had to endure such terrible mistreatment. Perhaps I described it in too much detail. At any rate, I heard one of the dignitaries say: 'Now it is time for us to proceed to the second point on the agenda.' The Chairman of the Conference, Bishop Theophil Wurm, who bravely opposed the authorities on the issue of euthanasia in 1940, accompanied me to the door and said, 'I thank you in the name of the brothers and wish God's blessing on you and your work.' That was one of the biggest disappointments I ever experienced. It was clear to me that I needed God's blessing, but I had hoped that these church leaders would help us" (H. Gruber, *Erinnerungen* [1968], p. 104ff.).

then in Berlin. Danicke claimed in a sermon that a pastor had been held in the safe of a branch office of the Reich bank.

I was told that you could provide me with further information on how this rumor had started. Unfortunately the facts about the whole matter are very unclear.

I even heard from one side that you were supposed to be the pastor who had started the rumor.

In the interests of Pastor Danicke I request an answer as soon as possible.

With German greetings!
Dr. Holstein
Attorney
by:
(signature)
Junior Clerk

(Handwritten note by Paul Schneider)
Responded with type-written letter
on September 28, 1937
a copy was put in my files.

Paul Schneider answers this very carefully phrased letter of the attorney from Eschbach in the Taunus region.

Pastor Schneider Eschbach near Usingen, Sept. 28, 1937
Dickenschied
Attorney and Notary
Dr. Horst Holstein, Berlin W 8, Mauerstrasse 18

Dear Dr. Holstein!

The claim made by Pastor Danicke, Strausberg is not incorrect in so far as I was kept in detention for eight weeks less two days in Koblenz in the basement of what had previously been the Reich bank building, in which the vaults of the Reich bank had been located.

This former Reich bank building has now been transformed into a Gestapo regional headquarters. A prison for detainees has been built in the basement that offers room for seven prisoners in five cells. The cells are regular prison cells with a meager amount of sunlight falling in. The air in the whole basement prison was also so damp and cold in the hot days of June and July that rubber and leather objects in the corridor or in the storage room got moldy.

It is generally known in the city that the safes were located in the basement of the former Reich bank building. It has not been proven and according to a statement a fellow prisoner made to me in prison, it cannot be assumed that the vaults were in the same location where the prison cells are now. Rather I understood it to mean that the vaults of the Reich bank were located in the front of the basement toward the street whereas our cells were built toward the back, toward the inner courtyard and partially under the inner courtyard (concrete ceiling).

I cannot say how the not quite accurate rumor got started. I was allowed to write only two letters to my wife in the first two weeks of my detention. In these letters I only told her that I had clean accommodations and that I was housed in an area of the basement where it was also cool during the hot days so that I could use warm underwear. Afterwards I was forbidden to write or receive mail until my release. On July 24 I was released from detention and could only tell my friends and brothers about the detention on the 24th and during the following days. I described the place of my detention in terms of the first two paragraphs above. In order to examine in greater detail the origin of the rumor it would be important to know on what Sunday Pastor Danicke made this claim in his sermon.

I am willing to give you further information if possible. The construction of the Gestapo regional headquarters, especially the prison in the basement, is of a rather recent date. It has been said that the cells were built only a few weeks before. This makes the rumor even more inexcusable. Perhaps the prison chaplain Appell in Arenberg near Koblenz can give you precise information on the date when the cells were built and where the former vaults were located. Or perhaps the residents of the Vogelsang I building can give you this information.

I would be grateful if you could let me know how the investigative detention turns out.

Sincerely,
Your . . .

(A handwritten note: I told about the cool basement only in a third letter that my wife no longer received. But my stay in Vogelsang was generally known.)

Before Paul Schneider leaves Eschbach, he has made a serious decision for himself and thus also for his family, which he communicates to the Reich chancellery and further high-ranking government offices with the candor that is typical of him.

Pastor Schneider
Dickenschied (Hunsrück)
Eschbach, September 30, 1937

To the Reich Chancellery of the German Reich in Berlin, Wilhelmstrasse. Copies were simultaneously sent to the Reich interior ministry and to the provincial governor in Koblenz.

With all respect I am honored to report the following information to these high-ranking government offices:

On May 30 of this year, shortly after being discharged from the hospital where I was treated for a fracture of the lower thigh, I was taken from my manse to Koblenz by officials of the Gestapo where I was interrogated and immediately taken into preventive detention in accordance with a disclosure made to me without allowing me to ask any questions.

The order for the preventive detention that was delivered to me during the first days of my detention appeals to Hindenburg's edict of February 1933 upholding public security and order and mentions as a reason for my arrest the general charge that my conduct was conducive to endangering the public security and order. Eight weeks less two days I was kept in preventive detention without any hearing or investigation being able to prove that I was guilty of a wrongful or rebellious act that would have justified this order for the preventive detention.

On July 24 they revealed to me that I was going to be deported from the Rhineland. As grounds for this action the deportation order again mentioned my conduct that was endangering public safety and order, this time in the whole Rhine province.

During the deportation hearing at the Gestapo headquarters in Koblenz I explained: In eight weeks of preventive detention you did not even make an attempt to prove that I was guilty of an unjust or rebellious act. The disclosure of my deportation that has just been made to me proves that the preventive detention represents a act of persecution targeted at the Confessing Church and thus at the church of Jesus Christ in Germany. I must characterize the order they issued for my preventive detention as unjust and untrue. For they issued it by appealing to Hindenburg's edict; I am going to rip it up as a sign of this injustice. Then I did rip it up. The word Hindenburg left as his legacy was: "Make sure that Christ is preached in Germany." The Confessing Church is doing nothing else. Of course, I also cannot recognize or accept the deportation. I know before God that he has assigned me to my congregation and I can not allow men, not even the authorities, to simply tear me away from it without any proof that I have done wrong. Consistent with this declaration I also reject the requirement that I name a place outside the Rhineland where I should reside. For two reasons I refused to sign the minutes taken by the inspector who presided at the hearing. I said that the minutes do not give an account of the whole hearing by leaving out my opening statement about the preventive detention and the order for the preventive detention as the grounds for my rejection of the deportation. I further said that all the previous statements I had candidly made to the Gestapo and signed in the minutes have only led to greater punishment—not "responsibility," as the minutes say. I viewed the long preventive detention as a punitive measure, which was also confirmed for me by a higher authority in the Gestapo prison. Only the second reason with the change the Gestapo made in my statement was recorded in the minutes.

Then I was taken by car across the border. In accordance with the statement I had made, I took the liberty of immediately returning to my congregation. On the following day I again preached the gospel of Jesus Christ in my two congregations, declaring that Jesus is Lord and that we must not deviate from this declaration of faith.

The rather long vacation I took, which I also needed because of the long preventive detention and because my leg is not yet fully healed, does not in any way change the decision I have made as a matter of principle to disobey an unjust human command. I have already borne witness to this decision and will continue to do so in the future. Without any legal grounds the deportation significantly interferes with the life of the church and congregation. It tears pastor and congregation apart although they were solemnly assigned to each other before God. The word of Holy Scripture applies to this joint assignment: "What God has joined together, let man not separate," just as much as it applies to Christian marriage. Congregations and pastors are thus urged to resist this unjust demand and order issued by persons in authority especially since such interference with the freedom and independence of church life made without legal grounds contradicts the solemn promises made by the highest authorities of the German Reich.

The threats of punishment, whether by fines or arrest or a new preventive detention, cannot frighten me. God can certainly rescue me from them if he wants, by making government authorities come to their senses or in whatever way God desires. Even if the punishments are applied, I still know that God will establish justice for all who suffer injustice, and that he will also judge between me and my government on his Day of Judgment as to the obedience we owe according to God's Word in Romans 13:1, a verse they held against me during my deportation, and as to the disobedience that is commanded according to God's Word in Acts 5:29: "We must obey God rather than men," a verse to which I also appealed when I refused to accept my deportation.

Permit me to mention a few points that do not actually account for the decision I have made, but that seem worthy of consideration from the perspective of the church's outward interests and from the perspective of political wisdom. My congregations have already been without regular pastoral care since March 20, half a year, and the Christian instruction of our young people has been left completely unattended. Furthermore, there is also the danger that if I followed the deportation order, the established church as a corporation of public law would no longer be able to find a new person to fill the pastorate in my parish since many small pastorates are being eliminated.

My six children see Dickenschied as their home, as I myself do, for I was also born in the Hunsrück. As a sign of my closeness to the congregation I have also acquired my own garden in Dickenschied.

My good reputation as a German citizen, as a human being, as a Christian, as a Protestant pastor, as a former officer and ex-serviceman who was on the front lines for three and a half years has been dishonored enough by having to endure the long preventive detention in prison under tightened prison rules. The continued persecution of my person and the continued harassment of the congregations that are willing to hold on to their rightful pastor would not be understood by all right thinking people in the congregation, and above all, it would not be understood by all the committed Christians of the congregation and would give rise to a great loss of confidence in the justice of the present leadership of the state. The outcry of the very few opponents of the Confessing Church in our congregation who have clearly proven to be destroyers of our church life, some of them for a long time, and who forced the session to fend them off with the necessary church discipline that is anchored in our confessions, cannot offset the support of the great majority.

Finally, I want to point out one final thing. I hope that the Christian congregation will still find the government to be a willing listener to its voice: Through their properly appointed sessions my two congregations have expressly asked me in writing to return and perform the duties of my office again. Thus I am no longer refusing to accept the deportation only because my conscience is captive to God. Rather, my sessions and congregations are also taking upon themselves the heavy burden and responsibility of disobeying a governmental order out of obedience to the Lord of the church who is at the same time also the Lord of the government.

I hereby commend my cause to the judgment of God, to whom the government and the church must give an account for the office he has bestowed on both of them, for he has given the government the worldly sword to punish the wicked and to protect the righteous, but he has given the church the spiritual sword of his holy and eternal Word until God's Kingdom comes in eternal and perfect righteousness when our Lord and Savior Jesus Christ himself will be both priest and king. Until then we hold to this truth: "Give to Caesar what is Caesar's and to God what is God's."

Pastor Schneider

If we only superficially examine the original copy of this letter that is kept in the federal archives in Koblenz, we must recognize that it hardly received any attention in the Reich chancellery. We find only the notice of receipt on it, but no indication that it was processed. They merely sent a brief note to Paul Schneider and then filed it away.

It must be asked whether Paul Schneider was ultimately asking too much of the powerful men in Berlin with his honesty. During the entire time of its existence the National Socialist state was never willing at any time to carry on a serious dialogue with the church about its nature, its temporal task and its confessional foundations. It wanted to make the church toe its line in order to then decree that it adopt the Nazi worldview. It was to be imbued with the "fighting spirit" of the National Socialist state and contribute to its display of power and its preservation of power. The Reich chancellery answers tersely:

The state secretary and head of the Reich Chancellery
RK 15547 B Berlin W 8, October 7, 1937

To
Pastor Schneider
Dickenschied
near Kirchberg (Hunsrück)

According to the address you also sent your petition of September 30 of this year concerning your preventive detention to the Reich and Prussian minister of the interior. He is the one primarily responsible for this matter. I will leave it to your discretion to turn to him for help if necessary.

pp (signed) Wienstein

Paul Schneider also properly informs the Brotherhood Council of his decision:

Pastor Schneider
Dickenschied, Hunsrück
Eschbach, Sept. 30, 1937

To the Brotherhood Council of the Protestant Confessing Synod in the Rhineland
For the attention of President Humburg

I hereby inform you of a letter I wrote to the state authorities concerning my deportation (a copy is enclosed) and give you notification of my return to my congregations planned for next Sunday, October 3.

On the part of the church leadership the way has been cleared for my return first by the visit and consultation of the deputy President, Pastor Schlingensiepen in Baden-Baden on August 17 and by a letter from brother Schlingensiepen of September 4.

Since a definite invitation to a meeting of all deported brothers has not been extended to this day, I do not feel justified in postponing the date of my return again, which I had already mentioned to the session in Dickenschied, in response to its request that I return as soon as possible.

The possibility of participating in such a conference still exists for me. Apart from that I feel justified by the fact of my return, knowing all its possible consequences, and by my letter to the state authorities.

Your brother,
Pastor Schneider

He had written to his friend Fritz Langensiepen earlier:

Eschbach, October 1, 1937

Dear Fritz!

"The die is cast." I have just sent letters of disobedience to the state authorities. Reif has requested my return for October 3 at two o'clock in the afternoon. He wants to be there himself. I will prepare for a thanksgiving sermon based on Psalm 145:12–21. I had informed the session that October 3 would be the date of my return in response to the letter of the Dickenschied session asking that I return as soon as possible. Until recently I had received urgent and sincere requests from Humburg to have patience and to keep waiting for the meeting, etc. But I had already decided to return. Then a new letter from the Council written by Beckmann arrived yesterday, completely clearing the way for me to return, especially since the meeting cannot take place.

I am not expecting any action by the state on October 3 since I already returned on July 25, but I leave it to you and the brothers whether you want to participate. If you could possibly say a few words . . . . But it would also be possible, and I would request this, for Reif to briefly address the congregations.

Womrath must first stand aside. Perhaps I could hold a worship service there in the evening. In any case, I will try to appear in my robe in the Dickenschied church without any prior announcement. How that happens must still be figured out. It is best that I am invisible before that.

I am enclosing a copy of my report to the state authorities for you and the brothers. I have already sent it to the Rhenish Council. Let us now hope that this matter in which you have taken such a sincere interest will turn out good for our congregations in that we may become more and more certain that this is the way the Lord is leading us. May he make us humble and reconciled to his will!

Send my sincere regards to you and your loved ones!
In faithfulness and gratitude,
Your, Paul
My wife, who is driving home today, greets you warmly!

This is a serious step that Paul Schneider announces here and then carries out. In his struggle for the truth of the gospel Paul Schneider stands alone in the concrete situation of fearlessly and wholeheartedly proclaiming what the

Word of God ultimately demands in its conflict with the powers arrayed against God. We do not know of any statement made by the leadership councils of the Confessing Church from this time in which it wholeheartedly supports Paul Schneider and signals to the Gestapo that he and the sessions of Dickenschied and Womrath have acted legally in terms of church law. This failure will remain an agonizing question addressed to the Confessing Church.

25

THE FINAL SERMON

"The eyes of all look to you, and you give them their food at the proper time. You open your hand and satisfy the desires of every living thing. The Lord is righteous in all his ways and loving toward all he has made. The Lord is near to all who call on him, to all who call on him in truth. He fulfills the desires of those who fear him; he hears their cry and saves them. The Lord watches over all who love him, but all the wicked he will destroy. My mouth will speak in praise of the Lord. Let every creature praise his holy name for ever and ever" (Ps. 145:15–21 NIV).

Dear members of the congregation!

What a privilege to celebrate thanksgiving even in this year of church distress! It was always an especially joyful festival in the church, in the village and even in the city, a time to thank God for the fruit of the field as the outward, visible blessing God has showered on our work, having filled our barns and cellars again. This year is no different, so we do not want to let anything rob us of our joy and gratitude even this year, we do not want to let the storms of hardship sweeping over our precious Protestant church stifle our songs of thanksgiving. Together with the Psalmist we want to praise God even today for giving and ruling over the gifts that he has given us anew.

How rich and good God is in his giving! The first verses of our text from Psalm 145 tell us this. For many it is a nice grace to say before meals. Today we want to pay special attention to two words from it. Many times the little word "you" is written in capital letters and at the same time approaches us with such close familiarity. The eyes of all look to *you*, and *you* give them their food at the proper time. *You* open your generous hand and satisfy the desires of every living thing. Here we see invisibly, yet in a living and real way, the personal, fatherly *You* of the living God and Father in heaven behind the strength of our arms as we work, behind the germinating power of the earth, behind all the mysterious, burgeoning growth. It is this *You* who still graciously preserves the order of nature on this sinful earth with its sinful human beings after making his promise in covenant with Noah: "As long as the earth endures, seedtime and harvest, cold and heat, summer and winter, day and night will never cease." Let us not rob God of his honor, let us not flee and hide behind laws of nature and the forces of nature, behind laws and forces of blood and soil to escape this great, personal You of the living God who approaches us in such a fatherly way. He is the One who comes to us so warmly, so intimately in his gifts on the day of Thanksgiving! There is also a second little word in our text that expresses to us the bounteous goodness of divine giving and that emphatically stresses it in its repetition: the little words *all* and *every*. The eyes of *all* look to you; you satisfy the desires of *every* living thing. This includes the creatures that lack the powers of reason, that search for their food with their animal instincts and wait for God's gifts. They are an example to us in the way they go about their work and our Savior points out how the birds in the sky are fed by our heavenly Father without having any cares in this world. The hen that finds a sip of water raises its little head to heaven as if thanking God, thus admonishing us who are human beings with the gift of reason to remember the Giver from whom all our food and drink comes. At night the beasts of prey go out and find their prey to satisfy their hunger. Likewise, man goes to work early and demands his food and wages. Everyone, even the wicked and godless human beings, whether they recognize and admit it or not, whether they thank God or not, wait for God's hand to open. Belshazzar was a godless, proud ruler in Babylon who elevated himself above God and proudly and defiantly said: "This is the great Babylon that I myself have built by my power, to the honor of my glory." Yet even Belshazzar only received this power on loan from God, as he soon had to realize to his own dismay. Even all those who do not thank God for his gifts, receive them from the One who in his bounteous goodness causes his sun to rise on the evil and the good and sends his rain on the righteous and the unrighteous.

But God's giving is even more abundant. He puts his blessing on the gifts of his hand from our fields and farmland as the fruits of our harvest on the altar of our church indicate. With our church he calls us into his house to worship him, so that we may call on him, the Giver, with prayer and supplication. The blessing of his gifts can only be revealed to us when we hear his holy, life-giving Word. Here we are privileged to recognize that God gives us everything as the Father of our Lord Jesus Christ, and through him, our Father as well. Here we learn that God still upholds the world by his gracious orders of preservation, not because of our ability and worthiness, but because the blood of his dear Son cries out to the Father in heaven from the cross of Golgotha to have mercy on us. Here God calls us with all the other gifts of his hand to accept the gift of all gifts, Jesus Christ. Here Jesus Christ gives himself to us as bread for our souls, as the One who brings eternal life.

Now we can appreciate the riches of God's goodness in the gifts he gives to meet our physical needs, realizing that he preserves our lives through these gifts so that salvation and redemption in Jesus Christ may be preached to us and many more may be saved. Then we will be kept from abusing God's gifts by anxiously hoarding them or arrogantly wasting them, while our hearts become hardened and proud and secure, just as the rich fool hardened his heart in the parable. May we never have the temerity to think that our souls can live on these earthly gifts: "You have plenty of good things laid up for many years. Take life easy; eat, drink and be merry!"

Only as we lift our hearts to the heart of God do our prayers of thanksgiving gain that full, warm sound of praise. We truly praise God's bounteous and gracious giving when we say with the Psalmist: The eyes of all look to you, and you give them their food at the proper time. You open your hand and satisfy the desires of every living thing.

The bounteous goodness of God in his giving is associated with the holiness and righteousness of his rule; so now we may exclaim: How holy and righteous is God in his rule! Just as God still upholds this world under the cross of his dear Son through his gracious orders of preservation, this precious, innocent blood shed for our sins is also the guarantee that God's rule is holy and righteous. For the sake of this blood God's goodness in giving and taking, in giving support and withholding it is intended to lead us to repentance. "If one does not want to convert, God has already drawn his bow." Woe to those who presume on God's grace, who become worldly and forgetful of God! For the sake of his righteousness and holiness God has also embedded malformed growth and inflationary times, drought and unfruitful years, poverty and sickness in his gracious orders of preservation. These hardships are his holy finger that he has lifted for the individual and for whole nations so that they would not forget God and take every gift from the gracious hand of the One who alone is holy and righteous, seeking his blessing in humility and repentance.

God's ways with the gift of his Word are also holy and righteous. Let us not forget that during this Thanksgiving festival and consider what it means! Worse for a nation than the rising price of bread is the rising price of God's Word. Our joy and our gratitude for this thanksgiving festival is dampened by the fact that we must fear such a time when the price of the Word of God will rise in the German nation, when many Protestant pastors who preach God's Word and God's will honestly and purely and without fear of displeasing the public authorities will endure captivity and persecution. There were also times in Israel when it was said that God's Word was expensive in the land. At the time of Elijah there was no prophet in the land except him because the godless queen Jezebel and her equally godless husband Ahab had exterminated the prophets of the Lord in the land. Such times were not blessed or good ones for Israel. They brought godless rule, the hardships of war, poverty and rising prices. But men and nations are to blame when such expensive times come for God's Word. We too have certainly deserved this time of church distress in Germany with our indifference toward the divine Word and our contempt for it. But woe to us when we are no longer permitted to do the work of sowing and harvesting the divine Word in the lives of young and old in our villages and communities! What good is it for a man to gain the whole world, yet forfeit his soul? Therefore, o country, listen to the Word of the Lord!

The holy and righteous rule of God divides into paths of mercy for those who pray earnestly, for those who fear God, for those who can and want to cry out to God in their distress, for those who love God, the Giver, more than all his gifts and his creatures, and into paths of judgment for all the godless. The Lord is near to all who call on him, all who earnestly call on him. If we earnestly desire something from him with a God-fearing heart, he will hear our cries and we will experience his help. This is true of our need for bread and our need for God's Word, our need for existence when the lives of so many people who fear God are threatened, and this is true of the churches and congregations that are in distress. God is asking us if we have allowed this distress in our church, congregation and school to seriously drive us to our knees in prayer. We were happy that our children were free to help us work because school and confirmation classes were cancelled in my absence, but were we equally concerned that they would receive their Christian instruction? O, we are not praying enough, we are not praying earnestly enough for our congregation and church and its Christian concerns! What is the reason for this? There are many who do not even want anyone to show them their need for God, their need for bread and for life, their need for the church and Word of God. There are many who have already turned to the ways of the world, to the crooked ways of hypocrisy, insincerity, lying, making compromises with the spirit of this world and the spirit of disobedience. But how are the people who do not want anyone to show them their need supposed to learn about receiving God's help? It is impossible. In this way they deprive themselves of experiencing the living God and his glorious help.

We should know today that declaring our faith in Jesus will cost us something, that we must enter into many hardships and dangers, into humiliation and persecution for his sake. Blessed is the one who does not avoid this distress! He is then privileged to experience the truth that God is a true help in times of need and can be found as such. He is privileged to experience what God promises to those who fear him: Even before they call, I will hear them; even before they cry out, I will answer them. He is privileged to comfort himself with this truth in his distress: "He who dwells in the shelter of the Most High will rest in the shadow of the Almighty. I will say of the Lord, 'He is my refuge and my fortress, my God, in whom I trust.'" (Ps. 91:1–2) Indeed, the one who is righteous and he alone is confident even in his death and says: "Whom have I in heaven but you? And earth has nothing I desire besides you. My flesh and my heart may fail, but God is the strength of my heart and my portion forever" (Ps. 73:25–26 NIV). The congregation and the church of Jesus Christ that does not refuse to accept the hardship will also experience the grace of God's wonderful help and will see how he helps us to get through it. In the midst of the storm this Word from the Lord is meant for his church: The gates of hell will not overcome it. He, the Lord himself, will bear witness to himself as the One who is alive and real in their midst: "And surely I am with you always, to the very end of the age!"

But something would be missing from the holiness and righteousness of God's rule if his ways were not also ways of judgment for all the godless. When Belshazzar, the Babylonian ruler of the world, had carried his godless, proud and profligate misuse of God's gifts too far, when he blasphemed God by drinking from the holy goblets of the temple with his nobles and his wives and concubines, when God's flaming handwriting appeared to him on the plaster of the wall in the royal palace and when even then he was only frightened instead of being willing to change his ways, then God's judgment came upon him: "That very night Belshazzar, king of the Babylonians, was slain." In the same way, the hour of judgment will come upon every farmer who neglects to build the Kingdom of God because he is so busy building and filling his barns, just as it came upon the rich fool in the parable: "You fool! This very night your life will be demanded from you!"

Woe to those seducers who seduce the people, a nation and its young people, to fall away from the living God and his Word, which alone can satisfy the soul and give it eternal life! Woe to those as well who allow themselves to be seduced, parents and children, because their earthly needs are more important to them than the eternal, divine bread of heaven! Woe to a whole generation—nothing more can be said about them than about the generation at the time of Noah: People were eating and drinking, marrying and giving in marriage. The only thing that still towers over it is the judicial power of God in his eternal Last Judgment. Whoever has ears to hear, let him hear! You who are indifferent, smug and self-righteous sinners, get ready to seek your Savior!

Thanksgiving! We praise the bounty of God's goodness in his gifts. We praise the righteousness and holiness of his rule. How then should we thank him? The last verse of our text tells us: "My mouth will speak in praise of the Lord." Not the mouth of another, for instance only the mouth of a pastor, rather your mouth should confess your God as the Father of our Lord Jesus Christ, here in the congregation and in front of it, but also outside the congregation in the world and in public, in front of those who want to hear it, and those who do not want to hear it, in front of the people, the state and the government. "Let every creature praise his holy name for ever and ever!" This means that God's praise and honor must not remain in a corner. Therefore, dear members of the congregation, if our journey is so full of trials and temptations today, as it obviously is, it is because people are talking about your steadfastness and confession of faith all around, because they do not want to have you praising the Lord and declaring your faith in the Lord and his church in this way. This should be an honor for you and an encouragement to continue following the path of the church that confesses its Lord to the whole world. May this be the way we express our gratitude for the harvest he has given us! Come, close the ranks!

> *I will sing in eternity of the Merciful One's grace.*
> *He faithfully loves his people, forgives and has patience.*
> *My mouth shall boldly proclaim his faithfulness and truth,*
> *So that even our grandchildren find God, as we found him.*
> *Yes, his grace rises, to be exalted eternally,*
> *and his truth remains firmly fixed in the heavens. Amen!*

Paul Schneider writes down his final sermon in the Gestapo prison in Koblenz for his congregation in Womrath after the Gestapo arrests him again while he is on the way to Womrath to hold the worship service there. He smuggles it out in a laundry bag. It is mimeographed by his wife and distributed to the members of the congregation in Womrath.

In a letter of March 18, 1935, when Paul Schneider is detained for refusing to sign a pledge not to read an announcement of the Confessing Church in the worship service, his wife writes to him:

> Do not push yourself to be a martyr! Sometimes I feel sorry for the other pastors who now appear in a poor light in the eyes of the people—or is it the other way around? In any case, I am satisfied with the decision you have made; I know well enough how something bothers you when you cannot do it wholeheartedly. You know that on the outside I can hold my own, but there are also tears that I have not cried. May God give us both strength to walk in his ways.

A long-standing friend of the Schneider family, Pastor Heinz Rolffs, who bore both joy and sorrow with the family, writes:[1]

> But in any case, his lifetime companion must not be missing from the portrait of his life. For her part in his martyrdom is that she released her husband amid much pain, giving up her rights as a wife and mother and refraining from exerting any influence on her husband's decision of conscience. This carries even greater weight since both of these

---

[1] A letter to the author.

human beings were very vital, independent-minded characters. Only God knows what inner struggles both had to surmount.

Superintendent Ernst Gillmann submits an impressive report to the consistory in Düsseldorf about the repeated arrest of Paul Schneider:

The Superintendent Simmern (Hunsrück), October 5, 1937
Tgb-Nr. 475/37

Concerning: Pastor Schneider, Dickenschied

To the Protestant Consistory of the Rhine province in Düsseldorf/ Rhineland

I hereby officially notify you that Pastor Paul Schneider from Dickenschied was arrested again toward evening on Sunday on the way to a thanksgiving service. He was put in the prison of the district court in Kirchberg and transported on the following day by car to Koblenz (?), apparently by the Gestapo. I do not know the more detailed circumstances. I have only heard the following facts: On Sunday, October 3, 1937 Paul Schneider surprisingly returned to his congregation from his exile. It is said that he sent an advance notice of his return to various higher government offices and then led the worship service in Dickenschied in the afternoon in place of the guest preacher I appointed. On the way to the yoked congregation of Womrath he was arrested by two policemen and put in prison according to the report of his wife. I do not know his whereabouts at the moment. The situation after his deportation is still remembered. At that time he returned from Wiesbaden where he had been brought by the Gestapo, led the worship service in both congregations, went on vacation to Baden-Baden and from there to the home of a friend. I do not know the location of his friend's home.

I am sorry that Schneider is now in detention again, mainly because of his wife and six children. One cannot do much, at least at the moment. There is great anger in the two congregations.

My very personal view is that it would have been more sensible for Schneider to let some more water flow down the Rhine before he took the second step of his return. But he did not consult with any of us, thus absolving us of our duty to dissuade him, which probably would have been of no use anyway; for he acts on the basis on his honest convictions. "To his own Master he stands or falls." (Rm. 14:4)

E. Gillmann

The sessions of the congregations in Dickenschied and Womrath once again do not remain silent in relation to the state authorities and declare their allegiance to their pastor.

The sessions of the congregations in
Dickenschied/Womrath

Dickenschied, October 13, 1937
(near Kirchberg/Hunsrück)

To the Reich and Prussian minister of the interior
Berlin

Before his return, which occurred at our request, our Pastor Schneider addressed a petition to the Reich Chancellery—the date was September 30. A copy of this petition was also sent to the Reich minister and the Prussian minister of the interior.

On the Sunday of his return, October 3, before eight o'clock in the evening Pastor Schneider was again taken into preventive detention on the way to his yoked congregation. He was first brought to Kirchberg in police custody. On Monday he was taken to the Gestapo prison in Koblenz, Vogelsang I. We lack any further news.

We make the petition of our pastor from September 30 and its contents fully our own. We especially want to point out that our congregations have been without a pastor since March of this year, having had to make do in our worship services with substitute pastors from the surrounding area. The sick could not be visited on a regular basis and the confirmands have not received any regular instruction etc.

We ask the Reich and Prussian minister of the interior to give us back our pastor soon.

Peter Klos, Jakob Scherer
Heinrich Diener, Peter Auler
Adolf Müller, Jakob Fuchs

The session of the Evangelical-Reformed Church in Dickenschied writes another report to the consistory:

> Our Pastor Paul Schneider has been in preventive detention again in Koblenz since October 3 of this year (Thanksgiving), as everyone knows. Pastor Schneider has been the pastor of our congregation and the congregation in Womrath since April 1, 1934. He has administered his office with great love and enthusiasm. The congregations are very satisfied with Pastor Schneider, apart from a few exceptions. Repeated, untruthful reports made to the party and local authorities by people who did this out of personal spitefulness intended to label Pastor Schneider as an enemy of the state. These individuals have been rather successful in doing this.

> We who serve on the session and almost the whole congregation with us, even the Catholic parish and the populace of the whole Hunsrück, who know Pastor Schneider, are of the view that he has not committed any acts that are hostile to the state, but every time has only courageously stood up for the pure doctrine of the gospel. In almost every worship service he has prayed for the Führer and his associates. He does not recognize and we also do not recognize the deportation from the Rhineland that was imposed on Pastor Schneider by the Gestapo without any reason after spending eight weeks in preventive detention in June and July of this year.

> If Pastor Schneider has now decided to resume his ministry among us after being separated several months from his congregations and his family (his wife and six little children), he has not done anything wrong. The congregations are greatly concerned and upset about the fate of their faithful pastor and hope that he can soon return again to his congregations.

The session of the
Evangelical-Reformed Church
Dickenschied, Hunsrück
Klos Diener Müller

The record of the interrogation made by the Gestapo in Koblenz (and copied with a pencil by Paul Schneider in his prison cell in Koblenz) clearly shows the injustice the organs of the state committed in their intoxication with power:

Copy

Responsibly questioned, Pastor Schneider from Dickenschied, born on August 29, 1897, gives the following information on his detention from May 31 to July 24, 1937, on his deportation from the Rhineland that occurred on July 24th and on being arrested again on October 3, 1937:

I sat in the prison of the Gestapo Koblenz, Vogelsang I for almost eight weeks of preventive detention. During this time they could not prove that the government was right in making the very serious accusations found in the preventive detention order—disturbance of the public safety and order—a charge seen by the legislature in terms of incitement to public rebellion. In particular, they did not bring me to trial. I was denied legal protection against the dishonorable punishment of an eight-week long detention under prison rules. But preventive detention is and can only be a preventive and temporary measure.

Yet in spite of the long duration of the preventive detention, in which my health was seriously endangered, and in spite of the absence of any legal protection to ascertain the offense, the preventive detention was ended with an almost even more serious punishment, my deportation from the Rhineland.

I explained at the deportation hearing that for the reasons mentioned above I had to view my preventive detention as a measure taken only to persecute the Confessing Church and thus had to consider it unjust and untrue. To demonstrate this injustice, I tore up the order for my preventive detention. For the reasons mentioned above I declared that

I did not intend to recognize or accept the deportation. Then they produced a receipt of the deportation order and shoved it into my hands, on the grounds that this was only a formal matter and that I could do with it whatever I wanted later. So I also tore up the receipt in Wiesbaden after my release.

I immediately returned to my congregations in keeping with the declaration I made in Koblenz and preached on Sunday, July 25th. In this way I demonstrated to my congregations that I was and would remain their pastor.

To protect my health and fully heal my broken leg from March 19, 1937 I took a rather long vacation that I spent outside the Rhineland. By taking this rest in between I wanted to give the offices of the Gestapo an opportunity to become reconciled with my stance on this issue that I clearly expressed when I was deported.

On Friday, October 1, I informed the Reich chancellery, the interior ministry and the provincial governor in Koblenz by certified letter that I could not obey the deportation order of the Gestapo. I gave them detailed reasons why I could not obey it based on my conscience that was captive to God's Word and will, and also cited several points that seem noteworthy to me in the outward interests of the church and for political reasons.

On October 3 I returned from vacation and resumed my ministry with the thanksgiving sermon in Dickenschied. I was arrested again even before I could perform my second official duty, an evening worship service in Womrath. The congregation had not had any worship service the whole day. The Sabbath rest of the congregation and its Sunday observance of hearing and learning the divine Word were grossly violated in this way.

I accepted the preventive detention on May 31 and a few days later took the order for the preventive detention and for eight weeks willingly submitted to the penalty imposed on me. I will also willingly bear what ultimately not human beings, but God, imposes on me and will not become an agitator. But it is clear to me that I cannot recognize or accept another preventive detention since the legitimacy of the first one was by no means proven. I cannot even create the impression of recognizing or accepting the preventive detention as lawful by accepting the order for another preventive detention.

On October 5 I signed the record of the objective report on my person and the two sermons I gave in my congregations in front of the inspector. Already on this occasion I referred to my petition addressed to the higher state authorities. I hereby do this again and ask either for my release so that I may have an unhindered ministry as the pastor of my congregations or for the opportunity to be taken to a proper German court where my guilt or innocence on the charge of disturbing the peace can be determined.

(Signature)

26

THE DIE IS CAST: BUCHENWALD

The petitions and reports go unheeded. Paul Schneider is put in the Buchenwald concentration camp on the Saturday before the first Sunday in Advent 1937. Before this happens he writes to his wife:

November 24, 1937

Now it seems as if the die has been cast. I am going to be sent to a camp, it does not matter whether it is a concentration camp or a detention camp. We are supposed to receive humane treatment and be able to keep in touch with our family members . . . make the congregations as independent as possible—I do not know the reason for this sudden turn of events. I presume that these decisions of a general nature were made at a higher level. What should I advise you to do now? From the outside it is so easy to give such cheap advice. I foresee a time when every sincere Christian will be compelled to openly confess and freely declare their faith. It will soon be your turn on account of our children. Then remember: "It is better to relinquish all creation than in the least thing to act against God's will," and at the same time trust the promise: "Whoever fears God has a secure refuge, and his children will also be shielded." Let us not go along with the tragedy of so many Christian parents. Remain loyal to the church . . . . God will give you the strength, my love, to go the right way. In all things always ask God for advice in all things first before you ask human beings; even our best friends will often not give us the right advise. The churches in Thuringia (Buchenwald) as well will stay as close to my heart as they were here in Koblenz . . . .

Mr. and Mrs. M. from O. are also going to be "transported" at the same time. I will go to the same camp with Mr. M. Yes, we will be put together with sectarians there. Yet surely we are called to serve one another. Mrs. M is in good spirits now after having endured many difficult hours and she is also more peaceful. Please give our friends and brothers my warm regards. Now we should not have high regard for our lives, knowing that the wolf has already forced his way into our flocks and lusts for the souls of our people and above all, for the souls of our young people. May the Lord not find us to be half-hearted! Wherever there are hirelings, the wolf catches and scatters the sheep. Let us remember, dearest, our afflictions are temporal and light and achieve for us an eternal glory that is important beyond all measure.

Our children belong to God through our faith and their baptism into Christ. Our faithful Lord will protect them body and soul.

Paul Schneider's wife remarks:

Paul was still able to write parting words to his children, our maid, old Sophie, and assistant pastor Kemper. Here is a quote from his letter to Kemper: "When you see the brothers and send them my regards, then ask them for me to do something now for God's sake and to step before their congregations, filling the breach with their most personal and ultimate commitment, and fight the spirit of abominable seduction and idolatry that has set out to seize power. It has already done so, even gaining intellectual and spiritual power over the people. Nothing will be salvaged any longer with all "wisdom" and "prudence"; rather what is left will also be lost. Just look at the bankruptcy of many colleagues in their congregations! In this situation everyone must now risk their life as well, otherwise they cannot gain it.

Mrs. Schneider stands up for her husband and after due consideration turns to various state authorities for help in gaining his release.

Margarete Schneider Dickenschied, January 8, 1938

Wife of Pastor Paul Schneider, presently detained in the concentration camp of Buchenwald near Weimar.

As the mother of six underage children (1/2 to ten years old), I would like to make the following request of you:

My husband has been in the Buchenwald concentration camp near Weimar since November 28, 1937 since as a Protestant pastor and an ordained servant of the divine Word, he could not accept the deportation from the whole Rhineland that was imposed on him, acting in obedience to the Holy Scriptures and the confession of our fathers. He himself gave detailed reasons for this in a lengthy letter that he wrote to the highest authorities (the Reich chancellery, and the Reich interior ministry) before he returned to his congregation on October 3. On the same evening he was arrested and taken to Koblenz in response to a report a woman made to the police—the rest of the congregation acted calmly. My husband is the pastor of two small Hunsrück congregations with a combined membership of 500 souls (5 kilometers from the rail line). He was assigned to them and has been called to proclaim the gospel to these congregations and to be vigilant in ensuring that God's Word is clearly and purely proclaimed and that they live according to it. He did this until his first arrest in May 1937, and on account of God's Word he was challenged by a few people in his congregation and finally reported to the police since they had no appreciation for the message of God's kingdom. The main reason they were offended was because of his uncompromising practice of Christian discipline on the basis of our book of confession, the Heidelberg Catechism, question 85. I can testify to the fact that during his whole ministry my husband has scrupulously guarded this point of Christian doctrine beginning in 1926—long before this church dispute arose. He has had to suffer many trials because of it.

The sessions of our two small congregations stand united behind him and in a letter addressed to the interior ministry dated June 8, 1937 they explained that they were very satisfied with the ministry of my husband and wanted him to return as their pastor. In addition, the great majority of the members of both congregations stand behind my husband and they have demonstrated this by signing a petition on his behalf (the lists of signatures were partially confiscated by the Gestapo). The church can testify that their pastor has lived with his poor farmers through times of both sorrow and joy in a genuine spirit of community and has stood by them, willing to help them in all things. As someone who was born in the Hunsrück, the Hunsrück has become his home and the home of his family. It would be very difficult for us to separate ourselves from it. Only a very few, who have given offense to the congregation by their walk, stand against him.

Since my husband as the pastor of these two small Hunsrück churches would never think of disturbing the peace and order of the Rhineland and has on principle always rejected the idea of being politically active (he went into battle as a war volunteer, having served three and a half years at the front; he is also a former officer, and having been wounded in action, he became a knight of the Iron Cross; his nationalistic views have surely been sufficiently proven by this distinguished record of service). Since he has been instructed to proclaim God's Word alone for the well-being and salvation of our fatherland, I sincerely request that you rescind the deportation order issued against my husband or cause it to be rescinded and release him so that he can return to his church and family.

I make this request with a serious concern for my husband's health. From March 19, 1937 to March 28, 1937 he was in the hospital for a complicated fracture of his lower thigh. When he was discharged from the hospital, his leg was not yet healed. As recently as October 1, 1937 the doctor sent by our car insurance company to examine Paul discovered that his leg was still 40 percent damaged.

(Signature)

The Nazi authorities close their mind to this letter. The Gestapo, as a power within the state that is independent of court decisions, continues to detain Paul Schneider in the concentration camp. The German-Christian consistory in Düsseldorf does not pay any attention to its Rhenish pastor—it drops him.

Mrs. Schneider does not give up. She drives to Berlin and stays for the better part of a week at the home of Superintendent Diestel. Six times she lodges a complaint with the Central Reich security office of the SS on Prince Albrecht Street 6. Five times she is put off with flimsy excuses: They told her that the file was temporarily not available, or that they could not say anything without the boss, who was absent. On her sixth visit a case worker at the SS central office for church affairs who passes himself off as a pastor's son, suggests to her that she should submit a declaration of loyalty to the present state in writing; he told her it could favorably influence the way things were handled. Her written declaration reads:

> My husband and I are in agreement that we recognize the validity of this biblical verse for us as well: "Everyone must submit himself to the governing authorities" (Rm. 13:1 NIV). We are not enemies of the state. We can also furnish evidence of this. However, we can also not recognize the deportation as lawful because it is based on malicious slander, and we ask that it be rescinded. Our congregation is fully in agreement with us on this point, as you can see from the letter I have enclosed. We believe we have no right to break trust with our congregation. During his solemn installation service my husband promised to be a faithful shepherd of the congregation, and feels bound by his conscience to keep this promise. For the sake of this faithfulness he has borne the charge of being disobedient and has willingly and without bitterness taken the punishment upon himself.
>
> We are willing to prove that we respect the laws of the state and are obedient to them. I know that my husband wants to do nothing but faithfully fulfil his duty of proclaiming the gospel to his congregations.
>
> Margarete Schneider

Kurt Scharf, who was later to become a president and bishop in the Protestant Church, personally submits this declaration to the central office of the SS. The caseworker for church affairs comments on it with these words: "Always the same thing . . . !"[1]

Pastor Fritz Langensiepen tries to help his friend and writes from Berlin to an influential acquaintance (the recipient of the letter was probably legation counselor first class Walther Hewel, who was a permanent representative of the Reich foreign minister with Hitler as assistant head of the department):

---

[1] Such petitions were not unproblematic in those days because the Nazi authorities linked the processing of the petition to a declaration of loyalty for one's conduct. Of course, Mrs. Schneider could not make such a declaration. Compare *Prediger*, p. 78.

Berlin, July 1938

Dear Mr. Hewel,

For the sake of an old friendship that has bound our families together
for many years, may I be so bold as to make a request of you.

It concerns Pastor Paul Schneider from Dickenschied in the Hunsrück
who is still in the concentration camp of Buchenwald/Weimar today.
A trial against Pastor Schneider on the charges of violating the pulpit
paragraph and the Treachery Act was pending at the special court in
Cologne. On June 10, 1938 this trial was abandoned on the basis of the
law granting immunity from prosecution at the expense of the national
treasury.

The reason for the arrest of Paul Schneider on May 31, 1937 was
the following: The small congregation of Dickenschied-Womrath is
unified. A few members of this congregation have been trying for years
to destroy this church unity. This caused offense in the congregation.
The leadership of the church, the session, thus felt compelled to exercise
discipline in accordance with the church's confession. The three
members were excluded from Holy Communion by the session until
they promised to "lead a better life" (Heidelberg Catechism, Question
85). The decision was only made after the pastor had first paid them a
pastoral visit and admonished them.

One of these members interpreted this measure of the session as a
"boycott." He reported it to the police and Pastor Schneider was taken
into preventive detention without any questioning. The decision of the
session had been announced to the congregation at the beginning of
March 1937, the arrest followed on May 31, 1937. In the meantime he
had had a serious accident in which he injured his leg (a complicated
fracture of the lower thigh). The arrest was made a few days after he
had been discharged from the hospital, incidentally fourteen days
after the birth of their sixth child, whose baptism had to occur in the
absence of the father.

Pastor Schneider spent eight weeks in the prison of the Gestapo in
Koblenz. Then it was revealed to him that he was being deported

from the whole Rhineland without even once being able to explain his viewpoint on the contested church discipline. He was told that the deportation order had been issued because he had "disturbed the public peace and safety of the Rhineland." It must not be forgotten that the community of Dickenschied is located in a very isolated area of the Hunsrück, five kilometers from the nearest little train station.

The legal protection Pastor Schneider requested was also denied to him. They merely handed him the deportation order that he had to reject since he could not just admit that he was a troublemaker. In addition, his health had suffered considerably from the first detention—the effects of the accident became even more noticeable. It must also not be forgotten that the dishonorable punishment cut him to the quick— Pastor Schneider went to war as a volunteer, was wounded, still carries the bullet in his abdomen today, was awarded the Iron Cross and returned from the war as an officer.

After Pastor Schneider had once again preached in his church, he took a necessary convalescent leave. In September 1937 the session of his congregation called on its lawful pastor to return to the church after having had to do without his ministry for several months and after the session and the great majority of the congregation had given him their full confidence, especially since Pastor Schneider took his official duties seriously.

Pastor Schneider then declared in a petition of September 30, 1937 to the Reich chancellery, the interior ministry and the provincial governor why he would return to his congregation. In his petition he emphasized that he was loyally committed to his congregation and that he was obligated to serve it by having solemnly taken a vow in front of the congregation. Pastor Schneider was also born in the Hunsrück and feels deeply attached to his home, as do his six children.

After he had preached again in his church on October 3, 1937, he was arrested again on the evening of the same day and was first taken to the prison in Koblenz for eight weeks. When he then did not feel able to accept the deportation, he was taken to the concentration camp on November 28, 1937 where he still is today. Even today he is still being given the option of deciding to accept the deportation, but he is not able to do so for the reasons described above. During the last three months he has only been allowed to write to his wife once a month and until now he has still not been allowed to receive any visits from his wife in the concentration camp.

Without any legal protection and without any court trial Pastor Schneider has already been held eight months in the concentration camp on the basis of a mere report to the police made by a spiteful enemy. Is an upright German man simply to be worn down and brought to his wife and his six children as a timeserver?

I would be deeply grateful to you if you would do your best to help secure the release of the pastor.

Sincerely Yours,
Fritz Langensiepen

The answer he hoped for does not come. The personal file of Paul Schneider is still the business of the consistory in Düsseldorf.

Protestant Consistory Düsseldorf, June 11, 1938
Nr. 448
To the Administrative Office of the Protestant Church
Berlin-Charlottenburg

Concerning: Pastor Schneider, Dickenschied
Dossier: the last decree from the 4th of this month-EO III 2466/38
Reporter: Junior court clerk Kolrep

Our repeated attempts to get a report on Pastor Schneider, Dickenschied, from the superintendent responsible for his case, Ernst Gillmann, have failed so far. Our caseworker expressed our concern about this when he spoke to your administrative office. The Gestapo informed the undersigned that Pastor Schneider is still in a concentration camp and his release promised for Christmas failed to materialize because he refused to sign a statement they submitted to him concerning his further conduct.

Rossler. Sinnig May 19, Kolrep May 15

The introductory remark shows how the consistory wanted to blame its indifference and uncertainty on the superintendent of the Simmern synod, Ernst Gillmann. Apparently it had forgotten or not taken notice of his report from October 5, 1937, Tgb.-Nr. 475/37 because such a petition would have inevitably caused them to draw serious consequences from it. For his part Superintendent Gillmann could have no interest in seeing a consistory packed with "German Christians" and National Socialists intervene in the internal affairs of the congregation in view of the confessional stance of the great majority of members in Dickenschied and Womrath.

In this context the next letter is of particular significance. It shows how the consistory sought to expand its influence and its own power without regard to the church. Düsseldorf took the initiative in proposing new church "enabling acts" to the administrative office in Berlin with the goal of deterrence and the use of force. These new laws were signed by Dr. Werner, the president of the church chancellery of the highest Protestant administrative office in Berlin and could be printed in the church's official gazette for the Rhine province as early as March 31, 1939. The following documentation will show what consequences these new laws had even before they went into effect.

The indifference of the Düsseldof consistory in handling the "case of Paul Schneider" is proven by the fact that it got in touch with the church's highest administrative office in Berlin only on June 11, 1938 and then again on September 7, 1938 although Paul Schneider had already been held in the Buchenwald concentration camp since November 1937. This circumstance as well as the way all the church authorities handled the case not only shows the indifference of the consistory and the church's highest administrative office, but also proves how these institutions were infiltrated by the National Socialist ideology.

The teamwork between the Gestapo and the Protestant consistory is one of the darkest chapters in the history of the Protestant Church in Germany.

Protestant Consistory September 7, 1938
4480 II
To the Highest Administrative Office of the Protestant Church
Berlin-Charlottenburg

Concerning: Pastor Schneider in Dickenschied
Without Decree
Reporter: Consistory junior clerk Kolrep

Consistory member D. Euler

With reference to our report made on June 11, 1938 we can now considerably supplement it on the basis of the notification issued to us by the Gestapo in Koblenz. According to the Gestapo Pastor Schneider has been in the concentration camp of Buchenwald near Weimar since November 25, 1937 and even today is still refusing to follow the orders of the state in spite of repeated questioning. Furthermore, a travel ban in the Rhine province has been imposed on Pastor Schneider. The confessional assistant pastor Kemper is temporarily officiating in his place in Dickenschied.

Both the Gestapo as well as the district leadership of the NSDAP in Koblenz-Trier have approached us about quickly transferring Pastor Schneider. In response, we first asked them to send us the legal files on Pastor Schneider so that we can initiate disciplinary proceedings against him. But we have not left the aforementioned authorities in doubt about the fact that we definitely consider it imperative to transfer the pastor because there is no other way to eliminate the political difficulties in Dickenschied. However, our present efforts are mainly focused on achieving a voluntary transfer of Schneider through appropriate negotiations. For this purpose we will take the opportunity to get in touch with the local authorities in the coming weeks and will also avail ourselves of the services of the local superintendent who would mediate in this case. We will report on the results of these efforts.

Finally, in this context, please allow us to make the suggestion that the case of Schneider as well as the trouble caused by the conduct of Pastor Boysen in Cologne-Lindenthal clearly demonstrate the necessity of offering the possibility of making it easier to take care of all such cases that can not be resolved satisfactorily in any other way by quite soon issuing a ruling on the transfer of pastors into temporary retirement. In such cases the main difficulty of finding another suitable parish for the pastors involved in a transfer would cease to apply.

Sinnig September 24 Euler September 23
Kolrep September 27

Mrs. Schneider, who was very close to Superintendent Martin Albertz and his wife Marianne, receives the following sympathetic letter from the Council of the Confessing Church in the Mark Brandenburg:

The Council of the Confessing Church
Berlin SW 42,
Dec. 26, 1938
in the Mark Brandenburg
Alexandrinen Street 101
Telephone: 173172

Dear Mrs. Schneider!

Your detailed letter to Mrs. Albertz and the quotes in it were deeply moving to me. May the Lord continue to give you both enough strength and patience to bear this particular trial.

You have probably heard by now that the application of the Rhenish Council for permission to speak to your husband has been rejected for the time being. Brother Schlingensiepen has been asked to submit in writing to the head of the local Gestapo office what he would like to discuss with your husband. I want to personally try to explain to the Gestapo officer, possibly today or tomorrow, that this is hardly possible. One can really have a pastoral influence on another person only if one sees him and his condition and hears him in person. I think it is a good idea that you, dear Mrs. Schneider, also apply for permission to speak to your husband yourself, independent of the Rhenish Council's attempt. In doing so, feel free to refer to Mrs. Niemöller and the routine that is followed there. That will not harm brother Niemöller at all. You probably know that Mrs. Niemöller has now received general permission to see her husband once a month at the police headquarters on Alexander Square and to take along one of the children each time. This can become known. It has been officially mentioned to various church delegations as evidence of the friendly way they are being treated. So it will not hurt if you refer to it.

Please address your petition to the Gestapo office, Berlin SW 11, Prince-Albrecht Street 8, and Department II B 2, booking number

873/73E. As soon as I know that you have made your application, I will personally inquire.

In sincere solidarity I send you my warm regards,
Your faithful,
(Scharf)

Although the Niemöller family was hit hard by the arrest of their father and uncle, their thoughts nevertheless went out to all those who were deprived of their freedom by the Gestapo. The children took pen in hand and wrote:

Dear Mr. Hitler!

We are very happy to have the privilege of writing our first letter to you, to which we add a request, namely the following request: We already know a lot about the church situation and would thus like to ask you to help our father and uncle (Pastor Niemöller, Dahlem) because he has been suffering innocently for over a year. Please help other pastors as well, especially Schneider (Dickenschied). Mrs. Niemöller and the other Confessing Church people are suffering very much because of this. We know what it is like to have no father. We miss him in so many ways. You can certainly understand us.

We greet you with a German salute!
(Signatures)

Herta Niemöller, the daughter of Martin Niemöller, and her ten year-old cousin Wilhelm Günther Niemöller, wrote this letter.

Within the Confessing Church of Germany intercessory prayer lists were passed around:

Protestant Confessing Synod Wuppertal-Barmen, Sept. 15, 1938
in the Rhineland
Intercessory Prayer List
(as of September 15, 1938)

I. The following men are in concentration camps:
    1. Pastor Schneider—Dickenschied/ Rhineland

2. Pastor Martin Niemöller—Berlin/Dahlem

3. Mr. Leikam, an intern in a notary's office—
Korb/Württemberg

4. Mr. Thiessies, businessman—
Altroggenrahmede/Westphalia

II. The following men are in preventive detention

5. Pastor Lucking—Dortmund

6. Mr. Suppert, businessman—Dortmund

7. Mr. Lohmeyer—Dortmund

8. Dr. Schmidt, an attorney—Dortmund

9. Pastor Krause—Kriescht/Neumark

III. 93 restraining orders, two expulsions, eleven travel bans, 39 men banned from staying in certain parts of the country, 37 men banned from speaking in public, 48 deportations.

Lord Jesus Christ, you have told your church that your disciples must suffer much for the sake of Your name; for the disciple is not above his master. Give your church a joyful faith so that they may sincerely thank you for all the suffering You allow to come over them and so that they may wholeheartedly worship you. But give all who are persecuted the ability to accept and recognize their suffering as your divine will, to remain strong in body and soul, not to deny You, but rather to praise you in all things. Please let their suffering come to an end soon and let them have justice. For you guide the hearts of all human beings like streams of water and can surely inspire those in power to let your children live in peace.

We praise you for the sake of your grace and faithfulness, by which you uphold and preserve your church. May Your name be praised throughout all eternity! Amen.

The informers from Womrath continue to cause trouble. Superintendent Gillmann receives the following dossier from the consistory:

Protestant Consistory Düsseldorf, June 27, 1938
of the Rhine Province Island Street 10
Nr. 4259

To the Superintendent in Simmern
2 enclosures (to be returned)

Enclosed we are sending you, Mr. Superintendent, a petition from Jakob Stumm and Erst Scherer from Womrath for your attention. Therefore, we ask you to give us a detailed report on this matter after hearing the session and its deputy chairman by July 10 of this year. On what order is the use of church discipline in the case of Stumm and Scherer based? We call your attention to the fact that the Heidelberg Catechism, irrespective of its character as a binding confession for the Reformed church within our provincial church, does not constitute an immediate norm to regulate the procedure used in imposing church discipline. On what facts was the use of church discipline based in the two cases mentioned here? Did those who were disciplined take steps to lodge a complaint with the session or the board of the district synod against the disciplinary measures imposed on them? Did the session rescind or modify the measures imposed on Stumm and Scherer after the departure of Pastor Schneider? We will use this opportunity to inform you that our financial department has promised to initiate an audit of church funds and bookkeeping in the Dickenschied and Womrath congregations in the near future.

Enclosures! Dr. Koch

Womrath, May 1, 1938

To the Protestant Consistory
in Düsseldorf, Island Street

Concerning: the complaint 1.of the farmer Friedrich Jakob Stumm and 2.of the farmer Ernst Adolf Scherer, both in Womrath, against the Protestant session in Womrath (the parish of Dickenschied)

1. I, Friedrich Jakob Stumm, have had ill feelings since my wedding in 1924 because my wife is Catholic and I am Protestant. Immediately after my wedding I was deprived of my church rights but the church taxes were demanded from me, and I also paid them up to and including 1934. Since I heard a speech of the Führer on the radio, declaring that

there are now only mixed marriages between Germans and Jews, but no longer between Aryans of different denominations, I refused to pay the church taxes. What makes it worse is that the session in Womrath with Pastor Schneider no longer wants to send the money to the consistory, but to the Brotherhood Council. Another reason I refuse to pay is that the session (including Pastor Schneider) have expressly declared their allegiance to the Brotherhood Council by carrying green membership cards which bear the signatures of the Brotherhood Council, Pastor Schneider and Jakob Fuchs.

2. The following reason applies to me, Ernst Scherer:

In December 1936 Pastor Schneider came from Dickenschied to my home in Womrath and revealed to me that he intended to expel me from the congregation because I was a lazy member, because I did not go to church and attend his worship services. This happened because he made attacks on the party and state in a covert way, which I could not accept as a National Socialist. On March 12, 1937 Pastor Schneider imposed church discipline on me, which had been announced from the pulpit in the church of Womrath. I am enclosing a copy of this letter. For this reason I refused to pay the church taxes.

As soon as what was said is taken back from the pulpit in Womrath, I am willing to pay all the back taxes, however, not to the Brotherhood Council, but to the consistory. If I am not given the right to do this, I will be compelled to leave the Protestant Church, unless I am assigned to a different congregation.

On April 28, 1938 assets were seized from the two of us because we were behind in paying church taxes for the years 1935/36 and 1937/38. In response we asked the tax office in Simmern to stop the seizure of our assets until this unresolved matter is settled.

We ask to be notified whether we have to pay the outstanding church taxes to the tax office now or whether a stoppage of the seizure can be secured from there until our matter is clarified.

We further ask to have the church funds from Womrath and Dickenschied audited by a certified auditor because we as well as others have doubts about its correctness.

Then we would like to also ask whether the Protestant congregation in Womrath has declared its allegiance to the Old Prussian Union? If this is true, then we ask whether the consistory has ordered prayers to be said during the worship service for Pastor Schneider, his wife and Pastor Niemöller, Berlin by the pastoral assistant Kemper and further, whether it has been decreed that today only one bell is to be rung for the worship service whereas this had previously been done with the three available bells.

We ask you to send us news soon; otherwise we will have to turn to the highest authority for help.

Heil Hitler!
Friedrich Jakob Stumm
Ernst Scherer

The following facts can be mentioned in response to the accusations that were made:

1. In 1924 Paul Schneider was not yet the pastor of Dickenschied and Womrath.

2. It is obvious that the initiative to draw up this petition had come from the functionaries of the radical "German Christians," for whom the unity of the "Confessing Church" of Dickenschied and Womrath had to be a thorn in the flesh.

3. They wanted to shake the congregation's confidence in the session; this could most easily be achieved by raising the suspicion that it had made illegal financial transactions.

4. Paul Schneider had already taken a position on the accusation made by Ernst Scherer.

5. At the end of the letter the spirit guiding the two persons who lodged the complaint can be clearly seen. They failed in their project of sowing distrust in the church; the congregations continue to see Paul Schneider as their lawful pastor.

6. President Humburg remitted the church tax revenue in Dickenschied and Womrath to the consistory in Düsseldorf by way of the Confessing Church's account. The examination of the respective church funds of the congregations in Dickenschied and Womrath raised no objections to their handling of the church's finances.

During this time Paul Schneider has already been in the notorious detention bunker in solitary confinement for several months because of his refusal to salute the swastika. In the detention bunker he becomes the pastor of Buchenwald as he endures the most severe mental torment and physical torture. A report testifies to what his fellow sufferers reported again and again.

Report
Concerning: Inmate Paul Schneider
Reference: without
Enclosures: none

To the Headquarters of the Concentration Camp
Buchenwald

The inmate Paul Schneider, born August 29, 1897 in Pferdsfeld, at present in solitary confinement, showed unbelievable behavior on August 28, 1938. Around 6:30 in the morning, during the morning report to me on the number of inmates in the camp, Schneider suddenly opened his cell window, and climbed up in his cell until his field of vision enabled him to clearly see the inmates who had lined up for roll call. In a loud voice Schneider preached to the lined-up inmates for about two minutes. He completely ignored my command to immediately stop preaching and to get away from the window. After that I gave the solitary confinement administrator the command to take Schneider away from the window by force.

I immediately reported this incident to the camp commander.

The 2. ranking camp leader for detaineees.
Signed (signature)
SS-Oberscharführer

The ordeal that is concealed behind such a report cannot be conveyed to the reader in a way that would enable him or her to understand this indescribable, horrendous experience.

An embarrassing administrative episode now interrupts the flow of our story; it shows how institutional bodies can be active in their own cause with great amounts of correspondence and supposed astuteness.

A letter of the Gestapo had fallen into the hands of the Confessing Church and was published by it. This incident led to a rather lengthy correspondence and various discussions between the Gestapo and the consistory.

The President of the consistory, Dr. Koch, who could be called a National Socialist who was loyal to the party line, initiated an extensive investigation and afterwards informed the Gestapo of its results:

The Consistory President Düsseldorf, January 17, 1939
-13890-
To the Gestapo
-the Gestapo office-
in Koblenz

Concerning: Pastor Schneider from Dickenschied

Following our letter of December 22, 1938-Nr. 4480 III-and with reference to the discussion that occurred on the 7th of this month, with Reich office manager Sohns and the undersigned participating, permit me most respectfully to give a concluding summary of the results of our investigations in the matter mentioned above. During the investigation of the question of how it could be explained that your letter of September 24, 1937-II B 355/37, at least a considerable part of it, was printed word for word in a brochure of the Confessional front, we first examined whether such a lead could be discovered within my office. This examination produced the following evidence: A copy of your letter dated October 6, 1937-Nr. 11226-was sent to the appropriate superintendent, Gillmann, in Simmern for his perusal and with the simultaneous request that he report on how the church in Dickenschied was being provided for. The order was signed by the following gentlemen who had previously served on the staff of the consistory: Judge Lengler as the case worker and author of the order, consistory member Hasenkamp as the theological case worker, general superintendent D. Stoltenhoff as co-signer, consistory member Spiess, who made the final signature, and finally, consistory member Dr. Jung, who put his endorsement on it as the office manager at that time. All the co-signers have left their jobs in my office with the exception of consistory member Spiess, who at my request made an official statement that he could not give any information about this incident and that he also had no idea how the aforementioned document could have ended up in the public eye. Since these men are no longer here, they cannot be called on to help solve this case. Furthermore, I also asked the registrars and all the consultants who were employed here at that time to make a statement about this matter without this effort yielding any clues.

As I already indicated during the discussion in Koblenz, the possibility that a visitor in the consistory office happened to gain unauthorized access to your letter and used this opportunity to immediately make a copy of it for later use can still not be rejected out of hand. However, a mere conjecture does not speak for either such a possibility or for the idea that such an indiscretion was committed by an official of the previous or present consistory. In any case, the observations I have made thus far cannot substantiate any suspicion pointing in the direction of this office.

It seems more likely that the solution points in a different direction. The fact that a copy was sent to Superintendent Gillman without my approval could give us further insight. I immediately asked him to make an official statement, which produced the following result. Gillmann says that he did not let the document out of his hands nor did he let anyone else peruse it, thus no one would have been able to make a copy. He said that there was no reason for him and his supporters (the confessional front) to pass it on because these incidents were already well known. According to the information provided by Gillmann the letter was put under lock and key without a file number. Thus Gillmann feels he is unable to make a statement on how this letter became known in confessional circles.

Although I have no reason to doubt the truth of Gillmann's explanation, I still have the suspicion that your letter found its way into the public eye from this office. It may well be that Superintendent Gillmann himself endeavored to take the document into safekeeping, which probably did not happen immediately. Therefore, it is easy to imagine that one of his frequent visitors had the opportunity to examine the letter. It could have been a person who had a special opportunity to take a look at the files as a result of his official position and in this way learned about the document. Therefore, my strong suspicion is centered on Pastor Kalthoff from the church in Horn, who is also a synod judge and is known to visit the manse quite often. With his close relationships to the confessional front I definitely believe he is capable of making such use of your letter if in fact he had learned about it. However, I have no evidence that he acted in this way and in spite of further investigations I do not think that we could produce such evidence. The possibility cannot be denied that perhaps another visitor who can no longer be discovered is responsible after all. During the time in question Superintendent Gillmann did not have any interns, so that no hint of the culprit can be derived from this source either. In any case, the composition of the pamphlet that deals extensively with Pastor Schneider-Dickenschied indicates that the trail of your letter that has fallen into the wrong hands almost surely points to Simmern, owing to the particularly strong interest that the Hunsrück shows in this matter.

To my regret the investigations we have conducted have not brought about a conclusive resolution of this case, which probably has something to do with the fact that the incident took place rather long ago. Unfortunately, I am somewhat dependent on mere assumptions but the suspicion I mentioned last appears to be the most plausible. However, any grounds for assuming that a member of my office was involved in this unpleasant incident have not been found. I am especially privileged to make this observation for my present office staff. Perhaps there is still a possibility of finding the solution to the puzzle by finding the names of those who wrote the pamphlet. Nevertheless, in conclusion permit me to add the remark that only a single regrettable incident is at issue here compared to the numerous confidential letters whose character has been strictly maintained. So now we can guarantee that you will not have to fear a repetition of this case.

Dr. Koch
For the attention of Reich office manager Sohns

This letter speaks for itself and shows how far a church institution had devoted itself to the forces arrayed against the church. At another point in our story it will become even more horribly clear what the alliance between the Gestapo and the consistory was capable of doing. It is obvious that Paul Schneider could expect no understanding, let alone help, from the consistory that was led by National Socialists.

A quite different letter is sent to the authorities in Berlin by the two sessions in Dickenschied and Womrath.

The sessions of the yoked
congregations of Dickenschied and Womrath
in the Hunsrück Dickenschied, March 10, 1939

To the Gestapo
Berlin SW 11
Prince-Albrecht-Street 8
Department II B 2
Booking Number 873/37E.

Concerning: A request to rescind the deportation order issued against our Pastor Paul Schneider and to release the detainee

We as the representatives of the yoked Protestant congregation of Dickenschied-Womrath in the Hunsrück repeat the request we made to the Gestapo central office on September 27, 1938 to release our pastor Paul Schneider who is still in the concentration camp of Buchenwald/Weimar today so that he can return to his congregations of Dickenschied and Womrath.

It will soon be 1½ years ago that our Pastor Schneider was arrested and removed from our congregations. He has already been in the concentration camp of Buchenwald/Weimar for one year and three months. He was arrested then because of a purely internal church affair and that is why a deportation order was also issued against him. The special court in Cologne dropped all other proceedings against him on the basis of the amnesty of April 30, 1938 since "no higher sentence or total prison sentence of six months was to be expected." Therefore, since the proceedings against our Pastor Schneider by the special court in Cologne have been dropped, i.e., he was given amnesty, we repeat our request to the Gestapo central office in Berlin to investigate the matter of our pastor again. We testify that our Pastor Schneider conscientiously performed the duties of his ministry and never incited the congregation or us to oppose the government. The pain and anxiety we feel over the fate of our pastor has been weighing on us and on his congregations since his arrest, for he remains faithful to his congregations and has proven this faithfulness by his deeds. Also the great majority of the congregations, including the Catholic populace, stands by our Pastor Schneider and is requesting his return. We also urgently implore the Gestapo head office to confer with the town council (the representation of the civil community) of Dickenschied, and possibly with the local group leader (the political leader) about the return of our pastor, since these men can also testify that law and order has prevailed and still prevails today in our communities and that nothing any longer stands in the way of Pastor Schneider's return. We once again ask that you rescind the deportation order issued against our pastor and release him.

(Signatures)

Mrs. Schneider keeps trying to secure the release of her husband, but at least to receive permission to talk to him. She calls on an attorney to look after their interests.

Dr. Schulze zur Wiesche Düsseldorf, March 24, 1939

In the deportation case against Pastor Paul Schneider from Dickenschied (Hunsrück) Mrs. Schneider has commissioned me to look after the interests of her husband. Pastor Schneider has been in the concentration camp at Buchenwald for longer than one year. It is essential that he be given the chance to speak with his legal counsel about how he should handle the deportation order in the future. For this reason I ask for permission to speak to Pastor Schneider.

Signed, Dr. Schulze zur Wiesche
Attorney at Law

The Gestapo in Berlin immediately notifies its office in Düsseldorf and requests information on the lawyer.

Gestapo Berlin, April 4, 1939
Gestapo Office
II B 2-873/37 E
A copy to be sent to the Gestapo office in Düsseldorf

Please examine this letter and inform us whether the attorney Dr. Schulze zur Wiesche has already called at your office about preventive detention cases and what is known about him.

By the decree of the Gestapo headquarters in Koblenz Pastor Paul Schneider from Dickenschied/Hunsrück was deported from the Rhine province on July 23, 1937. In case he violated this decree he was threatened with a coercive fine, or if necessary, preventive detention. Schneider did not follow this ban on staying in the Rhine province. Instead, he returned to his congregation and preached there. To enforce the ban Schneider was taken into preventive detention on October 3, 1937 and taken to the Buchenwald concentration camp where he still is.

pp, signed,
Roth
Seal Certified:
(Signature)

Chancellery Clerk
Gestapo Düsseldorf
II B 2/1671/80. 10/Schulze zur Wiesche
1.) To the Gestapo in Berlin
Concerning: Attorney Dr. Schulze zur Wiesche-Düsseldorf
Dossier: Decree of April 4, 1939-II B 2/873/37 E-

Attorney Paul Schulze zur Wiesche, born on August 17, 1905 in Duisburg, is living in Düsseldorf, Venloer Street 11a. He was previously a member of the Brotherhood Council of the Protestant Confessing Synod in the Rhineland and the head of the legal and administrative department of the Rhenish Confessing Synod. He has not been a member of either institution for about a year and a half; the legal and administrative department has been dissolved. It is not known here whether his departure from the Brotherhood Council as well occurred simultaneously with this or whether this was a tactical measure that was supposed to make him appear unbiased when he took action in legal matters for the Confessing Church. In any case, he is still commissioned today by the Rhenish Confessing Synod to look after the interests of the Confessing Church in legal disputes and to represent it in criminal cases against Confessing Church clergymen. In his capacity as a member of the Brotherhood Council and as the head of the legal and administrative department of the Rhenish Confessing Synod his conduct has repeatedly made a bad impression on us. However, his actions have not given us a handle to initiate special state police measures against him.

Schulze zur Wiesche has not yet called at our office about preventive detention cases.

2.) Subject card "Protestant Confessing Synod in the Rhineland"
Note: Attorney Schulze zur Wiesche-Düsseldorf has requested permission from the Gestapo to visit Pastor Paul Schneider, Dickenschied, who is in the concerntration camp at Buchenwald, for the purpose of discussing his deportation.

3.) II F
a) Supplement the personal card of Schulze zur Wiesche
Note: Applied for permission from the Gestapo to speak to Pastor Schneider-Dickenschied about his deportation. Schneider is in the concentration camp at Buchenwald.

Stamp

With the decree of April 4, 1939-IIB2/873/37E, the Gestapo card file asks for a report on what is known here about Schulze zur Wiesche.

(Initials)

Large sections of the population during the National Socialist era were of the opinion that Hitler knew nothing of the machinations of the Gestapo. This erroneous rumor causes the session of Dickenschied and Womrath to write a petition to the Führer and Reich chancellor. The assistant pastor Kemper who was pastoring in Dickenschied and Womrath at the time personally delivers the letter to the Reich chancellery in Berlin to be sure that it also reaches the correct office.

The Church Board of the yoked
Protestant congregations of Dickenschied and Womrath in the Hunsrück
Dickenschied, March 18, 1939

To the Führer and Reich Chancellor of the German Reich
Berlin

Concerning: The release of our pastor

With all respect we have the honor of reporting the following situation to the Führer and Chancellor of the German Reich.

Our Pastor Schneider was taken into preventive detention by the Gestapo on May 30, 1937 and was kept there eight weeks. A report by a man who interpreted a church discipline measure as a "boycott" led to his arrest although this church discipline is a purely church matter and is still anchored in our church laws today. On July 24, 1937 they revealed to him that he was being deported from the Rhineland. As grounds for this action the deportation order noted that his conduct endangered the public safety and order of the Rhineland. Pastor Schneider did not feel he was able to accept this deportation order since he had solemnly committed himself before God to his congregations and the congregations offered him their full confidence. He was also never questioned on the issue of church discipline although he had always asked for a hearing on this issue. In a letter addressed to the Reich chancellery dated September 30, 1937 he explained his reasons of conscience in detail.

On Thanksgiving Day in 1937 he was arrested again after returning to his congregation as we had asked him to do. He spent eight weeks in the prison of the Gestapo in Koblenz and was taken to the concentration camp at Buchenwald/Weimar on November 25, 1937. Since October 1938 his wife has been without any news from him. Schneider, who is 41 years old, was a war volunteer, and served three and a half years on the frontlines. He is deeply rooted in our Hunsrück region with his wife and his six under-aged children and has always stood at the side of those of us who are farmers during our field work, demonstrating true solidarity with the people. He has gained the confidence of the Protestant and Catholic population through his friendly nature. The church bears its sorrow with his wife and his six under-aged children. But above all our pastor served as a faithful provider of spiritual care and preached the Word of God to us according to the commission he was given. He has conscientiously performed the duties of his ministry and never incited his church or us to oppose the government. The pain of not knowing the fate of their pastor has weighed on his congregations since his detention. We know that he has been asked to make a decision time and again, aware of the fact that if he accepts the deportation he can be released. But with all respect we ask you, our Führer and chancellor of the German Reich, to consider that as a pastor, this man's conscience is captive to the Word of God and that he is committed to our church. Thus he has willingly taken upon himself this long period of detention and separation from his family out of loyalty to his congregations. Therefore, we ask as a church board that you release our pastor so that he can return to our congregations. Even the local town council (the representation of the civil community) can testify that there is law and order in our communities and nothing stands in the way of our pastor's return.

The church board of the Protestant congregations in Dickenschied and Womrath.

(Signatures)

27

DIABOLICAL TEAMWORK

On September 7, 1938 the Protestant consistory in Düsseldorf extended the request of the Gestapo and the party leadership of the NSDAP to transfer Paul Schneider from Dickenschied and Womrath. It did so by taking the initiative in persuading the highest administrative office of the Protestant Church to implement the new church "enabling acts" we have already mentioned. On the basis of these laws clergymen could be forced into temporary retirement by decree.

The official church office existed in a realm far removed from the cause of the gospel and the Reformational confessions. It administered the church as an institution according to opportunistic official standards. It did not pay attention to the motivations of those who had come into conflict with the ruling power—motivations that could be justified on ethical and theological grounds. It accepted the "Aryan paragraphs" and ignored those who saw them as an obvious injustice and who openly expressed their opinion. They pushed aside the biblical view of man in favor of a neo-pagan one. Members of the church did not get a hearing if they supported the retention of the Old Testament, resisted the political conformity forced on the Protestant youth groups and the Protestant press or rejected the controversial oath to the "Führer."

The following documents are part of the darkest chapter in the history of the Protestant Church in Germany.

The Protestant Consistory Düsseldorf, April 5, 1939
138990 II
To the Gestapo
Gestapo headquarters Koblenz in Koblenz/Rhine

Concerning: the implementation of the decree of March 18, 1939 on the transfer of clergymen for official reasons

As we had always said at our various personal discussions, we had to first await the enactment of the aforementioned decrees on the transfer of clergymen in order to take such measures against the pastors who are under consideration for this. Now the legal handle to take action against intolerable clergymen has finally been provided for us by this decree—something we have long desired to use in the public interest.

The names of pastors Schneider, Dickenschied and Langensiepen, Godenroth were mentioned first during the examination of pastors that took place by mutual agreement. The consensus was that this decree on the transfer of clergymen should probably first be applied to these pastors in our official area. We are still convinced that it is absolutely necessary to take immediate action against these gentlemen on the basis of the legal grounds now available to us.

We would thus like to draw your attention to the fact that we will take the necessary steps after the Easter holidays based on the personal hearings we have conducted. We will soon have more detailed announcements sent out; perhaps in the meantime the opportunity for another discussion in Koblenz will present itself for the undersigned. Both the details of the practical implementation of the decree and any additional cases that are similar to these could be discussed.

We are enclosing a copy of our church gazette containing the text of the decree on the transfer of clergymen for your personal examination.

Rössler April 5, Kolrep April 5

The collaboration between the Gestapo and the Protestant Consistory cannot be shown more clearly. From now on everything was possible, giving free reign to the arbitrary use of power. "Troublesome" clergymen could now be removed from their office by decree.

We find another note for use within the consistory's office.

Protestant Consistory Düsseldorf, May 2, 1939

Confidential file, only for personal office use!

1. File Note

The discussion carried on between the deputy head of the Gestapo in Koblenz, Dr. Hoffmann, and the Consistory President Dr. Koch with the participation of the undersigned on April 29 of this year on the basis of a prior arrangement, which dealt primarily with the practical implementation of the recently issued so-called Decree on the Transfer of Clergymen, produced the following results, briefly summarized here:

In view of the various, quite different cases that are under consideration for such a transfer in the Koblenz governmental district, two groups were distinguished, which are to be treated separately, depending on the seriousness of the incriminating political or other evidence. These cases are to be dealt with concurrently. In this regard the representative of the Gestapo labeled the pastors Schneider, Dickenschied and Gross, Freusburg as top priority. The Gestapo has a special interest in the implementation of these two transfer procedures. Only after we have dealt with these two cases should we proceed to transfer the remaining pastors named at the end of our conversation.

The treatment of the case of Schneider, Dickenschied, occupied a large part of the discussion. His transfer into temporary retirement should be pursued without delay. This measure would be based on the fact that he is not able to have a fruitful ministry as a result of his rather lengthy stay in a concentration camp that will probably not be ended for the foreseeable future. It is also necessitated by the circumstance that the maintenance of order in the Dickenschied congregation demands that we finally implement the transfer procedure in order to set things straight there. During the discussion it came to light that Pastor Schneider has committed numerous political offenses stretching back to 1934. Upon our request the Gestapo will soon send us a confidential listing of all these incriminating individual points for our files. The state has a special interest in establishing peaceful church conditions in the area of Dickenschied because this is our border area located very close to our Western fortifications.

On the question of implementing the transfer procedure against Schneider it was decided that upon our request the Gestapo would assume the responsibility of holding the required hearing of the pastor in Buchenwald, the concentration camp at which he is presently being detained, and that they would give this job to an experienced police official in Weimar. Likewise, the Gestapo will provide for the orderly delivery of the transfer decree itself. The counterstatement of the corporation of the local congregation provided for in the transfer decree is to be effectively dealt with by summoning two elders here for an oral hearing.

Furthermore, Pastor Gross, Freusburg, was mentioned as the second person whose transfer into temporary retirement will be viewed as especially urgent. Based on information provided by the Gestapo extensive incriminating material against him is also available, comprising a total of thirteen complaints. The tension caused in the congregation by the politically intolerable behavior of the pastor has become so dangerous that any day we can expect serious disturbances in the populace and even the venting of emotions in the form of individual actions that emphatically document the tremendous anger of the National Socialist part of the congregation. Therefore, it is necessary to take the same action against him as we did against Pastor Schneider.

When we discussed the repercussions of our transfer order in the congregation—for example, when the manse is vacated, but the pastor involved continues to stay in the community, be it in the home of a neighbor, we came to the conclusion that in these especially difficult cases, namely in the case of Schneider, Dickenschied—the Gestapo would come to our help with suitable measures, for instance, by imposing a ban that prohibits him from staying in the Rhine province or a ban that prohibits him from speaking in public.

Then the names of Knuth, Graeber, Hoetzel, Langensiepen and van de Loo were additionally mentioned as pastors who would be considered as candidates for such a transfer when this decree is implemented in the governmental district of Koblenz. During this discussion we also mentioned Pastor Morchen. He appears to be urgently in need of being transferred. All of these gentlemen described by the Gestapo show a more or less significant amount of incriminating political material. In the case of Pastor Graeber it is a matter of thirteen such points. In view of the strong support Graeber seems to find from Prince zu Wied, a corresponding attempt to work on the prince in this direction would be beneficial in the opinion of the Gestapo.

With reference to our recent visit with the government in Koblenz where the question of cutting off state allowances to a number of the aforementioned pastors had been discussed, it was stated in this discussion that concerted action between the government, the Gestapo and us must take place as much as possible. The cooperation would take place in such a way that our measures to transfer troublesome pastors would be taken at the same time the Gestapo would be cutting off state allowances to them. But in any case, regular, mutual communication with the government and the Gestapo on the measures and steps we intend to take should occur in all these matters to increase our clout and to build the level of trust in our collaborative efforts.

Rössler Kolrep

This paper had been declared a classified document and shows how correctly Paul Schneider had acted when he could no longer see the consistory as his church leadership or even as one that deserved the name; this is additionally confirmed by the following letter.

Protestant Consistory Düsseldorf, June 5, 1939
Nr. 5581
To the Gestapo
Gestapo Headquarters Koblenz in Koblenz

Concerning: The implementation of the transfer procedure against the pastors Schneider, Dickenschied and Gross, Freusburg.

The urgent necessity of taking action against the two aforementioned clergymen in accordance with the decree issued on the transfer of pastors was clearly brought out in the discussion that recently took place here with the deputy director of your office. But their incriminating political actions would in no way allow us to transfer them to a different parish where the same difficulties would easily show up again. Instead, only temporary retirement can be considered as a real remedy.

Therefore, if you no longer have any fundamental objections, we must attach great importance to the more detailed evidence you promised us with regard to these two gentlemen for the practical implementation of this procedure. Therefore, we would be very grateful if you would kindly transmit this information to us in the interests of implementing this procedure as quickly as possible. In addition we would like to ask you to express the fact that in the case of Pastor Schneider you do not expect his release from the concentration camp in the foreseeable future.

Signed June 10, Wa.

In examining the few and often incomplete files it is striking that the Gestapo took its time in responding to all these inquires, in contrast to the consistory. It was not so open, but rather reserved until its dialogue partner had fallen in line with its position. On the same day the consistory issued a report to the district leadership of the NSDAP, with which it maintained good relations.

Protestant Consistory Düsseldorf, June 5, 1939
Nr. 5581
To the District Leadershp of the NSDAP in Koblenz

Concerning: the Procedure Against Clergymen on the basis of the Transfer Decree of March 18, 1939

The issue mentioned above was especially dealt with in the discussion that recently took place between the deputy district leader Neumann and our legal caseworker, consistory member Kolrep. During their discussion on how to practically handle this decree whose more detailed regulations are found in the official copy enclosed for your examination, it was clarified from our side that we must start these measures by taking action against the seriously incriminated pastors who have gotten involved in politics. After this the transfer cases necessary in other respects would be dealt with.

In the area of this governmental district it is mainly the pastors Schneider, Dickenschied and Gross, Freusburg, who require an immediate transfer to temporary retirement since the possibility of using them in another pastorate is ruled out. The Gestapo will send the extensive incriminating evidence that exists in both cases to us shortly. We have already been in contact with the Gestapo for some time now on account of this matter.

We ask that you view the above report first as a general confirmation of the discussion we mentioned. We have welcomed your desire to be regularly informed of the steps we have taken on the issue of transferring pastors. Therefore, we will promptly inform you both of the two transfer cases now being handled and of all subsequent cases. Furthermore, it should contribute to a fruitful collaboration if your office would influence the subordinate district leaderships in terms of mutually communicating on political complaints about the pastors there. The non-intervention of the office could be explained until now by the absence of a legal opportunity to take such action.

Now, where this legal gap has been filled by the decree mentioned above, we face a quite different situation, making it possible for us to cleanse and free our church province from such seriously incriminated elements. In the meantime, the administrative office in Berlin has asked us to transfer Pastor Reif in Veldenz as well. We then reported to them that we thought it would be highly advisable to consider such a transfer, and requested further details on how to proceed.

Heil Hitler!
Rössler, Kolrep June 5

The teamwork between the "Protestant" consistory and the district leadership of the NSDAP itself could not be demonstrated more clearly.

On May 16, 1939 the provincial governor to whom the Gestapo has reported the individual "criminal offenses," filed a petition with the Reich minister of church affairs to cut off the Dickenschied pastor's state allowance used to pay the pastor's salary. The reason given read as follows: "Schneider is a fanatical Confessing Church pastor and has been in the concentration camp of Buchenwald near Weimar since November 1937." The minister decreed:

The Reich minister for Church Affairs Leipziger Strasse 3
I 13 102/39 Berlin W 8, June 15, 1939
To the Provincial Governor in Koblenz

Concerning: Cutting off the 400.-RM annual state salary of the Protestant pastor Paul Robert Schneider in Dickenschied, presently in the concentration camp of Buchenwald.

Report of May 16, 1939-IIa Nr. 144-

I request that you see to it that his state salary is cut off on the basis of the circular edict of September 24, 1938-11415/38 II,III and to notify me of what you have done.

pp.
Dr. Richter

A copy of the order mentioned above was also transmitted to the administrative office of the Protestant Church in Berlin.

It makes us wonder why the authorities start to move and deal with Paul Schneider precisely in the spring and summer of 1939. For him it is the time when he is tormented by the SS-bunker guard at Buchenwald in the midst of unimaginable suffering in the "bunker," i.e., in a small cell in solitary confinement.

From Dickenschied Mrs. Schneider tries again to get permission to speak to her husband:

Mrs. Schneider Dickenschied,
June 23, 1939
Post Office in Kirchberg, H. Nr. 8
Hunsrück

To the Gestapo
Berlin SW 11

Prince Albrecht Street 8
Department II B 2
Booking Number 873/37

As a mother of six under-aged children I repeat the request I already
made in August of last year that you allow me to at least visit my husband
who will soon have been in the concentration camp of Buchenwald for
two years, since I would like to hear my husband's advice in matters
pertaining to my children. If visits are forbidden in the camp, I ask
that you take my husband to the prison in Weimar, so that I can speak
to him there, which is what happens in the case of Pastor Niemöller.
Therefore, I kindly ask you again for permission and would be very
grateful to hear from you soon.

Margarete Schneider

She was not given permission to speak to or visit her husband. The Gestapo
could not show his wife a man it tortured almost beyond recognition.

The church and state authorities are jointly making enormous efforts
to remove Paul Schneider from his office. The Gestapo grants the request of
the consistory from June 5, 1939 and officially informs it: "We do not expect
Schneider, who has been in the concentration camp of Buchenwald near
Weimar since November 1937, to be released in the foreseeable future . . . ."

His total "criminal record" reads:

Gestapo
Gestapo Headquarters Koblenz
In Vogelsang I
Telephone Nr. 2291
Koblenz, June 17, 1939
Br.-Nr. II B-74/39
Please indicate the above business number and date in your response

To the Protestant Consistory
of the Rhine Province
Düsseldorf
Insel Street 10

Concerning: The implementation of the Transfer Decree from March 18, 1939 against the Protestant Pastor Paul Robert Schneider, born August 29, 1897 in Pferdsfeld, residing in Dickenschied, in the district of Simmern, presently in the concentration camp of Buchenwald

Dossier: The letter there from June 5, 1939 Nr. 5581

The Protestant Pastor Paul Robert Schneider who lives in Dickenschied, in the district of Simmern, and has been detained in the Buchenwald concentration camp since November 1937, has demonstrated through his behavior that he is unworthy of ever again occupying the office of a pastor.

Therefore, I request that you transfer him to retirement on the basis of the decree on the transfer of clergymen for official reasons of March 18, 1939 (section 2). We do not expect Schneider, who has been in the Buchenwald concentration camp near Weimar since November 1937, to be released in the foreseeable future, since he refuses to make a declaration that he will refrain from making any statement or taking any action that is hostile to the state in the future. The following facts are known about Schneider:

On June 12, 1934 a Hitler youth was buried in Gemünden, in the district of Simmern. The district leader spoke at the gravesite and said among other things that the deceased had now entered the storm of Horst Wessel. Schneider, who had already spoken before, stepped up to the grave again and declared: "I do not know if there is a storm of Horst Wessel in the life to come, but I do know that Karl Moog has gone home and entered eternity." Afterwards there was an argument between the district leader and Pastor Schneider. Since this incident greatly angered the populace, Schneider was taken into preventive detention from June 12 to June 20 1934. Criminal proceedings were not initiated.

On February 16, 1936 Schneider explained in a sermon that the German youth belonged neither to Adolf Hitler nor to Baldur von Schirach, but solely to Christ. The criminal proceedings for violating 130 3 of the Penal Code were suspended by the district attorney in Koblenz-Js347/36-on the following grounds: "According to the statement of the witness the defendant spoke about the relationship of youth to the state, thus making matters of state an object of discussion. Because the witness, however, can give no information on the exact wording and context in which the statements were made, it cannot be proved with certainty that the discussion occurred in a way that would endanger the public peace. Moreover, the impunity law of April 30, 1938 would probably apply here."

In June 1936 Schneider disseminated an inflammatory paper of the confessional front in Dickenschied. In the paper the Reich government is accused of falsifying the results of the election. The criminal proceedings were suspended by the special court-1 S Js 1355/36-on June 10, 1938 based on the impunity law.

During a conversation in Womrath in June 1936 Schneider called National Socialism a work of the devil. The criminal proceedings for violating the Treachery Act were suspended on June 10, 1938 by the special court in Cologne-I S Js331/37-on the basis of the Impunity Law of April 30, 1938.

Schneider made disparaging remarks about the books *Mein Kampf* and *The Myth of the 20. Century* during a sermon on June 25, 1936 in Isselhorst, in the district of Bielefeld. On June 10, 1938 the special court in Cologne-I S Js 331/37-suspended the criminal proceedings initiated against him for violating the Treachery Act on the basis of the Impunity Law of April 30, 1938.

In the middle of December 1936 Schneider expressed this idea on the occasion of a discussion: "The brown crowd does not belong in the church."

Criminal proceedings initiated by the district attorney were pending in the special court in Cologne. Pastor Schneider was charged with organizing an illegal church collection on Sunday, May 24, 1937, in the church of Isselhorst. The outcome of the trial and the file number are not known here.

Schneider made matters of state the object of discussion in a way that endangered the public peace in his sermon on January 31, 1937.

Criminal proceedings were suspended by the special court in Cologne-30 S Js 72/37-on June 10, 1938 on the basis of the Impunity Law of April 30, 1938.

In March 1937 Schneider imposed Christian discipline on members of his congregation because they were opponents of the confessional front. He called on the congregation to break off Christian and church fellowship with these persons. Pastor Schneider was taken into preventive custody on May 31, 1937 on the basis of these events. When he was released from preventive detention on July 24, 1937, a ban on staying in the Rhine province was imposed on him. In spite of this ban Schneider returned to Dickenschied and began his agitation again. Therefore, he was taken into preventive detention again on October 3, 1937. His release could not occur since he stubbornly refused to follow the ban forbidding him from staying in the Rhine province.

On November 25, 1937 he was taken to the Buchenwald concentration camp near Weimar where he still is today.

On September 29, 1937 Schneider took up an illegal church collection in Eschbach in the Taunus region. Criminal proceedings are pending at the district attorney's office in Frankfurt/Main-6 B Js 694/37-.

In November 1937 Schneider made disparaging remarks about the state in a sermon in Hausen/Hunsrück. The special court in Cologne-30 S Js 312/37-suspended criminal proceedings on June 10, 1938 on the basis of the Impunity Law of April 30, 1938.

I request that you send me notification of what you have initiated from there.

In proxy:
Signed, Dr. Braune
Certified:
Signed, Klein

In enumerating his "criminal deeds," the Gestapo made a mistake. In the letter it is claimed that Paul Schneider made "disparaging remarks" in Hausen/Hunsrück in November 1937. In making their indictment, the Gestapo did not notice that he could not have been in Hausen/Hunsrück since he had already been in the custody of the Gestapo since October 3, 1937.

After receiving the letter requested by the consistory in Düsseldorf, it took action and issued a decree that was supposed to be delivered to Paul Schneider in the concentration camp, but did not reach him on account of the coming events. It was, by the way, the only letter that the consistory sent to him in Buchenwald.

28

THE GESTAPO'S INTENTION TO FORCE HIM INTO TEMPORARY RETIREMENT

Protestant Consistory Düsseldorf, June 15, 1939
of the Rhine province Insel Street 10
Nr. 6568 II

Concerning: Implementation of Your Transfer to Temporary Retirement

To Pastor Schneider, presently in Buchenwald, at the concentration camp

For a rather long time now the party and the Gestapo have repeatedly and emphatically called our attention to your conduct that is hostile to the state. Long ago you were made aware of the serious and detailed evidence that has been gathered to incriminate you in this respect. Thus a special enumeration of these complaints would be superfluous at this point. Such an accurate assessment of your negative attitude toward the Third Reich finds further confirmation by the fact that your stay at the concentration camp has continued without interruption since November 1937. If no change in your views concerning a positive and unreserved affirmation of the present state has occurred in this time, but because of your previous attitude there is no prospect that you could be released from the concentration camp in the foreseeable future, then we see ourselves confronted with the absolute necessity of taking action against you for the purpose of transferring you to temporary retirement on the basis of the Decree on the Transfer of

Clergymen For Official Reasons of March 18, 1939 (Statute Book I. of the German Protestant Church Nr. 4 for 1939).

In accordance with Article 1 of the decree this transfer is based on the fact that a fruitful ministry in your pastorate is no longer possible for you because of a long absence from your congregation that is of your own making and because there is no prospect of an improvement in this situation by your listening to reason. Moreover, maintaining order in the Dickenschied congregation and setting things straight in the life of the church there requires that we relieve you of your office.

Since you will be given the opportunity to make a counterstatement before our final decision in accordance with article 2 of the aforementioned decree, but since in your case this hearing is particularly difficult to arrange, we will avail ourselves of the office of the Gestapo for this purpose. It will soon send us its opinion.

The special copy sent to the Gestapo has the following addition:

We are sending you the above copy for your personal examination with reference to your official letter of June 17-Nr. II B-741/39-and the personal discussion you had with Dr. Venter. Since you kindly agreed to hold the required hearing of the clergyman, we hereby make this request and enclose two additional carbon copies of our decree. In the meantime we will expediently arrange the required hearing of the Dickenschied session in such a way that we will summon the members of this body here, perhaps a select group, and briefly fill them in on our measure . . . .

The following remark is found under this plan:

3) Resubmit because of the hearing of the session and the meeting of the theological case worker. (Furthermore, notify the district leadership of the NSDAP. Report to the administrative office of the Protestant Church.)

A hearing of Paul Schneider in the concentration camp did not take place based on our present state of knowledge. In the same way, an indication that members of the Dickenschied session were summoned to the consistory in Düsseldorf to accept a declaration cannot be found anywhere. The events that must still be described prevented it from happening. Or did the Gestapo recognize that their plan was inevitably doomed to failure because Paul Schneider would not go along with it? For only if he had consented to being transferred to temporary retirement,would a document have been available that the gentlemen of the consistory could have used to declare his official transfer. Then they could have submitted this declaration to the elders of Dickenschied and Womrath, which would have made the elders feel unsure of themselves. The plan of the consistory and the Gestapo fails. So the Gestapo finds another way to get a solution—a "final solution."[1]

Although Paul Schneider is brought to the sickbay under guard, he still succeeds in exchanging a few words with the Buchenwald inmate Peter Propst. He reports later:

> Paul roughly said: "I have swollen feet and fluid around the heart. There is no spot on me that has not been beaten black and blue. They have given me injections; since the second injection my heart has been beating very irregularly. I will probably not live much longer. I want to bless you as I say good-bye and also pray for you, asking that you will follow the right path."[2]

---

[1] There are three versions: 1. Was Paul Schneider to be "gotten ready" for a conversation with an "experienced" detective in order to give them the signature they needed to transfer him to temporary retirement? The Gestapo in Koblenz had taken over this part of implementing the transfer procedure. The consistory has assumed the other part, the notification of the two sessions. A further question in this context is whether the Gestapo headquarters in Berlin had approved this "official help." For it alone was responsible for Buchenwald; 2. Could the Gestapo even have been interested in providing such services? For its demand, his banishment from the Rhine province, would not have been fulfilled with his transfer to temporary retirement. What the inspector of the political department, Schott, said to Mrs. Schneider, that Paul Schneider's release was dependent on his agreement to no longer return to the Rhineland, is only partially true; 3. A further question: Could the Gestapo still afford to release Paul Schneider from the concentration camp at all? His release would have been linked to a commitment on his part in lieu of an oath to be silent about the events and experiences in the Buchenwald concentration camp. Paul Schneider would not have signed such a commitment at any time. The Gestapo was ultimately afraid of Paul Schneider. This is proven simply by the long period of detention, which can hardly be shown to be the case elsewhere.

[2] *Prediger*, p. 208.

29

THE END IN THIS AGE

On July 18, 1939 the following telegram arrives at the Dickenschied manse:

> Paul Schneider, born on August 29, 1897, died today. If you desire to transport the body at your own expense, you must make your application to the morgue in Weimar within 24 hours. Otherwise the body will be cremated. The Camp Commander of Buchenwald.

Mrs. Schneider drives to Buchenwald immediately, accompanied by Pastor Petry who had just brought an assistant pastor of the Confessing Church to fill in for Paul Schneider in Dickenschied and Womrath. She takes a car and trailer, arriving in Weimar around ten o'clock in the morning on July 19, 1939. Around noon they are able to proceed to Buchenwald.

They drive up to the camp on Karachow Road. Armed SS-guards stand behind the trees at the edge of the forest. Three barricades must be passed; the SS-men who check their passes have instructions to let the car with the trailer and its passengers pass. Nevertheless, they assure themselves of who is sitting in the car. At the third barrier two armed SS-men jump up on the two running boards of the car and ride along up to the square in front of the administration building. Mrs. Schneider and her companion are welcomed by the SS-leader and deputy camp commander Rodl, SS-leader and camp physician Dr. Ding and the inspector of the political department, Schott, with real politeness. Mrs. Schneider reports:

> On July 19 the prisoners Poller and Peix laid out Paul's body in a car garage on the orders of the camp leadership after our call from Weimar. I was permitted to briefly see Paul's face again. There was no make-up

on him, as several books claim, however the body was lightly powdered. Red and white flowers lay around his head that were supposed to cover up the cuts made during the autopsy; the body, and his hands as well, were covered with a blanket. The peace and the majestic look of the redeemed lay on Paul's face. I was privileged to see Paul in this brief moment with the eyes of faith: "Formed in the best image, pure, and free and completely perfect . . . ." "How blissful is that peace with Jesus in the light, one does not know death, sin and pain there."

My companion Pastor Petry spoke these words: "Because You are risen from the dead, I will not remain in the grave; Your ascension is my greatest comfort, it can drive away the fear of death. For you are mine and I am yours, and where you are, there I will be, that is why I go there with joy in my heart." Then he prayed the Lord's prayer.

After Mrs. Schneider has seen her husband, she goes to the administrative building. She reports: "The prisoners I had mentioned put Paul in the casket we had brought along and sealed the casket seven times while I took care of the formalities in the business office of the Gestapo inspector. The Gestapo inspector offered to answer any questions I might have. I wanted to know why my husband had not written for five and a half months: "He was so stubborn and did not want to write." I responded: "But in the first letter after this long interruption Paul wrote: 'How glad I am that I am permitted to write again.'" Or this question: Did my husband have a Bible? At first it was vaguely answered in the affirmative, but then he generalized: "We have 2,000 books in our camp library." The inspector also claimed he had the papers for the release of my husband lying on his desk—only one small condition was attached to it, no longer returning to the Rhineland. They said my husband had refused to accept it."[1]

The following description (a letter to the author) comes from the former Buchenwald prisoner Arthur Dietzsch:

In response to your deeply appreciated letter of May 7, 1966 I will gladly tell you what I experienced with Paul Schneider, especially since we had more in common than companionship. The following incident was the main reason for this:

---

[1] *Prediger*, p. 208.

For weeks Paul Schneider and I were pulling on the same lever of a dump car in the unit assigned to the SS-housing estate under the "greenhorn" overseer Berg or the "greenhorn" foreman Pfeiffer. I had not yet been with this unit very long when a guard pulled the cap off my head and threw it far away. Involuntarily I wanted to let go of the lever and run after my cap. Then Paul Schneider called to me between his teeth; "Don't let go of it! Stay here!" I understood. After we had arrived at the unloading place, the guard summoned me and said I should fetch my cap. Instead of following his summons, I ripped apart the shirt on my chest and said, if they wanted to finish me off, then they should shoot, but right away and not from behind. The guard raised his rifle, but another guard remarked apathetically: "Leave him alone, he knows!"

The guards were given three days of vacation and a special payment of money for each "attempted escape" that had failed because of their vigorous response. Moreover, they were given special preference when it came time for promotions. The evidence for an attempted escape was always there when a bullet hit a prisoner in the back. Paul Schneider thus literally saved my life by giving me his warning.

Not only during work, but also at roll call I frequently stood near Paul Schneider. That was the case on May 1, 1938 where a flag raising took place for the first and the last time, and those of us who were prisoners had to participate in it. After the command: "Caps off!" Paul Schneider kept his cap on his head to the horror of all those standing around him. He did not react when I softly called out to him: "Paul, don't do anything stupid!" After we were dismissed, I immediately ran toward Paul Schneider and asked him why he had not taken off his cap. "I will not salute this criminal symbol," he answered with unusual intensity. While I was reproaching him for not thinking of his wife and his children, this command rang out from the loudspeaker: "The prisoner who did not take off his cap at roll call, go immediately to the gate," and shortly after that, we heard it again: "If the prisoner does not immediately report, the whole camp will be punished!" After that Paul Schneider started jogging toward the gate, and I only saw him again many months later when he was led off to the prisoners' sickbay by Koch and Sommer.[2]

We take the following report from the magazine *"Appell"* printed as a manuscript:

> Karl Trzmiel, the former Buchenwald prisoner Nr. 320/38 who makes his home in Dippoldiswalde (Saxony) and who became very familiar with Schneider's fate in Buchenwald, reports the following story about Pastor Schneider and his steadfast work in the Buchenwald concentration camp: I was informed on by an overseer named Heidenfelder and reported to the camp commandant Koch. They accused me of holding a resistance meeting in block 6. While getting a terrible beating, I was picked up from the construction site by the camp elder Richter and taken to the commander who sentenced me to death before a firing squad "because I had glorified Stalin." I do not know why they did not carry out the sentence. I was first whipped 28 times with a cane and then put in a darkened cell. I was freed after being detained there for seven weeks because they needed the detention cells for the "campaign against the Jews" they were waging at that time.
>
> In the bunker where the darkened cells were located I got to know Pastor Schneider who lay next to me in the cell. Every morning he held morning devotions for us prisoners for which he always had to take beatings and mistreatment from the guards Sommer and Pleissner. By reducing his food rations to half the regular amount, by often even completely taking away all his food, Pastor Schneider, who had already been in this bunker over a year when I was admitted, was continually being tormented and tortured. But he did not let himself be shaken at all and continued his work. I still clearly remember an incident when the camp leader Schober appeared in the bunker and told the pastor: "Your wife and youngest child have had a fatal accident,

---

[2] Here Arthur Dietzsch was probably wrong. Based on detailed investigative work the SS-Commander Koch was not seen in the sickbay in connection with Paul Schneider. I also would like to point out the description of Paul Schneider in Buchenwald by Eugen Kogon in *Der SS-Staat* (1974), p. 206f. He could appeal to only a single witness; he himself confirmed that for Mrs. Schneider. Such a thing could easily happen considering the structure of the camp that was confusing to the prisoners, since most of them were dependent only on what was passed on by word of mouth.

doesn't that grieve you deeply?" Pastor Schneider replied after a short pause: "Certainly, that grieves me very deeply, but the way you treat the prisoners so terribly is far more depressing to me." Camp leader Schober was now furious and replied: "I'm going to make sure you pay for that, you scoundrel!" A short time later Pastor Schneider was no longer among the living.

A letter from Karl Trzmiel to Mrs. Schneider supplements the report:

When I was put in a darkened cell in 1938 I got to know your husband better. I already knew your husband from the beginning of my detention in Buchenwald because every morning when we had lined up for roll call, the voice of your husband rang out through his cell window when he preached to the prisoners. A short time after that we could hear from outside how your husband's preaching was disrupted by their beatings. Now I would like to tell you a few things from my life in the bunker (solitary confinement). Early in the morning at the first sound of the whistle everyone had to step outside to shave and wash. That had to be done in five minutes. We had to trot to the washroom, and as we went, there were beatings and they tried to trip us so that we would fall down; if a prisoner fell down and spilled his night pail, he had to wipe it up while they beat him; this happened to each of us at least once, and it also happened to your husband. In the cell there was a bed that was attached to the wall during the day; there was no place to sit. In the morning your husband got 150 grams of bread, and a half-liter of coffee or soup. At noon he got a half-liter of food, in the evening he got a half-liter of soup or coffee, because bread was counted for the whole day. Often your husband only got half of a daily ration. When he was confined to the darkened cell, which often happened, he only got a regular meal once every four days. Beatings were nothing unusual for your husband. There was nothing to read. Guard Pleissner and guard Sommer were the tyrants of your husband, mainly Sommer. When they had the campaign against the Jews, a prisoner was beaten out of his mind, and he was locked in the cell with the prisoner Willi Mohr. When Willi refused, this lunatic was put in the cell with your husband. Your husband did not allow himself to become bitter, and when we said he should refuse to have him in his cell, your husband told us: "Love your neighbor as yourself, be helpful and good." This lunatic died by an injection (we called it a suicide shot) in your husband's cell. Nevertheless, the cell was not disinfected, but your husband stayed in it as if nothing of the kind had happened. The prisoner Willi Mohr who also came from the Rhineland had to die in solitary confinement. Although I am no longer in any church, my wife still belongs to the church, and I must say that your husband was a hero. If all the communists were such heroes, we could all be proud.

Alfred Leikam, who later became a notary, had come into conflict with National Socialism on the basis of his Christian stance and was put in the Buchenwald concentration camp. He reports:

> On November 5, 1938 I arrived in the Buchenwald camp. At that time Paul Schneider was already in solitary confinement, i.e., in a small detention cell, called a bunker, at the entrance of the camp. There he was subject to arbitrary treatment and was completely at the mercy of the more or less sadistic overseers (prisoners who were considered trustworthy and granted special privileges, including the right to guard other prisoners). Thus I no longer came into direct contact with Paul Schneider or had any chance to talk to him. The following reports thus come from conversations with other prisoners. Paul Schneider's journey in the camp can roughly be described as follows:
>
> Paul Schneider came to Buchenwald in November 1937. At first he was assigned to a work unit outside the camp (stone quarry, digging ditches, construction work, etc.). In the morning the work units marched to work and came back to the camp again in the evening. Schneider never denied his calling as a pastor to the other prisoners; he tried to win his fellow prisoners for Christ by encouraging and admonishing them with Christian truth, praying for them and actively assisting them. At first an outward success could not be observed in his conversation partners . . . . Now I come to his death. In the summer of 1939 it seemed as if Schneider was to be released. The camp physician at that time, Dr. Ding, had to confirm in writing every week to Berlin that Schneider was physically able to remain in detention. The medical certification regularly confirmed his weakened physical condition, his latent weak heart, but stated that he was able to remain in camp detention. I myself have seen his medical files; they were hidden away by Dr. Ding in 1943.
>
> In June/July 1939, probably as a result of his increasingly weak heart, a glucose treatment with strophantin was begun. The injections were

administered in the prisoners' infirmary, prisoner Rudolf Gottschalk from Frankfurt/Main reported to me. By the way, he hardly recognized Schneider any more after his long period of solitary confinement although he had earlier worked together with him. For this purpose Schneider was led by an SS-man from his cell to the prisoners' infirmary. Prisoner Gottschalk, who on this occasion provided Schneider with food, (fruit, dietary food, etc.) as best he could, assured me that he made the mixture for each injection himself and was present at each injection. During one of these injections Schneider suddenly collapsed and died as a result of a heart collapse. The unofficial autopsy determined that an overdose of strophantin with advanced weakness of the heart muscle was the cause of death. Prisoner Gottschalk believed that Schneider also got additional strophantin injections in his cell besides the injections with the medically correct dosage in the prisoners' infirmary, unless the normal dosage for Schneider that was set at the lower end of the norm was still set too high in view of his weakened condition. However, it must be clearly stated that this acute cause of death was the result of his solitary confinement, an ordeal that lasted one and a half years.

Arthur Dietzsch comes to similar conclusions about the death of Paul Schneider at the end of his report:

> The personal treatment by the camp physician at that time, Dr. Ding, caused a stir among those of us who were prisoners. We naturally tried to start a conversation with Paul Schneider, but we were only successful the third or fourth time he was being treated in the infirmary. When we asked him about how he was doing, he explained that he was to be released and was getting glucose injections to accelerate his recovery.
>
> Paul Schneider was terribly emaciated; his bright, blue eyes positively glowed in his dark eye sockets, his body showed numerous black and blue welts, his lower thighs were swollen in an unimaginable way. Horrified by his appearance and overwhelmed by his brave attitude, none of us could bring ourselves to take away Paul Schneider's belief that he was going to be released, for we could not resist the uneasy feeling that they had nothing good planned for him, and our gloomy suspicion was not mistaken.
>
> About a week later Dr. Ding burst into his business office: "What a dirty trick! Schneider has just died!" We prisoners looked at each other

in stunned silence and quietly bowed our heads over our work. After a short while Walter Krämer, the infirmary overseer who had waited in the business office, went to the convection room, which was later to become our laboratory, to examine the empty ampoules. Except for some traces of glucose and strophantin he found nothing that would force someone to conclude that Paul Schneider had died a violent death. Perhaps Paul Schneider had really succumbed to a heart attack after all that he had to endure, but perhaps it was also an overdose of strophantin . . . .

We must still let the former Buchenwald prisoner Walter Poller speak as a further contemporary witness, who had to prepare the body of Paul Schneider and then helped to put it in the coffin. Later, i.e., after 1945 until his retirement, Walter Poller was the editor-in-chief of the *"Westfälische Rundschau."* As a political prisoner Walter Poller was put on duty as a recorder of medical records in Buchenwald. We first quote from his book *The Medical Recorder of Buchenwald.*

> Pastor Paul Schneider from Dickenschied was in Buchenwald for two years . . . . When he refused during the roll call to salute the murderous flag of the thousand-year Reich that he detested, he was laid over a sawhorse, punished with twenty-five lashes with a cane and then locked in the solitary confinement building because he steadfastly refused to give the salute they demanded. That was the beginning of his end. We knew that a death sentence was already pronounced over him because even in the camp he still made no secret of his Christian convictions and his opposition to Nazism and because he enjoyed great popularity and general respect among the prisoners, literally sharing everything with his fellow inmates from the first day of his detention in the camp, sharing even the bread and the little money he had. But no one suspected on this day that the sentence would only be carried out after more than one endlessly long year.
> I was present at the execution.
> Many times Schneider's voice was heard, ringing out loudly and clearly from the solitary confinement building almost across the whole square, when the ten thousands lined up for roll call: "Friends, listen to me. Pastor Paul Schneider is speaking here. They are torturing and murdering people here. For the sake of Christ, have mercy. Pray to

God. Remain steadfast and true. God, the almighty Father, will take this evil from us."

It was clear to us: Paul Schneider was a zealous advocate of the Faith, a deeply religious man who found his comfort and strength in the passion story of his religious ideal, enabling him to take upon himself the heavy load, even to the point of being willing to die. Paul Schneider believed in redemption through Jesus Christ, his Lord. After such preaching he knew what had to come with the inevitability of a law of nature, but the moral law in him compelled him to act in such an exemplary, courageous way.

After such preaching Schneider was always taken out of his cell in the solitary confinement building and brought to the central square where roll call was taken. There he was whipped until the blood oozed through his clothes. And then he was dragged back to the solitary confinement building half-conscious.

I do not know what else Paul Schneider had to endure in solitary confinement, but it must have been horrible. For there he was in the hands of the overseer of solitary confinement, the sadistic SS-man Sommer, who took great delight in beating the inmates, and even hung them upside down from trees with perverse pleasure. Time and again he had the pharmacy of the prisoners' infirmary give him poison and afterwards a death was always recorded in the solitary confinement building. In the summer of 1939 I got to see Paul Schneider up close for the first time. Prison guard Sommer suddenly took him to the prisoners' infirmary.

What a sight! I have never felt the deep tragedy of Pilate's words, "Ecce homo" (behold the man) in a more deeply moving way than then. The large, noble, pale yellow face with its bright, open eyes was furrowed by suffering, and yet full of that transfiguration that the most noble and determined humanity will etch on every fighter's brow. The body was nothing but skin and bones, the arms were unshapely and swollen, on the wrists there were bluish-red, green and bloody cuts. And the legs—they were no longer human legs, but elephant legs.

Water! We who had seen many prisoners die from cardiovascular trouble faced a puzzle: How was it possible that this man was still living? How was it possible that he was able to walk the long way across the large square where roll call was taken, through the endlessly long rows of barracks and through the forest down to the prisoners' infirmary in this condition? To be sure, he was clumsy and wobbly, yet he was still walking by his own effort!

SS-guard Sommer's dirty face, as cunning as a jaguar's with its stupid, yet brutal features, stood in sharp contrast to Schneider's. He never left Schneider's side for a moment, and we prisoners could not exchange a word with our friend to find out more details. What was going to happen in this case? Another murder? As desensitized as we had become to the huge number of deaths every day, this case somehow touched us much more deeply. Paul Schneider was not just some nameless, unknown prisoner, although for that reason he was no less pitiable and wretched than the others. Paul Schneider was one of those whose death would have wide repercussions, stretching as far as Holland, England, Sweden and America. And Paul Schneider was our friend, whose convictions were perhaps not ours, but whose integrity and Christianity of loving deeds was beyond any doubt.

But our hardened features betrayed to the SS-guard Sommer nothing of what was going on inside of us. Only the closest prisoners exchanged glances with each other that told the schooled insider what we felt and how we were inwardly trembling with emotion. We did not stop doing the job assigned to us for even a fraction of a second, and slowly the hawk-like, searching look in the eyes of the henchman Sommer, who was probing for symptoms in Schneider, lulled us into a false sense of security.

Then the camp physician Dr. Ding came.

"Why didn't you let us know that you were sick, Schneider?" Ding addressed him in a calm, business-like tone of voice that an exemplary doctor would use. Paul Schneider wanted to get up from the bench on which he was allowed to sit down, but Ding immediately said: "Keep sitting."

Now Paul Schneider looked up to Ding somewhat helplessly, obviously surprised by the way in which he was addressed. But I clearly saw in his eyes that he did not trust his tone of voice. He made a gesture with his right hand, as if he did not quite know how he should respond.

Ding repeated his question again in a most kindly and suggestive way: "You are surely sick. You must notify us when you don't feel well." Schneider did not say anything. Was not this Dr. Ding the camp physician in the Buchenwald concentration camp? Was he an unsuspecting angel from another world? Did he not see that this person here had obviously been tortured to the brink of death? The prisoners in the area acted as if the matter were completely unimportant to them. "Come along," Ding then continued, "I will examine you." Paul Schneider struggled to his feet and staggered behind Ding into another room in the barracks where Ding felt Schneider's body and listened with a stethoscope.

Will Ding now give him an injection?

No! He doesn't do it!

He gives this order: "Put ointment bandages around his wrists. Give him glucose, and a cardiac stimulant. Massage him carefully. Apply red light to the sections of his back, buttocks and upper thighs that are suffused with blood."

And he leaves Paul Schneider's fellow prisoners with the responsibility of carrying out the orders.

What's going on here? Do they want to treat Paul Schneider differently now? Humanely? The way the external and internal law commands it?

The prison orderlies try to help Paul Schneider, but they cannot exchange a word with him that could give them an explanation, an answer to our questions, because even now Sommer does not leave Schneider's side. When Ding leaves the room, he orders: "The treatment will be continued tomorrow. Sommer, you will bring Schneider to the infirmary again tomorrow morning after the roll call."

The treatment was continued for about eight to ten days. Schneider recovered surprisingly fast.

During this time I am there once when Ding asks him: "Well, Schneider, how do you feel now?"

Schneider smiles: "Good, Dr. Ding." Ding asks another question: "Do you have a proper bed in your cell?"

Schneider: "Yes, Dr. Ding."

Ding: "Stop this nonsense, Schneider. You can see that you are treated properly when you fit into the camp discipline."

Paul Schneider does not answer, he only smiles, but his eyes are sparkling. Ding continues: "I will speak to the camp commandant to see if you can be released from solitary confinement."

In the meantime the orderlies have been able to speak to Schneider. He had been chained again in the cell for about two weeks day and night, without interruption, as if he had been nailed to the cross. SS-guard Sommer, whom he called a murderer and a torturer, had mistreated him very horribly during this whole time. But he did not know how to explain to himself why he was now suddenly being treated so decently. Was he perhaps to be released?

When the treatment reaches somewhat of a conclusion with surprisingly quick and good success, Ding does another thorough physical examination with a stethoscopy of the heart and lungs and then says: "You see, Schneider, you have recovered beautifully. You still have only a little cardiac insufficiency. Well, that's certainly understandable considering this whole affair you've been through. But we'll be able to cure that too. Let's inject a cardiac stimulant."

Ding gets an ampoule from the pharmacy, fills up the injection needle in Schneider's presence and injects it.

The next day I am there when Sommer brings Schneider to the infirmary. According to the reports of the orderlies Ding asked Schneider how he was feeling after the injection he was given yesterday. Schneider replied that on the whole he felt good, only he was somewhat dizzy. That should actually not have been the case, Ding responded, but perhaps you have a certain allergy to the medication, because otherwise we have always gotten very good results with it. "Let's try a different medication and see how you take that."

When I enter the treatment room, Ding is not present. Schneider is sitting under the ultraviolet lamp. He returns my morning greeting, smiling gently. He has made an excellent recovery. His arms and legs are normal again, only his body is still unusually gaunt, but his chest swells broadly and strongly and Schneider's posture is again straightened.

Ding comes into the room. He has a full injection needle in his hand. He is surprisingly animated. Oh, I know this feature of his! I cannot be part of this, so I leave the room and go to the doctor's office.

I am absolutely shattered. Had I not already begun to believe that Paul Schneider could survive Buchenwald? And now this sudden change again! I go to the waste paper basket into which Ding usually throws the empty ampoules, more mechanically than anything else and only reluctantly, following an inner compulsion. And five empty strophantin ampoules are lying there. Two of them injected at once are fatal. A short time later Ding comes into the doctor's office, sits down at his desk, and I hand him the folder with documents needing his signature. He signs them and does not read through any of the documents. I can clearly see that his thoughts are completely elsewhere.

Peix, the orderly of the inner ward, steps into the room. So, now it's coming, Ding is acting busy. I look at Peix. The seconds are becoming an eternity.

"Doctor," Peix says, "should Schneider be taken back to his cell now?"

"What?" Ding asks with a surprised look on his face, staring into space for a moment, as someone usually does when he is thinking a thousand thoughts in that fraction of a second when he is suddenly startled. "What? Right! No." An atmosphere of limitless incomprehensibility fills the room, and Ding is still staring into space. But then he says, as if it's only a matter of a harmless therapy: "No, put him under the ultraviolet lamp for another half hour."

Peix walks out of the room. Ding keeps on signing documents. Could I have been wrong? But it is simply not possible for any human heart to outlast this dose of poison longer than a few minutes! Am I seeing ghosts? Ding is perfectly calm, asks me questions, and discusses this and that. I must have been wrong.

Then Peix comes rushing into the room: "Dr. Ding, please come quickly." Ding jumps up, doesn't even ask first what has happened, and runs with quick steps behind Peix. For a moment I have to hold on tightly to the edge of the table. Then I also go into the room where the ultraviolet radiation treatments are given. Paul Schneider is lying there, stretched out lengthwise on the floor. Dead. Ding kneels alongside the corpse, opening the closed eyelids. Peix stands next to him like a wooden column.

Later I find out that Paul Schneider complained about a sudden dizzy feeling under the ultraviolet lamp. After that the orderly removed the ultraviolet lamp, and when Paul Schneider was walking toward the chair on which his clothes lay, he fell down.

In his doctor's office Ding dictates to me a completely false medical history he simply made up.

A fever curve is drawn, although Schneider was never in the infirmary for in-patient treatment. In the report on his death it says that Schneider had already been discharged from his in-patient treatment in the infirmary and was still only in outpatient treatment. It goes on to say that death occurred surprisingly in the vicinity of the infirmary barracks after a treatment. It says the cause of death was probably a weak heart.

The camp commander is immediately notified. This is the first time that such a thing happens. Berlin receives news of his death by telex. The falsified medical reports, in which the story of several in-patient treatments in the infirmary is made up, are compiled with great care, so that they can be immediately sent to Berlin upon request, and of course, they are promptly requested.

And while the orderlies transport the corpse into the wretched morgue housed in a barracks outside the camp, I am racking my brain: Why all this expenditure of time and effort? Usually they make short work of it. Now even a postmortem examination of the corpse is being ordered. This puzzling question is becoming even more inextricable for me. The next day the head of the Pathological Institute of the University of Jena comes to perform the autopsy on the corpse. I have to write the autopsy report. Once again I see Paul Schneider on the plank bed. No signs of any mistreatment, no signs of all the suffering that this man had to endure. Only there in the bend of his right arm there is a small, hardly visible puncture wound, the place at which the murderer injected the poison into the bloodstream, the poison that did not want to work, who knows for what reason, and that finally took effect under the ultraviolet light that acted as a cardiac depressant.

The corpse is opened. All his organs are fine. Nowhere is there a trace of any sickness that could have led to death. The heart is opened, this large, overly strong, believing heart. The autopsy report closes with the words:

Cause of death—cardiac insufficiency.

And here is the epilogue. It also brings the answer to the questions that had still puzzled me until then.

Schneider's corpse is not taken to Weimar to be incinerated in the crematorium. A few days later Peix and I are given the job of putting the corpse in a coffin for viewing and are told to be there when it is picked up.[3]

In the course of corresponding with Walter Poller, the author of this documentation asked whether he ever saw the commander of the concentration camp, Koch, with Sommer and Paul Schneider in the prisoners' infirmary. Walter Poller answered:

---

[3] W. Poller, *Der Arztschreiber von Buchenwald* (1960), p. 194 ff.

I can only confirm that Sommer alone took Paul Schneider out of the solitary confinement building to the prisoners' infirmary and that Koch was never together with Paul Schneider in the prisoners' infirmary. To be sure, there is every reason to believe that in taking Schneider to the infirmary Sommer was acting on the orders of Koch. In addition, the behavior of the camp physician Dr. Ding toward Schneider and Schneider's behavior during the first examination in the prisoners' infirmary point to the fact that the camp commandant Koch had ordered the medical treatment and that the order was part of an intentional plan to murder Schneider, a plan that could only be triggered or carried out on the orders of Koch, based on all the other experiences I had learned from. It can hardly be clarified today if Koch acted on his own initiative or followed a pertinent tip from "above."

A further question addressed to Walter Poller was meant to clarify if Paul Schneider could have been a patient in the infirmary at any time, as other reports claim to know. Walter Poller answered:

And now to your second question: It depends on what you want to express by saying "Paul Schneider was a patient in the infirmary." If you mean by that what is generally expressed with the parallel phrase: "He is a patient in the hospital," I can assure you with absolute certainty that Paul Schneider was not a patient in the infirmary in the final year before his death. At least since the middle of 1938 medical records were kept on each patient. A few minutes after the death of Paul Schneider I myself looked in the card file for such a medical record and found nothing in spite of a very extensive search. I also did not find any record in the so-called outpatient card file, which, however, was not kept very reliably. I definitely know that because Dr. Ding expressly asked me shortly after Paul Schneider's death for his medical record or his card in the card file and because then I had to make a new medical record on the orders of Dr. Ding. Ding then made entries on the record that were pure fabrications. In my presence Dr. Ding drew a fever chart to supplement the entries on the medical record. I no longer remember the exact date of this fever chart, but I remember exactly that the dates entered on it were all made up. I myself had been employed in the infirmary since the end of January 1939. From this point in time to his death Paul Schneider was not treated as an in-patient in the infirmary, as I can definitely testify from my own experience, and in all probability he was not an in-patient at an earlier time either! A number of people claim that Schneider was said to have been an in-patient in the infirmary. This claim can probably be explained by the following circumstance, if such people are presenting it in a trustworthy or credible way. In the report on Schneider's death that Dr. Ding himself dictated to me as I typed, it explicitly stated that his sudden death occurred on the way from the infirmary to his cell after an out-patient treatment. When Dr. Ding dictated this passage to me, I was not at all surprised by it, because I had grown accustomed to his practice of giving untrue descriptions in his reports time and again. He probably thought he could somehow protect himself by doing so. Of course, I also immediately spoke to my trustworthy friends about this untrue description by Dr. Ding and there is every reason to believe that this phrase was used in these conversations about Paul Schneider's death: "Schneider was in the infirmary," which could be understood in terms of Paul Schneider being in the infirmary not as a patient, but as a dead man . . . .

30

THE UNNERVED AUTHORITIES

While the Protestant consistory in Düsseldorf is orchestrating Paul Schneider's removal from office in cooperation with the Gestapo, the events in Buchenwald described in the previous chapter are running their course.

Superintendent Ernst Gillmann announces the death of Paul Schneider to the consistory. The consistory notifies the administrative office of the Protestant Church in Berlin:

> The Consistory President Düsseldorf, July 26, 1939
> 7806
>
> To the Protestant Administrative Office
> Berlin
>
> Concerning: Pastor Schneider, Dickenschied
> Edict of the 15th of this month on 80 III 4930 II/38
>
> After we had just initiated the procedure of transferring Pastor Schneider into temporary retirement, we received the news of his sudden death in these days. As the superintendent responsible for his district, Gillmann, told us in Simmern, Schneider succumbed to a heart attack in the Buchenwald concentration camp near Weimar.
>
> If it appears that the political difficulties having to do with the person of Schneider are mainly settled based on this news, I feel especially compelled to make the following report as a result of the rumors we

have heard and the actual information we received about the manner in which the funeral services took place in Dickenschied.

The previously dissected body was laid out in Weimar and then was taken in a sealed casket to Dickenschied after the widow had seen the face of the dead man again. Considering the special significance of this case it was supposedly doubtful to the police until shortly before the beginning of the funeral whether they could even justify the release of the body. When they decided to oblige the family, it was at once apparent that an immense crowd of visitors had flocked together from all directions. People were said to have come from far away, even from East Prussia, Bavaria and Schleswig-Holstein. The impressive character of this rally was impressively underscored by the presence of a large number of clergymen in robes, about 150. An additional 50 pastors or so had shown up in civilian clothes to pay him their last respects.

Superintendent Gillmann conducted the funeral. From what I heard, Pastor Schlingensiepen gave the funeral sermon, but in a moderate tone. This was followed by about twenty eulogies at the graveside; the bearing of the widow is said to have been such that she found general admiration.

Since Superintendent Gillmann had explained to the police that he would do his best to ensure that no unpleasant incidents would occur, the authorities trusted his assurances. In fact, the ceremony proceeded in a calm and dignified fashion. The police were said to have had not the slightest reason to intervene.

If one disregards the regrettable death, it is astonishing that such a powerful demonstration could even take place at the present time, even more so in this immediate border region. If people always did justice to the merits of Schneider's personality, we must not ignore the fact that he was considered to be an opponent of the state and the aforementioned measure taken against him had become necessary. Until the end there was no prospect that he could have been released from the concentration camp in the foreseeable future. We had to see for ourselves that his continuation in the ministry was no longer acceptable. Furthermore, if one considers that these funeral services did not fail to make a deep impression on the populace of this region that is known to be very difficult with regard to its church politics, the whole event was probably not suitable to contribute to the pacification of the church situation there and does not fit in well with our continued efforts to create peaceful conditions. Moreover, since we are in the process of restoring order in the various neighboring congregations, our work will probably be made considerably more difficult by the anger that has been stirred up again in large parts of the population. Schneider's grave in Dickenschied is being adopted as a place of great significance; this is certainly an unwelcome development. The eyes of many will be fixed on it as if on a place of pilgrimage.

The danger of foreigners exploiting this event for propaganda purposes should not be considered insignificant. This idea suggests itself because it has become known to us that Schneider's death is said to have been announced to the public much earlier by foreign radio stations before the family members or any church authorities knew about it.

The preceding serious assessment of this matter makes it my duty to report on it in detail. Considering the unusual nature of this case, I have enclosed an additional copy of this letter which I ask you to please send to the minister of church affairs.

Dr. Koch

This letter joins those that are among the darkest chapters in recent church history, as this documentation shows. About four weeks later another letter is sent to the church administration in Berlin, in which the cynicism of the consistory once again becomes evident in the way they argue their case. The report of the Gestapo was business-like in its approach; the subject of the consistory's report is the charge that the Gestapo should not have given its permission to hold this funeral. The consistory would certainly have preferred that Paul Schneider's body be cremated in Weimar so that every memory of Paul Schneider could be blotted out. The lines in their letter reveal great insecurity: "Without decree"— they are meant to serve the purpose of justifying themselves.

Protestant Consistory Düsseldorf, August 21, 1939
8122

To the Protestant Church Administrative Office in Berlin-Charlottenburg

Concerning: the death of Pastor Paul Schneider, Dickenschied
Without decree
Reporter: consistory member Kolrep
Co-reporter: consistory member D. Euler
1 enclosure

We present the following information to further supplement the report made by the consistory president dated July 28 of this year-Nr. 8122:

In the meantime we have gotten in touch with the Gestapo headquarters in Koblenz to get as complete a picture as possible of the funeral and its attendant circumstances. They were willing to give us further details. We have enclosed a copy of the report made by Dr. Venter who personally observed the funeral as the leading official of the Gestapo. It provides information on this event. Moreover, it is apparent that the official statements of the Gestapo essentially agree with the information already reported. We also gained the impression from our conversation with the Gestapo that our assessment of these events can be seen as quite accurate. These gentlemen especially approved of our reference to the fact that the decision to grant permission for such a sensational funeral ceremony, which also did not remain unnoticed overseas, can only be regretted and that the existence of the burial site in Dickenschied will always keep the memory of Pastor Schneider alive.

Likewise, we were confidentially informed by the Gestapo of a statement made by the regional Brotherhood Councils on the second of this month about the following subject: Schneider is to be regularly remembered on his birthday or on the Sunday after August 29, 1939. In the same way the congregations of the Confessing Church are to remember Schneider with thanksgiving and intercessory prayer on the Sunday before Advent, on which the dead are commemorated.

Finally, a "Schneider-Foundation" is supposed to be established for his widow and the children as well as for general church purposes. However, we could not find out further details about all this.

If we should get our hands on any other material in this matter, we will make another report on it. Our only additional comment is that we must refrain from filling this pastorate again in view of the difficult conditions in Dickenschied. At the present time we are busy examining the question of whether the Dickenschied congregation can permanently receive its pulpit supply from the neighboring congregation in Kirchberg in order to eliminate the pastoral position in this way.

Per proxy:
Kolrep August 18
To be submitted to Reich office manager Sohns for his further examination and to President Koch after he returns from vacation.

The enclosure:

The Gestapo Koblenz, July 26, 1939
Gestapo headquarters
Koblenz
II B Nr. 355/37
Per proxy

On July 21, 1939 the funeral of Pastor Paul Schneider took place in Dickenschied, in the district of Simmern. The interment followed from the Protestant church, in which a funeral service took place at two o'clock. Shortly after two o'clock the funeral procession started to move from the church. At the head of the procession about 45 females carried wreaths and flower arrangements. 20 young men and 150 pastors in their vestments from all parts of the Reich followed them. The family members of the deceased and the population of Dickenschied and the neighboring villages walked behind the casket that was carried by residents of the village.

At the grave a clergyman from Barmen gave the funeral oration. He was followed by a large number of the participating pastors who gave eulogies. These pastors of the Confessing Church were from Bavaria, East Prussia, Württemberg, Silesia, Oldenburg, Baden, Berlin and its suburbs, Hessen-Nassau, Schleswig-Holstein, Saxony, Thuringia, Pomerania, the Rhine province, Westphalia, and Hannover. After that, a clergyman of the United Church of Germany spoke, then clergymen from the Rhenish Mission, the City Mission of Baden-Baden and a representative of the Rhenish assistant pastors and vicars (etc.).

In their remarks they portrayed Pastor Schneider as a champion of their faith, who suffered according to the will of the Lord and who died for his Lord. There were no incidents whatsoever.

Per Proxy
Dr. Venter

Superintendent Albertz writes to the sessions of Dickenschied and Womrath:

The Provisional Leadership Berlin-Spandau, July 20, 1939
of the German Protestant Church

Superintendent Lic. Albertz
Schlemminger Strasse 21

To the Elders of the congregations of Dickenschied and Womrath

Dear Gentlemen and Brothers!

Tomorrow innumerable thoughts and prayers from all over Christendom will surround your dear congregation, especially your brave pastor's wife and the pastor's sons and daughters, when you pay your final respects to your lawful pastor. The whole Confessing Church sympathizes with your great loss and the fate of our dear brother Schneider from the bottom of our hearts. It is my task to express these thoughts to you through this letter in the name of all the members of the provisional leadership of the German Protestant Church. Since my colleagues Müller and Dr. Böhm and I myself are restricted to Berlin by a Gestapo ban, the provisional church leadership will be represented tomorrow by our member Pastor Forck from Hamburg and he will also lay a wreath on our behalf.

As the Reformed member of the provisional church leadership I feel especially close to you, your dear pastor and your congregations. In those days you tried to practice Christian discipline according to the rule of the New Testament and on the basis of the teaching of the Heidelberg Catechism, and precisely this action of yours, which you took jointly with you brother who has now gone home, will certainly now occupy your attention in a special way.

Brother Schneider was never doubtful about his conviction that he had to go the way he had been led, his conscience being captive to the Holy Scriptures. So I ask you as the fellow elders of our brother to take as his legacy what he left you and your church when he bore witness to and followed the way of Christ by his actions and his suffering.

We remind you and ourselves of the comfort offered by the 52nd question of our Catechism. To paraphrase the answer, "In all his distress and persecution our dear brother Schneider turned his eyes to the heavens and confidently awaited as judge the very One who has already stood trial in his place before God and so has removed the whole curse from him." All of us in the Confessing Church must thank him at his grave for the favor he did all of us. At a time when church discipline on the foundation of God's Word, which our fathers practiced, was completely buried, he has reestablished it and reminded Christians in Germany of something they have neglected to their detriment through the centuries. When he went to prison, he set an example for all of us by demonstrating the great, unchanging faithfulness of a pastor to his congregation, to which he was assigned, but especially by addressing a great question to our conscience. Is it really true that only the will of God is recognized and done in the realm of the church? Finally, he was a courageous witness for his Lord in the concentration camp itself. So now he has gone home to God, as we hope, and entered the joy of his Lord.

We know how much you have lost in your pastor. All the more wholeheartedly we ask you to look after his wife and his children, helping them and praying for them, and together with the young brother who is standing in for brother Schneider, to continue to lead the congregations of Dickenschied and Womrath in all steadfastness and wisdom as churches reformed by God's Word.

May the God of all comfort comfort you with his mercy.

For the provisional leadership of the
German Protestant Church
Albertz

Pastor Wilhelm Niesel, a member of the council of the Protestant Church of
the Old Prussian Union, turns for help to the Reich chancellery with a petition
that is processed by the permanent secretary of the chancellery, Friedrich-
Wilhelm Kritzinger, a committed National Socialist, who later, on January 20,
1942, participated in the notorious Wannsee Conference.[1] He passes the letter
on to the Reich leader of the SS who answers it. This event shows again how
the rulers at that time used purely internal church measures as an opportunity
to eliminate pastors who were not acceptable to them, whose pastoral "actions"
at the same time constituted an appeal to the congregations. The historian
Gunther van Norden sees it in these terms:

> The church struggle gained a political dimension, going beyond the
> intentions of the church leadership, as the believers were activated to
> participate in religious life and as the appeals to the political leadership
> to stop following the path they had embarked on were aggressively
> presented and targeted at the largest sections of the population as
> possible. Hurten even speaks of the "mass basis" that the church protest
> possessed as a "power factor." The regime itself considered this power
> factor to be more dangerous than the resistance of the Communist
> Party of Germany (KPD).[2]

The intrepid nature and deep faith of Paul Schneider, which the SS could
not break with their inhumane methods, showed the National Socialists their
limits and ultimately their powerlessness. The events already reported as well
as the following documents allow us to take a further look at the prevalent
conditions in those days.

The Council of the Old Prussian Union
of the Protestant Church

---

[1] The "final solution" to the "Jewish question" was decided at this conference.

[2] G. van Norden, "Zwischen Kooperation und Teilwiderstand: Die Rolle der Kirchen
und Konfessionen" in *Der Widerstand gegen den Nationalsozialismus* (1986), p. 231.

Berlin-Lichterfelde, July 29, 1939
Drakestrasse 32
Telephone: 76 224 41/42

To the Reich Minister and
Head of the Reich Chancellery
Dr. Lammers
Berlin W 8
Wilhelmplatz

On July 18, 1939 the Protestant pastor Paul Schneider from Dickenschied (Rhineland) died in the Buchenwald concentration camp near Weimar. Pastor Schneider would have completed his 42nd year in August. He leaves behind his wife and six small children. The reasons that had led to his arrest are explained in the enclosed report. It follows that Pastor Schneider was arrested on the occasion of a purely church matter. In accordance with the Reformed confession and in agreement with the leadership of his congregation, the session in Dickenschied, he had taken a church disciplinary action.

His death has deeply shaken the Protestant congregations in all of Germany. Especially in the Rhineland emotions are running high far beyond the circles of the Protestant Church.

We feel obligated to inform you of these events and also ask you to use your influence to ensure that the constantly increasing actions taken against Protestant pastors and church members are stopped.

Lic. Niesel
Enclosure

The following information has been reported to us about Pastor Schneider from Dickenschied:

Dickenschied is a small village in the Hunsrück, an area where the church is very much alive. The village has 500 inhabitants, of which the smaller half is Protestant. In addition, there is a daughter village with a somewhat larger congregation. The church is of the Reformed confession and holds to the old traditions of the Reformed Church.

Confirmation instruction is given on the basis of the Heidelberg Catechism.

In 1934 Pastor Schneider came to this church, a man of radiant warm-heartedness, an essentially German figure. He is not at all a fanatic, but a conscientious pastor who provided loving pastoral care to each individual member and knew how to talk evangelistically to the people. He was a man of ultimate truthfulness, for whom many things were unacceptable that others thought they could still accept.

Pastor Schneider saw that there were forces at work in his congregation that threatened to fragment their church life. He came to the realization that the way religion was taught in the school was contrary to biblical Christianity, and that a celebration of Christmas was being observed that was inconsistent with the Christian significance of the Christmas season. It was found that parents were keeping their children away from confirmation classes and from the childrens' worship service, something that had never happened in the church. The session and the pastor were often mocked. Signatures were collected to make it possible for a Thuringian German Christian to preach in the congregation.

Pastor Schneider discussed these incidents with his session. They agreed that in view of this development article 85 of the Heidelberg Catechism had to be applied, the article that deals with so-called discipline toward repentance in the congregation.

After that Pastor Schneider went to the congregation and explained to it how this Christian discipline was to be understood according to the Reformed confession. He said the congregation must not incur the charge that it was partly responsible for the destruction and secularization of the Christian life of their congregation. Christian discipline, as the Reformed faith requires it, is not a matter of anger or hatred, but of love. For the Reformers church discipline was the means they used to practice real love for a human being, because the congregation confronts the individual with his sins and especially drives him to repentance through the seriousness with which it does this.

Two members of the congregation were the first ones to be affected by this action of the session, including the teacher in the daughter village of Womrath. The session addressed the following letter to him:

"Last Sunday on May 1 the session announced Christian discipline toward repentance, which we had announced to you with your summons to the session meeting.

In accordance with the announcement the officers exclude you from the Christian fellowship, by withholding the sacraments from you. God himself excludes you from the kingdom of Christ until you promise to lead a better life and show evidence of it (Heidelberg Catechism, Question 85). You are familiar with the reasons. In addition, you have mocked the leadership, discipline and order of the congregation and accused the session of lying without producing the least bit of evidence for it. You have also brought dissension into the congregation by collecting signatures with the intention of paving the way for the proclamation of a pastor in this congregation who cannot be considered by the Confessing Church and this congregation to be standing any longer on the foundation of the gospel and the church of Christ. He belongs to the Thuringian German Christians, a sect that even the Chairman of the Reich Church Committee Dr. Zollner in a theological opinion called a false teaching that stood outside the bounds of the church.

The congregation is urged to break off Christian and church fellowship with you, but to treat you kindly in all necessary interactions, just as church discipline as a whole does not want your damnation, but seeks your repentance and your readmission into the membership of the congregation.

You retain the right to hear the proclamation of the Word and to receive pastoral care in the congregation. Church contributions (church taxes) will not be collected from you.

Next Sunday Christian discipline will again be proclaimed to the congregation in a gentle form that does not mention your name. Only if you then do not choose to listen to the congregation will the discipline toward repentance become effective with the third announcement.

May God prepare your heart to receive his truth and mercy and may he allow you to recognize his holy, Christian church on earth, apart from which no salvation and blessedness can be found."

After that Pastor Schneider was taken into preventive detention on May 31, 1937. The Gestapo indicated as the reason for this action that Pastor Schneider had irresponsibly called on the congregation from the pulpit to boycott a national comrade. On July 24 he was let go again without a hearing on his case having taken place. He was simultaneously deported from the Rhineland. Pastor Schneider declared that he could not accept this deportation since he was committed to his congregation by his ordination vow. He preached the following day in his two congregations, but began a convalescent leave on the same evening, which he spent outside the Rhineland. When the vacation was over— that was on August 28—he filled in for a friend in Nassau-Hessen in order to await a revision of the actions taken against him by the state authorities and in order to make his final decision in inner peace. During this time he was able to find out for himself that his congregation was awaiting his return and that especially his session, to whom he felt particularly bound on the basis of the Reformed confession, took the view that a true shepherd did not leave the flock entrusted to him. After that he returned to his congregation on October 3, 1937. He gave his reasons for this step in a detailed letter he sent to the Reich chancellery. Yet on the very same evening he was arrested on the way to the evening worship service he intended to hold in the daughter village and was taken to Koblenz. The Gestapo headquarters in Koblenz wrote to the consistory in Düsseldorf about their action:

"Pastor Schneider is a fanatical supporter of the Confessing Church who has used every opportunity to agitate against the National Socialist state. This is why several criminal proceedings are pending against him in the special court in Cologne. He is charge with violating the Treachery Act and Article 30a of the Penal Code.

His detention was absolutely necessary at that time because he had announced Christian discipline against two national comrades from the pulpit. One of the members on whom this discipline was imposed was a supporter of the German Christians. Pastor Schneider was taken into preventive detention because of this action that is reminiscent of medieval conditions as well as because he disparaged a national comrade from the pulpit . . . ."

On November 25, 1937 Pastor Schneider was taken to the Buchenwald concentration camp near Weimar. During his whole time in the camp he was never allowed to receive visitors, thus he also never saw his wife. From the fall of 1938 to the spring of 1939 she got no mail whatsoever from him.

On July 18 of this year Mrs. Schneider received the news that her husband had died in the concentration camp of a heart attack. She immediately drove to Buchenwald. The coffin, sealed with seven seals, was handed over to her for burial in Dickenschied. On the way home a contingent of police made sure that the coffin arrived in Dickenschied only on the day of burial and that it was not set up in the manse, but was immediately taken to the church. The funeral took place in a peaceful way and was attended by large numbers of the population and by representatives from almost all the Protestant regional churches and church provinces.

   The petition is directly answered by the Gestapo and was personally signed by its boss, in whose hands all power was concentrated.

The Reich leader-SS Berlin SW 11, September 27, 1939
and Prince Albrecht Street 8
Head of the German Police Telephone: 12 00 40
in the Reich ministry of the interior
S-PP (II B) 131/39g

To the Council of the Protestant Church of the Old Prussian Union in Berlin-Lichterfelde
Drake Street 32

In response to your letter of July 29, 1939

Your view that Pastor Schneider was arrested on the occasion of a purely church matter is not accurate. Pastor Schneider tried in early 1937 to impose the so-called Christian discipline toward repentance on a national comrade because this man did not want to let his son attend the Confessing Church instruction of Pastor Schneider, but wanted his son to attend the church instruction of another pastor. Pastor Schneider publicly called on his congregation from the pulpit to break off all Christian and church fellowship with the two national comrades concerned. By making this appeal he turned this Christian discipline into a punitive measure, far exceeding the sphere of the church and amounting to the complete boycott of a national comrade. Pastor Schneider was taken into preventive detention because of this summons to a boycott that went beyond the church realm and was targeted at the national community. Later he was released from preventive detention and a ban was issued against him, forbidding him from staying in the Rhine province. When Pastor Schneider was released, it was pointed out to him that his return to the Rhine province would result in the Gestapo taking action against him. In spite of this oral and written notice Pastor Schneider returned to his congregation. Once again Pastor Schneider had to be taken into preventive detention because he obviously failed to heed the orders of the Gestapo. When Pastor Schneider then continued to declare that he would not obey the deportation order and would not follow the orders of the state in the future, his transfer to a concentration camp had to be ordered.

Even in the concentration camp it was revealed to Pastor Schneider several times that nothing stood in the way of his release from the concentration camp if he would commit himself to obey the deportation order. Pastor Schneider had always refused to make this commitment and thus had only himself to blame for his continued stay in the camp.

With reference to the last paragraph of your letter I hereby inform you that I do not have to take any measures against pastors if they stay within the framework of the current laws.

Heinrich Himmler

Before we focus our attention on what happened after the death of Paul Schneider, let us recall two statements made by former Buchenwald prisoners. First, the Social Democrat Walter Poller, who could not submit to the dictates of the National Socialists because of his political convictions and thus became a prisoner in Buchenwald after a long prison term. He writes:

Paul Schneider was a fanatic of faith, a deeply religious person, who found in the passion story of his religious ideal the comfort and the strength to take upon himself heavy trials to the point that he was willing to die. Paul Schneider believed in redemption through Jesus Christ, his Lord . . . .

Alfred Leikam, who had seen through the machinations of the National Socialists as a confessing Christian and had to offer resistance from a sense of Christian responsibility, was locked up in prisons without the order of a court of law and then was put in the Buchenwald concentration camp. He writes:

All the prisoners were respectful of the memory of Schneider and full of praise for his life. This word was true of his life: "His bond with Christ had become completely manifest." In my opinion he is the only one in Germany who so consciously took upon himself the cross of Christ to the point of death, overcoming all human fear and who was so deeply influenced by this word of faith: "Our faith is the victory that has overcome the world." If anyone wears "Christ's robe of honor" and was "deemed worthy of his suffering," it was Pastor Schneider. I could and I can hold his memory only in the highest regard. Which of us would like to boast of this mystery of Christ!

31

THE GESTAPO CONTINUES ITS PERSECUTION

The funeral services for Paul Schneider had a great effect that could not be anticipated by any side. We have seen that the German Christian consistory criticized the decision of the Gestapo to let the burial take place in Dickenschied. The Gestapo was surprised by the manner in which the funeral was conducted and thus became a witness to a Christian burial in the truest sense of the word. The notes that were struck there were so new for them that they return to Koblenz speechless, as we know. Nevertheless, they remain on the trail of Paul Schneider. Since he is no longer among the living, his family, his colleagues, and his church, which can now be found in the whole German Reich and beyond its borders, takes his place for the Gestapo.

On August 7, 1939 at 7:30 p.m. the Gestapo sends a telex in Wesermünde that is received by the Gestapo headquarters in Düsseldorf at ten o'clock.

Wesermünde Nr. 6958 August 7, 1939, 7:10 p.m.
To all Gestapo headquarters and offices

Concerning: The conference of the regional Brotherhood Councils on August 2, 1939
Dossier: none

A letter was intercepted here that the Confessing Church produced on a typewriter and disseminated by making carbon copies. Among other things it deals with Pastor Schneider who died in the concentration camp. The letter is titled: "Report on the Conference of the Regional Brotherhood Councils in August 1939" and was addressed to Pastor

Udo Smidt, Wesermünde-Lehe, Lange Street 92. It bears the postmark Hamburg-Altona, August 4, 1939, four o'clock. The report begins: 25 representatives were present. To open the meeting Asmussen[1] gave a moving devotional of a liturgical nature in view of the death of Brother Schneider. A bearer of the holy office in the Christian church was for the sake of his office first stripped of his freedom and then died in one way or another (God knows exactly how), daring to answer to God for what he did. In another place we read literally: He is one of the souls under the altar (Rv. 6). They were told to wait a little longer, until the number of their fellow servants and brothers who were to be killed as they had been was completed. (Rv. 6:11) We may be there. Niemöller, Leikam, Steinbauer, Pinn, Tiemann-Gronau, von Kameke, Schlingensiepen-Siegen among others are in the hands of those who held Schneider. We should ask God that the fruit of Schneider's suffering and death does not pass. Every congregation must know about his case. Not to cause trouble or to achieve something tactically, but to affirm our connection with the righteous who have been perfected, a connection that is there.

Schneider would have had a birthday in August. The pastors who have not yet remembered Schneider in front of the congregation should use it. They should do it now and intercede for this family in the worship service (August 29). In another place we read: The following items have been decided:

1. Kodlab (Conference of the Regional Brotherhood Councils) asks the Lbrr (the regional Brotherhood Councils), to instruct the pastors in their regions to remember Schneider on his birthday, Sunday, August 28
    a) with a brief factual report
    b) with intercessory prayer for the family
    c) with thanksgiving for Brother Schneider.

2. After interceding for the suffering and persecuted we should regularly thank God in our worship services for those who have overcome.

---

[1] Compare W. Lehmann, *Hans Asmussen* (1988), p. 94f.

3. On the Sunday before Advent when the dead in Christ are commemorated Schneider should be remembered by name with prayers of thanksgiving and intercession.

4. A Schneider Foundation should be established.
>   a) for the children
>   b) for general church purposes, etc. The collected funds should be brought along to the next Kodlab, etc.

The letter is signed: With warmest regards, Justus. The following men spoke at the conference: Asmussen, Albertz, Boehm, Scharf, Beckmann, Staemler, Kloppenburg, Dahlkotter and Rumpf.

Undoubtedly these persons are pastors. Where do they work? Or where have they appeared with regard to the Gestapo? Where did the Conference of the Regional Brotherhood Councils take place on August 2? Not answering by August 11, 1939 is considered a failure.

Additional remark of the Gestapo. The original of the intercepted letter is being sent there by express letter.

Additional remark for the staff leadership in Hamburg. A copy of the intercepted letter is being sent there by express letter.

Gestapo Wesermünde-Bremerhaven Rom 2 B 1 Nr. 1462/39
SB. Kleine-Loegte

This telex is sent to all the offices of the Gestapo. The Gestapo office in Halle an der Saale goes into action immediately and arrests Superintendent Stämmler a few hours after receiving the telex. It sends the following telex to the Gestapo-offices:

Halle 2631 August 8, 1939 8:30 p.m.

To all Gestapo headquarters and offices
Urgent. Submit immediately

Concerning: The Conference of the Regional Brotherhood Councils on August 2, 1939 in Berlin

Dossier: FS of the Gestapo Wesermünde, Nr. 6958 of August 7, 1939, Rom 2 B i i462/39

The representative of the local provincial Brotherhood Council, Pastor and Superintendent Dr. Wolfgang Staemmler, born September 2, 1889 in Duschnik, living in Grosskugel, was arrested early this morning. Besides him about 20 persons attended the Conference of the Kodlab on August 2 in Berlin from 10:00 a.m. to 5:30 p.m. in the Protestant parish hall in Berlin-Steglitz. Pastor Scharf from Sachsenhausen near Oranienburg chaired the meeting. Further participants:

1. Pastor Niesel, Berlin-Lichterfelde,
2. Pastor Dr. Böhm, Berlin,
3. Pastor von Rabenau, Berlin-Schöneberg,
4. Pastor Asmussen, Berlin,
5. Pastor Vogel, Dobrikow near Luckenwalde,
6. Pastor Beckmann, Düsseldorf,
7. Pastor Dahlkotter, Lippstadt,
8. Pastor Hildebrand, Goldap,
9. Pastor Mittendorf, Hamburg-Altona
10. Pastor Rumpf, Wiesbaden,
11. Pastor Werner, Gossma/Thuringia
12. Superintendent Albertz, Spandau
13. Pastor Kloppenburg, Oldenburg,
14. A representative from Württemberg whose name is unknown
15. and from Hessen.

The death of Pastor Schneider is said to have been the first point on the agenda. Stämmler claims

1) that he joined the meeting for the first time an hour after the start of the meeting during the debate on this point and

2) furthermore, that he was not always a witness to this discussion. He claims that he expressed no doubts about Schneider's death, but that he had a calming influence in terms of saying that we should be "grateful for the fact that a witness has been given to a church that was believed to be dead, a witness who remained faithful unto death." Further decisions or instructions of the kind mentioned in the FS were

not made in his presence. He says he rejects as outrageous the remarks made in the circular letter of the Confessing Church disclosed to him here and also refuses to accept any responsibility for them. Not even a directive matching the intention of the circular letter was issued at the meeting of the Prussian Brotherhood Council that took place following the Kodlab. These pastors also attended this meeting:

1. Pastor Schulze, Stettin,
2. Pastor Kelner from Pomerania,
3. Pastor Kleiner or Kelner (Kellner) from Silesia,
4. Pastor Buhre from Berlin and
5. Pastor Dibelius from Berlin.

I ask that all the pastors mentioned here be responsibly questioned about the information given by Stämmler on the meeting of the Kodlab in general and also in particular on the remarks of the Confessing Church made in the circular letter that was intercepted by the Gestapo in Wesermünde. I also ask that you inform me of any facts incriminating Stämmler.

According to the information provided by Stämmler the main railroad station here in Halle is supposed to be the site for a meeting of the provincial Brotherhood Council of Saxony tomorrow morning, Wednesday at 9:45 a.m. The participants:

1. Pastor Müller, Heiligenstadt,
2. Superintendent Deipser, Breesenstedt,
3. Pastor Jänicke, Magdeburg,
4. Pastor Schnapper, Grossmöringen.

Further details on this will follow.
Gestapo Halle Rom 2B 2E 7047/39

In Düsseldorf Dr. Joachim Beckmann, who later became the President of the Rhenish church, is ordered to the Gestapo office. He is no stranger to them.

Düsseldorf, August 9, 1939

On being summoned, Dr. Joachim Beckmann appears. He resides in Düsseldorf, Kopernikus Street 9c, and explains in response to our questioning:

On August 2, 1939 I attended the Conference of the Regional Brotherhood Councils in Berlin-Steglitz in the Protestant parish hall. The conference is a working group to which the individual regional Brotherhood Councils and a few other members of the Confessing Church send representatives. It does not have the authority to make decisions. This conference convenes once every two to three months. Usually the date for the next conference is set at the respective meeting. The conference on August 2, 1939 had already been set for this date a long time ago. The number of participants comes to about 30 persons.

As the deputy representative of the Prussian Brotherhood Council I myself attended there on August 2, 1939.

The conferences have the purpose of facilitating an exchange of views and sharing opinions on the issues facing the Confessing Church in the area of church politics. It does not have the character of an organ of church leadership for the Confessing Church. Only ideas are given there whose implementation is left up to the individual Brotherhood Councils.

At the last conference on August 2, 1939 Pastor Scharf chaired the meeting. On the whole I also recall the names of participants you held in front of me. I was not personally familiar with several other participants.

No special lectures are given at the conferences. It is almost always only a discussion.

I can only say about the conference on August 2, 1939 that after an introductory devotional by Pastor Asmussen a discussion about the death of Pastor Schneider followed. The results of the discussion were summarized in terms of these ideas: Intercessory prayers for the family of Pastor Schneider on Pastor Schneider's birthday or on the Sunday before Advent when the dead in Christ are commemorated, prayers of thanksgiving that Pastor Schneider was called home as a faithful witness to his Lord. We also expressed concern for the family of Pastor Schneider, discussing ideas about how we could ensure that they would not suffer any material want. A member suggested the creation of a special "foundation," but it was not set down in writing as a consensus view.

In response to your question I can also comment on the devotional given at the beginning of the conference. Pastor Asmussen made reference to the death of Pastor Schneider in it. I can no longer recall precise details. I can still remember the Bible verse, Revelation 6:11, that you held in front of me. Otherwise, I can only say about the devotional of Pastor Asmussen that it was very serious and dignified and did not contain any statements that were ambiguous and would allow one to draw the conclusion that it was the opinion of the speaker that Pastor Schneider was possibly killed. To understand the remarks made in the devotional it is useful to point out that the participants of the conference were familiar with the remark the camp doctor made to Mrs. Schneider: "Pastor Schneider had been suffering from a heart defect for six months. He also suddenly died in the infirmary from a heart attack." The shared conviction of the participants was that in the long run Schneider was not up to the great strains and stresses of the camp.

I cannot recall any critical statements made by conference participants on the remarks of Pastor Asmussen and the treatment of Schneider's case. This must have happened when I left the room for a short time.

The report you showed me on the conference of the Regional Brotherhood Councils is by no means authentic. It must be the private notes of a participant that he wrote up later. In my opinion it contains various mistakes about the views expressed and the statements made at the conference. For instance, I did not give any talk, but merely made a remark in the discussion on an issue that was raised.

Besides the treatment of Schneider's case, which took about two hours, other issues were also dealt with, for example: The situation of the Christian non-Aryans (the office of Gruber), and the last decree on the

Reich citizenship law. The conference may have lasted from 10:00 a.m. to 5:30 p.m. with about a two-hour break for lunch.

I am not familiar with the paper you submitted to me in which the conference also took a position on the death of Schneider. At any rate, the Rhenish Council did not issue it. The letters of the Rhenish Council have always borne the signature of the council. Moreover, since the imposition of the ban on our circular letters no circulars have been issued.

Read and signed:
Dr. Beckmann
Confirmed:
Eisel
(Signature)
Political Inspector Junior Civil Servant

Note:

Pastor Joachim Beckmann, born on July 18, 1901 in Wanne-Eickel, resides in Düsseldorf, Kopernikus Street 9c, and is—by his own account—not a member of the Prussian Brotherhood Council. He is merely a delegate to the Kodlab.

Signature Eisel
Political Inspector Junior Civil Servant

The report on the funeral services in Dickenschied is feared and sought by the Gestapo. The reader could relive the events at the cemetery in it. The spirit that permeated everything was discernable in every word, whether in the form of the address, the songs or remarks. On the one hand, all who were there or who got their hands on the publication were drawn into the aura of the Christian faith's confidence in ultimate victory. On the other hand, the injustice, the satanic aspect of the persecution, was directly present, even if it was not expressed publicly.

In February 1940, at the beginning of the war (1939–1945), the Gestapo again strikes it rich. The war unleashed by the National Socialists does not in any way prevent them from continuing its actions on the issue of Paul Schneider. The following letter is sent from Trier to Koblenz:

Certified copy
Gestapo
Gestapo office in Trier Trier, February 9, 1940
Br.-Nr. 834/40-II B 2-17/40 E
To the Gestapo
Gestapo office
Koblenz

Concerning: Implementation of the Collection Act of November 5, 1934-Collections of the Confessing Church
Dossier: None
Enclosures: 1 photocopy

Enclosed I am sending you a photocopy of a intercepted letter written by the Confessing Church pastor Heinz Friedrich Wilhelm Rolffs, who was born on June 28, 1900 in Stade, and resides in Bell (in the district of Simmern/Hunsrück), that was addressed to the local Confessing Church pastor Otto Kirstner, who was born on March 6, 1907 in Koblenz, and resides in Trier, Weberbach Street 52. The letter was mimeographed and mailed on February 8, 1940 in Kastellaun.

Contrary to the regulations of the financial department of the Protestant Consistory, Rolffs is here calling on the Confessing Church pastors, who have joined together in the Hunsrück Brotherhood, not to send in their collections to the special account A of the financial department of the consistory, but to remit them directly to the associations or institutions or to keep the contributions at home or to bring them along to the convention.

Furthermore, he is calling on the Confessing Church pastors to take up a monthly "thank offering" collection for the Confessing Church and to collect monetary donations for the widow of Pastor Schneider from Dickenschied/Hunsrück, who died in the concentration camp. These funds are to be remitted to his postal checking account Cologne Nr. 59022.

Signed, Nolle
Distributor
Central Reich Security Office pp. Seal F.d.R.d.A. from II B 109/40
Koblenz, March 7, 1940
(Signature)
Chancellery clerk

Central Reich Security Office Berlin SW 11, February 15, 1940
IV/4 A b 99/40

To the Gestapo Office in Trier
Concerning: Pastor Wilhelm Rolffs in Bell
Dossier: report of February 9, 1940-834/49-II B 2-17/40E

I request that you initiate criminal proceedings against Pastor Rolffs in Bell for calling on pastors to collect funds for the widow of the Confessing Church Pastor Schneider and that you report to me on the outcome at the appropriate time.

On orders:
Signed: Hahnenbruch

An investigation of Pastor Rolffs is immediately initiated. He does not hesitate for a moment to openly tell the Gestapo that he did what he could to secure financial support for Mrs. Schneider. The coordinator of this campaign to support the Schneiders is Pastor Voget in Elberfeld. Mrs. Schneider with her six children received only a very modest pension. He and others now come under fire from the Gestapo.

The circular letter intercepted by the Gestapo reads as follows:

Bell, February 6, 1940

Dear Brothers!

As a result of travel difficulties our convention on January 30 was so poorly attended that I feel compelled to inform you in writing of several important items: 1) The huge loss of students now studying theology indicates more clearly than anything else the end of the established Protestant Church. Caring for our future pastors will be the exclusive responsibility of our congregations. In every synod we must seek out one young man who can be recruited to study theology and who should be cared for and supported by the Confessing Church. 2) The task and responsibility of the Confessing Church has grown because of the war just as much as its distress has. The war is going to bring neither a pause nor the decision in our struggle. 3) The matter of the collections has not progressed beyond the pre-war level. The collections cannot be paid into "account A," instead it would be best to bring them along to the convention or keep them temporarily in your own church accounts or send them directly to the institutions or associations. Every month a thank offering is to be requested for the Confessing Church. The gifts are to be wrapped with a label indicating the purpose of the funds or are to be handed in with the label "to be used at the discretion of the local pastor." 4) I ask that you immediately request from me the number of green cards you will need to collect the freewill offerings for "The Church Under the Word" 1940. 5) Every colleague has to raise about 50 marks in his congregation for the future provision of sister Schneider and her family (to be paid into my postal checking account Cologne 59022 with the note "for the Schneider family").

With warm regards from your brother,
Signed, Rolffs

The Gestapo takes aim at point 5 of the letter in particular, where Pastor Rolffs does his best to help the Schneider family. This conflict drags on for about a year. What is significant about it is the fact that the district attorney does not target the suggested collection for the Schneider family, but looks for a collection outside the framework of the collection plan issued by the German Christian consistory. If it were publicly organized, it could thus be categorized as a punishable act.

Gestapo Koblenz, March 18, 1940
Gestapo headquarters In Vogelsang I
Telephone: Nr. 2291
Br.-Nr. II B 109/40
To the Gestapo

Gestapo Headquarters in Düsseldorf

Concerning: Plans to organize collections for the widow Margarete Schneider, nee Dieterich, who was born January 8, 1904 in Wildberg, and resides in Dickenschied, in the district of Simmern

Dossier: none
Enclosures: 1
I am sending you the enclosed dossier, and request that you examine it.

I will initiate criminal proceedings against Pastor Heinz Rolffs for violating the Collection Act. I will leave it up to you to decide if you want to also initiate criminal proceedings against Pastor Voget. I request that you inform me of the outcome of the proceedings.

The Protestant pastor
Paul Robert Schneider
born on August 29, 1897 in Pferdsfeld, resided in Dickenschied, in the district of Simmern.

He was a fanatical supporter of the Confessing Church and was taken into preventive detention on May 31, 1937. He was later taken to the Buchenwald concentration camp near Weimar where he died on July 18, 1939.

(Signature)

The bookkeeping of the Gestapo needs to be corrected here: Paul Schneider was indeed arrested on May 31, 1937, but released on July 24, 1937 and deported from the Rhineland. Then he was arrested again on October 3, 1937 and put in the concentration camp on November 25, 1937. This has already been laid out above. The district attorney informs the district court in Kastellaun:

The district attorney Koblenz, June 11, 1940
Business number: 2 Js 207/40

1. Original copy with files sent to the Gestapo

Gestapo Office in Koblenz

The defendant is guilty of violating the Collection Act because he admittedly organized an unapproved collection (namely a thank offering) in January 1940.

Furthermore, we have a violation of #111 of the State Legal Code in so far as the defendant called on the Confessing Church to commit a punishable act, i.e., to organize a public collection (a thank offering) "by disseminating a written document"—namely, a circular letter.

In my opinion a punishable act cannot be proven in so far as the defendant asked in the circular letter that donations be raised for the widow of Schneider. It cannot be proven that the collection Rolffs asked them to support was to be taken publicly—in the church in particular—which would make this collection a punishable offense. The possibility exists that the collection was to be taken only in the circle of their friends—therefore not publicly.

2. After two weeks
by proxy
Signed Dr. Zbikowski

The district court decides to issue an order of summary punishment against Pastor Rolffs, which the district attorney approves on June 26, 1940. Pastor Rolffs files an appeal through his attorney Dr. Schulze zur Wiesche against the imposition of a fine of 157.50 RM. It goes to trial, and the district attorney persists in imposing the fine. Nevertheless, on January 7, 1941 the district court drops the case. The Gestapo in Koblenz informs the Gestapo in Düsseldorf:

Gestapo Koblenz, February 3, 1941
Gestapo Headquarters Vogelsang I
Koblenz
Br.-Nr. II B 109/40
Please indicate the above business number and date in your reply.

To the Gestapo
-Gestapo Headquarters-

Düsseldorf

Concerning: Organizing a collection of monetary donations for the widow of Pastor Paul Schneider, Dickenschied, who died in the concentration camp.

Dossier: The letter there of February 24, 1940
II B 2/80, 10/Voget
Enclosures: 1

The trial initiated against the Protestant pastor Heinz Rolffs, who was born on June 28, 1900 in Stade, is married and resides in Bell, in the district of Simmern, for violating the Collection Act was suspended on January 7, 1941 by the district court in Kastellaun-1 Cs. 11/40. I request that you examine the reasons why the case was dropped from the enclosed copies.

I request that you notify me of the outcome of the proceedings initiated against Pastor Voget.

(Signature)

Although the district attorney clearly stated in Koblenz: "In my opinion a punishable act cannot be proven in so far as the defendant asked in the circular letter that donations be raised for the widow of Schneider," the Gestapo sticks to its plan to persecute those who offer support for the Schneider family.

Pastor Karl Immer had written in a circular letter for the "Coetus of Reformed pastors in Germany":

At the present time housing is being purchased in Wuppertal for Mrs. Schneider, whose husband was a member of the coetus from the beginning, so that her children will have the room to pursue their activities in a house with a yard. We need money for this. We will be out of the woods if every brother sends in a collection from his Bible study class to postal checking account Nr. 2399 at the Dorp. Stadt Savings and Loan, branch Wuppertal-Barmen Confessing Church Nr. 144400 Essen . . . .

Questioned by the Gestapo about this matter, Pastor Immer explains:

> In July 1939 it was decided at the funeral of Pastor Schneider, Dickenschied/Hunsrück, which representatives from almost all the Protestant churches in Germany attended, to grant assistance to the widow. We thought of purchasing a house so that Mrs. Schneider, who only gets a small widow's pension, can make a decent living with her children. This news quickly spread through the whole Confessing Church . . . .

Pastor Julius Voget made a similar statement to the Gestapo. While the investigations against pastors Immer and Voeget are in full swing, the Gestapo in Koblenz is pressing the district attorney and the courts again and again for information on the status of this matter. In examining the files that can be found, one cannot help feeling that the Gestapo in Koblenz had a "special interest" in the family of Paul Schneider since it wanted to make any kind of help for them a punishable offense. But ultimately, it fails because of the solidarity of Schneider's pastoral colleagues and their congregations. Pastor Voget gives his testimony about this matter to the Gestapo:

> The deceased Pastor Paul Robert Schneider was a covenant brother of mine. I have been a good friend of his wife for such a long time that it seemed natural for me to drive to his funeral with my wife. Even on the day of the funeral numerous colleagues expressed the desire to somehow show their gratitude for Paul Schneider's life.
>
> Later it was discussed in pastoral circles. The best suggestion that emerged was to help Schneider's widow acquire a suitable house in a city where her six children could attend the various schools. I offered Mrs. Schneider my help in looking for a suitable single-family home in Wuppertal. Mrs. Schneider agreed to that.
>
> I contacted the architect Reusch from Wuppertal-Barmen. He made several suggestions, but especially called my attention to the house at Bau Street 38 in Wuppertal-Elberfeld. The house belonged to the "Evangelical Society for Germany" in Wuppertal-Elberfeld, in which most recently the deceased pastor Sporri had lived. After Mrs. Schneider looked at it, the house was purchased . . . .

By moving away from Dickenschied, the family of Paul Schneider is no longer in the area controlled by the Gestapo headquarters in Koblenz. But it passes the dossier on to the next Gestapo office that will keep her under surveillance.

Gestapo Koblenz, April 29, 1940
Gestapo headquarters in Koblenz In Vogelsang 1
Telephone: Nr. 22291
Br.-Nr. II B 109/40
Please indicate the above business number and date in your response.

To the Gestapo
-Gestapo headquarters-
in Düsseldorf

Concerning: efforts to organize a collection for the widow Margarete Schneider, nee Dietrich, born January 8, 1904 in Wildberg.
Dossier: none

Following my letters of March 18 and April 15 I further inform you that the widow of Schneider has moved from Dickenschied in the district of Simmern to Elberfeld.

By proxy:
Pruss

32

EPILOGUE

Even during the typesetting reports and remarks arrived that deal with Paul Schneider's life of suffering. What is so lamentable is that the reports—often very brief, although important, can be found scattered in various publications.

The former French Buchenwald prisoner Pierre Durand published a book *The Beast of Buchenwald* in the military publishing company of the former East Germany. In this report he tells of an observation made by the prisoner Adolf Pauer, who as a plumber had to repair the roof of the camp commander Karl Koch's villa. He notes: "When Paul Schneider had to level the landscape around the commander's house, Ilse Koch sicced her dog on the pastor, afterwards she forbade the orderlies to bind up the bleeding wounds caused by the dog bites, and forced Schneider to keep on working at a fast pace." (Pastor Elsa-Ulrike Ross from the Paul-Schneider-Community Center in Weimar pointed out this story to me. This center is a place that feels committed to the spiritual legacy of Paul Schneider.) Ilse Koch took her own life after the war.

If one compares the reports, conspicuous differences are inevitable; this can be exclusively explained by the conditions prevalent in the concentration camp at that time and by the structure of the camp. Then the correspondence in the details can be recognized. First, I would like to quote from sections of a work titled *Paul Schneider, Brothers, Be Strong . . .* whose second edition was published by the Union Publishing Company (the former East Germany) in 1984. Walter Feurich wrote the book. We read in it:

> The incredible attitude of Paul Schneider deeply impressed his Marxist fellow prisoners in Buchenwald as well, as some of them later testified orally or in writing. In this work Feurich lets the well-known Communist writer Bruno Apitz have a chance to speak through a newspaper article from 1958. He tells in the article that Paul Schneider

would have gone free if he had signed a declaration of loyalty to the National Socialist state: "But he did not sign! He never signed . . . . He preferred death to betrayal . . . . Loyalty to his cause, steadfastness and courage gave the one who died in his lonely Buchenwald cell a moral greatness that today, almost 20 years after his torturous death, still shines and will always shine. You believers, Pastor Schneider is yours! But he is also ours! He is a brother and companion to all human beings who want to have peace on earth.

Anneliese Feurich, the widow of Walter Feurich, reports in her article "A Brother and Companion" from the East German Protestant monthly magazine "Standpunkt" in July 1989 on page 188: "The illegal camp leadership of the Marxists (in Buchenwald) discussed how they could assist Schneider in his cell. One person from their ranks volunteered for the job, and they actually succeeded in smuggling this man into his cell . . . ." The volunteer in the truest sense of the word was the Communist prisoner Fritz Männchen, who survived Buchenwald and gave the following report:

January 31, 1939:

Around eight o'clock in the evening I was in prisoner block 37. The Gestapo secretary Leclair summoned me to follow him. Our path led to the bunker. In the bunker the notorious prison guard Martin Sommer welcomed me. He opened a cell and pushed me in. Here I noticed a prisoner who was praying, kneeling by the steam heating unit. I bumped him lightly on the shoulder. Then I saw that it was Pastor Schneider. He stood up, and we embraced. After that Pastor Schneider said to me: "Fritz, what are you doing here in my cell?" I answered: "Dear God sent me to you so that you are not alone." I got the following response: "Do you believe, Fritz, that my God sent you to me?" I responded to him; "Yes, I believe it!" Since it was on a Friday that I came to his cell, it was a day of fasting for Pastor Schneider. We conversed, and he asked me: "What are our companions doing in the camp? Have you heard something from my wife and my six children?" Since I didn't want to make his heart even more heavy than it was, I told him that his wife and his six children were doing fine. After that Schneider kneeled again and prayed that God would make him strong so that he could return home to his loved ones and that he may stay healthy. Pastor Schneider then told me about the time of suffering he had endured in the bunker until now. Every day he was beaten again and again with the bullwhip. He showed me his body, and I was so shaken that I could not say anything. There were gaping holes the size of a fist on both sides of his hip joint that were caused by lying on the wooden plank bed. No blanket, no straw mattress, nothing was in the cell where Pastor Schneider lived from June to January. The cold that enveloped the cell—the steam heating was not turned on—forced us to do exercises so that we could get a little warmer. Suddenly the cell door was opened, and the prison guard went straight for Pastor Schneider with the bullwhip and beat him with the words: "You bastard!" In response Pastor Schneider said in a soft voice: "I am not a bastard, sir!" After that the prison guard beat up Pastor Schneider until he bled, collapsing in the corner of the cell. I tried to look after Pastor Schneider. Unfortunately I could not put him on the wooden plank bed because it was attached to the wall during the day. On the cold floor I wiped off his bloody face with my coat, ripped out the inner lining and bound up Pastor Schneider's wounds with it somehow or other. Eight days later the trusty was dismissed from the bunker. Prison guard Rodel had me taken out of the cell one day and explained to me that I was to temporarily do the job of the trusty. I had to pass out the food and was responsible for the cleanliness of the solitary confinement building. I had to pass out the food to most of the prisoners myself; however, there were companions of ours in the cells to whom jailer Sommer passed out the food himself. I myself watched how Sommer poured a fluid into different bowls before passing out the food; he also poured it into Pastor Schneider's bowl, among others. At first I could not find out what kind of substance it was. However, while cleaning the room of prison guard Sommer I could determine that the fluid in the cupboard was a cardiac depressant.

The last reference must be seen in connection with the reports given above; he corroborates the thesis of the premeditated murder of Paul Schneider. Now we come to a letter written by Pastor Petry who accompanied Mrs. Schneider to Buchenwald to pick up the body of her husband:

Wirschweiler, August 1, 1939

Dear friends! Thank you very much for Anita's letter! Since I did not meet Walther at the funeral of brother Schneider, I assumed that you were already in Boltenhagen.[1] How difficult it must have been for you to get this news during what was hopefully a happy vacation until then. We arrived home on Tuesday, July 18. Our return had been somewhat delayed since I took in the Rhenish Confessing Synod on the Lower Rhine on the way home, which had met from July 16 at one o'clock in the afternoon to about noon on the 17th. We stayed there overnight. When we had been home an hour, Müsse[2] gave me the news of Schneider's death on the telephone and asked me to go with him to Dickenschied right away. So I got in my car again and we drove to Dickenschied. We met Mrs. Schneider there—she was still in a bright summer dress—as she was giving instructions to some people in her bright and clear voice. In all these days Mrs. Schneider manifested a wonderfully composed and calm bearing. She is really a brave woman. And you can only appreciate her composure when you know how she really depended on her husband. We not only cried, but also laughed during those days in Dickenschied and on the way to Weimar. In the afternoon she had received the telegram with the news that her husband had died and that she could take him home at her own cost, or else he would be cremated after 24 hours. A little later the policeman told her that Schneider had died of a heart attack. Schneider had written three very confident and cheerful letters since Easter. He wrote that he was bright and healthy. But it also came out in these letters that he was constantly struggling between the strong hope of freedom and the complete surrender of his life there. Around two o'clock at night Mrs. Schneider and I drove to Weimar with a Mercedes to which a trailer was attached that carried the casket. We were there at 10 o'clock in the morning. From a city office I announced to the camp that we were coming and presented Mrs. Schneider's request to see her husband. This was promised; they told us we should come in two hours. Around noon we were in the camp. We were welcomed very

---

[1] Anita and Walther (Pastor) Disselnkotter; close friends and confidents of the Schneider family.

[2] Müsse, a pastor in Hausen, not far from Dickenschied.

politely at the entrance by two camp leaders and the camp physician. They told us that Schneider had been dissected since the cause of death had not been clear. But he had had a heart defect for about six months and he had been in the infirmary for the last three days and was being treated for it. He also had swollen legs in the final weeks. His death had occurred quite suddenly in the presence of the camp physician.

We were then led to Schneider's coffin. He was covered with a white sheet up to his neck. His face bore the expression of one who had peacefully passed away. Mrs. Schneider said: Dead, but not defeated. We both recited a verse from a hymn and then prayed the Lord's Prayer. Mrs. Schneider stood alone with her husband for the final minute while our escort and I withdrew to the entrance. That was the way we said good-bye. Then brother Schneider was put in the casket we had purchased. This casket was sealed seven times and we were no longer permitted to open it in Dickenschied. In the meantime we took care of some formalities at an office in the camp. Mrs. Schneider was still able to ask a few questions. My mouth was sealed. We were not permitted to lay out the body in the manse in Dickenschied, but certainly in the church. We were satisfied with that. Then we set out on our sad journey home.

Around midnight we were on the outskirts of Simmern when two policemen stopped us with instructions to leave the casket in the hospital's mortuary in Simmern until the funeral. In the meantime the congregation had gathered in the Dickenschied church to receive their dead pastor there. We told the people in front of the manse what we had experienced, and it was remarkable how clearly and comfortingly Mrs. Schneider told the Womrath women everything. I then drove home in the middle of the night. The funeral was at noon on Friday. Brother Schneider had been laid out in the church before the service. So he had now returned to his church this way! Langensiepen said in the ceremony that was held there for the family members and the Dickenschied congregation: His mouth is silent—but his witness is alive.[3] A large congregation gathered at the grave, also approximately 150 pastors in their robes. We were all under the immediate impression

---

[3] Langensiepen, a pastor in Godenroth, a friend and confident of the Schneider family.

that we were witnessing a significant hour in the history of the church. Schlingensiepen[4] gave the sermon. Then representatives from the whole country made remarks: VKL, East Prussia, Silesia, Berlin, Brandenburg, Bavaria (Putz for Meiser!),[5] Württemberg, Nassau and Hessen, Westphalia, Hamburg, Oldenburg, Ippach[6] and many others. In conclusion we sang: My hope is built on nothing less than Jesus' blood and righteousness . . . .

Mrs. Schneider has received 500 letters in the past week, and also some quite impressive financial gifts. Meyer is temporarily filling the pulpit in Dickenschied.[7] The consistory wants to temporarily leave the job of finding a replacement to Gillmann. Tomorrow I will drive again to Dickenschied.

Otherwise, we are fine in spite of the salary ban that Mr. Sohns will not repeal. Meyer stirred up the congregation in our absence. In the two weeks since our return we have been able to sell natural produce worth 40 RM. By the way, since our return someone is constantly sick in our house. Marianne[8] took along your children's cough as a souvenir from Zuschen.[9] Her barking was at times quite considerable. But now she is over the worst. Yesterday evening I was at the Brunks home in Bruchweiler.[10] When I wanted to return, the air had been let out of three tires and the vents were screwed out. After I had tried to tinker with it for an hour and a half in vain, I rode home on a bicycle. The Ladies Aid festival held only in the church in Thalfang was very good.

---

[4] Schlingensiepen, a pastor and member of the Rhenish Brotherhood Council.

[5] Meiser was bishop of the Evangelical-Lutheran Church of Bavaria at that time.

[6] Ippach, a free church pastor. He along with his wife had made it possible for the Schneiders to spend their last vacation unobserved by the Gestapo in Baden-Baden through the arrangements Pastor Disselnkotter had made.

[7] Meyer, a assistant pastor of the Confessing Church, who had filled in for Schneider in Dickenschied.

[8] Marianne Petry, daughter of Pastor Gerhard Petry.

[9] Zuschen, the parish of Pastor Walter Disselnkotter, who was so kind to make this letter available.

[10] Bruchweiler was pastorally cared for by Pastor Petry.

Reif[11] has been transferred "in the interests of the ministry." Langensiepen already wants to be transferred to temporary retirement. When will it be our turn? Truly! After the storm we will travel safely through the waves.

We greet you with deep affection,
Your, Gerhard

Time and again people have asked me what happened after the end of the war to the followers of Hitler who played their diabolical game in the Buchenwald concentration camp with the people there.

Mr. Wolfgang Roll, department head of the Historical Department of the "Buchenwald National Memorial" helped me track them down and provided the following information:

Karl Koch, SS-Standartenführer, born August 2, 1897 in Darmstadt; NSDAP-member Nr. 475586; SS-member Nr. 14830; 1935 commander of the guard company in the Esterwegen concentration camp. In April 1936 commander of the Columbiahaus concentration camp in Berlin; commander of the Sachsenhausen concentration camp from 1936–1937; commander of the Buchenwald concentration camp from July 1937 to December 1941; in December 1941 removed from his post for corruption and financial embezzlement, but on the recommendation of Himmler he was appointed in January 1941 to be the commander of the Majdanek concentration camp in Lublin until August 22, 1942; August 24, 1943 arrest and investigative detention by the Gestapo in Weimar; December 19, 1944 sentenced to death by the SS and the Police Court of Prien/Chiemsee for corruption, accepting stolen goods, embezzlement and immoral behavior; May 3, 1945 executed by firing squad on the shooting range of the SS in Buchenwald.

Martin Sommer, born February 8, 1915 in Schkölm in the district of Weissenfels; 1931 joined the NSDAP and the SA; 1933 transferred to the general SS; 1934 a member of the barracked SS in the "Special Political Department of Saxony" (at the end of 1934 renamed the "SS-Death Head Division of Saxony"); 1935 guard duty in the Sachsenburg and Lichtenburg concentration

---

[11] Reif, pastor in Veldenz.

camps; 1937 transfer of this SS-unit to Buchenwald; after moving up through various commando units, from 1938 he was the second in command, from September 1939 first in command as the supervisor of solitary confinement; had a part in multiple murders in the so-called bunker of the Buchenwald concentration camp; member of Commando 99 to murder Soviet prisoners of war (commissary order); 1943 transferred to the Military-SS, stationed in France as a member of the 9th SS-tank regiment; in the course of the "Koch" affair ordered to Buchenwald; investigative detention in the police and court prison in Weimar; 1944 indictment within the framework of the trial against Koch, in September 1944 given a separate trial; in early March 1945 assigned to a special combat group; wounded in the area of Eisenach on April 8, 1945; after the end of the war arrested by the Americans, 1947 officially released; 1950 arrest warrant and the opening of a preliminary investigation by the district attorney of Augsburg; 1951 the trial transferred to the state court of appeal in Bayreuth; 1959 sentenced to "life in prison"; 1971 released to a nursing home where he could live as a free man. He had at his disposal not only a modern, battery-driven wheelchair, but also a television set and a telephone. From the very scant news that has been passed on to us from conversations with him, it can be recognized that he did not regret his past up to his death in 1988. The management of the nursing home did not allow the author a visit with Sommer.

Dr. Erwin Ding-Schuler, was born September 19, 1912 in Bitterfeld; Sturmbannführer; doctor on location for the Military-SS. Since August 31, 1943 he served as the head of the department for typhus and viral research at the Hygiene Institute of the Military-SS at the Buchenwald concentration camp. He conducted medical experiments on about 1,000 persons with poison, typhus, yellow fever, smallpox and cholera; 1945 in American detention; committed suicide on August 14, 1945 in Freising.

I have also provided several brief biographical sketches of leading figures in the Confessing Church who are mentioned in the book.

Otto Dibelius was born May 15, 1880 in Berlin, and died January 31, 1967 in Berlin. He served as a pastor since 1907. In 1921 he became a member of the consistory; from 1925 to 1933 he served as the General Superintendent of the Lutheran regional church in Kurmark. He was favorably inclined to National

Socialism until they seized power. Soon he showed his distance from the anti-Christian goals of the Nazis, thus he was forced to retire in June 1933. From the fall of 1934 he belonged to the Confessing Church; he resisted the intervention of the totalitarian state, and was temporarily held in detention; he was banned from speaking in public, but was acquitted of the charge of high treason in 1937. From 1945–1966 he was the Protestant bishop of Berlin-Brandenburg. He also collaborated on the Stuttgart Confession of October 19, 1945. Dibelius was one of the prominent members of the Confessing Church. However, his protest merely focused on National Socialist interference in church affairs, although Kurt Gerstein, a high-ranking SS-officer had told him details about the destruction of European Jewry in the East.

Martin Niemöller was born January 14, 1892 in Lippstadt/Westphalia, and he died on March 6, 1984 in Wiesbaden. He was a Protestant pastor and theologian. In 1910 he entered the Kaiser's navy and became a submarine commander in World War 1. From 1924–30 he worked for the homeland mission in Westphalia. Since July 1, 1931 he was the pastor of St. Annen Church in Berlin-Dahlem. In 1934 he published his patriotic autobiography, *From the Submarine to the Pulpit.* The takeover of the National Socialists fit in well with his nationalistic mindset and his skepticism toward the Weimar Republic; yet the attempts of the National Socialists to force the church into political conformity and to infiltrate it with their ideology kindled his resistance. Together with the so-called Young Reformers he founded the Pastors' Emergency League on September 21, 1933. His participation in an audience with Hitler on January 25, 1934 led to a heated exchange between him and the Chancellor. As a result, the Gestapo put him under constant surveillance. In March of 1934 he was removed from his office as pastor, which he ignored; after protests of the congregation and the verdict of the district court in Berlin he was officially reinstated on July 5, 1934. The Barmen Confessing Synod can be considered the constituent assembly of the Confessing Church in which Niemöller played a leading role in the struggle against the German Christians and the National Socialists. His passionate and popular sermons led to his arrest on charges of abusing the pulpit and violating the Treachery Act. In a trial before the special court in Berlin-Moabit he was sentenced on March 2, 1938 to seven months in prison, which he had already served. Nevertheless, he was kept in various concentration camps as the "personal prisoner of the Führer" until the end of the war. In May 1945 he was liberated by American troops as he was being transported from Dachau to Southern Tyrol. After the war he was a co-author of the Stuttgart Confession of October 1945. After the war he continued to serve the Protestant Church of Germany in various leadership roles. As an opponent of German rearmament and the nuclear arms race he supported the German peace movement and the ecumenical movement. To the end of his life in 1984 he remained a valiant, courageous and at times controversial witness to Jesus Christ.

Heinrich Gruber was born June 24, 1891 in Stolberg/Rhineland, and died on November 29, 1975 in Berlin. Gruber was a pastor in Berlin-Kaulsdorf beginning in 1934. As an opponent of National Socialism he joined the Confessing Church and in 1937 established the "Gruber Office" that looked after Christians of Jewish descent, advising them on emigration issues and on employment opportunities overseas. From 1940–1943 he was a prisoner in the Sachsenhausen and Dachau concentration camps. After his release in 1943 he resumed his illegal help. After the war he was the representative of the Protestant Church in East Germany to the Communist government. He gave up this office after vehemently criticizing the communist policies of the GDR that were hostile to the church and anti-Christian. In the 1950s he moved to West Germany where he began a dogged struggle against rearmament and nuclear weapons. In 1961 he was the only German to testify at the Eichmann trial. In the last years of his life he consistently warned the nation about the dangers inherent in the Neo-Nazi movement.

IMPORTANT DATES IN THE LIFE OF PAUL SCHNEIDER

1897   Born in Pferdsfeld (Soonwald) in the Hunsrück region on August 29 as the son of Pastor Adolf Schneider and his wife Elisabeth, nee Schnorr.

1915   Passed his school-leaving exam and qualified for study at the university level; war volunteer in Hofgeismar.

1916   Wounded in Russia, infantry artillery in France.

1918   Lieutenant of the reserves.

1919   Participation in the battles fought in Thuringia after the war as a member of the Marburg student corps; begins his study of theology in Giessen; continues his studies in Marburg, Tübingen and again in Marburg.

1922   First Theological Examination in Koblenz; afterwards a blue-collar worker at the blast furnace in the Ruhr area (voluntary industrial internship); the seminary in Soest (Westphalia).

1923   Second Theological Examination.

1924   Worked at the Berlin City Mission.

1925   Ordination (January), assisant pastor in the Ruhr area.

1926   Succeeds his father as pastor of the yoked congregations of Hochelheim
        and Dornholzhausen in the church district of Wetzlar; marries the
        pastor's daughter Margarete Dieterich, born January 8, 1904 in
        Wildberg, in Weilheim (Württemberg); six children come from their
        marriage.

1932   First complaint of the district leadership of the NSDAP in Frankfurt/
        Main to the superintendent of the church district of Wetzlar.

1933   First open clash with the NSDAP.

1934   Suspension at the instigation of the NSDAP and later transfer; Pastor
        of Dickenschied and Womrath in the Hunsrück; first arrest as a result
        of a clash with the district leader of the NSDAP on the occasion of a
        funeral in Gemünden.

1935   Second arrest in March in connection with the reading of a declaration
        written by the Old Prussian Confessing Synod from the pulpit.

1937   Third arrest; in the Gestapo prison of Koblenz from May to July 24;
        deported from the Rhine province. Nevertheless, gives the sermon
        in Dickenschied and Womrath on July 25, 1937, followed by a
        convalescent leave in Baden-Baden (at the city mission). On October
        3 returns to the congregations of Dickenschied and Womrath at the
        urgent request of both sessions; Thanksgiving worship service in
        Dickenschied. Fourth arrest on the same day at the edge of the forest
        on the outskirts of Womrath on the way to the Thanksgiving service
        there; on November 27 he is taken to the Buchenwald concentration
        camp near Weimar.

1939   At the instigation of the consistory in Düsseldorf the highest
        administrative office of the Protestant Church in Berlin issues the
        "Decree on the Transfer of Clergymen for Official Reasons"; by means
        of this decree Paul Schneider is to be transferred into temporary
        retirement after consultations between the consistory and the Gestapo;
        on July 15 the consistory initiates the procedure to transfer him into
        temporary retirement, but it can no longer be implemented; on July 18

his wife receives notification by telegraph of Paul Schneider's death in the Buchenwald concentration camp near Weimar; on July 21 funeral service and burial in Dickenschied. The whole Protestant and Catholic population of Dickenschied and Womrath and the surrounding area attend the funeral, including 150 pastors in their vestments and 50 additional pastors in civilian clothes from all the regional churches in Germany. Shock and dismay in the ranks of the Gestapo, the NSDAP and the Protestant Consistory in Düsseldorf. The Protestant Consistory reproaches the Gestapo for giving permission to the family to hold the funeral and interment in Dickenschied; the family of Paul Schneider and its helpers continue to be observed by the Gestapo.

GLOSSARY

BK=*Bekennende Kirche* ("Confessing Church"). The Nazis were forced to tolerate religion in Germany, but as Martin Bormann exclaimed: "National Socialism and Christianity are irreconcilable." Hitler supported this view, stating: "One day we want to be in a position where only complete idiots stand in the pulpit and preach to old women." The Nazis viewed Christianity as a faith tainted by the Jews. In response, the Nazis offered the German people a new religion based on blood, soil, Germanic folklore and the Thousand Year Reich. Racial supremacy played a large part in the new "religion" that sought to usher in a brave new secular world.

Nazis who still wanted a spiritual home were offered a faith called *gottgläubig* ("believers in God") as an alternative to the established churches. The movement was heavily tainted with peculiar pagan practices. It was given official sanction by the Nazi authorities, and by 1939 the number of "God believers" exceeded three million. The Nazis stressed romantic notions of a pagan past, while simultaneously repressing the established churches. The Nazis were unwilling to tolerate (as with the family) an alternative power center in the Christian religion. The rituals of life associated with the church—birth, marriage and death—were all criticized. As part of this attack, the Nazis also changed the calendar to downplay Christian celebrations and emphasize non-Christian ceremonies. Thus, in 1938 carols and the nativity play were forbidden in schools; at the same time, Christmas was replaced with the new term "Yuletide."

The Nazis wanted to extend the Nazi policy of *Gleichschaltung* (enforced political conformity) to the churches. This policy of coordination aimed to fuse all areas of German life together into a supreme Nazi machine. Anything or anyone opposed to this process was suspect, and a collection of Nazi organizations tried to bring together all areas of German life under Nazi authority. The churches were an obvious target and in April 1933 hard-line Nazis demanded the immediate conformity, *Gleichschaltung*, of all Protestant Churches. The response was mixed: some churchmen acquiesced to Nazi demands; others met the new threat with determined opposition. Nazi Protestants were called "Deutsche Christen" (DC). These "German Christians" believed that Jesus Christ had been sent to them in the form of Hitler, that God had sanctified the Aryan way of life and that racial mixing was wrong. With this in mind, the "German Christians" attempted to pass a motion that required Aryan origin as a basis for the pastoral office. Pastor Martin Niemöller assumed leadership of this opposition movement within the German Protestant Church and formed the Pastors' Emergency League (*Pfarrernotbund*) to oppose the hardliners. Some 7,000 pastors joined Niemöller in forming the Confessing Church (*Bekennende Kirche*), which claimed to be the true Protestant Church in Germany and set up alternative structures of church government and pastoral training to counter the German Christian threat to the integrity of the Church. Its first national synod held in Barmen in 1934 formulated the famous "Barmen Declaration" (whose primary author was the theologian Karl Barth) which boldly affirmed its allegiance to Jesus Christ as the "one Word of God whom we must obey in life and in death" and denied the German Christians' claim that Adolf Hitler and National Socialism were a new source of revelation that God had sent to the German people to renew the nation and restore its national pride. Following the Nazi's anti-Semitic ideology the German Christians also attacked the Old Testament and those parts of the New Testament considered tainted by Judaism. These blatant attacks on the Christian faith and the German Christians' power grab in the church, pushing through the appointment of a national bishop with complete authority to implement *Gleichschaltung* in the churches, were heavily criticized by the Confessing Church and were attacked by its leaders such as Niemöller, Barth and Bonhoeffer, and courageous pastors such as Paul Schneider, Asmussen and Albertz.

In the end, the Nazis' attempt at *Gleichschaltung* for Protestantism failed. But this did not stop the Nazis from persecuting religious opponents, including Niemöller, who was imprisoned in 1937 and subsequently sent to a concentration camp. When the Confessing Church went on record in 1935 to say that the entire Nazi racial-folkish world-view (*Weltanschauung*) was nonsense, 700 ministers were arrested, humiliated and their civil liberties restricted. Ultimately, while the Nazis failed to absorb these churches, by the late 1930s the policies of repression had effectively stifled open opposition within the Protestant movement, and it was left to a few brave churchmen such as Bonhoeffer and Schneider to speak out against the Nazi excesses.

NSDAP=*Nationalsozialistische Deutsche Arbeiterpartei* ("National Socialist German Workers' Party"). After World War I Hitler was employed by the German army to monitor extremist organizations, including a small right-wing group in Bavaria called the DAP—*Deutsche Arbeiterpartei* (German Workers' Party). This group attracted Hitler's attention the most and in September 1919 the 30-year old Hitler joined the DAP as number 555. Hitler proved to be good at talking and soon his speeches attracted new members for the DAP. In 1921 he moved to take over the party and give it a new name: The National Socialist German Workers' Party (*Nationalsozialistische Deutsche Arbeiterpartei*). This was shortened to the acronym "Nazi" from the first syllable of *Na-tional* and the second syllable of *So-zi-alist*. With the term Nazi came all the symbols of fascism that helped draw in new recruits. There were uniforms and a new greeting to replace *Guten Tag: "Heil Hitler!"* Eventually, school classes were opened with *Heil Hitler* and every child was expected to say *Heil Hitler* over 100 times per day. The infamous raised right-arm salute was part of this greeting. The Nazis also appropriated a powerful symbol in the Swastika (*Hakenkreuz*). This was an ancient symbol that appeared on ceramics as far back as 4,000 B.C. Under the Nazis, the black Swastika on a white circular background against red came to denote the superior "Aryan" race.

The use of symbols and greetings was complemented by Hitler's program of simple political slogans backed up by the use of newspapers and Storm Troopers for battles on the streets with the communists and social democrats. Hitler pushed the message that all Germany's woes were the result of international Jewry and Marxists, and many in the population angered by the Treaty of Versailles and suffering from economic dislocation eagerly received his message. Hitler's ideas of racial superiority and extreme nationalism were not new, but he colored them with showmanship and eloquence, all carefully contrived to build up a mythical status around the former Austrian corporal and failed painter.

Once the Nazis took over in 1933, Hitler's personality and ideas naturally played the key role. One of his most critical beliefs was in social Darwinism— the idea that within society or politics struggle would lead the fittest to survive. Thus, Hitler encouraged his subordinates to use their initiative and carve out their own power bases. If they were the "strongest and fittest" they would succeed. In a speech in 1928 Hitler said, "The idea of struggle is as old as life itself." He went on to say: "In this struggle the stronger, the more able win while the less able, the weak, lose. Struggle is the father of all things."

SA=*Sturmabteilung* ("Storm Troopers"). They were also known as the Brown shirts, uniformed Nazi Party supporters recruited from 1921 by Ernst Röhm. Mostly ex-soldiers and ex-*Freikorps* members, they grew in number until banned after the Munich "Beer Hall Putsch" in 1923. However, following the reformation of the party the SA rose in numbers. When Hitler became Chancellor in 1933, the SA numbered 500,000. Fearing Röhm and the SA would become a rival power base, Hitler ordered the SS to emasculate the SA during the "Night of the Long Knives." On June 30 Hitler ordered the SS to begin executing those individuals considered to be "enemies of the regime." Some 1,000 were killed, including Röhm and Gregor Strasser.

SS=*Schutzstaffel* ("Protection Squad"). Originally the personal bodyguard of Adolf Hitler, under Heinrich Himmler the SS became a state within a state, an army within an army. It eventually developed into an organization with many branches, such as the *Waffen-SS* (armed SS), concentration camps, the Race and Resettlement Office, and numerous business enterprises. This SS business empire controlled twenty concentration camps and 165 labor camps. At the Nuremberg Tribunal, the SS was declared a criminal organization.

Gestapo=*Geheime Staatspolizei* ("Secret State Police"). The secret police of the Nazi state used terror to keep control of the state and its population. Its main task was to track down subversives who threatened the Nazis' iron grip. It had no restrictions as to its powers of arrest. Its activities extended into occupied countries during the war years. At its height, in 1943, there were 45,000 Gestapo members controlling 60,000 agents and 100,000 informers, who acted as its eyes and ears. Each large apartment building, for example, had its own resident Gestapo informer who kept an eye on fellow tenants. To be denounced by an informer meant being taken into custody, where officials had the right under the law to extract confessions by beating (which could go on for days at a time, the prisoner lapsing in and out of consciousness). The terrified prisoner could then be dispatched to a concentration camp, never to be seen again. Through its use of intimidation and terror the Gestapo kept a strict control on the state and its people. *SS-Gruppenführer* Heinrich Müller headed the organization.

RSHA=*Reichsicherheitshauptamt* ("Central Reich Security Office"). The shadow cast across everyday life in Nazi Germany was Himmler's SS, the empire within an empire. Within this immense organization, the Central Reich Security Office under the command of *SS-Obergruppenführer* Reinhard Heydrich had the most impact on life in the Third Reich. The most important sections within the RSHA were the Gestapo (described above), *Die Kriminalpolizei* (*Kripo*) ("The Criminal Investigation Department") under *SS-Gruppenführer* Arthur Nebe, the *Ausland-Sicherheitsdienst* (SD) ("The External Intelligence Service") under *SS-Brigadeführer* Walter Schellenberg, whose main task was to gather foreign intelligence, and the *Inland-Sicherheitsdienst* (SD) ("The Internal Intelligence Service") under *SS-Brigadeführer* Otto Ohlendorf. Its main task was to gather domestic intelligence on groups and individuals who resisted the Nazi regime. It was another key component of the RSHA that helped maintain internal state security after the Nazis came to power in 1933.

RAD=*Reichsarbeitsdienst* ("The Labor Service of the Third Reich"). By a law of June 26, 1933, the RAD enforced six months' labor service for all males between the ages of nineteen and 25. This was later extended to women also.

HJ=*Hitler-Jugend* ("Hitler Youth"). A highly militarized organization for German boys between the ages of fourteen and eighteen that prepared them for military service and war. Everything about the Hitler Youth stressed the martial and physical, so they learned the basics of marksmanship on the firing range, practiced marching and performed military drills. Once war started, Hitler youth were expected to play their part, helping with civil defense on the home front. The education of the Hitler Youth was carefully regulated. When a boy turned ten, he would have to register with the Reich Youth Headquarters. After a thorough investigation of the youth's background for racial purity, he was admitted to the *Deutsches Jungvolk* ("German Young People") for boys between the ages of ten and fourteen. He was required to undergo an initiation test where he recited Nazi dogma, all the verses of the "Horst Wessel Song" (a Nazi anthem in honor of an SA man killed in a street fight with communists), ran 180 feet in twelve seconds and completed a one and a half day cross-country hike. As a *Pimpf,* he was expected to learn semaphore, lay telephone wires and participate in small arms drills. If successful at his tests as a *Pimpf,* the boy entered the Hitler youth proper at fourteen. When they turned eighteen, Hitler Youth members entered the NSDAP. At nineteen they entered the State Labor Service before joining the armed forces. Thus the Hitler Youth provided a means of indoctrinating and forming young boys for Nazism and military service. The Nazis monopolized every free hour and parents did not dare to object for fear of being seen as troublemakers. Young people, living more and more with their comrades, were gradually weaned away from their families. Their Reich youth leader was Baldur von Schirach.

BdM=*Bund deutscher Mädchen* ("League of German Girls"). Organized along similar lines to the Hitler Youth for boys. It was also under the control of the Reich youth leader and took in girls at the age of ten. The girls' groups were organized along military lines. All of the girls in the *BdM* were constantly reminded that the whole task of schooling was to prepare them to be "carriers of the National Socialist world view." They were to devote themselves to comradeship, service and physical fitness so as to become good German mothers. By 1936, more than two million girls were enrolled in the *BdM.*

KdF=*Kraft durch Freude* ("Strength through Joy"). Successful and popular Nazi organization that coordinated sports and leisure-time activities. It gave ordinary Germans access to foreign travel, tourist areas and entertainment. It was of great propaganda value to the Third Reich.

Das Amt für die Überwachung der gesamten geistigen und weltanschaulichen Schulung und Erziehung der NSDAP ("Office for the Supervision of the Total Intellectual and Ideological Training and Education of the NDSAP"). This office grew out of the earlier League of Struggle for German Culture (*Kampfbund für Deutsche Kultur KfDK*). The League of Struggle had been founded in 1929 to combat "Jewish" influence on German culture. Its founder was Alfred Rosenberg, one of the Nazi's ideological thinkers. In its new form after 1933, Rosenberg's Office for the Supervision of Ideological Training developed blacklists, burned books and emptied museums of anything considered "decadent." Rosenberg was an early anti-Semitic writer whose *The Myth of the Twentieth Century* (published in 1930) was required Nazi reading. Its premise was that liberalism had wrecked the ascendancy of the Nordic people, allowing "lesser" races to take power, and that Germany's duty was to rule them. In 1940 he set up a task force to loot art treasures from conquered Europe, and a year later he became minister for the occupied Eastern territories. He was hanged as a war criminal in 1946.

Arier=("Aryan"). This term was first used by the linguistic scholar Friedrich Max Müller to describe a group of peoples who migrated into northwest Europe in ancient history. As seen by the Nazis, the "Nordic" peoples of Europe formed the heartland of the so-called superior "Aryan race."

* Quotations are taken from the life story of Paul Schneider that he submitted for his First Theological Examination.

** Quotations are taken from the diary of Paul Schneider.

CPSIA information can be obtained at www.ICGtesting.com
Printed in the USA
BVOW02s0806251113

337258BV00001B/10/P